Romantic Narrative

Romantic Narrative

Shelley, Hays, Godwin, Wollstonecraft

TILOTTAMA RAJAN

The Johns Hopkins University Press

Baltimore

The Johns Hopkins University Press
2715 North Charles Street
Baltimore, Maryland 21218-4363
www.press.jhu.edu

Library of Congress Cataloging-in-Publication Data

Rajan, Tilottama.
    Romantic narrative : Shelley, Hays, Godwin, Wollstonecraft / Tilottama Rajan.
      p.   cm.
    Includes bibliographical references and index.
    ISBN-13: 978-0-8018-9721-4 (hardcover : alk. paper)
    ISBN-10: 0-8018-9721-1 (hardcover : alk. paper)
      1. English literature—18th century—History and criticism—Theory, etc.
2. English literature—19th century—History and criticism—Theory, etc. 3. English
fiction—18th century—History and criticism—Theory, etc. 4. Shelley, Percy Bysshe,
1792–1822—Criticism and interpretation. 5. Hays, Mary, 1759 or 60–1843—
Criticism and interpretation. 6. Godwin, William, 1756–1836—Criticism and
interpretation. 7. Wollstonecraft, Mary, 1759–1797—Criticism and interpretation. 8. Romanticism—Great Britain. I. Title.
    PR447.R28 2010
    820.9'145—dc22   2010001218

A catalog record for this book is available from the British Library.

*Special discounts are available for bulk purchases of this book. For more information,
please contact Special Sales at 410-516-6936 or specialsales@press.jhu.edu.*

The Johns Hopkins University Press uses environmentally friendly book materials,
including recycled text paper that is composed of at least 30 percent post-consumer
waste, whenever possible. All of our book papers are acid-free, and our jackets and
covers are printed on paper with recycled content.

In memory of my father,
Balachandra Rajan,
March 24, 1920–January 23, 2009,
the reason for everything I have achieved
and for my mother,
Chandra Rajan

CONTENTS

ACKNOWLEDGMENTS

I struggled to finish this book before my father's death, and completed a long prospectus (a first version of the Introduction) on the day he died. It was cremated with him: my final tribute to someone who was my intellectual and personal example. Writing of Flaubert, Michel Foucault says that his "entire work is dedicated to the conflagration" of the archive, "this primary discourse: its precious ashes, its black, unmalleable coal." For me that has not occurred yet, but this book is dedicated to my parents: my father, Balachandra Rajan (well known as a scholar of English literature), and my mother, Chandra Rajan (an eminent translator of Sanskrit texts), who has been a constant personal support.

I also want to acknowledge the past and recent support of many friends and colleagues, particularly Anand and Madhu Bhalla, Shemim Chaudhry, Angela Cozea, Chris Keep, Sally Vernon, and Susan Wallace for their understanding and loyalty during a difficult time. I am also grateful to Steven Bruhm, Kul and Louise Bhatia, Nandi Bhatia, Antonio Calcagno, David Clark, Milda Danys, Corinne Davies, Helen Fielding, Bush Gulati, Linda Hutcheon, Monika Lee, Madeline and Tom Lennon, Penelope Lister, Mervyn Nicholson, Jan Plug, Chitra Reddin, Eric Savoy, Peter Schwenger, Clara Thomas, Jane Toswell, Brian Young, Charlotte Wolters, Julia Wright, and Archie and Mary Young. I have been blessed with students and former students, whom I respect and admire, both personally and intellectually. My particular thanks go to John Vanderheide, who has done much more than help with the preparation of this manuscript. My thanks also go to Naqaa Abbas, Adina Arvatu, Chris Bundock, Rebecca Gagan, Josh Lambier, and Jonathan Murphy. Thomas Pfau has read the entire manuscript, and I am grateful to him for his incisive comments and intellectual and professional support. Although I do not like to burden people with reading my work, given all of the claims on our time, Ross Woodman and Joel Faflak have read parts of the manuscript, and their interest in seeing me set aside my abstruser researches in German Idealism to return to work that, in its earliest form, was done many years ago was important in encouraging me to complete this book. I am particularly grateful to Ross Woodman for his ongoing support and that rare negative capability that allows him to enter into another person's work. Beyond that I have benefited from the work and the presence in the field of many fellow Romanticists, who have heard parts of this project at conferences and offered intellectual and personal support over the years: in addition to some of those mentioned above, Ian Balfour, Christoph Bode, Marshall Brown, Julie Carlson, David Collings, Elizabeth Fay, David Ferris, Denise Gigante, Gary Handwerk, Mary Jacobus, Theresa Kelley, Jacques Khalip, David Farrell Krell, Arkady Plotnitsky, Marc Redfield, and Richard Sha.

This project was initially funded by a grant from the Social Sciences and Humanities Research Council of Canada, to which I am grateful not only for financial support but also for my self-instilled guilt, which made me feel that, inasmuch as I had received money, I ought to consolidate my thinking into a book. I am also grateful to the Canada Research Chairs program for continued funding and release time. A shorter and substantially different version of Chapter 3, with the same title, "Autonarration and Genotext in Mary Hays's *Memoirs of Emma Courtney*," appeared in *Studies in Romanticism* 32. 2 (1993): 149–76; copyright Trustees of Boston University. A much shorter and different version of Chapter 2 appeared under the title "Promethean Narrative: Overdetermined Form in Shelley's Gothic Fiction," in *Shelley: Poet and Legislator of the World,* ed. Betty T. Bennett and Stuart Curran (Baltimore: Johns Hopkins University Press, 1995), 240–52; permission to reprint is hereby acknowledged. Finally, I am also grateful to Greg Nicholl and Trevor Lipscombe, at the Johns Hopkins University Press, for their support, and to Barbara Lamb and Kim Johnson, for their help with the manuscript.

ARLY IN MARY WOLLSTONECRAFT'S unfinished text, *The Wrongs of Woman; or, Maria* (1798), the heroine gives up writing lyrical effusions to begin a narrative of her life, which is circulated, also in unfinished form, among various readers inside the text. Her choice raises several issues about the relative value of literary modes. In *Modern Romance and Transformations of the Novel* Ian Duncan, using Sir Walter Scott as his centerpiece, argues that by the early nineteenth century the (masculine) novel had absorbed a (feminine) romance, thus gendering narrative for generations thereafter.[1] Yet Wollstonecraft sees narrative as a means to authority and contestation, even as she struggles with the plots into which Maria is written by both romance and realism. *Wrongs* does not, however, support the argument that the Romantic novel was a marginalized female form—on and increasingly by women—while men claimed the higher status of "poetry."[2] For it is poetry that is conventionalized as feminine, while narrative initiates Maria's growth as a political and individual subject. Indeed, as Mary Favret notes, writing on the fetishized use of poetic inserts in novels by Charlotte Smith and Anne Radcliffe, these inserts, which are "separable, artificial, and disposable," "correct, contain, and hypostatize the feminine in the novel,"[3] instituting poetry itself as feminine. At the same time, Maria does not actually dismiss poetry, but only a specific form of poetry: what she calls "rhapsodies descriptive of the state of [her] mind."[4] Nor is it clear that she writes a novel in Duncan's sense, unless we take "*novel*" nongenerically, as the literary vehicle of the "new(s)" or in Mikhail Bakhtin's sense of the novel as marking a new sense of time oriented to the future rather than the past and resulting in the "novelization" of adjacent genres.[5]

Starting from the unwritten theory in Wollstonecraft's text, this book has three general aims. First, it offers a theory of narrative or, rather, of a "narrativity" opposed to the disciplinary apparatus of the Novel, where the word *Novel*, with a capital N, signifies a sociopolitical institution that developed through the nineteenth century and on whose normalizing role in the public sphere critics from Jürgen Habermas to Clifford Siskin have written.[6] Second, in focusing on this narrativity, this study questions the association of narrative with what Peter Brooks calls "reading for plot,"[7] which derives from a unigeneric reduction of narrative to the (Victorian) Novel. And finally, it reflects on what the category of Romantic narrative can tell us about disciplinary issues raised by historical study that are of particular urgency at this point. These include the role of poetry versus prose as epistemic practices in an emergent modernity and the place of Romanticism itself within a reorganization of knowledge that has subsumed it into a "nineteenth century," the understanding of which is informed by the late-twentieth-century's shift from literature to culture.

The idea for this book began several years ago with two articles, "Romanticism and the Death of Lyric Consciousness" and "The Web of Human Things: Lyric and Narrative in Shelley's *Alastor*" (an earlier and quite different version of chapter 1 of the present book).[8] These articles argued against a synecdoche that had identified Romanticism with lyric, based on the assumption that the Romantics definitively replaced the triad epic/tragedy/comedy with that of epic/drama/lyric.[9] For a long time lyric was thus cast as the dominant mode—if not genre—of a Romanticism that internalized the quest romance (in John Keats' *Endymion* and Percy Shelley's *Alastor*) or lyricized an array of forms including the ballad, the epic (in William Wordsworth's *The Prelude),* and drama (in Shelley's *Prometheus Unbound*).[10] In a tropology that persists from the New Criticism's penchant for analyzing even narrative poetry in short (lyric) segments, to the New Historicism's critique of a Romanticism metonymically identified with Wordsworth, *lyricization* had signified internalization, a retreat into a transcendental identity, and a certain idealism and resistance to materiality.[11] On the other hand, if one argues that the Romantics questioned an identity transcendentally sealed by the abstraction of poetry into lyric, narrative too had not been formulated in the reigning metaphorics of form as a category receptive to "*différance*" (either linguistic or ideological). It was portrayed as linear and logocentric: whether sympathetically, in Paul Ricoeur's argument for a "configurative mean-ing," which puts together the fragments of our lives; ambivalently, in Hayden White's discussion of the "value" of such myths of integration; or critically, in Teresa de Lauretis's claim that the very deployment of characters in a plot (modeled on the subject/verb/object structure of the sentence) is embedded in a patriarchal syntax.[12] D. A. Miller's interest in the "discontents" of narrative was more a concessive clause than a new proposition about narrative, since he continued to make narrative the cause rather than the expression of these discontents. An exception was J. Hillis Miller's *Ariadne's Thread: Story Lines,* which used the figure of the labyrinth to characterize narratological components such as plot and character as lines that split and disseminate, thus extending Yale decon-struction from poetry to the novel and providing a valuable poststructur-alist sequel to structuralist narratology.[13] But since dissemination for Hil-lis Miller characterizes all language, his analysis robbed narrative of any specificity as a mode different from others: a specificity registered, for example, in Maria's turn from rhapsody to narrative in *The Wrongs of Woman.*

At the time, then, the work I saw performed by a study focused on *narrative* for the mapping of Romanticism within a broader ideological field was to argue against the growing critique of the period in terms of what Jerome McGann famously called "the Romantic Ideology." Origi-nally I had meant to focus equally on this narrativity in both prose and poetry. But while I by no means see narrative as limited to the novel (with a small *n*), demographic and curricular changes in the profession over the past two decades have resulted in a shift of attention from poetry to prose, to which this book now responds by focusing primarily on a *poet-ics* of narrative as it emerges in Romantic prose fiction. Prose fiction, for its part, is a broader category than the Novel, including texts such as Percy Shelley's Gothic novels (juvenilia, which I treat, on the model of closet drama, as "closet novels"); Mary Hays's *Memoirs of Emma Court-ney* (which I discuss as an "autonarration," which at points thematizes the Novel and takes issue with it but which is somewhere between auto-biography and fiction); and Wollstonecraft's *Wrongs* (which comes to us as an unfinished part-narrative-cum-manifesto with autonarrational ele-ments and which William Godwin published in a state that was deliber-ately not ready for the publicness of the Novel).

The work of this prose fiction, I suggest, is fundamentally different from that of the Novel as it began to emerge in the nineteenth century and in the Regency period in the work of Scott and Jane Austen. Using this pair of figures to represent Romantic fiction, current criticism and curricular practice has absorbed "Romanticism" into a Victorianized "nineteenth century," which divides the cultural field of the novel between the nation-building of Scott's historical novels and a domestic sphere disciplined by the Austenian novel of manners.[14] The novel of manners, in turn, is a form in which private feelings exist only insofar as private individuals come together as a public, to evoke Habermas's definition of the public sphere, of which the private is merely an epiphenomenon.[15] Accompanying this reduction of Romanticism's contribution to the now-privileged genre of prose is a tendency to identify the period with "poetry," thus diminishing the place of Romanticism within the disciplinary field of the "nineteenth century." For "nineteenth century" is by no means a neutral chronological term; it signals an epistemic redescription analogous to the one that occurred when the Renaissance was renamed "early modern." This latter term had allowed us to study late Medieval and Renaissance culture in terms of the emergence of issues central to our own modernity: gender, new economic formations, travel, and the beginnings of colonialism. In a similar way, the term "nineteenth century" results in a retrodetermination of Romanticism by what the late twentieth century sees as the Victorians' concern with nationalism, imperialism, commodification, and the strictly contained resistance to these forces in various forms of identity and sexual politics. Both redescriptions—early modern and nineteenth century—are part of our own paradigm shift towards an almost exclusive concern with literature's relation to civil society: its contribution to what Kant termed "pragmatic anthropology," which, as Gianni Vattimo argues, is a positivist discipline focused on what "man makes, can, or should make of himself as a freely acting" and enlightened being, "a citizen of the world."[16]

Within this reorganization of knowledge, which has also entailed a shift from "theory" to "cultural studies" (in the loosely thematic sense in which that term is used to protect most work done in English departments under the more rigorous umbrella of thinkers such as Friedrich Kittler), the turn to prose metonymizes a turn to culture and responsibility. The result has been a redistribution of power among the historical fields that has seen the Victorian Novel assume the preeminence once accorded to Romantic "poetry" during the heyday of deconstruction.[17] But arguably this reduction of Romanticism to poetry, as opposed to prose, objectivity, and criticism, had already begun with Victorians such as Robert Browning, John Stuart Mill, and Matthew Arnold and before that with Thomas Love Peacock's *Four Ages of Poetry*. And this in turn has allowed poetry to be disciplined within the development from Romantic prematurity to Victorian sobriety in what Andrew Elfenbein identifies as one of the nineteenth century's "master-narrative[s] of transition."[18]

The Novel is the very crystallization of this master-narrative, given its association with *Bildung* as what Marc Redfield calls aesthetic ideology. This *Bildung* may be figurally concentrated in the maturation of the protagonist, but just as often, given that the *Bildungsroman* is a "semimythical genre,"[19] it consists in an education of the reader within the field of shared judgments—what Immanuel Kant calls the *sensus communis*—for which the Novel functions as an invisible substrate. If only implicitly, the historical role of the Novel in an emergent "contest of faculties"—to quote Kant again—has been well covered. Thus this study tries to make a theoretical as well as a historical contribution. Within the spectrum of existing narrative and narratological theory, it argues for a poetics of narrative that unbinds the closure of plot and thus the ideologemes that plot as mimesis naturalizes. This poetics, I suggest, is the legacy of the Romantic texts discussed here (as well as others) to a theory of narrative as well as an age of prose. I therefore take up an undeveloped comment by Teresa de Lauretis in "Desire in Narrative," where she suggests that we replace "structural analyses" of narrative (Propp, Greimas, etc.) with a "dynamic, processual view of signification as a work(ing) of the codes," which focuses on "narrativity" or the "structuring and destructuring . . . processes at work in textual" production.[20] Narratology, or the *structuralist* theory of narrative, is particularly useful as an object of critique because it conceals ideology within the claim of a pure formalism. At the same time this very formalism lets us see the arbitrary nature of the codes thus inscribed, in contrast to theories oriented to content, which naturalize ideology. As against narrative theory's consent to ideology (whether formal or mimetic), the "work on form, or the deformation of form," as David Carroll calls it in *Paraesthetics*,[21] is at the heart of the narrativity I explore in Romantic prose fiction through, for example, Shelley's attempt in *Alastor* to write a poem that takes form neither as lyric nor story; the distorted forms of his Gothic novels; or Godwin's decision to present *The Wrongs of Woman* in an unfinalized state so as to make us focus on the process of its shaping.

In speaking of a *poetics* of narrative in Romantic prose fiction or in suggesting that "poetry is the idea of prose" (to quote Giorgio Agamben), I use the word "poetry" as Shelley uses it in *The Defence of Poetry*, to connote a faculty or mode of thinking rather than a genre. For it is poetry, or *poiesis*, which, as it "dissolves, diffuses and dissipates" forms in order to "re-create" them, gives us access to the structuring and destructuring processes at work in textual production. Samuel Taylor Coleridge's famous definition is usually seen as crediting the secondary imagination with synthesizing powers, but it is significant that the "struggle to idealize and unify" is underwritten and made possible by a more radically deconstructive activity, a *poiesis* or semiosis.[22] As Joel Faflak argues, drawing on Ross Woodman's work on sanity, madness, and transformation, we "forget this 'poetry' at [our] peril," since it is poetry, or more accurately, *poiesis*, that "returns the public sphere to its creative functioning" by disclosing the "radically chaotic moment" of the "articulation" of a culture's discourses as "fantasy," which Coleridge himself disavows in abstracting imagination from fancy.[23] As this formulation also intimates, poetry is part of the work of the negative; it is not an essence or a positivity. Instead, because poetry in Shelley's words "create[s] afresh . . . associations" that have become "disorganized,"[24] a poetics of narrative allows for an ongoing process of unmaking the codes reified by a culture buried in its institutions so that we can reimagine those institutions. It is in this sense that Shelley can provocatively describe Plato and Francis Bacon as poets (*DP*, 514–15).

This study, in short, takes up the functioning of narrativity in the context of the epistemologies at stake in poetry and prose from Shelley and Peacock to our own Victorianism. At the early end of this history it is worth mentioning Friedrich Schlegel, who thinks of the novel outside the genre distinction between poetry and prose and thus thinks of it as *poiesis* in Coleridge's and Shelley's sense. As Rudolph Haym says, the "genuine novel" for Schlegel is "a *summa* of all that is poetic, and he consistently designates this poetic ideal with the name 'romantic' poetry." Or as Schlegel himself says in his "Letter on the Novel," which is part of his *Dialogue on Poetry:* "Ein Roman ist ein romantisches Buch."[25] To be sure, Schlegel's "poetry" is a plenitude that does not quite take account of the work of the negative explored in this study. Focusing on this work, which includes the deformation of form as a crucial part of the work on form, I begin with two complementary propositions. In *The Concept of Criticism in German Romanticism,* Walter Benjamin suggests that "the Idea of poetry is prose," where prose means criticism and reflection, sobriety rather than enthusiasm or "mania." Against Benjamin's insistence that poetry increasingly turns towards its "prosaic kernel,"[26] Agamben sees prose itself as having to take up a "poetic inheritance with which thought must come to terms." While sharing Benjamin's view that prose and poetry are not distinct genres but exist in relation to each other, Agamben insists that poetry is "the Idea of prose," poetry being a form of negative capability that is crystallized (in the actual genre of poetry) in an irresolution between "syntax" and "rhythm," the larger logic of the poem and the unformulated drives—what Julia Kristeva calls the "semiotic"—for which rhythm itself is no more than a figure.[27] In our own context, and in a debate that goes back to the nineteenth century, prose has come to signify social engagement and has become cathected with a certain social positivism and resistance to Theory, which I take up in chapter 5 and throughout the book in an implicit homology between poetry and Theory as forms of "difficult thought." Narrative as outlined here is at once poetry made responsible to its prosaic kernel and prose cognizant of its poietic inheritance.

Within this framing set of issues, *Romantic Narrative* consists of six intersecting chapters, which explore different ways in which the processes of narrative are thematized and operate in texts by Percy Shelley, Mary Hays, William Godwin, and Mary Wollstonecraft. The first chapter sets the agenda for the book by discussing Shelley's *Alastor* as engaged in an unfinished dialogue with itself about the nature of poetry on the threshold of a world of prose and (Arnoldian) criticism evoked in the poem's Preface. Shelley had to confront prose as the genre of an emergent modernity in Peacock's *Four Ages of Poetry,* which provides a Scottish Enlightenment history of the progressive outmoding of poetry in commercial society. He further had to confront it through the work of his wife, Mary Shelley, whose turn to prose and conflicted relation to poetry as "the Idea of prose" I also discuss in chapter 1. This chapter, "The Trauma of Lyric:

Shelley's Missed Encounter with Poetry in *Alastor*," therefore reads *Alastor* alongside Mary Shelley's novels, Wordsworth's *The Ruined Cottage* and Keats' *The Fall of Hyperion,* and through Browning's distinction between subjective and objective poetry in his essay on Percy Shelley, as well as through the latter's own distinction between "poem" and "story" in *The Defence.*

My discussion of *Alastor* begins with the aporia of a Narrator writing a poem about a lyric "Poet" that withdraws from gathering itself together as either lyric or narrative. Lacking characters and events, the poem's structure is consumed by its texture, to borrow John Crowe Ransom's terms in his defense of poetry against an Aristotelian Chicago School, which constitutes literature around plot and argument. Or, in Allen Tate's terms, the poem's "ex-tension" keeps collapsing into an "intension," which deconstructs any clarity of plot and argument,[28] yet also frustrates the simplicity, concentration, and closure of lyric idealization. Shelley's resistance to shaping the Poet's life into a plot that reduces texture to structure has to do with the poetry omitted by what he calls "the *story* of particular facts" (*DP,* 515). Hence his Narrator hangs on to a lyricism that does not describe the genre of the poem but subsists in its affect and in buried references to Wordsworth. But what the Narrator protects by restricting poetry to the ineffability of lyric is not really lyric, but a trauma cathected with lyric: the trauma of the foreclosure of poetry. For the Poet of *Alastor* is not Browning's subjective poet, as I suggest by reading him through work by Maurice Blanchot and Jean-Luc Nancy on literature and death. In this sense, we can see Shelley's Poet as a precursor of later poets such as Hölderlin, Nerval, and Rilke. Of this literature as the underside of modernity Michel Foucault writes that it "breaks with the whole definition of *genres* as forms adapted to an order of representations" and "encloses itself within a radical intransitivity." Interestingly, Foucault sees the emergence of literature as linked to that of philology, the subject of this book's last chapter: "At the beginning of the nineteenth century," he writes, "at a time when language was burying itself within its own density as an object . . . it was also reconstituting itself elsewhere, in an independent form, difficult of access, folded back upon the enigma of its own origin."[29] But writing a half century before the literature Foucault describes here, the Narrator of *Alastor* misrecognizes as lyric a poetry of involution, self-reflection, and negativity that is profoundly at odds with lyric ideality purely as a resistance to narrative. At the same time, *Alastor* is impelled by an insistent narrativity. The Narrator, that is, needs to tell the Poet's story and to pass on the poem's missed encounter with itself, as the problem of thinking the work of this more modern "poetry" in culture: a problem more thoroughly engaged in poems such as *The Fall of Hyperion* or *The Triumph of Life* or in the prose fiction taken up in this book. At the end of the text, then, it is not so much that the Poet dies as that the Poet as "phantasm" and "image" is returned to a cultural archive—what Yeats calls "the foul rag-and-bone shop of the heart"[30]—so that the High Romantic poetry unworked in *Alastor* can be thought anew.

Chapter 2 begins from the curious fact that Shelley had actually written two novels before turning to serious poetry, implicitly recognizing that poetry as the vehicle of the "Romantic Ideology" always exists in the shadow of its novelization. Indeed, it is not just that these prose fictions trouble what will become the Victorian identification of Shelley with a pure poetry. Anticipating his debate with Peacock's essay on the demise of poetry by writing his own *Nightmare Abbey* ten years earlier, Shelley also crosses the boundary between high and low culture upon which more conservative concepts of Romantic "poetry" are constituted. Thus the second chapter, "Shelley's Promethean Narratives: Gothic Anamorphoses in *Zastrozzi, St. Irvyne,* and *Prometheus Unbound,*" therefore reads Shelley's novels *Zastrozzi* (1810) and *St. Irvyne* (1811) in conjunction with *Prometheus Unbound* and, intermittently, with other cannibalized bits of his past and future poetry (*Alastor, The Triumph of Life*). It explores two contrary movements: the narrativity underlying the seemingly High Romantic closure of Shelley's lyrical drama, and the poetry that Shelley wants to restore to the work performed by narrative in the (de)construction of his culture's fantasies. Drawing on G. W. F. Hegel's theorization of the Symbolic and Romantic as modes in which the "Idea" does not find an adequate embodiment in material forms, and taking up Julia Kristeva's notion of the "adolescent novel," I discuss Shelley's juvenilia as what I call closet novels: texts whose ideas are not ready to be performed and which are thus composed of semiautonomous parts, which foreground a disconnection between acts, agents, and ideas. The novels are a pastiche, and in styling them as such Shelley deconstructs them into the "phrase regimes"—in Jean-François Lyotard's term—from which the

Promethean ideology they project is compounded. He thus dissolves and recycles these phrases and ideas so as to make them available for further thought. Anticipating Shelley's similar composition of *Prometheus Unbound,* the novels allow us to read the latter as well against the grain of a critical unification imposed on it by theories of organic form, not to mention that they explore the darker underside of Promethean transgression, thus disclosing the prosaic kernel of Shelley's poetry.

As texts almost entirely reducible to their form—their malconstruction and the stereotyped plot and character positions they explode—the Gothic novels can also be seen as containing an embedded narratology. In other words, they are parodies of a narratology whose structural mechanisms they defamiliarize, so as to unbind the *narrativity* that exists within the novels and between the novels and Shelley's poetry. Turning to a more obviously "realistic" text, chapter 3, "Unbinding the Personal: Autonarration, Epistolarity, and Genotext in Mary Hays's *Memoirs of Emma Courtney,*" looks at Hays's unworking of the structural discipline of the Novel through what I call "autonarration." *Memoirs* is infamously based on Hays's failed relationship with the Cambridge radical William Frend, which she uses in conjunction with her letters to Godwin as a theater for negotiating political justice, by exploring the psychodynamics of desires and drives that cannot be expressed within the social scripts available to her. Indeed, the very syntagm of romantic love as defining women's desire is one such script that Hays projects and negates. Far from being a narcissistic transfer of life into text, autonarration (a term I extend to other Romantic writers, such as Mary Shelley) involves a double textualization of both life and fiction. It does not unfold at the level of either life or text, but through the differences between the novel and the "events" or facts that it symbolically transforms or anamorphically deforms. These differences, rather than the ideologically reified (counter) positions of things as they are *or* their romantic, feminist subversion, constitute the work of the negative that the narrativity of this text (which is often misunderstood as fetishizing desire) seeks to set in motion.

One such difference between Hays's "life" and her text is the sordid, secret marriage of the novel's hero, Augustus Harley, which unbinds us from a plot of romantic failure that would dismiss Emma/Hays's desire, yet without positing marriage as the goal of this desire. Such differences make narrative a zone of possibilities wherein we can recover what Gerald Prince calls "the disnarrated,"[31] what has not been but could yet be said. Focusing on such differences, chapter 3 tries to access an underlying *poiesis* that makes autonarration the site where a culture's narratives can be dissolved and dissipated in order to be reimagined. In order to theorize this *poiesis,* I expand the concept of the archive introduced in both previous chapters and drawn from Foucault and Jacques Derrida. Over the course of his work Foucault uses the term "archive" in quite contrary senses. In "Fantasia of the Library" (1967), the archive is the amorphous mass of everything that has been or *could be* said, like the world underneath the grave described by Shelley in *Prometheus Unbound,* which contains the phantasms of "of all forms that think and live" as well as "Dreams and the light imaginings of men" (1.1.198–200). But in *The Archeology of Knowledge* (1969), this amorphous mass is renamed the "corpus," while the archive is limited to the "law of what can be said," the "*langue* that defines the system of constructing" sentences and events within accepted phrase regimes.[32] The narrativity released in Romantic texts, I suggest, constantly opposes the systems of archiving experience within predictable plots to a corpus that unbinds the phrases and syntagms of narrative from their ideological closure. The deconstruction of these systems requires what Derrida calls an archiviolithic process, a kind of death drive that ex-terminates existing terms and syntagms.[33] Thus chapter 3 also draws on D. W. Winnicott's analysis of playing to develop a psychopathology of narrative as a "potential space" in which the author plays with the social text by projecting, abjecting, and ex-terminating characters and plot positions. In so doing, to evoke Shelley, narrative "create[s] afresh" the "associations" that have become "disorganized" in the process of what Godwin calls "institution" as the reification of ideology.

Taking up this notion of institution, by which Godwin means not only political and social institutions but also anything that has been discursively instituted, chapter 4 turns to Godwin himself and asks how narrative can help us think before the universality of institution. In other words, it asks how narrative can help us think anarchically, in the root sense of an-arche: before *arche,* or foundation, or before the aesthetic and juridical practices that a culture develops to archive experience. Such practices include character, which Godwin calls into question when Caleb says: "I have now no character";[34] and they include "story" or "tale," words Godwin uses to suggest a sequencing or reduction of the explosive particulars of the event within the (ideo)logic of plot. Focusing on *Caleb Williams* and more briefly on *Fleetwood* and *Mandeville*, this chapter, "The Scene of Justice: Trial and Confession in Godwin's *Caleb Williams* and Other Fiction," extends the poetics of narrative into an ethics of narrativity as the perpetual unsettling of the stories we tell about ourselves and others. It thus develops further a concept of pathological reading introduced in chapter 3 with reference to Emma Courtney, by describing the anarchic effects of our "perverse identification" as part-subjects with parts of characters such as Caleb, Falkland, and Fleetwood—these particulars being the unstable ground for a reimagining of culture.

More specifically, chapter 4 is concerned with how the texture of narrative—its "minute shades [of] character" and minute particulars[35]—raises the issue of *judgment,* which is thematized by the novel's juridical framework as a metaphor for the disciplinary apparatus of the Novel. For judgment is at the heart of the Novel as socialization and normalization, and it is inscribed in its very terminology, where "deciding" the plot connotes a legal-moral decision that Godwin unsettles by writing an ending for his first novel that he immediately crosses out. In taking up judgment in a philosophical, ethical, and juridical sense, I read Godwin alongside his contemporary Kant, who distinguishes between reflective and determinant judgment in the third *Critique,* so as to make Godwinian narrative part of a radical Enlightenment, which calls into question the Novel as an institution of the public sphere. I also read Godwin through Lyotard (to whom Kant was important) and suggest that narrative is a mode uniquely suited to doing justice to the other as opposed to passing judgment, since it is through the particulars of narrative that we access the "differends," which cannot be captured in a judgment. For Lyotard the differend is the resistant kernel of difference that eludes capture in a litigation (or argument), which requires judgments to be made in the terms of one or the other party.[36] Paradoxically, it is the very realism of the novel that discloses these differends by eliciting a poietic practice of close reading focused on the novel's in-tension rather than its plot and extension. Realism here converges with Idealism. For, as I argue elsewhere, there is a unique symbiosis between empiricism and Idealism in Romantic thought that is also a differend between Godwin and Kant. In other words, far from being reducible to John Locke's tabula rasa (as opposed to Kant's prestructuring of experience by existing concepts), empiricism entails a *sensitivity* towards the minute particulars that disrupt our concepts: particulars that must be developed towards their "ideality" (in Hegel's words) if we are to grasp their larger significance for these concepts.[37]

Departing from previous chapters (as the novel itself differs in style from others discussed here), chapter 5, on Godwin's *St. Leon,* takes up Romantic narrative, not in terms of the deconstructive texture of narrativity, but in terms of the disciplinarity of the Novel on the cusp of the nineteenth century and the disciplinary discourse network in which the privileging of the Novel participates at the turn of our own century. Novels began to be taught in Scottish universities as part of a "wholesale restructuring of the public sphere," in which literature, as the discipline of rhetoric and belles-lettres, was being configured under the umbrella of political economy. This reorganization of knowledge was part of the emergence of "civil or commercial society,"[38] and it is still with us in more populist form, in a cultural studies that adds ever new subjects and objects to the corpus (from Indians to parrots), according to a liberal principle of representative democracy and wealth creation. Insofar as rhetoric and belles-lettres were part of civil society's discourse of improvement, "the roots of the modern university disciplines of anthropology and of English Literature," as Robert Crawford points out, "are mutually entwined," and "both are linked to the development of modern economics."[39] The Novel was uniquely homologous with the rise of anthropology, which is still a key discipline in the academic postmodern, as David Simpson argues: differently, to be sure, and yet not so differently, since we remain the inheritors of a discourse of improvement that Theodor Adorno and Max Horkheimer have critiqued as "enlightenment."[40] For Adam Smith, who planned "a grand synthesis of the human sciences . . . across the civic and pedagogic domain of the university curriculum,"[41] saw the supersession of romance by the Novel as part of the "improvement" at the heart of anthropology: a narrative of transition that is taken over in Peacock's "four ages" of poetry.[42] It is no accident that Smith, who played a key role in the modern disciplining of literature as *techne,* what Redfield calls aesthetic ideology, was also the father of modern economics. Nor is it surprising that the principle of economy is throughout the coded individualism of the Novel, as well as the more apparently eccentric individualism of cultural studies, as a consent to seeing man as an epiphenomenon of the economic and a constraint to contribute to the general "good."

Reading against the grain of the Novel as economy, the fifth chapter, "Gambling, Alchemy, Speculation: Godwin's Critique of Pure Reason in *St. Leon*," focuses on Godwin's second novel, which is about a sixteenth-century aristocrat and gambler who acquires the philosopher's stone. It takes up the two operational metaphors of the text, gambling and alchemy, as figures through which Godwin speculates on what is and is not sayable within the discourse of the Novel and the increasingly middle-class, anti-Romantic ideology of his time. The chapter continues the previous chapter's reading of Godwin alongside Kant, some of whose work, including his utopian political essays, was translated in the 1790s. In reading Godwin with Kant I raise two larger issues: that of the place of Romanticism in a culture increasingly hostile to (German) speculative philosophy and thus, as David Simpson has shown, resistant to what was then called "Theory";[43] and that of the place of theoretical and philosophical approaches in our own culture, which is to say, the issue of what Derrida calls the *"philosophical* continents" that divide our own culture.[44] Speculation in Godwin's novel functions as a hinge for the debate he sets up around his central character, whose use of the confessional form requires that we perversely identify with his choice of experiment over thrift and family values. "Speculation" here encompasses intellectual speculation, economic speculation, or gambling, and the gamble that is alchemy as a metaphor for perfectibility. Because of the incredible situation of a character who lives forever, the novel unfolds as a potential space in which St. Leon can be dismissed and brought back, and in which ideologemes such as family and nation can be ex-terminated without consequence. Within this narrativity, chapter 5 continues to explore the issue of judgment (and specifically how we judge St. Leon) as a process of reflecting on judgment itself. This process in turn stages a differend between speculative Idealism and Common Sense, the antieconomy of romance and the episteme of the Novel as a form increasingly committed to the family as the sentimental, private manifestation of governmentality.

Finally, chapter 6 returns to the figure of the archive by way of Godwin's (literally) archival work on Wollstonecraft's *The Wrongs of Woman*. For the text we have was compiled by Godwin from two manuscript states and published not as what we now call an eclectic text but as a text in which he carefully marks lacunae, points of (in)decision, and his own editorial insertions. This chapter, "Whose Text? Godwin's Editing of

Mary Wollstonecraft's *Wrongs of Woman*," therefore tries to imagine Wollstonecraft's novel apart from her husband's editing of it. In particular I focus on what it might mean to read the text as ending with the trial scene in its last complete chapter and without the fragments in "The Conclusion, By the Editor," which may well not have been the last fragments Wollstonecraft wrote (as Godwin mournfully implies). Taking up court procedures and divorce and separation laws at the time, I suggest that Godwin's narrativizing of the text through the addition of the Conclusion is different from the alternately polemical, sentimental, and enthusiastic narratives that Wollstonecraft herself (de)constructs. But the point of discerning two (or more) voices in the text is not to restore a supposed "original" text. It is rather to disclose the part-narratives embedded in Godwin's editing and the other narratives they occlude as part of a general narrativity released by the publication of the text as a draft, an edited text. More specifically, by drawing attention to his own editorial activity, Godwin (to evoke Lyotard, on whom I draw throughout this book) decomposes the text into the phrases from which it is assembled. He halts any premature narrativizing of its episodes and affects within a genre such as sentimental romance or feminist communal narrative, and instead asks us to focus on the very process of phrasing and on the structuring and destructuring processes at work in textuality. Wollstonecraft's "text," Godwin's editing, and others' readings of the text over time all form part of an archive that includes both her writing and the thinking that has been and still can be done around her work. This is to say that by phrasing the text in the philological genre, which demands a careful attention to texture, Godwin restores a certain "poetry" both to prose and its reading.

ABBREVIATIONS

A	G. W. F. Hegel, *Aesthetics*
CJ	Immanuel Kant, *Critique of Judgment*
CPR	Immanuel Kant, *Critique of Pure Reason*
CW	William Godwin, *Caleb Williams*
D	Jean-François Lyotard, *The Differend*
DP	Percy Shelley, *Defence of Poetry*
E	*The Complete Poetry and Prose of William Blake*
HR	William Godwin. "Of History and Romance," in *Caleb Williams*
L	Letters by Mary Hays, in Mary Hays, *Memoirs of Emma Courtney*
M	Mary Hays, *Memoirs of Emma Courtney*
MV	William Godwin, *Memoirs of the Author of "A Vindication of the Rights of Woman"*
PJ	William Godwin, *Enquiry Concerning Political Justice*
PU	Percy Shelley, *Prometheus Unbound*
R	Julia Kristeva, *Revolution in Poetic Language*
St.L	William Godwin, *St. Leon*
W	Mary Wollstonecraft, *The Wrongs of Woman; or, Maria: A Fragment*

Romantic Narrative

CHAPTER ONE

The Trauma of Lyric

Shelley's Missed Encounter with Poetry in Alastor

L ABYRINTHS, WEAVINGS, and related figures are ubiquitous in Shelley's texts, whether they are used to characterize language or other ways of grasping the world, such as thought, emotion, even vision. Thus, in *Prometheus Unbound* (1820), language rules with "Daedal harmony a throng / Of thoughts and forms," whose complexity it does not eliminate so much as contain within its own labyrinthine structure (4.416–17).[1] In an essay on imagery Shelley describes the mind as "a wilderness of intricate paths . . . a world within a world."[2] Perhaps the most famous of such images occurs in the *Revolt of Islam* (1817), where Cythna describes the tracing of signs on the sand to range:

> These woofs, as they were woven of my thought:
> Clear, elemental shapes, whose smallest change
> A subtler language within language wrought.   (7.32)

The phrasing here anticipates Shelley's description of the epipsyche, in the essay "On Love" (1818), as a "soul within our soul," wherein we

> dimly see within our intellectual nature a miniature as it were of our entire self, yet deprived of all that we condemn or despise, the ideal prototype of every thing excellent or lovely that we are capable of conceiving as belonging to the nature of man. Not only the portrait of our external being, but an assemblage of the minutest particulars of which our nature is composed: a mirror whose surface reflects only the forms of purity and brightness: a soul within our soul that describes a circle around its proper Paradise which pain and sorrow or evil dare not overleap. (504)

As a cognitive figure, the epipsyche is at once a "surface" idealization of the psyche it projects and a mirror of this psyche's "minutest particulars": a tension or disavowal echoed in *The Defence of Poetry* (1821), where poetry is a "mirror which makes beautiful that which is distorted," while the story of particular facts "is as a mirror which distorts . . . that which should be beautiful" (515). Similarly, language in Cythna's account, as the lure of inwardness, promises a grasping of identity but is implicated in intricacies and involutions that displace any definitive meaning. For it seems that the process of "composition" generates a secondary discourse, by which the clear elemental shapes with which we begin in "inspiration" are subtly shifted (*DP,* 531), and that representation is a turning inwards that is not the finding of a center. Taken together these images suggest that Shelley senses in language a disturbing disseminative potential: "senses," because, unlike the contemporary theorists whom he so strikingly antici-pates, he also wants to elide this potential. In short, language and thought, which is significantly conceived *as* language in *The Revolt,* form a mirror stage that discloses hidden articulations and fragmentations in the clear elemental shapes projected on the plane of the imaginary.

These descriptions of intricacy and complexity aptly describe *Alastor* (1816), a poem characterized by what Allen Tate calls "*in*tension," as the failure to achieve a "tension" between structure and texture. In intension connotative inwardness and obscurity overwhelm the drive to "*exten*-sion," or summarizable statement,[3] hence the number of "'short-circuited comparisons,' 'self-inwoven similes,' and other reflexive locutions in the poem."[4] The poem's intension marks its resistance both to the lyric crys-tallization that its speaker craves and to the story into which he also tries to shape the Poet's life as lyricism fails him: a story that remains "a half told and mangled tale," to evoke Godwin.[5] At the heart of the poem stands the speaker, who is almost universally referred to as the Narrator.[6] This Narrator struggles to find a mode in which to represent the Poet, that struggle being tied up with what we can call the differing "onto-poetics" of lyric and story. As the medium through whom inspiration passes into composition, the Narrator has the task of mediating literature to the world, and he stands on the threshold between poetry and a prose held off in the Preface, just outside the protected space of the text. As such *Alastor* can usefully frame the issues I raise in this study around a nar-rativity that resists being disciplined as the Novel, which are really issues about the place of Romanticism in relation to the disciplinary structures of modernity. To be sure, *Alastor* is not like the texts to be explored in subsequent chapters, since its engagement with the complex intertexture of relations that underlies narrative is abstracted to the level of linguistic complexity rather than particularized as narrative. In the *Defence,* too, Shelley analyzes these relations in terms of the system of language rather than a narratological system with psychic as well as epistemological materiality. Nevertheless, *Alastor* stands at the cusp of a turn from a poetry identified with lyric and its cognates to a narrative that crosses the categories of both prose and poetry. Unable to form his text as poem or story, the Narrator harks back to the receding origin of a "lyric encryption," which is already presented as troubled in Wordsworth. His double resistance to both poem and story thus poses crucial questions not only about the limits of a lyricization and inwardization that we associate with the "Romantic Ideology" but also about what is foreclosed by the objectivity of prose, considered not as a genre but, like poetry in the *Defence,* as an epistemology.

In what follows I approach *Alastor* as the autonarration of Shelley projecting himself as the Poet, the Preface writer who is uncomfortably on the cusp between poetry and an emergent Peacockian world of utility, and the Narrator who tells, or cannot tell, the story of the poet he (is not quite sure he) wants to be. Shelley, that is, projects himself as a subject still in process, through a series of part-objects by way of whom he negotiates his relation to poetry. The Poet, who returns melodramatically as Keats wounded by reviewers in the hysterical self-performance of *Adonais,* is certainly how Mary Shelley projects Percy both in her editing and in her bitterly idealized de-jection of him as Woodville in *Mathilda.* As Mary Favret argues, Shelley's editing of her husband's poetry, accompanied by some fifty pages of commentary in the form of prefaces and notes, "models the definition of genres for the rest of the nineteenth century" and raises the question of the political stakes of genre. In this passive-aggressive "labour of love" Shelley, according to Favret, constructs Percy as esoteric, "ethereal and insubstantial," even "pitiable." She effeminizes the poet so as to claim for the woman writer "an immediate social and ideological influence" connected to "the various modes of prose fiction," in contrast to which poetry is disallowed from having a "political effect."[7] Favret's argument has even more resonance today than in 1993, as "cultural studies" in its current recension has radically leveled the ground or, rather, reversed the hierarchy between poetry and prose, high and low culture, not to mention "theory" and cultural studies itself. Yet this contest of faculties already frames the work of Kierkegaard in his distinction between a passionate, revolutionary age and a leveling, average age, and of Arnold, in his distinction between epochs of creation and criticism.[8] Before them, it also frames the work of the second generation of Romantic poets, including Byron, who wrote poetry as "the prose of the world" in *Don Juan,* and Shelley himself, who wrote prose as well as poetry. Indeed, the Poet who crystallizes the transcendental blindness of the Romantic Ideology is already a subject of Peacockian mockery as Fitzeustace, in Shelley's *St. Irvyne,* published five years earlier than *Alastor.*

As a poem that makes poetry and story (if not actually prose) its objects of reflection, *Alastor* is thus the unfinished autonarration of Shelley's struggle to think through the task of literature in the modern world. As I suggest at the end of this chapter, Mary Shelley's shifting inscription of "Shelley" from *Mathilda* to *The Last Man* expands this autonarration into a process that extends across and between her corpus and Percy's. Contrary to Favret's argument, which constructs her as an oppositional subject in relation to "masculine Romanticism," Mary Shelley's own corpus can also be seen autonarratively, as a repeating and working through of her relationship to Romanticism through a series of part-subjects that includes Percy, Byron, and her parents. The medium for this process is a narrative, or rather narrativity, that operates between texts and is not to be aligned strictly with the genres of prose or poetry. Interestingly, Shelley himself links this narrativity to the *spirit* of poetry when he speaks, albeit somewhat rhapsodically, of a "cyclic poem," in the making of which "all poets, like the co-operating thoughts of one great mind," participate (*DP,* 512, 522). By poetry Shelley does not mean poetry in its "restricted sense," as an arrangement "of "metrical language," but as an underlying "faculty" that is at the heart of "revolutions in opinion" (513, 515) and the renewal of "language [and] institution" in Godwin's sense (521) and that composes from its initiating thoughts, "as from elements, other thoughts, each containing within itself the principle of its own integrity" (510). As a text that emerges from this narrativity, *Alastor* does not conclude the Poet's story. Rather it restores him to an "archive" of images that lie "underneath the grave" (*PU,* 1.197): a world of "charnels" and "coffins," like Yeats' "foul rag and bone shop of the heart." It is from this liminal space that the Narrator summons the Poet's "phantasm" at the beginning of *Alastor*, and it is to this space that he returns his "image" at the end, allowing Shelley to depotentialize the figure of the Poet and make it available for further reflection (40, 71).

Of course, the Poet in *Alastor* is not the poet of *The Defence*, being almost a cliché of High Romanticism. Rather, he is at once abjected and protected as a lyric poet. For Shelley has yet to work through the place of "poetry" in the modern world, and arguably one outcome of this process is a text such as *Prometheus Unbound*, which I discuss in chapter 2 in relation to Shelley's relatively unremarked foray into prose fiction and thus narrativity. In this chapter I therefore approach *Alastor* on two levels. On a thematic or *metathematic* level the poem, as an attempted narrative about a lyric poet, is an unresolved reflection on what is foreclosed by both lyric and "story" as the form of narrative most oriented to plot. Here lyric, as an avoidance of (hi)story, figures a transcendence that has been critiqued as the Romantic Ideology, even as the hysteria of this over-idealization encrypts and protects a trauma, which is the trauma of the foreclosure of poetry. Yet *Alastor* is not a lyric, its very length resulting in the dissipation rather than concentration of lyric affect.[9] Nor is it a story, since it is profoundly lacking in what Paul Ricoeur calls "followability," forcing us to think about the limitations of this followability, "thanks to which the plot construes significant wholes out of scattered events."[10] In fact, *Alastor* is profoundly "unreadable" in Paul de Man's sense: a poem that dis-figures itself, as its figures, including those of genre, recede towards the ground from which all figure and all self-fashioning emerge as simplifications. At its most fundamental level, the poem raises the issue of "shape," which de Man discerns in his analysis of the "shape all light" in *The Triumph of Life*.[11] Hence, before any thematization of genre or mode, *Alastor* also asks to be approached at an *archeological* level as Shelley's most intense encounter with a complexity that underlies and swallows up the text's attempts to conventionalize itself as lyric, elegy, or story. In the *Defence* Shelley will come up against the fact that this complexity inheres in the very system of language. And insofar as the linguistic system after Ferdinand de Saussure becomes the analogical basis for narratology, Shelley's theorizing of language in the *Defence* can double as a theory of narrative complexity that unsettles narratology's attempt to make narrative a form of "institution," albeit in a neutrally structural way, which conceals the ideological stakes of this narratology.

This complexity and intension operate aslant any thematization of lyric or story to raise a larger issue at the heart of my discussion of "narrative": that of poetry versus prose, not as genres but as epistemologies and practices. In *The Idea of Prose,* Giorgio Agamben argues that there is no absolutely distinct identity to poetry: prose and poetry exist in a diacritical relation, in their difference from each other. Briefly, poetry is "the discourse in which it is possible to set a metrical limit against a syntactical one," such that, as Alexander García Düttman explains in his commentary on Agamben, there is a suspension or hesitation between "signification" and *"melos"* as that which "resist[s] any translation."[12] Hence Shelley's emphasis in *The Defence* on meter and sound as constitutive of poetry, even though this emphasis may seem at odds with his desire not to restrict poetry to a genre. Agamben's focus on the legacy of poetry forms a symmetrical pair with Walter Benjamin's argument, in *The Concept of Criticism in German Romanticism,* for the absolute privilege of prose in German Romanticism. For Benjamin "the idea of poetry is prose," and prose is the "ground of poetic forms, all of which are mediated in it and dissolved as though in their canonical creative ground." Benjamin's paradoxical assertion that prose can be poetry echoes Friedrich Schlegel's decoupling of the novel from the form of prose, when he famously writes that "Ein Roman ist ein romantisches Buch."[13] But by a sleight of hand Benjamin, unlike Schlegel, also *does* equate Romanticism with the mechanisms of prose, identifying the prose of the novel with the prosaic. For Benjamin, then, the "idea of poetry" is prose, where prose means criticism and reflection, sobriety rather than "ecstasy" or "mania."[14]

Against Benjamin's insistence that poetry finds its "idea," the "a priori of a method," in its "prosaic kernel," Agamben sees prose itself as having to take up a "poetic inheritance with which thought must come to terms." For Agamben, then, the "idea," or a priori method, of prose is poetry, the memory of which continues to inhabit the prose in which poetry seeks its idea. Agamben's synecdoche for poetry is *"enjambement"* as a "disconnection . . . between sounding rhythm and meaning." Thus, "contrary to the received opinion that sees in poetry a perfect fit between sound and meaning," an aesthetic ideology, "poetry lives, instead, only in their inner disagreement." One must not underestimate the importance of Benjamin's understanding of the Romantics in terms of a criticism and a reflection that move beyond both the eighteenth century's celebration of conventional aesthetic rules and the Sturm und Drang's "boundless cult of creative power understood as the mere expressive force of the creator."[15] Crucial to this reading is the recognition that the Romantics release "reflection . . . from the restriction to a self-positing I that it had in Fichte" and extend it to "thinking in general."[16] In an Anglo-American context, Benjamin's reading of Romanticism can be posed against critiques of the Romantic Ideology as "aesthetic ideology" from Irving Babbitt to Jerome McGann. For the Narrator, far from displaying "an uncritical absorption in Romanticism's own self-representations,"[17] summons up the Poet only as an obscure "phantasm"; to a degree, the Narrator therefore represents a principle of sobriety, as Wasserman first argued in opposing him to the Poet.[18] Nevertheless, given that Benjamin, as Rodolphe Gasché suggests, does finally want to move beyond reflection as it plays out in Romanticism,[19] we must ask what it is that impedes this movement: what it is that stalls the Narrator's criticism of the Poet and makes "reflection" not reducible to "criticism." Or why is it that the Narrator resists prose as the idea of poetry, a resistance we feel even in the prose of the Preface-writer?

On the one hand, the Preface-writer constructs the Poet's life as a lesson in which the Poet's exclusive pursuit of a "prototype" without equivalent in experience rightly leads to a disappointment in which his "self-centred seclusion [is] avenged by the furies of an irresistible passion" (73). This "allegory" (73) tellingly anticipates the binaries set up more sympathetically in Browning's *Essay* on Percy Shelley, which is one of the earlier texts to introduce prose as the idea of poetry. Browning, as is well known, distinguishes between "objective" and "subjective" poetry, inaugurating the Victorians' dissociation of the Romantics—except for Wordsworth—from prose. For Browning, who mirrors standard distinctions between the classical and the Romantic in Friedrich Schiller and Hegel, the objective work "speaks for itself": "the thing fashioned, [the] poetry" is "substantive, projected from [the poet] and distinct." On the other hand, the subjective or Romantic work is not fully separated from the poet, forming, we could say, a part-object. To be sure, Browning idealizes the inwardness of the subjective poet. He does not speak of part-objects but recasts Shelley's corpus as a "sublime, fragmentary essay" in which immaturity is the unfinishedness of inspiration rather than hesitation. Thus the subjective poet is a "seer," whereas the objective poet is a "fashioner," who sees "more clearly, widely, and deeply, than is possible to the average mind." As one who sees ex-tensively and is oriented to the world, the "aggregate human mind," the objective poet reproduces "things external (whether the phenomena of the scenic universe or the manifested action of the human heart and brain) with an immediate reference . . . to the common eye and apprehension of his fellow men." By contrast, the subjective poet embodies what he perceives with reference not "to the many below [but] to the One above him," the "absolute Mind." His words are the "*Ideas* of Plato, seeds of creation, lying burningly on the Divine Hand."[20] This poet is the "Poet" of *Alastor* and *Adonais,* whose life the Preface-writer, with Victorian prescience, characterizes as "not barren of instruction to actual men" (73) and which he, unlike Browning, judges from the perspective of an objective literature allied with prose.

No sooner, however, has the Preface-writer dismissed the Poet as removed from "actual men" than he turns round and fervidly praises the Poet's generosity of spirit, claiming that those who are "instigated by no sacred thirst of doubtful knowledge, . . . loving nothing on this earth, and cherishing no hopes beyond" are "morally dead" (73). Standing on the edge of a Victorian period in which Browning, despite his sympathy for Shelley, would choose objective over subjective poetry, and in which Arnold would valorize criticism over creation, Shelley in *Alastor* occupies a liminal space: a differend, in Jean-François Lyotard's terms, between poetry and the emergent spirit of prose. As the Preface-writer he looks forward to criticism rather than creation, even as he evokes Wordsworth in the antechapel to his poem so as to proclaim the aridity of surviving into one's own maturity. But as the Narrator Shelley, though feeling the pressure of prose, harks back to a lyricism he deconstructs, yet almost unconsciously, as if not taking responsibility for his sobriety. For the Narrator's tone, contrary to Wasserman's view of him as a realist, is characterized by a certain sentimentality, a staged "mawkish[ness]," to evoke Keats' sober criticism of his own *Isabella.*[21] Through its very conflictedness, its resistance to itself, the poem inaugurates the question that remains the horizon for Romanticism as prose: that of poetry's legacy to prose. And this question returns in the Preface, which we can take to be both before and after the poem it prefaces. For the Preface ends not with prose but with a quotation from Wordsworth: with verse, which, in its etymological root as *versus*, signifies the "turning" or "hanging" back that Agamben sees as the essence of poetry.[22]

Yet *Alastor* is a missed encounter with this question of poetry, to which Keats returns in *The Fall of Hyperion,* where he works through the differend between the objective poet, who feels the pressure of being useful to humanity, and the dreamer, who is not quite the subjective poet criticized by the Preface-writer. In contrast to Keats, Shelley at this point can conceive of the Poet only as someone whose "genius," in Browning's words, "operate[s] by a different law." This simplification forces Shelley into the equally unconvincing criticism of the Preface, which lays the ground for a dismissal of the Poet as ineffectual angel, resulting in a further hysterical retreat from criticism in the second paragraph of the Preface. What *Alastor* misses is what Browning also misses when he contrasts the objective poet, who reproduces "things external," with his subjective counterpart, who "rather carries them on the retina of his own eyes."[23] Browning's phrase fleetingly grasps subjective poetry as inwardness—a reflection caught in its own reflex, as in the many instances of reflection in *Alastor,* to which we shall return—only to sublimate this inwardness into a less troubling idealism, which is directed not within but above, to the Platonic ideas. Shelley similarly mistakes the intension of poetry for a vision of "knowledge and truth and virtue" (158), which is belied by the vacancy that befalls the Poet after his visionary episodes: a vacancy that suggests a more modern experience of poetry. Lacking a vocabulary for this experience, Shelley can only convert the Narrator's self-reflection of himself as and through the Poet into criticism, as a form of objectivity that the poem then dis-figures in being unable to tell the Poet's story either objectively or subjectively.

Reflection, which is throughout the poem's method and imagery, is what the Narrator wants to avoid. For, if the Narrator represents a Romanticism that has "forfeited its transcendence,"[24] he also imagines himself at the receding origin of a lyricism whose transcendence protects a poetry he has not yet thought through. Through the Poet, but in an overwrought rather than a chaste way, the Narrator presents a thematic cluster that

Shelley had inherited from Wordsworth's Lucy poems and to which he returns in *Adonais*. That cluster figures a way of living that is visionary rather than ordinary, invested in a special being, whose life and death are understood only by nature and whose memory becomes for his survivors the site of a bitter separation between private and public, between poetry and prose. Writing from the other side of this divide, the Narrator struggles to bring back the Poet, idealizing him as a "prototype" much as the Poet does with his epipsyche. But this sentimentalization is haunted by doubts that the Narrator is barely able to repress about the value of the visionary life, and the symptom of these doubts is the poem's inability to concatenate itself either as lyric or story, subjective or objective literature.

Thus, at the beginning of the poem the Narrator, evoking the figure of the Aeolian harp, pictures himself as a "long-forgotten lyre" awaiting inspiration from nature (42). Yet he also speaks of searching for some "lone ghost" to "render up the *tale* of what we are" (27–29) and casts doubt on the immediacy of lyric inspiration in addressing his muse as mother of an "unfathomable world" (18; emphasis mine). Representing himself both as lyricist and narrator, Shelley encounters in the process of representation, and specifically in the problematic of genre, a mirror stage in which the identity of literature is enacted and called in question through the Narrator's troubled construction of the Poet. On the one hand, the Narrator finds a language within his language, in which his lyricism is subtly displaced by the pressures of narrative; on the other hand, he also finds that this narrativity cannot be contained within the succinct form of a tale: a particular kind of narrative, which, as Benjamin says, "contains . . . something useful" and possesses a "chaste compactness which precludes psychological analysis."[25] The Narrator's attempt to tell the Poet's story, in other words, discloses that narrative is not simply the objective form of a presumed lyric totality, but something quite different.

This is to say that *Alastor* is essentially an autonarration of its own composition and the unresolved epistemic stakes of genre, rather than a poem about a real being called the Poet. For one of the curious things about the text is that its main figure never comes alive, speaking only once and reverting at the end to an "image, silent, cold, and motionless" (661). Summoned up from a realm of "incommunicable dream, / And twilight phantasms" (39–40), the Poet seems an archetype or semiotype in the

Narrator's consciousness, and the poem of which he is the subject is thus a poem about itself: about making figures true, and whether it is possible to find a mode of language that will confer identity on the Poet and his author the Narrator. This displacement of interest from the mimetic to the discursive is connected to another phenomenon: the unwilling transposition of the visionary theme from the lyric to the narrative mode. For as we have said, the pre-text for *Alastor* is the Wordsworthian crystallization in lyric of the visionary self: the sensitive soul who, like Lucy or the Boy of Winander, dies young. Thus the Narrator's initial "There was a Poet" (50) recalls Wordsworth's "There was a boy." The depiction of the Poet as unrecognized except by nature recalls Lucy, who dwelt by the untrodden ways and whose death made a difference only to the speaker. And the final reabsorption of the Poet by nature resembles, though more nihilistically, Lucy in "A slumber did My spirit seal": "Roll'd round in earth's diurnal course/With rocks and stones and trees" (7–8).[26]

The figure of the sensitive soul is by no means uncomplicated in Wordsworth. For leaving aside the text evoked in the prose of *Alastor*'s Preface, even in its simplest inscription as the visionary child this figure is rendered ambiguous by the child's death, which seals it in an identity with its essence yet denies it any being in the world, as though in some sense it has not been or has not yet been. But in those Wordsworthian pre-texts, which comprise for Shelley's Narrator an ideal limit, the figure of the beautiful soul is sealed against any probing of its liminality by being recalled in the mode of lyric rather than narrative. Lyric thus becomes for the Narrator the mode in which he can best approximate a discourse that will make the figure of the subjective poet identical with itself. For the autonomous (as opposed to the intertextual) lyric comes as close as is possible in language to the forgetting of difference. Lyric concentrates on a single spot of time: on someone like Lucy seen in a single moment, not in a series of situations in which she might appear differently. In reducing time to a moment it also selects the moment that most expresses the essence of the subject's life: the moment that is, like the epipsyche, or more darkly, like the Wordsworthian epitaph, a "soul within our soul."[27] Unfolding as voice rather than narrative, lyric does not posit a narrator different from the subject of his story or caught in relationships of (non)identity with characters who displace him from his desire. Finally lyric, as Northrop Frye points out, is overheard rather than heard.[28] By forgetting its reader, or at least by eliding its reader as someone different from the author, it simulates a hermeneutics of identity that confirms the oneness of the speaker with his subject.

The lyricization of the beautiful soul is thus part of an attempt to embody it in a language that will not displace it. At least in theory, the lyrical consciousness is present to itself, able to bypass the reflective and reflexive mode of language in song, or at least to make language the true voice of feeling. To be sure, there are deconstructions of lyric and music, such as those of Arthur Schopenhauer and Friedrich Nietzsche, both of whom see feeling as itself a mobile army of metaphors and both of whom see the quintessentially lyric attunement of "mood" as a conflictual site.[29] But the conventionally Romantic representations of lyric in terms of nightingales and Aeolian harps largely ignore this association of music with the subconscious and the will, and thus with the trace of nonidentity. Instead they assimilate art into nature, while conceiving of nature immediately as song and not as the "unfathomable world" it actually becomes in *Alastor* (18). If lyric functions in terms of an ontopoetics of presence, it also involves a suppression of temporality. Lyric compression, as Sharon Cameron points out, produces an abridgement of time: a concentration on the moment rather than the sequence, which has the effect of exempting the self from action, from involvement in the complex intertexture of events,[30] and thus from a reading that would situate its values. Often focusing on experiences of loss or death that confirm the triumph of a life that thwarts the desires of the subject, lyric protects the subject's interiority from what is merely exterior through an idealism that sublates material circumstance into its metaphoric figuration. For lyrics, as Cameron suggests, "oppose speech to the action from which it exempts itself, oppose voice as it rises momentarily from the enthusiasms of temporal advance to the flow of time that ultimately rushes over and drowns it." Or as Adorno puts it, lyric is a "self-forgetting in which the subject submerges in language."[31]

Narrative, by contrast, is the insertion of the subject into a temporal and historical world: a space populated by other people and no longer defined purely by the subject. If *Alastor*, which is concerned with only one character, is in this respect an ellipsis of the mode, the pressure of narrative is still felt in the presence of figures like the Arab maiden and the veiled woman. For the episodic appearance of these others hints at something untold, while their very resistance to a complete interiorization within the Poet's consciousness renders interiority symptomatically as an effacement of, rather than an exemption from, being-in-the-world. The chronotope of narrative, its configuration of space as something inhabited by others and of time as something that continues beyond the moment of speech, necessarily generates a more complex hermeneutic than that of lyric. That the narrator is telling the story *of* someone other than himself reminds us that he is telling it *to* someone other than himself, a fact emphasized in more complex narratives by the presence of characters telling each other things. But as importantly in *Alastor*, as in most narratives, the time of the poem is not identical with the time of the Poet's story, still less with a moment of that story expressive of a single mood. Wordsworth's "There was a boy," in its form as an autonomous lyric, ends with the epiphanic absorption of the boy in nature. The time of the poem is the time of the poet's memory, and the poem ceases when the poet stops speaking. By contrast, in *Alastor*, as in book 5 of *The Prelude*, into which Wordsworth's autonomous lyric is later absorbed, the Narrator survives the Poet, reflecting on his death not for two lines but at length, thus breaking the mood he has created. Inserting the past into the present, the format of narrative as a story told to someone necessarily implicates it in a future in which the story may be retold, re-visioned. The time of narrative is a space that others will come to inhabit, as the text recognizes in the gesture of a Preface: a Preface, moreover, whose uncertainty as to whether it should idealize or didactically dismiss the Poet reflects a division in the poem's audience.

The vulnerability of narrative to a hermeneutics of difference is corroborated by other features of the mode. Narrative is both psychologically and structurally a mode of difference at odds with unmediated vision or direct cognition. That texts like *Alastor* are not narratives in the way that novels are, and seem closer to the lyric in making the main character a version of the speaker, is not crucial. For if they interiorize narrative so as to conserve lyric identity, that identity is now articulated in terms of a splitting of the subject. Subjective narratives of the sort the Romantics write project the self in the form of an alter ego who is then inside and outside the narrative voice. Where the lyric poet is undivided and speaks in *propria persona*, the Narrator of *Alastor* projects himself as the Poet, seeking to identify with a visionary ideology that he also constructs through someone he is not. Endemic to such narrative is a doubling of the subject into narrator and character, author and narrator, by which the self is repeated as something outside itself and displaced from itself. Put differently, narrative is also the removal of the self into an objective world that will disclose it as other than itself. The events of the Poet's life, the path followed by the Narrator's (poetic) desire in the actual world, divide him from this desire and force him to know its gaps and inadequacies, however reluctantly. Narrative is, in this sense, the mirror stage of lyric. Even as it promises the subject an identity in the objective world, it also marks the unsettling insertion of the imaginary ego both into what Jacques Lacan calls the symbolic and into what Julia Kristeva calls the semiotic order.[32]

If, from a psychological point of view, narrative is a process in which the self discloses its difference from itself, on a structural level its very length creates complications elided by the brevity of the lyric, which wants to submerge itself within a mood. For narratives contain characters and episodes that are linked to one another in relations of connection and difference. This intratextual complexity is the source of interpretive difference, as the various characters provide more than one perspective from which the reader can view the protagonist. Moreover, the elements of a narrative are interimplicated, present within each other, in such a way that no element exists in and of itself. A narrative thus forms an intratextual network of differences, much like what Shelley had described in *The Revolt of Islam* or what Derrida later describes as writing, or *écriture:* "The play of differences supposes, in effect, syntheses and referrals which forbid at any moment, or in any sense, that a simple element be *present* in and of itself, referring only to itself, . . . no element can function like a sign without referring to another element which itself is not simply present. This interweaving results in each 'element' . . . being constituted on the basis of the trace within it of other elements of the chain or system."[33] Given this complexity, the syntagmatic arrangement of events in a plot is suspended by paradigmatic relations between these events, which render the reading of plot recursive rather than progressive. Thus the Poet, in his wanderings through lands whose foreignness registers his self-estrangement, seems to proceed from the Middle East to India, cradle of the human race, in a journey towards what German Romanticism located as the origins of civilization and being. But the vacancy that follows his vision of the veiled maid in Cashmire recalls the similar vacancy of his mind in Ethiopia and makes us wonder whether the second episode retains traces of the first, where inspiration is asserted but not described, so that it seems to reproduce the very vacancy it replaces (106–28).

Shelley himself comes up against the difference at the heart of language, which he resists, like the Narrator wanting to be a lyric poet, when, in the *Defence,* he fails to sustain an opposition between language and other artistic media. Shelley initially claims that "language is arbitrarily produced by the Imagination and has relation to thoughts alone; but all other materials, instruments and conditions of art have relations among each other, which limit and interpose between conception and expression. The former is as a mirror which reflects, the latter as a cloud which enfeebles, the light of which both are mediums of communication" (*DP,* 513). A word directly evokes its referent, we are told, whereas a painting distracts us from viewing it mimetically by allowing us to be caught up in the interplay between its parts, between its forms and its colors. Words, in this formulation, have positive, univocal identities, which produce direct cognition, whereas all other semiotic systems are diacritical. Yet, only a page later, Shelley writes that "sounds as well as thoughts have relations, both between each other and towards that which they represent" (514). His hesitations about "story" in the *Defence* may be due, among other things, to a distrust of forms that fail to abstract the poetical "parts of a composition" from the "intertexture," which is produced when the hermeneutic whole conceived by inspiration is executed in parts that develop relations among one another as well as towards the whole they are supposed to create (515, 532).

That intertexture is troubling on semantic as well as syntactic grounds. Distinguishing prose from poetry, Shelley criticizes the "story of particular facts" for failing to idealize that "which is distorted" (515), for not being "a mirror whose surface reflects only the forms of purity and brightness," as he says of the epipsyche ("On Love," 504):

> There is this difference between a story and a poem, that a story is a
> catalogue of detached facts, which have no other bond of connexion
> than time, place, circumstance, cause and effect; the other is the cre-
> ation of actions according to the unchangeable forms of human
> nature, as existing in the mind of the creator, which is itself the image
> of all other minds. The one is partial, and applies only to a definite

period of time, . . . the other is universal. . . . The story of particular facts is as a mirror which obscures and distorts that which should be beautiful: Poetry is a mirror which makes beautiful that which is distorted. (*DP,* 515)

Whereas poetry, according to Shelley, omits those elements of chronology and circumstance whose interference prevents the text from resolving into a single impression, narrative is episodic rather than epipsychic. It introduces scenes and considerations at odds with a causality that would make plot into the text's self-explanation, and it thus inhibits the closure that allows literature to refer directly to what it represents. Telling the story of the Poet chronologically rather than according to principles of retrospective selection, which would make each episode a stage in an argument, the Narrator includes in it an encounter with an Arab maid who plays no further part in the poem. The episodic character of her appearance is visually marked by her insertion into an unusually short verse-paragraph that is simply dropped into the poem, unintegrated with anything else. We can read her as constellating a phase in the phenomenology of the Poet's mind and can thus absorb her into the poem's causal structure as a shadowy material type of the more spiritual veiled maid. But some of the questions she raises—about the Poet's metaphysical quest as an evasion of his existence in the material world—challenge the phenomenology she is supposed to subserve. Yet these questions, which are repeated in/from the Preface, do not recur in the poem, which raises epistemological but not ethical doubts about the Poet's quest. They remain loose ends in the poem, which are symptomatic of the narrative's tendency to generate complications that it is not always able to integrate into a more complex unity: subplots that contain within themselves the principle of their own integrity.

What Shelley calls "the story of particular facts" is not quite what Benjamin famously calls story or tale in "The Storyteller." The Benjaminian tale is chaste and compact and comes to a point, which is some sort of "counsel for [its] readers." It is characterized by the listener's "interest in retaining what he is told" so that he can "reproduc[e] the story," which means that it must possess what Ricoeur calls "followability." Followability results from the "successive actions, thoughts, and feelings in question" having a "certain directedness," and thus from the story's ability to convert the "episodic dimension" into a "configurational dimension, according to which the plot construes significant wholes out of scattered events."[34] Story, according to this characterization, is actually closer to what Shelley calls *poetry* in conveying universals, although in a more prosaic form. It is for this reason that Wordsworth, in the poem to which Shelley alludes in his epigraph, sees no contradiction between the "tale" of Margaret (1.609, 615, 636, 682) and a poetry that he opposes to the "degrading thirst after outrageous stimulants" in German tragedies and verse narratives.[35] For Wordsworth lyric and tale stand in a mutually supplementary relationship, in which the anaesthetic of sensibility supports the distillation of Margaret's narrative into an affecting "story" that circulates between Poet and Pedlar to reaffirm a shared wisdom. On the one hand, then, the tale for Wordsworth is a way of containing a certain excessiveness of lyric feeling. Storytelling is nostalgically linked to an artisanal community recalled by the Pedlar though belied by the specifics of Margaret's experience, and the telling of her "homely tale" (615) thus economizes lyric loss within a community (of men). On the other hand, lyricism provides an exit from the depressing materiality of the tale. For when the events of Margaret's story become too painful, when the configurational cannot subsume the episodic, the "simple tale" is reduced to pure lyricism, "pass[ing]" from the Pedlar's mind "like a forgotten sound" that is "hardly clothed/In bodily form" (609–10, 638–39).

Yet in evoking Wordsworth, Shelley harks back to a lyric compact that is already profoundly troubled. For the history of Margaret's tale, especially in its textual genesis from its pre-texts to book 1 of *The Excursion,* is that of Wordsworth's own attempt to find a form for what begins neither as lyric nor as story: a traumatic spot of time focused on a speck of glass and a part-narrative about a woman and a baker's cart.[36] In "The Baker's Cart" and "Incipient Madness" Wordsworth starts with the barest form of "particular facts": facts that are not clearly facts, not quite empirical or psychic, objective or subjective. Attempting to fit them into a larger whole, he begins in MS A to write a story, but only in unconnected bits and pieces. As the text evolves, Wordsworth wavers between poetry and "prose," between the lyrical, the elegiac, the narrative, and a form of sententious philosophizing or "criticism" oriented to composing the "FIRST GENUINE PHILOSOPHIC POEM" that Coleridge was insistent he write.[37] He restlessly combines and separates Margaret's "short bare narrative of unrelieved distress" and the Pedlar's autobiography.[38] In adding the latter to Margaret's story through various stages of MS B, only to partially withdraw it onto the verso of the pages of *The Ruined Cottage* in MS D,[39] Wordsworth foregrounds the issue between her story as a catalogue of detached facts and the "poetry which *should* invest them" and has been "stript" from them and which he yet cannot entirely renounce (*DP*, 515; emphasis mine).

But the issue of what this poetry is does not end with the Pedlar's autobiography. For Wordsworth's removal of his self-absorption in the Pedlar to the verso of MS D is as interesting as his transference, when he composed the fragment "Incipient Madness,"of the lines about his night trip to the ruin onto the verso of the notebook in which he wrote MS A, because as Butler puts it, these lines "had no place in his calm, straightforward tale of Margaret." Butler cordons off the poet's "madness" from Margaret's tale according to a criterion of objectivity in which "the work speaks for itself" and is independent of the poet.[40] But these verso pages of the MS A notebook function as what Gasché calls the "tain of the mirror" in the process of self-reflection that constitutes writing. The tain, from the French word "*étain*," "refers to the tinfoil, the silver lining, the lustreless back of the mirror," which has "no place . . . in reflection's scintillating play" but is yet the condition of possibility for "specular and speculative activity." Such activity involves "the action by mirroring surfaces of throwing back light, and in particular a mirror's exhibition or reproduction of objects in the form of images." The verso pages, then, are the dark reflection cast by the text, a reflection that does not give back an image,[41] unlike Wordsworth's self-imaging through the Pedlar.

In short, whether "Incipient Madness" precedes, follows, or accompanies MS A,[42] the point is that the "overflow" from Margaret's tale, the material having to do with the speaker's response to the tale, cathects two very different notions of poetry. The chastening of Margaret's story produces, in the Pedlar, a philosophizing whose hysterical sententiousness betrays Wordsworth's uneasiness about making the story meaningful. However, the verso pages are also the space of a certain abjection, a dejection of the work of literature by a nameless shadowy speaker not even called a poet. In this space, poetry becomes fascination, unemployment, worklessness, rather than the work of meaning. The terms are Blanchot's,[43] and they aptly describe the speaker's fixation on the "speck of glass," like the "film" in which Coleridge tries to see a "companionable form" that only "vexes meditation."[44] But the broken glass, as part-object rather than part-subject, marks the unusable negativity of the poem's slow time, in which objects fail to be represented in the form of images, as the dialectic of reflection itself fails. For the speaker stays endlessly in the ruin: for "three weeks" he watches a glow worm hanging its "light" in a bramble's "dusky shade" till it is "seen no more," and for "two summers" he listens to the "melancholy song" of a linnet, which then also "vanish[es]" (36–46). At the end he has produced nothing, no images: only "an unform'd/Dark vacuity," as Blake says of Los's stalled creation in *The Book of Los* (E 94, 5.49–50).[45] Yet these experiences of vacancy are in a "sickly" way nurturing, like the spots of time, as the speaker perversely intimates in comparing his fixation to that of a "sucking babe," "fastening on all things/That promise food" ("Incipient Madness," 9–12).

The poem's textual history, in other words, is the autonarrative of Wordsworth's struggle to define the work of literature in relation to an experience of worklessness and ruin that is conveyed in naked form in Margaret's history, and more "poetically" in Keats' *Fall of Hyperion*. For Keats' speaker, not quite a "poet" yet not just a dreamer, also spends a "long awful time" in Moneta's ruined sanctuary, brooding on "three fixed shapes" and bearing "the load of an eternal quietude" for "a whole moon" before he begins to write (1.388–92).[46] In Wordsworth's turn from his night thoughts, the self-reflective struggle of composition generates the proto-Wordsworthian persona of the Pedlar: as Wordsworth was to say, "the character I have represented in his person is chiefly an idea of what I fancied my own character might have become in his circumstances."[47] Yet the autogenetic scene of the poem's composition also raises the question of what "poetry" is in the present age, insofar as the anachronism of the Pedlar in the period of the Industrial Revolution puts the poetry he represents at an odd distance from the present. Hence the doubling of the speaker into the Pedlar and an anonymous narrator who is not the Pedlar. This empty position of the narrator is the space, as yet not clearly defined, within which Wordsworth himself circulated "the story of Margaret" to Charles Lamb and Coleridge long before the publication of *The Excursion*.[48] In a longer history, *The Ruined Cottage* and its various recensions and *avant-textes*, including the autonarrational scene of their circulation, form a textual web within which the question we have been pursuing first emerges: that of what poetry as the "idea" of prose is. Does it consist in the Pedlar's lyric sublimation of the prosaic substance of his tale? And is this lyricism, which some might see as a form of Romantic Ideology, quite the same thing as the philosophizing that Wordsworth adds to the tale as a further layer of sublimation? Or is lyricism itself a trope for giving a different kind of attention to the story's detached facts, one that would hear in its core experience of depression and unemployment something not reducible to the prosaic, economic content of those words? One that might even hear in the Pedlar's out-of-dateness a figure for poetry's necessary untimeliness?

Underlying this autonarration, in which Wordsworth projects himself as a part-self whom he adds to and subtracts from the text, is a narrativity that compels him to tell Margaret's story over and over through successive versions of the text. This narrativity crystallizes in the MS D version known as *The Ruined Cottage,* which abstracts the Pedlar's telling of the story to the anonymous narrator from the larger whole into which it would be absorbed in *The Excursion,* becoming in effect a poem about its own narrating. But of course the version of the poem that Shelley knew would have seemed to close off the radical rethinking of poetry opened by this textual history, providing a model for silencing this narrativity by converting it into lyrical feeling, sententious criticism, or pragmatic tale.[49] Against Wordsworth, the resistance to narrative in *Alastor* actually comes from two directions, which open up the questions closed off in *The Excursion.* On the one hand, narrative as Shelley defines it in *The Defence* and as he writes it in *Alastor* is not the supplement to lyric, which Wordsworth intends in shaping Margaret's history as a "tale." It does not "render up the tale of what we are," whether the immediate cognition that the Narrator craves here is ontological or, failing that, didactic. And the Narrator therefore eschews a form whose very length disallows him from construing a significant whole out of scattered events. On the other hand, his inability to tell the Poet's story comes precisely from his reluctance to reduce the poet's life to an "epitome," which Shelley, as if disagreeing with his own criticism of "story" for lacking a configurational dimension, assails for "eat[ing] out the poetry" from history (*DP*, 515). This is to say, unlike the Pedlar, who *does* want to distill Margaret's life into an epitome, the Narrator does not want to construe a whole out of the differences that make up the Poet's story. He does not want to reach a judgment about poetry and the Poet, to bring his story to a conclusion. And the narrativity at the heart of the poem, which is in excess of its configurational impulses, is what keeps it from having to reach a conclusion.

From the invocation, where the Narrator describes himself as a "long-forgotten lyre" and asks nature to favor his "solemn song" (42, 18), to the end, where the dead Poet is described with lurid poignancy as a "lute" and the Narrator refers to his own poem as a "simple strain" (667, 706), lyric and not narrative is the desired mode of *Alastor*. Nevertheless, the Narrator describes his own previous history as given over to narration, though he tries to view this stage as merely preliminary:

> I have made my bed
> In charnels and on coffins, where black death
> Keeps record of the trophies won from thee,
> Hoping to still these obstinate questionings
> Of thee and thine, by forcing some lone ghost,
> Thy messenger, to render up the tale
> Of what we are.   (23–29)

What is interesting here is that the narrative process does not culminate in a tale. The tale, insofar as it can be told, does not "render" an account of its subject and, analogically, its listener. Indeed, it does not have its origin in the speaker: it does not seem to come from him, but to him, from an unknowable source. As important, narrativity is not associated with a configurative act but with a process of "obstinate questionings." Narrative is in effect pictured as an autonarration, a psychoanalysis in which characters function as part-objects through whom the narrating subject tries to constitute himself but which yields only inadequate self-representations. Proclaiming that he has had enough of such "twilight phantasms" (39–40), the Narrator sees himself as about to emerge from this interminable analysis through a resumption of his long-forgotten lyre. But what he constructs in the poem is another narrative, in which the Poet's failure to find his ideal through a series of part-subjects reproduces the Narrator's failure to create a figure that will render up the tale of what he is. The poem, in other words, is the record of the Narrator's failure to fulfil his lyric intention. Moreover, if lyric ideally is a transcendence of narrative, its belatedness in the Narrator's career suggests that it has no more than a liminal status, as a desire produced by what it seeks to forget. For the Narrator symptomatically describes the music produced by his Aeolian lyre as a "woven" hymn (48), suggesting that he cannot really conceive of a form of expression that points single-mindedly outwards, to a referent or source or affective state, rather than inwards, to its own textural complications. As we have seen, images of weaving are the site of a crossing in Shelley's aesthetics from a univocal to a differential concept of language. In the passage cited from *The Revolt of Islam,* it is arguable that the subtler language within language produced by the woof of thought is meant to be a form of pure expression, like that soul within a soul defined as the epipsyche, more identical with itself as it becomes more refined and complex. But this desired univocality—like lyric's attempt to synthesize multiple emotions into a single mood—is constantly decentered by the complexity on which Shelley tries to base it.

The (un)weaving of lyric desire is thematized in the poem's most important episode: the scene of the Poet's creative origination, in which he sees the veiled maid in the vale of Cashmire. This Muse/*anima* develops from simple to complex as she is unveiled, as her ideality turns out to contain a darker subtext, and as the attempt to articulate concretely what begins as a dreamy abstraction discloses a resistant materiality in what had seemed spiritual and pure. The intense physicality of what the Poet projects as a Platonic form, so troubling that he swoons rather than consummate his love, enacts the embodiment of vision: the linguistic process by which the Idea is given a body in words that do not exist by themselves but inevitably refer to other elements in the chain or system. To begin with, the veiled woman is characterized in terms of allegorical abstractions that allow her song (or that of the Poet who projects her as muse) to bear a direct relation to transcendental referents:

Knowledge and truth and virtue were her theme,
And lofty hopes of divine liberty,
Thoughts the most dear to him, and poesy,
Herself a poet. (158–61)

In the beginning the Poet is figured, through the supplementary figure of his Muse, as Browning's subjective poet, who, in Shelley's own words, "participates in the eternal, the infinite, and the one" (*DP,* 513). Yet the multiplication of transcendental referents in *Alastor* makes us wonder if the Muse is indeed simple in essence: whether knowledge, truth, and virtue are the same thing, and whether there lies beneath these simple terms a philosophic mythology, which makes these concepts into figures in a series of stories and family romances. This diffusion of reference is linked to the presence of the woman's body, or rather to the body of her emotions: her "tremulous sobs," "beating heart," and her "pure mind," which is confusingly experienced only through her body, kindling "through all her frame/A permeating fire" (161–72). For the body has been linked by Nietzsche and more recently by Julia Kristeva to the problem of representation. The female body is, for Kristeva, the site of pulsions that disturb the order of both the symbolic and the imaginary: of what cannot be said or imagined and thus of something felt in language only in terms of gaps and absences.[50] Resisting clear representation, the body of the veiled woman disrupts the Poet's attempt to link her to a transcendental signified or to make the music she sings the vehicle of a disembodied and simple lyricism, "scarcely clothed in bodily form."

The multivocality of the veiled woman corresponds to her profound ambiguity as a figure for poetry and for a lyricism linked not just to the feelings but de-idealized and complicated by the association of feeling itself with the female body. The veiled woman is both epipsyche and Muse, "Herself a poet" who plays upon a harp. As lyric poet, she produces a Wagnerian music strangely lacking in lyric serenity: "wild numbers then/She raised, with voice stifled in tremulous sobs" (163–64). Her music, moreover, tells an "ineffable tale" (168), a tale curiously like the poem itself in that it cannot be interpreted so as to render up the tale of what we are. Describing it as ineffable rather than obscure, the Narrator etherealizes a disruptiveness that Shelley unravels through the "shape all light" in The Triumph of Life as the figure for a poetry entrammeled in history. For in Shelley's last poem the names of history evoked as "poets" in The Defence are reduced to "epitomes" within a precession of simulacra, as the "wondrous music" heard by Rousseau unfolds bleakly into a history of particular facts (Triumph of Life, 369). And yet this poetry, as a suspension between signification and melos, subsists rhythmically in the enjambment of the terza rima, the "ghost of a forgotten form of sleep" (428): the dream-work of a poetry exposed to psychosis and trauma, whose dis-figurations are necessary to restore to its creative functioning a culture buried in the practico-inert of its discourses.

One could equally see, behind the references to truth and liberty in *Alastor,* the unreadable history of the French Revolution, which Shelley's last poem dis-figures. But the Poet in *Alastor* moves quickly to suppress narrative in music by figuring its silences as unheard melodies. Yet the song he creates in his mind is "intermitted" (172), full of gaps and absences, as if there is more to be told about this woman who never becomes present in the song she sings and must be pursued beyond the "realm of dream" (206) if the Poet is to discover to what the song refers. As a *mise-en-abîme* of the larger poem, the vision of the veiled woman thus deconstructs lyric as the epipsyche of narrative, just as much as it deconstructs story or tale as the epitome of narrative. Lyric is not so much the antitype of narrative as a sublimation, maintained only by the absence of narrative. As the withholding of narrative, the woman's song is present only as the absence of something that the Poet must recover if the song is to be fully self-present but that, paradoxically, might deconstruct its identity as song.

That lyric is no more than the absence of narrative, constituted on the trace of what it does not tell, is suggested by the association of the woman's song with weaving. We shall return to this image, which is Shelley's image for the differential texture, or in his term, "intertexture," of language (*DP,* 532). At the end of *Alastor* "the web of human things" (719) becomes an image for everything that the Poet seeks to forget in imagining an epipsyche that "reflects only the forms of purity and brightness" ("On Love," 504). It becomes an image for "Nature's vast frame, . . ./Birth and the grave" (*Alastor,* 719–20), and thus for the complex intertexture of existence in which nothing is present without the alternatives that it has deselected. As a mode that tells of life from birth to the grave, narrative inevitably recreates this intertexture. By contrast, lyric, as the attempt to abstract a single moment and thus a single referent from life, brackets the interconnections between this and other moments so as to reduce existence to some simple essence. But it is precisely this simplicity that the Poet fails to find through the veiled woman, who seems a natural rather than a transcendental muse, associated with "streams and breezes" (155), and whose voice creates no single mood:

> Her voice was like the voice of his own soul
> Heard in the calm of thought; its music long,

Like woven sounds of streams and breezes, held
His inmost sense suspended in its web
Of many-coloured woof and shifting hues.   (153–57)

As already observed, images of weaving are the site of an unfolding complication in Shelley's aesthetics, in which the very notion of lyric as an *epoche* achieved through interiorization is here implicated. Associated with interiority and thus with the promise of a deep truth, these images reveal the Poet's inmost sense, not as a center, but as a place of dissemination. As used in *The Triumph of Life*, where the place in which the shape all light appears is filled with "many sounds woven into one/Oblivious melody" (340–41), weaving is explicitly presented as the fantasizing of a Platonic abstraction: of something that seems a single fabric only because we are oblivious to how it is woven of multiple strands. As weaving, lyric is thus no more than the illusory unification of that web of differences that unravels in more extensive structures, such as narrative. For the more elaborate the structure, the more our attention is riveted on the interrelations of its parts, and the more parts there are to generate such interrelations.

❧

The development of *Alastor* as a web of differences is everywhere apparent, most obviously in the way the Narrator tells the Poet's story twice over, and also in the very syntax of the poem, which at the most local level is the basis for the syntagmatic unfolding of the text as argument and story. Put differently, the emergence of the syntagmatic line of plot depends on a balance between what John Crowe Ransom has called "structure," as the schema for a "logical object or universal," and "texture," as "incessant particularity" and a "tissue of irrelevance from which" poetry "does not really emerge." For Ransom, plot (or in the case of lyric, argument) is the crystallization of structure and of the "prose" in literature. Plot is "the logical construct; the big presentable object which most gives its own shape and extension to the whole poem," thus asserting the text's "right in the world of affairs" and making it "social and ethical . . . reputable and useful"[51]— in short, objective.

But in *Alastor* texture, the intension of the poem, swallows up structure, leading to an indeterminacy and involution of reference. William Keach has written compellingly about this involution, in the form of "figures within figures," and "Shelley's frequent resort to an imagery lacking in individuation" wherein, rather than "a firmly held, developed image," we have "a flood of images which one must grasp momentarily in one aspect and then release."⁵² The texture of Shelley's poetry, in other words, eludes any settling in denotation, any hypostasis. Keach goes on to discuss Shelley's style in terms of "speed" as a short-circuiting of syntax; "evanescence" and "erasure," although not in the nihilistic mode elaborated by Paul de Man in "Shelley Disfigured"; and reflexive imagery. The reflexive nature of the poem's syntax, in which "a phrase or clause turns back on itself,"⁵³ is figured in several *scenes* of reflection: the Poet gazing into a lake (211–19); almost being swallowed up in a whirlpool that "reflect[s], yet distort[s] every cloud" (384–86); coming to a well where his eyes behold "Their own wan light through the reflected lines/Of his thin hair" (469–71); and reflecting on the wandering stream that images his life (505–8)—not to mention the Poet reflecting on himself through the veiled maid, "Whose voice was like the voice of his own soul" (153–54), and the Narrator reflecting on himself through the Poet.

These scenes, typical of Shelley's tendency to write poetry whose imagery is "drawn from the operations of the human mind" ("Preface" to *PU*, 133), constitute reflection rather than criticism as the mode of *Alastor*. They, moreover, constitute reflection as poetry's legacy to prose. For if lyric is the desired mode of the Narrator and the Poet, the poem itself enacts poetry as reflection, "the calm of thought," which turns out to be a "treacherous" calm, yielding not clarity, but something "searchless," "invisible" (*Alastor*, 386, 507). Hence Benjamin's dissociation of criticism from the reflection of the Romantics, because in their work reflection "expands without limit or check," and "the thinking given form" in it "turns into formless thinking which directs itself upon the absolute." As a result, the absolute "becomes characterized by increasing, and ultimately inextricable . . . ambiguity."⁵⁴ For in *Alastor*, rather than a polished surface that throws back light, the medium of reflection is most often a lake, a river, a well, a shifting surface whose volume cannot be gauged and which absorbs rather than returns what is reflected in it. The poem, then, is characterized by what Gasché describes as the turning away from a straightforward consideration of objects and experience into "a consideration of the very experience in which objects are given." But this reflection does not result in the constitution of being as self-consciousness through a Kantian reflection on the transcendental structures of cognition. It is not the case that the play of reflections, even though it includes a "mirroring of the mirror," eventually results in the reflecting and the reflected being reintegrated to "form a totality in which they are reflected into one another, leaving absolutely no remainder.[55]

Structurally, this reflection in *Alastor* emerges from the poem's very extensiveness as an unraveling of lyric brevity. For extended structures, as we have seen through Shelley's discussion of language, develop complex internal interrelations, which is to say that *Alastor*'s extensiveness, paradoxically, is the source of its intension.[56] Such structures repeat themselves, repeating images, formulations, or characters and episodes, like the encounters with the Arab woman and the veiled maid. Repeating themselves, they go back over themselves and reflect on themselves. Repetition, then, far from confirming meaning as denotation, functions somewhat like *enjambement*. *Enjambement*, according to Agamben, is "the *versura*, the turning point . . . unspoken-of in treatises on metrics" that gives poetry its "versatility." It is an "ambiguous gesture that turns in two opposed directions at once: backwards (*versus*), and forwards (*pro versa*)," so as to create a "hanging back" which is "the poetic inheritance with which thought must come to terms."[57] In effect *enjambement* for Agamben has the same structure as reflection, *reflectere*, which, as Gasché explains, "means to 'bend' or 'to turn back' or backward, as well as to bring back."[58]

A key instance of the intension of repetition as well as the enjambment of syntax in a scene of reflection is the passage that follows the Poet's attempt to pursue the veiled woman beyond the "realms of dream." What the lines *say* is crucial to determining what is at issue in the Poet's being-towards-death and whether this choice is legitimized by the existence of a transcendent realm. But the passage is by no means easy to read, since at a crucial point it sets against the syntactical progression, in Agamben's terms, a limit that is at once metrical or asym-metrical and grammatical:

> Does the dark gate of death
> Conduct to thy mysterious paradise,
> O Sleep? Does the bright arch of rainbow clouds,
> And pendent mountains seen in the calm lake,
> Lead only to a black and watery depth,

While death's blue vault, with loathliest vapours hung,
Where every shade which the foul grave exhales
Hides its dead eye from the detested day,
Conducts, O Sleep, to thy delightful realms?   (211–19)

In a syntagmatic reading, which tries to construct an argument by following the syntax of the passage, the Narrator's question could be said to
repeat itself in a second question, intended to provide a more extensive
gloss on the first. Thus the first question, we can argue, begins with the
paradox of something that appears negative yielding its opposite: the
dark gate of death leading to the paradise of sleep. In that very moment
of metaphoric conversion, however, "the verse," to evoke Agamben, "is
irresistibly drawn into bending over into the next line to lay hold of what
it has thrown out of itself."[59] The negative alternative reasserts itself as
the Narrator realizes that the "paradise" of clouds and mountains seen in
the lake is an atmospheric illusion that conceals the tangled undergrowth
of the lake's "black and watery depth." Nevertheless, the Narrator presses
on, introducing a more complex system of paradoxes. He asks whether
the apparently negative paradox of appearance and reality might not conceal its own re-reversal into a positive paradox. Does the fact that the
reality of death by drowning may lie hidden in the promise of the rainbow
clouds seen in the lake yield, in turn, to the possibility that this ugly and
dark appearance hides the more positive reality of sleep? Such a re-reversal
would also entail a valorizing of the transcendent over the natural realm
that justifies the additional lines, which are otherwise redundant. For it is
nature that tricks us with the appearance of beauty only to reveal the
clouds in the lake as an atmospheric illusion, while the reality of ugliness
ceases to be a reality as soon as we move beyond the merely material
world.

But this reading, a philosophic story as it were, is far from easy to
extract from the passage, the syntax of which jams or at least retards our
attempts at paraphrase. The problem lies in the labyrinthine complexity
of the second question, which introduces a long and not clearly subordinate clause between the grammatical subject "death's blue vault" and the
main verb, "Conducts." This syntactic detour allows various other grammatical possibilities to come into play, and while they may not finally
prevail, the story constructed above is unsettled by the way it seems to

hide these other possibilities within itself. Initially it seems that the first three lines of the second question provide an alternative to the first question, and that the Narrator, having asked whether death leads to the positive condition of sleep, raises the possibility that what seems beneficent may hide something threatening. It becomes clear in the next line that this is not the Narrator's intention and that he wants to overturn the negative alternative with a further positive paradox. But this reversal (though only in the form of a question) is a long time in coming, as the depressing description of death's blue vault takes over the sentence. This is all the more true because the subordinate clause on death contains a further subordinate clause, beginning, "Where every shade which the foul grave exhales." The effect is to convert the larger subordinate clause into a main clause in relation to the subordinate clause it contains and thus to give it a certain autonomy in relation to the main sentence, in which it is contained. It is not immediately clear where the second question ends and whether the verb "hides" or the verb "conducts" is the main verb of the sentence. Indeed, the visual stacking of what seems to be a main verb on top of another main verb jams the syntactical progression, turning any resolution of the Narrator's doubts back on itself.

Syntax is not the only source of complications in this sentence. The second question is organized around an opposition between the deceptive paradoxes of nature and the saving paradoxes of transcendence. But the image of death's blue "vault"—both a "dome," as Shelley figures it in *Adonais* (462), and a crypt—uneasily recalls the earlier image of rainbow clouds in the lake: again a transcendence projected downwards into a depth. Even as we hope that death's vault will prove an exit to something better, the image reminds us that all constructions of hope may lead "only to a black and watery depth" and that even the Poet's deferral of his ideal to the afterlife may be futile. Or perhaps death does lead to sleep, but perhaps sleep is not "delightful," not rest, but "nocturnal wandering," what Blanchot calls "the essence of night" as "the *other* night,"[60] an eternal vigilance that Keats describes as "deathwards progressing/To no death" (*Fall,* 1.260–61).

In the background of this passage is also its Wordsworthian pre-text, "There was a boy," a lyric poem about a lyric poet who is as close to nature as art can be, his music created by using his mouth as an instrument. The poem exists in subtly different versions: as a first-person lyric in the 1799 version from MS JJ, as a third-person lyric in *Lyrical Ballads* (1800), as part of the fifth book in the 1805 and 1850 versions of *The Prelude*, and again as an autonomous third-person lyric under the classification "Poems of Imagination" in *Poems in Two Volumes* (1815). As I argue elsewhere, the minute pronominal and grammatical shifts that occur between the 1799 version and all subsequent versions harbor the trace of a narrative encrypted in what seems a lyrical idyll.[61] The *Prelude* versions are the most significant, in that their absorption of the short poem into a larger structure, which contains episodes of drowning, intimates a death that is made prosaically explicit in the next verse paragraph, where we are told "This boy was taken from his mates, and died/In childhood ere he was full ten years old" (1805, 5.414–15; 1850, 5.389–90). Yet thereafter, even when the poem is reexcerpted from *The Prelude* so as to return it to its original form as a lyric, these traces mark lyric autonomy as a simulation, for in these versions, the single poem always moves from the idyll on the boy to some form of the lines on his early death, turning from poetry to "prose," ecstasy to sobriety.

More specifically, after 1799 Wordsworth makes two crucial changes. In the 1799 version the shift from the third person opening, "There was a boy," to the first person in the remainder of the poem, had covered over the ominousness of the past tense by suggesting that the boy is simply a past self: one, moreover, who returns again and again in the moment of writing. But subsequently, the entire poem is phrased in the third person, thus introducing a speaker different from the young Poet. And, whereas the 1799 version had used the past imperfect, the tense of repeated action, to describe the boy's intercourse with nature, the subsequent versions oddly introduce one phrase ("has carried") in which the tense marks off a single, finite event. These changes give a troubling pastness and finality to the poem's concluding segment, which becomes uncertainly figural and literal:

> And when it chanced
> That pauses of deep silence mocked his skill,
> Then sometimes in that silence, while he hung
> Listening, a gentle shock of mild surprize
> *Has carried* far into his heart the voice
> Of mountain torrents; or the visible scene
> *Would enter* unawares into his mind

With all its solemn imagery, its rocks,
Its woods, and that uncertain heaven, received
Into the bosom of the steady lake.   (1805, 5.404–13; emphasis mine)

On the one hand, the identity of inside and outside in this scene of reflection functions according to the logic of what M. H. Abrams calls the greater romantic lyric, which merges the reflecting and reflected so as to leave no remainder. The sky is reflected in the lake, and the entire "visible scene," so internalized as to become part of the mind's "imagery," is "received" into the reflective medium of the boy's mind as landscape and consciousness become identical. On the other hand, why is it that at one barely noticed moment a gentle shock "has carried" the voice of mountain torrents into the boy's heart, where in 1799 Wordsworth uses the tense of habitual action ("would carry")? The new phrasing, echoed in *Alastor*,[62] triggers a doubt as to what the fusion of boy and waterfall means and discloses a wavering between the literal and the figural. Perhaps the phrase "uncertain heaven" does not just refer literally to the clouds reflected in the water but also metaphorically to the tenuousness of a paradise the boy constructs out of a material world that he sees as the alphabet of his imagination. Perhaps the voice of mountain torrents is literally and not just figurally carried into the boy's heart. Perhaps, then, this metaphoric heaven is actually received into the lake as the boy drowns, "rolled round," like Lucy, in "earth's diurnal course." In the last lines of Wordsworth's lyric, reflection expands without limit or check, as it becomes impossible to tell what is received into what, to draw a boundary between the reflection and the reflected. The "visible scene" enters the mind in reflection, this scene itself being one in which the reflection of the sky in the lake produces an "uncertain Heaven," which is somehow confirmed as it is "received" into the "steady lake" as figure for the reflecting consciousness yet is also deconstructed as this consciousness itself is literally received, reflected back, like Narcissus, into the "bosom" of an impassive nature.

Returning to this scene of reflection and the "fair paradise" that (dis)appears in it, *Alastor* ghoulishly unravels Wordsworth's text into the story of particular facts encrypted in the elision of trauma made possible by lyric compression. For Shelley, who would only have known the version in

Lyrical Ballads, tells at great length the story of the Poet's death by water, barely hinted at even in the *Prelude* version. Yet curiously, in transferring his account of the Poet from lyric to narrative, the Narrator also cannot tell the Poet's story: not the story of particular facts, but a story as something that has wholeness. As Ricoeur says, a story in this sense "must be more than an enumeration of events in a serial order; it must make an intelligible whole of the incidents," in such a way as to convey "the point of the story."[63] But one of the curious things about *Alastor* is a doubling of the narration in which this point is lost, whether because the Narrator actually tells the Poet's story twice or because he has him go through a similar sequence of events more than once in a vain attempt to construct his life as a history with a beginning, a middle, and an end.[64] This repetition, or rereflection, as we have seen, is already foreshadowed in the poem's syntax. For given that syntax is the linguistic equivalent of the syntagmatic axis along which plot is generated in narrative, the involution of the poem's syntax is the first site of its resistance to achieving "followability."

Arguably, the events of the Poet's story up to the point when he dreams of the veiled maid are relatively clear. An account of his early education and wanderings, not among the hills of Athol but in more distant places like Tyre and Balbec, is followed by his brief encounter with the Arab maiden, whom he scarcely notices. He then arrives in the vale of Cashmire, where he dreams of a veiled maid who phantasmatically appears, only to slip from his grasp as "sleep/. . ./Roll[s] back its impulse on his vacant brain" (189–91). Pursuing her "Beyond the realms of dream" (206), and having already wondered whether "the dark gate of death" leads to a "mysterious paradise" or only to a "black and watery depth" (211–22), the Poet comes to a "lone Chorasmian shore," where he sees a swan (272–75). Creatures other than man, he concludes, have companions, a home, and achieve a certain contentment; by contrast he, with a "frame more attuned/To beauty," wastes his "surpassing powers" on an earth that "echoes not [his] thoughts" (287–90).

At this point, the Poet presumably decides to die, and it is here that the story becomes more involved and endlessly elaborate. For the Poet's will-to-death (if indeed it is *his* will) makes it incumbent on the Narrator to make the narrative do what stories do: reach a conclusion, a decision, about the Poet. And it is this decision, on whether the Poet's tale is to render up the objective lesson of the Preface or whether he is a compelling embodiment of Browning's subjective poet in search of the Platonic ideas, that the Narrator is apparently unable to reach. Thus the story starts confusingly to repeat itself. Briefly, the Poet has already seen a veiled woman in Cashmire (140 ff.) and, failing to find her again, has been seized by a daemonic passion that rouses him from his couch, "As an eagle grasped/In folds of the green serpent" (227ff.). At the point where he glimpses the swan, the futility of his quest has already led him to waste away, as his limbs grow "lean" and his "scattered hair/Sered by the autumn of strange suffering" sings "dirges in the wind" (248–50). Shortly after seeing the swan, he leaps into a boat, exclaiming:

> "Vision and Love!"
> "I have beheld
> The path of thy departure. Sleep and Death
> Shall not divide us long!"   (366–69)

Finally, after a turbulent and confusing journey, he seems to arrive in a spot that is nature's "cradle, and his sepulchre" (430), where he sees a landscape reflected in water (433–37), which takes us back to the initial reflection on "death's blue vault."

But now, when we expect everything to be over, the Poet again sees a feminine spirit (469ff.), is roused from his couch by a "joyous madness" (517), ages in a ghastly way (531ff.) as his journey by water continues, and again arrives in a cove, where he does presumably expire (571ff.). The repetition of the story undoes the Narrator's attempt at mimesis, giving the Poet's life a phantasmatic quality. For as Hillis Miller has pointed out, repetition can function in a Nietzschean way, creating a world of "simulacra" or "phantasms," a series of "ungrounded doublings which arise from differential interrelations among elements which are all on the same plane."[65] It is as if, in the course of the initial narration, the Narrator has discovered gaps and possibilities that make it necessary to weave the strands of his fantasy about the Poet differently, so as to achieve a closure that will again be impossible because the reenactment of the Poet's life simply opens up different gaps and loose ends.

It is impossible to separate neatly the different figural intentions behind the two phases of the Narrator's telling of the Poet's story, if indeed they are two, since these intentions are swallowed up in the intratextual complications of the poem. But the crucial problem in the text is the significance of the Poet's life and death. Although the Narrator, in the conventionalized opening and closing of the poem, hysterically idealizes the Poet, his postponement of the latter's death some two hundred and fifty lines beyond its announcement, and his seemingly endless protraction of the story, manifest an emergent doubt as to whether the death is climactic. Indeed, the Narrator has no clear view of what the Poet's story "means," and he produces accounts that try to determine this meaning as they work themselves out and that tacitly reread themselves as they proceed. Thus perhaps in the first phase, the Narrator sees the Poet's vision as having an external sanction, which legitimizes his pursuit of it beyond the realm of life. If so, perhaps he wants to see the Poet's life as having come full circle, bringing him to a sepulcher that is also the cradle of his mother nature, an end that is an origin. But there are numerous instabilities in this representation of the Poet. For one thing, it is never clear whether the Poet is in sympathy with nature or at odds with her, whether the benediction of circularity that the Narrator has nature confer on the Poet's death is an empty formula. Even at the beginning of the poem, where there are no "human hands" to build the Poet's "untimely tomb," the pyramid of mouldering leaves that shelters his remains seems assembled more by the random movements of the wind than by design (50–54), creating a dissension between the prosaic fact and the poetry with which the Narrator tries to invest it. Then at the end, although the Poet's blood is described as having beaten in "mystic sympathy/With nature's ebb and flow," heaven remains "Utterly black" at the moment of his death (651–60), as if there is nothing beyond this death. Nor is it clear that the veiled woman is anything but a narcissistic projection. Her voice is, after all, like the voice "of his own soul/Heard in the calm of thought" (153–54).

Because of the many questions that the first narration raises, we can speculate that the Narrator recasts the Poet's death as the conscious pursuit of an interior ideal. This time the scene of his encounter with the female spirit is overtly narcissistic. She appears just after he has seen his reflection in a well and is without links to the transcendent or to nature:

> clothed in no bright robes
> Of shadowy silver or enshrining light.
> Borrowed from aught the visible world affords   (480–82)

On looking up, the Poet sees only "two eyes,/Two starry eyes," which "hung in the gloom of thought" (489–90). Following the "Spirit" (479), the Poet now moves in obedience to "the light/That shone within his soul" (492–93), and thereafter he consciously interiorizes the landscape by seeing it as an image of his life (502–8), exploring whether meaning can be found in the landscape of the self when it cannot be found outside or beyond the self. If, in this second attempt at configuring the Poet's life, the Narrator engages in what an earlier Romantic criticism called "the internalization of quest-romance,"[66] we should logically expect the Poet to die at peace with himself. And the Narrator does try to create the sense of an ending by suggesting that the Poet has finally made the mind its own place:

> Yet the grey precipice and solemn pine
> And torrent, were not all;—one silent nook
> Was there.   (571–73)

My narrativization of the Narrator's second attempt at configuration, however, while resolving some of the contradictions in the previous story, is not without its complications, for the landscape of the self is no less labyrinthine than that of nature. As the Poet follows "the windings of the dell," commenting that the stream's "darksome stillness," "searchless fountain, and invisible course/Have each their type in me" (494, 505–8), he is once again involved in reflections that do not give back an image. Thus neither we nor he ever make contact with the Poet's "self," his "character" in Godwin's word, except as displaced from itself into some specular image, reflected in the water in the form of a "treacherous likeness" (474). Nor do we make contact with his death, for as Blanchot writes, there are two deaths. On the one hand, there is the death that "circulates in the language of possibility" and has for its "horizon the freedom to die and the capacity to take mortal risks"; this is the death the Narrator wants to make the climax of the Poet's story. On the other hand, there is "its double, which is ungraspable" and "not linked to *me* by any relation of any sort."[67] At points it seems that the Poet's death is this second death, which cannot be narrated because it is not a finite event but is always there.

Hence the closing description of the nook, in which the Narrator wants to think of the Poet as peacefully dying, unravels on closer inspection:

> Even on the edge of that vast mountain,
> Upheld by knotty roots and fallen rocks,
> It overlooked in its serenity
> The dark earth, and the bending vault of stars.
> It was a tranquil spot, that seemed to smile
> Even in the lap of horror.   (573–78)

The spatial position of the nook is ambiguous. It is described as overlooking or being above the dark earth, as though its serenity comes from its having transcended the complications of life; but it is also described as being in the "*lap* of horror," as though it is surrounded by what it seeks to forget, to overlook. What the repetition of the story makes clear is that narrative is a potentially endless process: not a closed structure, but a proliferating web of speculation.

This is not, however, what the Narrator has in mind in telling the Poet's story, which he configures as quest-narrative: a circuitous return to an identity of author and work that is not merely unreflective. Through the self-repetition of himself as the Poet, the Narrator tries to gain access to himself, to construct himself to himself, so as to find an alter ego who will no longer make a ghost of the self but will instead render up the tale of what we are. This alter ego must be a unity; it must not be different from itself if it is to tell its tale clearly. Yet no representation of this part-object that is the Poet really succeeds in making the Narrator's conception fully present within the order of representation. Because the Poet is rarely pictured as speaking, we know him only from the outside, like the pyramids among which he wanders in search of meaning, which similarly present an exterior that baffles penetration and perhaps conceals an absence. His mind is repeatedly described as "vacant" (126, 191), and though we are once told that "meaning" flashed on it "like strong inspiration" (126–28), we have no sense of what that meaning is and infer from the parenthetical way in which the claim is made that it may simply be a trick of light. Onto this empty schema the Narrator projects different and contradictory interpretations that constantly unravel each other.

The repetitive narration, which fragments the poem's structure by showing the Narrator as assembling and disassembling an identity for the Poet, is reflected at the textural level in the poem's blurred, almost unreadable descriptions: descriptions in which the figure and its ground do not seem to come together. There is, for instance, the passage in which the Poet embarks in the death-boat:

> Following his eager soul, the wanderer
> Leaped in the boat, he spread his cloak aloft
> On the bare mast, and took his lonely seat,
> And felt the boat speed o'er the tranquil sea
> Like a torn cloud before the hurricane.
>
> As one that in a silver vision floats
> Obedient to the sweep of odorous winds
> Upon resplendent clouds, so rapidly
> Along the dark and ruffled waters fled
> The straining boat.   (311–20)

It is unclear here whether the weather—both physical and emotional—is calm or stormy. The sea is tranquil, yet the boat proceeds as if driven by a hurricane. The Poet floats in a silver dream but moves rapidly along the dark waters. He seems at peace with himself, in control of his destiny as he stands at the steady helm (333), having chosen freely to embrace death in the pursuit of his ideal. However, he appears harried, a victim of forces without and within that push him helplessly towards destruction. The radical contradictions that occur in the space of a few lines impede any attempt at visualization, as the Narrator is seemingly left with the collapse of his attempt to construct the Poet as a coherent figure.

And yet, as Shelley says, the details of the Poet's story "[are] not all." At stake in the Narrator's almost schizophrenic representation of the Poet is the issue of poetry versus prose: the obstinate restoration, to the prose in which we are tempted to phrase the Poet's story, of the poetry "eat[en] out" of it in Shelley's dis-figuration of Wordsworthian lyric (*DP*, 485). For the in-tense mode (in Tate's sense) in which the Narrator tells the story produces a jamming of the story's extension by a lyricism that takes the form of ungrounded affect and superfluous loco-descriptive details. The result is a hanging on to the Poet and his quest that is really a "hanging back" from resolution that Agamben associates with poetry. It is this hanging back that we also see more chastely in the poem on the Boy of Winander. Not only does the Boy "hang" listening to the sounds we cannot hear in everyday life, as if halting for a moment the ephemerality of what he does. Wordsworth too hangs back from determining the figural as the literal event of the Boy's death. He hangs onto this poem, reproducing it in successive texts that always return to the prose of actuality, while always protecting the lyric on the Boy in a separate verse paragraph, which keeps a space for poetry.

❦

The Narrator's failure is a failure of both narrative and lyric, but it also provides the generative ground for rethinking the very nature of literature. Unable to bring the Poet into focus as a character, the Narrator is also unable to give his life the status of factuality. But it is just as possible to say that the contradictions haunting the narrative process generate productive differences: differences between the Narrator and a character who is other than him and between the Narrator and assumed readers whose penumbral presence complicates his relationship to his protagonist. Insofar as he (mis)conceives narrative in terms of plot as the signifier of interpretive closure, the Narrator resists this narrativity: a resistance manifested in a nostalgia for lyric and in a concluding attempt to bring back lyric as elegy. Yet by writing the beautiful soul into a more extensive form, the Narrator also wants to give it a substantiality it lacks for Wordsworth. Given no voice and scarcely spoken of in a poem whose brevity feels language to be a profanation, Wordsworth's Lucy exists only as an unheard melody, at once protected and ephemeralized in lyric as the mode of childhood.[68] Though the figure of genius in *Alastor* is similarly silent, his Narrator is not. In describing the Poet's life at such length, the poem presses beyond the modesty of the Lucy poems. Similarly, in describing the Poet's displaced wanderings through foreign cultures, the Narrator pleads, albeit by negation, for the Poet's place in contemporary culture. And by the same token, unlike Wordsworth, he opens the Poet to an ideological contestation reflected in his inability to sustain an idealized portrayal of his character as Browning's subjective poet.

Importantly this very idealization, rather than being merely sentimental, is part of what André Green, borrowing a phrase from Hegel, calls "the work of the negative." As Green argues, pushing further Melanie Klein's psychoanalysis of idealization, idealization is not just an inability to integrate the good object into the ego and thus a failure on the part of the subject. It is also part of the *work* of the negative, albeit a process of working through that is disavowed. In other words, as a pushing away of the good, it is a disguised form of the negative, which withdraws from integrating the idealized object because there is something missing in it that prevents it from being posited except as fantasy.[69] Hence the Narrator exalts the Poet as a "surpassing Spirit," but with such excessive zeal that he seems a "vapour fed with golden beams" (714, 663). Yet it would be wrong to dismiss as hysterical the lyricism that houses this idealization. For lyricism, which subsists in the poem as affect rather than reference, constructs a space of protection and encryption that is like what Jean-Luc Nancy calls the sacred. Whereas religion "is the observance of a rite" that "maintains a bond," the sacred signifies "the separate, what is set aside, removed, cut off." It is "at a distance . . . what one cannot touch . . . *the distinct*," which is fundamentally "heterogeneous"and "unbindable":[70] a strangeness also signified by the poem's title, "Alastor," meaning a wanderer who " is what the Greeks called the specter of the unburied," which cannot be stabilized as an ancestor or housed in a literary tradition.[71]

The distinct is not exalted or transcendent but is "what is separated by marks . . . what is withdrawn and set apart by a line or trait, by being marked also as withdrawn [*retrait*]."[72] Wandering among sphinxes and obelisks (106–16), the Poet is stigmatized as distinct, like the dreamer among the remnants of the Titans' lost story in Keats' *Fall of Hyperion*. These remnants —girdles, draperies, and other "decrepit things" that the dreamer hangs on to—are ordinary objects, like the "useless fragment" of Margaret's wooden bowl in *The Ruined Cottage*. But they are also archeological traces that Keats marks as sacred when he describes the "strange vessels" and "holy jewelries" that survive in this "place the moth could not corrupt." The reference is to the medieval trope of the "incorruptible corpse." However, here it is not the body that is incorrupt but a "mingled heap" of objects, which, no longer being available for use as things, survive as "imageries from a sombre loom," open to a different kind of reflection, made possible by the untimeliness of poetry (*Fall*, 1.70–80). Within this space of "safety" the dreamer and not the more conventional "poet" is marked out, "favored for unworthiness" in the poem's difficult negotiation of what literature is (1.144, 182). For on the one hand, in contrast to the "poet," who is of his own time, Keats' dreamer is of no "benefit" to the "great world." He is a "fever" of himself (166–68) and a wanderer in and from a different time, like the Poet of

Alastor in his "self-centred seclusion." On the other hand, so that "happiness be somewhat shar'd," such "things" as he are granted access to the sanctuary (*Fall*, 1.177–78). Meanwhile, those who "labour for mortal good" and seek to be "humanist[s]" and "physician[s]to all men," find a "haven in the world" and have no need to enter the sanctuary (1.159, 190, 150). By the same token, they "rot on the pavement," (1.153),[73] like the Wordsworthian poet/Pastor whose heart "burn[s] to the socket" in the quotation from *The Excursion* that concludes the Preface to *Alastor* (70).

But *Alastor* is not quite *The Fall of Hyperion*, which is written in the first person and is more ready to confront the question of what literature is. What is set apart in *Alastor* is not the Poet himself as a special being, since one can scarcely think of a character more obscure or ineffectual than this "frail exhalation" (687). What is set apart is poetry, for which the Poet is merely a figure and for which lyric is only a shell covering over an inexpressible kernel. Hence the vacancy with which the Poet is associated, since he never adequately embodies what he figures. And hence the fact that poetry is given nonpositively in "the trait and in the line that separates it,"[74] in the image of a Poet that, at the end, is vacated of the content projected into it. For at the end, the Poet, whose words often seem ventriloquized by the Narrator, reverts to being an "image, silent, cold, and motionless" (661), like the empty forms that subsist "underneath the grave" in *Prometheus Unbound*, waiting to be thought differently (1.197). As Nancy suggests, the image is not so much referential—an image *of* something—as is it is a form in which the thing is given to us. Or withheld from us. For the essence of the image is that it is "detached, placed outside and before one's eyes" and is "inseparable from a hidden surface, from which it cannot . . . be peeled away: the dark side of the picture" or the tain of the mirror. As such, the image is what withdraws from "the world of things considered as a world of availability."[75]

The Narrator, in other words, constructs the Poet as a way of gesturing towards poetry as the radically heterogeneous, which cannot be bound in his own projection and recuperation of the Poet as Browning's visionary. Wanting to conserve the spirit of poetry, he allows the "charmed eddies" of lyric to build an "untimely tomb" for the Poet, only to describe this memorial as a "pyramid/Of mouldering leaves" (52–54), which cannot gather in what it seeks to bind. For the Poet is only spasmodically linked to "all of great/Or good, or lovely" that "the past . . . consecrates" (72–

73). More often, like Keats' dreamer brooding on Moneta's statuary for three moons, he "linger[s]," gazing on "speechless shapes . . . through the long burning day" and not "suspend[ing]" his "task" even at night (121–26). Rather than producing ideas that "lie burningly on the divine hand," he seeks, or finds, a reflex of the external world "on the retina of his own eyes": what Foucault, following Blanchot, calls "the unthought," what reflection cannot see, since the eye cannot see itself. Although the Narrator represents the Poet as frantically launched on a quest for permanence, the Poet often seems more like Blanchot's Orpheus turning towards Eurydice. For Blanchot, "Eurydice is the furthest that art can reach. Under a name that hides her and a veil that covers her, she is the profoundly obscure point toward which art and desire, death and night, seem to tend," the form in which "the essence of night approaches as the *other* night" and the other death.[76]

Orpheus's "*work*" as artist is not to descend into this night, which Blanchot calls "madness" and which is the condition of possibility for representation, but to bring it " back to the light of day" by giving it "form, shape, and reality." By turning towards Eurydice, as the Poet does in following the veiled maid, Blanchot's Orpheus "betrays the work, and Eurydice, and the night"; he betrays the night by disappearing into it. Hence the Narrator struggles to give shape to the Poet's life, often using phrases borrowed from others such as Wordsworth. He tries to represent the Poet as a lyric poet, although neither the Poet nor the poem itself are really lyrical. Having failed in this attempt, the Narrator then tries to configure the Poet's death in terms of "the power to finish," so that death, rather than being a failure, can at least be "the force of the negative" and "the cutting edge of decision." But "not to turn towards Eurydice would be no less untrue."[77] Thus the Narrator, evoking "Medea," "poisons," and "dark magician[s]" at the end, cannot avoid including, in the fragmentary memorial of the Poet, that turning towards death and madness that he also resists in portraying the Poet as a "surpassing Spirit" (672–84, 714).

Gathering up Shelley's posthumous poems in 1824 and his collected poems in 1839, Mary Shelley becomes his Narrator and the guardian of his literary remains. She becomes the Narrator who survives the Poet in *Alastor*, which she curiously includes in the *Posthumous Poems*.[78] It has been argued, with justification, that she constructs Shelley's legacy in terms of a politics of genre that is tied up with her own anxieties about his reputation, her rivalry with him, and the cultural fate of poetry itself. Thus Neil Fraistat contrasts her editions of Shelley with the pirated edition by William Benbow, arguing that she foregrounds the lyrics and "non-narrative fragments" so as to produce an "etherealized, disembodied and virtually depoliticized poet," who was to become for the Victorians a signifier of the "pure poetry" to which they wanted to reduce (Romantic) poetry. Mary Favret, extending the disembodiment of lyric to all poetry, argues that the personal agon between the Shelleys aligned prose with realism and poetry with ineffectual idealism within the frame of judgment of an emergent modernity. The motives assigned to Mary Shelley in these accounts are different, namely, a competitive effeminizing of poetry in the case of Favret and a protective aestheticizing of Percy Shelley's work in the case of Fraistat. But both stories concur in the way they see Mary Shelley as disallowing to poetry, as lyrical poetry, any effect outside an obscure and increasingly restricted sphere.[79]

Indeed, Mary Shelley does represent Shelley's lyrics in *Prometheus Unbound* as the distilled essence of his "abstruse and imaginative theories," and she also speaks of his intention to write "prose metaphysical essays," which would have explained "much of what is obscure in his poetry." She comments that he "loved to idealize reality" and that he used poetry to "obliterate all that would otherwise" have been "too harsh or hideous." She further follows the Preface-writer in condemning Shelley for lacking "sympathies with our kind," because he is "too brilliant" and "too subtle."[80] But her narratives about Shelley and the place of poetry are far less settled than these phrases suggest. Her inclusion of so many fragments in *Posthumous Poems* may not just be a way of attenuating and marginalizing Shelley, as Fraistat suggests.[81] It may also be, at least visually and paratextually, a way of presenting his work as unfinished and open to different narrativizations. Indeed, as I suggest in the last chapter, which deals with Godwin's editing of Wollstonecraft, the very process of editing as an archival activity returns Shelley's poems and "Shelley" himself to a cultural archive possessed of further narrativity. But this narrativity has already been opened up in *Alastor* between the Narrator, Poet, and Preface-writer, as well as by Shelley's own archiving of his poem as a text passed on to a further reader and in his circulation of the figure of "Shelley" through his corpus.

Thus, as Susan Wolfson points out, Mary Shelley does not wholly dismiss her husband as ineffectual. As his Narrator rather than Preface-writer, she also tries to rehabilitate him as a political thinker, pointing out that he had "from youth been the victim of the state of feeling inspired by the reaction of the French Revolution."[82] More specifically, while her Prefaces contribute to a pathologizing of Shelley and poetry that would entrench itself by the Victorian period,[83] they also identify Shelley as a type of the Romantic poet who is committed to what does not find a place in the discourse of prose: a restless wandering and exile, an orphic will to death, and an obsessive delving into the particularities of nature as a trope for seeking outside the social the texture of feelings occluded by a life with a more determinate and instituted structure.[84] Moreover, this Romanticism—European more than English—is its own inwardly directed revolution, part of the state of feeling inspired by "the reaction of the French Revolution." Mary Shelley's phrasing is interesting here, for the ambiguous genitive leaves it unclear whether the "reaction" involved refers to the Revolution itself or to the complex, disparate reaction(s) it produced. She thus intimates that Shelley's poetry and indeed his idealism are part of the reaction of this general turbulence rather than simple entities in themselves, part of what Philippe Lacoue-Labarthe and Nancy call *retrait du politique*, wherein Shelley's very abstraction, rather than being simple aloofness, takes its place in a symptomatic network with a certain critical force.[85]

To be sure, Mary Shelley could be seen as recontaining the space she opens for Romanticism by deflecting what is really an ontology and an aesthetic into the biographical. She repeatedly apologizes for her husband, stressing the "ill health and perpetual pain" that "preyed" on Shelley's powers. Nevertheless, the Prefaces exhibit the same pattern that we find in *Alastor*, which they echo at several points. They idealize Shelley as "the wise, the brave, the gentle," damning him with fulsome praise. But they also want to delve beneath an idealization that is its own form of negation, so as to grasp a principle of "internal irritability" and "excitement" that is not captured by their ineffectual Platonisms.[86] "Irritability" and "excitement" are medical terms from Albrecht Haller and John Brown, with a revolutionary genealogy and a serious philosophical afterlife in the work of Schelling and Hegel. Mary Shelley recognizes the larger force of Shelley's irritability in *The Last Man*, where it is the enervated and withdrawn Adrian who curiously revives as a political figure in the last part of the novel, regenerated and "medicin'd," in Keats' words, "by sickness not ignoble." Meanwhile, more conventional political forms such as re-publicanism and the nation-state, and political leaders more convinced that they can be "physician[s] to all men," fall victim to the plague (Keats, *Fall*, 1.183–84, 190). In short, the Prefaces are part of the complex au-tonarration, or rather psychonarration,[87] of Mary Shelley's own relation-ship to the irritable legacy of Romanticism and poetry. Taken together with her fiction, they do not clearly put forward prose as the future of poetry. Rather, they record a conflicted process of reflecting on the role of poetry in relation to society: a role that is not easy to grasp except symp-tomatically, because poetry is itself an effect of, even a crypt for, their inner disagreement. Poetry is an effect and a repository for a missed en-counter that is the essence of the relation between literature and society, which is to say that the "prose" Mary Shelley writes is itself a symptom-atic effect of the imperative she feels not to write poetry.

As Mary Jacobus compellingly argues, it is this poetry that in its very absence informs Mary Shelley's *Mathilda*, where the nameless shadowy Father wanders through scenes of exile, like the Poet in *Alastor*, and where Mathilda, like Orpheus, finally turns towards death, the night, and her father. Following the same pattern of disavowal in her novella as in her Prefaces, Mary Shelley abjects poetry by giving it "an ideal form" in the poet Woodville or locating it in "the 'elsewhere' of quotation from Dante, Spenser, and Wordsworth." This de-jection of poetry, however, marks her "failure to own—to take credit for—the strained and over-wrought 'poetry' of her lyrical prose": what Jacobus calls a "subtractive lyricism," following my own description of Mathilda's lyricism as "less a positive identity than a subtraction from narrative."[88] This lyricism, in other words, is not so much in the text as it mimes a "lost object," a fac-ulty cut off from itself in lines from Wordsworth and Dante that are only the image—silent, cold, and motionless—of a poetry that is still (to be) born. Yet it is this stranded lyricism that, through what Jacobus calls a "negative empathy," lets us "listen to a literary text that speaks with such profound elisions that the listener is unable to hear it." And despite Mary Shelley's casting off of Shelley as the angelic Woodville, it is Shelley's po-etry and its dark spirit of solitude that is the condition of possibility for a " '*nescience*' or unrecognized knowledge," "the bearer of a buried parental secret,"[89] which the text conveys in the form of a letter that cannot be opened and that is addressed, for lack of another, to the wrong reader. A letter addressed within the diegesis to Woodville but in reality also to Godwin: the nameless shadowy father of a prose whose elisions his daughter hears only when the Symbolic father has been put to death.

Alastor too is addressed to the wrong reader or to no reader, there being no one in the solitude of the text's diegesis to hear the poem except the Preface-writer. For this reason it is also addressed to us in the wrong form. That form, as the Narrator initially conceives it, is lyric, even though lyric proves to be neither the form nor the content of the poem. As Heather Dubrow suggests, lyric is often represented as "something extraordinary, atypical," the repository of what is "precious but imperiled in the current climate." And yet, curiously, what is protected by the poem's stranded lyricism is the loss of lyric, buried in references to Wordsworth, whose own elegy on Lucy, "rolled round . . . with rocks and stones," encrypts the story of poetry's *failure* as lyric to move rocks and stones in the mode of Orpheus and Amphion.[90] Hence, at the end the Narrator abandons lyric when, in a Gothic parody of the Aeolian harp, he allows the Poet's "divinest lineaments" to be "Worn by the senseless wind" (704–5). Protecting its failure, *Alastor* as "lyric" does not protect lyric so much as the trauma with which lyric is cathected in the nineteenth century: the trauma of a larger foreclosure of poetry. But the poem is also insistently a narrative that wants to make poetry's legacy, the legacy of its untimeliness and obscurity, an object for further speculation. As such it is driven by the urgency of passing on the Poet, poetry, and "Shelley" to a world of prose represented by Mary Shelley in her missed encounter with her own work, but anticipated by Shelley himself as his own Preface-writer, archivist, and posthumous voice.

CHAPTER TWO

Shelley's Promethean Narratives

Gothic Anamorphoses in Zastrozzi, St. Irvyne, and Prometheus Unbound

S HELLEY'S EARLY NOVEL *St. Irvyne* breaks off hastily with the formulaic declaration that Ginotti and Nempere are the same person, and that Eloise is Wolfstein's sister.

> Ginotti is Nempere. Eloise is the sister of Wolfstein. Let then the memory of these victims to hell and malice live in the remembrance of those who can pity the wanderings of error; let remorse and repentance expiate the offences which arise from the delusion of the passions, and let endless life be sought from Him alone who can give an eternity of happiness. (252)[1]

This hurriedly tacked-on ending, at which Shelley's publisher Stockdale protested, seems almost to parody the facile binding up of loose ends in the overdetermined genre of Gothic romance, which impossibly yokes together violence and abjection with the utopianism of the sentimental novel. In the baroque double plot of Shelley's second novel, Eloise is the young innocent who embarks on a journey away from her home in St. Irvyne to improve her mother's health—an evocation of a stock motif from Anne Radcliffe. Nempere is the casuistical seducer of Eloise, who, like Christabel, innocently wanders into her unconscious. Eloise is rescued by Nempere's equally libertine friend Mountjoy, who wins her in gambling and later kills Nempere in a duel. In the last chapter she marries the Shelleyan poet Fitzeustace, who accepts her even though she is carrying Nempere's child, and the two presumably live happily ever after. Then, to please his parents, they give up the ideal of free love, "procuring moral expediency, at a slight sacrifice of what we conceive to be right" (250), in an obvious reminiscence of the marriage of Godwin and Wollstonecraft.

The romance plot, centered on Eloise, takes up four chapters (7, 9, 11, and 12). The Gothic plot, focusing on Ginotti and Wolfstein, is more extensive, occupying the first four chapters, chapters 7, 10, and the Conclusion. Ginotti is the obscure figure who sanctions Wolfstein's poisoning of the bandit Cavigni in order to obtain the lovely Megalena de Metastasio. In this frame story, Ginotti functions as the shadow and Dark Interpreter of the increasingly dissolute Wolfstein, until the plot disposes of both of them in its Faustian Conclusion, just as Ginotti is about to give his pupil the elixir of life. Meanwhile, Megalena too has grown increasingly jealous and depraved, forcing Wolfstein to kill the innocent Olympia as proof of his loyalty. Megalena initially shares with Eloise the position of the abducted victim who forms a strange bond with her seducer, and Ginotti and Nempere are both described as being of gigantic stature. Nevertheless, until the end the Wolfstein and Eloise stories seem completely unconnected, to the point that Shelley actually omits the chapters that might have linked them: chapters 5 and 6. The equations in the last paragraph merge these plots, announcing that Eloise is Wolfstein's sister, and summarily disposing not only of Wolfstein but also of Ginotti, Eloise (even though she is supposed to live happily after) and any residues of Nempere.

At the same time, the hastiness of this algebra foregrounds the failure of the conventionally moralistic resolution to close the gaps opened by constructing the novel out of semiautonomous pieces. Why, for instance, does Nempere, who has already been killed in chapter 12, return to die in another time and place and in another plot, as Ginotti? And if Ginotti needs to die twice, is he actually dead at the end? Or is he simply dead by convention, surviving as the text's unconscious, its botched figure for what it has not yet articulated? To be sure, the desired unity of Radcliffe's *Mysteries of Udolpho* is similarly threatened by the semiautonomy of certain recesses and subplots, such as the story of Laurentini. But *St. Irvyne* actually emphasizes the ways in which it fails to cohere. Its two plots share a character, Ginotti/Nempere, who performs different functions in each one; likewise, they share plot positions that are occupied differently by characters in each story. This shifting of plot positions makes the character of Ginotti unreadable, and his return displaces us from any sense that the simple story of Eloise united with Fitzeustace is where the story actually ends. For as the uncanny link between the two plots, Ginotti's return as a phantasm the text must recall does not simply repeat the death of Nempere so as to confirm it in both narrative sectors; it also inscribes the utopian story of a heroine saved by a Shelleyan poet within another set of signifiers, marking the Gothic plot as the unconscious of the romance story and reminding us of a darker side to the revolutionary idealism of the latter.

It is interesting that before turning to the genre of poetry, and despite the lyric simplification he entertains but finally defers in *Alastor*, Shelley had written two novels, as if poetry always exists in the shadow of its novelization. *Zastrozzi* was written when Shelley was still at Eton and was published under the signature of "P.B.S." in 1810; *St. Irvyne*, by a "gentleman of Oxford," was published a year later. Both thus bear only a partial signature, occupying a space between publication and writing, which indicates that the identity of literature for Shelley was still under negotiation.[2] Not surprisingly, the two novels have largely been dismissed as juvenilia. But what role might the very notion of juvenilia or prematurity play in the economy of narrative as a medium of speculation rather than cognition? And what role might narrative correspondingly play in poetry as an unbinding of its lyric or epic closure that returns the products of poetry to their underlying *poiesis?* Structurally and thematically there are enough connections between the novels and the later poetry to suggest that the novels are at once a laboratory for the later work, a way of placing this work permanently under erasure, and yet still a closet for a poetry that Shelley felt nervously compelled to disavow. Indeed, *St. Irvyne*, brought before the public again in 1822,[3] comes both before and after the "mature" work, returning Shelley's mythmaking to its underlying narrativity. The division between poetry and narrative at issue in the intertextual relations between the later texts and the Gothic novels also aligns itself in this case with a difference between high and low culture. Thus the "novelization" of poetry that occurs between these texts already calls in question the "high" Romanticism canonized by a certain phase of literary criticism and then critiqued by Jerome McGann and others. This is to say that because the novels are pastiche and because they draw on one of the most commodified literary forms of the period, the Gothic, they already preview what has been seen as Romanticism's marketing of itself to itself: a buying into its own fantasies, which McGann has called the Romantic Ideology. These fantasies or ideologemes include the "Poet" opposed to the prose of the world, who is the subject of *Alastor, Adonais,* and the *Defence of Poetry* and who is first introduced with Peacockian irony as Fitzeustace in *St. Irvyne.* They also include the "deep ecology" of the last act of *Prometheus Unbound* and romantic dreams of perfectibility and Promethean transgression.[4]

It is of course the parallels with *Prometheus Unbound* that are the most obvious. These range from the rocky landscape of the novels, where we see the first novel's hero Verezzi in chains, to its eponymous antihero, Zastrozzi, as Promethean transgressor. As important, the phantasmal repetition of characters in *St. Irvyne* also strikingly anticipates what Shelley does in *Prometheus,* where he has a character speak through the phantasm of another character rather than in *propria persona,* and where Demogorgon occupies roles in the plot that are radically incommensurable. The amorphous and troubling Demogorgon of act 2 is the unconscious of the figure conjured up in the final act by Asia's desire, not in the sense that he is the reality behind appearance, but in the sense that he (or it) is the other within her own language. Shelley's metaphor for this doubling of the self as its other is the underworld visited by the Magus Zoroaster in act 1, where "do inhabit the shadows of all forms that think and live" (1.198). It is from something like this underworld that the phantasm Ginotti reappears, as the shadow or unresolved remainder left after the destruction of Nempere. In *Prometheus Unbound* this sense of the self as laterally related to an other, which remains to trouble thought and which cannot be reintegrated as Jungian hidden depth, also takes the structural form of an action whose parts exceed the whole one tries to construct out of them. For the play, rather than unfolding as a linear plot, occurs in disconnected segments: Prometheus, in act 1, trying to break the cycle of victim and torturer by "recalling" his curse, in the double sense of remembering and revoking it; Asia, in act 2, simultaneously trying to read Panthea's dreams so that she can emplot history as a narrative culminating in her union with Prometheus; and Demogorgon, in act 3, taking the drama out of the closet in dethroning Jove. In this montage of mutually supplementary spaces, Prometheus' attempt to renounce hatred is simply not consistent with Demogorgon's violently Jovian overthrow of Jove, as if private and public, ideality and history, have missed each other. In this respect *Prometheus Unbound* resembles *St. Irvyne,* as an assemblage that finally disassembles itself—a kind of monster made of bits and pieces whose role as an ontological metaphor for the Gothic's traversal of Enlightenment phantasms Mary Shelley will inscribe seven years later. For *St. Irvyne,* too, is composed of semiautonomous parts, in which the marriage of Eloise and Fitzeustace is only tenuously supported by the destruction of Nempere, who, like Jove, may well return again.

These parallels, combined with *St. Irvyne*'s echoing of Godwin's *St. Leon* (1798), mark Shelley's later work as a return to an archive of revolutionary ideas, phrases, and motifs that began to form itself in the 1790s. Shelley's title actually does not refer to a character, as in *St. Leon,* whose eponymous protagonist is a gambler and alchemist who, ironically, figures Godwin's search for perfectibility. *St. Irvyne* names a place reminiscent of Wordsworth's Tintern Abbey, whose pastoral idealism Shelley (r)evokes: St. Irvyne, we are told, "was the same as when [Eloise] had left it five years ago" (209). Nevertheless, the title and the motif of alchemy hastily introduced at the end do point us towards ideas of perfectibility that are also taken up in *Frankenstein* and that Shelley associates with the radical thought- and life-experiments made possible by Godwin and the philosophes. These experiments, which in Shelley's novel include libertinism and atheism, mark a darker side of the Enlightenment, which Shelley associates in *The Triumph of Life* with the drug nepenthe and in *St. Irvyne* with alchemy, which never quite manages to turn "to potable gold the poisonous waters which flow from death through life" (*DP,* 505).

In addition, there is Ginotti's strange vision, which occupies most of chapter 10 of *St. Irvyne,* introducing an unexpected metaphysical depth into what has seemed a second-rate imitation of the Gothic. Just before giving Wolfstein the formula for the elixir of life (238), Ginotti tells the story of his own quest for eternal life. By seventeen he had delved into the secrets of "natural philosophy" and "metaphysical calculations," convincing himself of "the non-existence of a First Cause" (234). The death of God is the intellectual basis for the transgression of all socially imposed codes and institutions. This absolute transgression leads Ginotti to experiment with poison, trying it out on a youth who had offended him (235), in anticipation of Wolfstein's more sordid poisoning of Cavigni, wherein the *acte gratuit* of murder aims at an ex-termination of conventional characters, relations, and terms. Yet the materialism of the philosophes and the knowledge that his own "muscles and fibres" cannot logically be "made of stuff more durable than those of other men" (235) also pushes Ginotti to a despairing nihilism, which makes him all the more avid for the secret of eternal life. Inconsistently for someone who does not believe in a hereafter, he fears more than ever "to die . . . [to] perish, perhaps *everlastingly*" (235; emphasis mine). In despair, he contemplates suicide, when, "gazing on the expansive gulf which yawned" before him, he sees a "form of most exact and superior symmetry." The passage is worth quoting at length:

> The phantasm advanced towards me; it seemed then, to my imagination, that his figure was borne on the sweet strain of music which filled the circumambient air. In a voice which was fascination itself, the being addressed me, saying, "Wilt thou come with me? wilt thou be mine?" I felt a decided wish never to be his. "No, no," I unhesitatingly cried, with a feeling which no language can either explain or describe. No sooner had I uttered these words, than methought a sensation of deadly horror chilled my sickening frame . . . the beautiful being vanished; clouds, as of chaos, rolled around, and from their dark masses flashed incesant meteors. . . . My neck was grasped firmly, and, turning round in an agony of horror, I beheld a form more hideous than the imagination of man is capable of portraying, whose proportions, gigantic and deformed, were seemingly blackened by the inerasible traces of the thunderbolts of God; yet in its hideous and detestable countenance, though seemingly far different, I thought I could recognize that of the lovely vision. (236–37)

The passage strikingly anticipates the primal scene of Rousseau's spiritual birth at the dawn of a new era in *The Triumph of Life*. In this scene the shape all light changes into the deformed shape in the Car, yet never quite ceases to be present in the "severe excess" of the sobriety that follows and whose illumination it haunts: "The ghost of a forgotten form of sleep" (424–28). Ginotti's vision, in other words, condenses many of the paradoxes to which Shelley was to return: his fascination with avantgarde thought and behavior and what they opened up, along with an idealism for which he still craved a transcendental grounding that this thought made impossible; the cycle of illusion and disillusion or mania and sobriety characteristic of revolutionary thought and encapsulated in Rousseau's symbolic autobiography; and the sense that, despite the depravity unleashed by the period's intellectual and historical ferment, "something not yet made good pushes its essence forward" in the deformation of idealism, to quote Habermas on the utopianism of Ernst Bloch.[5] Shelley's Gothic novels, in other words, begin an experiment with the pre-texts and leitmotifs of a revolutionary Romanticism that is replayed in his later poetry as part of a self-conscious resumption of the structural and ideological problems in which the early work is caught. To be sure, these novels are *jeux d'esprit,* whose plots verge on the ridiculous, and the resemblances to Godwin, the philosophes, revenge tragedy, Charlotte Dacre's *Zofloya,* and Shelley's own future work make for something of a mishmash. But rather than dismissing the novels as juvenilia, we might recall Julia Kristeva's characterization of the novel itself as an adolescent form connected to a polymorphous "perversity." Arguing that the novelistic mode provides for an experimentation in which the writer dresses up as her characters, Kristeva suggests that it creates a space withdrawn from reality-testing that the writer is then free to reorganize "in the time before an ideally postulated maturity."[6] Significantly, the text she uses as a paradigm for the novel is Antoine de la Sale's *Little Jehan de Saintré* (1446): not an example of the Novel, but a medieval text drawn from the period that Hegel and A. W. Schlegel saw as the beginning of Romanticism. In *Alastor* the adolescent Romantic "Poet" must be set aside by the more Victorian Narrator, who then melancholically dis-figures "the narrative of particular facts" he has been compelled to write. But in *Prometheus Unbound* Shelley once again returns to the pre-mature, when Asia and Prometheus, having been ceremonially married, retreat, "Like human babes in their brief innocence," to their cave as the space of fantasy (3.3.33). This marriage, if stripped of its mythopoeic dignity, is no more credible than that of Eloise and Fitzeustace in *St. Irvyne,* except insofar as adolescence provides the writer with metaphors of "what is not yet formed . . . what awaits the writer . . . what calls to him."[7]

Given their Gothic mode, we might think of these early novels as Symbolic forms in Hegel's sense, where the Symbolic (best exemplified by the monstrous or fantastic) dis-figures the "adequate embodiment" and hypostasis of "the Idea."[8] For the point made by the aesthetic of these novels is that what is not yet formed is necessarily deformed in the process of its formation. Indeed, Hegel's account of the Symbolic—which is very different from the conventional understanding of the symbol in Goethe or Coleridge—captures a "manic" quality, which Kristeva discerns in the adolescent's transition to the symbol, which for her is still part of what Melanie Klein sees as the paranoid-schizoid position.[9] In the *Aesthetics* Hegel elaborates three forms of art that involve different relations between "inwardness" and its "externalization" the "idea," and its "embodiment," or in Kristeva's terms "word and drive."[10] In the earliest or Symbolic phase, which is pre-art, pre-mature, art fails to achieve identity with itself because of a deficiency in self-consciousness that is reflected in the Idea still being "indeterminate" (*A*, 1.76). In this mode external forms are warped and dis-figured by the inadequacy of their Idea. This problem is overcome in the Classical mode, as art becomes "the adequate embodiment of the Idea" in plastic form, an adequacy Lukács also attributes to the realist novel.[11] Then, in the Romantic phase, form and content are again separated, this time because of a deficiency in matter that repeats and reverses the problems of the Symbolic (1.77–79). Both act 4 of *Prometheus Unbound* and act 2, scene 1, where Asia can grasp her sister's dreams only by reading Panthea's "written soul" in her eyes (110), are examples of this Romanticism, which presses beyond mediation. Thus, while the Idea in the Symbolic fails to embody itself because of its own deficiency, in the Romantic the Idea is fully developed but "can no longer find its adequate reality" in the "shapes" available to it within culture (*A*, 1.422).

As I argue elsewhere, Hegel's criteria of beauty and adequacy should lead him to privilege the adequate embodiment of the Idea in Classicism, but he is drawn rather to the dis-integration of meaning and shape in the Symbolic and Romantic as a place for the work of the negative. And while the Romantic is more aesthetically acceptable and mature than the Symbolic, the two are simply different versions of this dis-integration. Indeed, the Romantic is arguably an alibi for revisiting Symbolic dis-integration.[12] This being said, the two are also stylistically very different: the Romantic is Christian and spiritual, the Symbolic uncouth and pagan. More specifically, the Romantic withdraws from making the "Idea" present except in ineffable forms "pinnacled dim in the intense inane" (*PU*, 3.4.204). The Idea in the Romantic mode is imagined as still to come—*à venir*, as Derrida puts it. But the Symbolic tries to force the "Idea" into the material actually available to it, resulting in what Hegel calls "the bad and untrue determinacy" of the grotesque or the cliché (*A*, 1.76–77). Yet the other side of the greater aestheticism of the Romantic is that it can be charged with what Derrida calls "bad infinity." The Romantic, in other words, avoids thinking the Idea "now," deferring it into the infinite future, which makes it a form of bad infinity.[13] By contrast, the crudity of the Symbolic comes from its engagement with culture as it stands. In *Zastrozzi*, then, the Idea takes the form of perversion, which as Slavoj Žižek says, always occurs within the law,[14] as a dis-figuration of the law that becomes "like what [it] contemplate[s]" (*PU*, 1.1.450). The Symbolic, in short, is committed to a certain "base materialism," in Georges Bataille's phrase.[15] It does its work at the site of the material in attempting to realize the Idea in the here and now, even if this means that the Idea can be imagined only in a warped form. This difference is reflected in the esotericism of Shelley's imagining an audience of no more than five to twenty-five for his "Romantic" lyrical drama, whereas the novels (whatever their actual sales) are aimed at a mass market.

It is clear that Zastrozzi and, more cynically, Ginotti/Wolfstein, are Symbolic, adolescent masks for the Promethean transgression whose incoherences they unmask. Unable to think through the contradictions of the desire to which he gives a premature determinacy in Zastrozzi, Shelley hastily destroys his monster according to the conventions of revenge tragedy and Faustian melodrama. But he then also undoes this destruction by allowing the first novel to return in the second as a revenant, or specter, with which he is not entirely done. The novels are pastiche and do not refer to the "real world" so much as to other texts: literary, social, and moral. They shamelessly reuse names from previous texts, mostly Gothic. In effect, the novels are part of a new form of literature that Foucault sees as emerging in the nineteenth century, where texts are "linked to the vast world of print" and develop "within the recognizable institution of writing": what Clifford Siskin calls the work of writing. This new epistemic technology opens a "space wholly dependent on the network formed by the books of the past" and as such "serves to circulate the fiction of books." The work of writing as the condition of possibility for a text that is pure textuality emerges from and returns to the archive as theorized by Foucault in his seminal essay "Fantasia of the Library." Foucault's starting point is Flaubert's early work, *The Temptation of St. Anthony*, whose protagonist is exposed to a myriad books and ideas from the past. The

disciplining of his imagination, necessary for Flaubert to produce something more akin to the Novel, can occur only through a "conflagration of
the archive," through which " 'Temptation' among the ruins of an ancient
world populated by spirits is transformed into an 'education' in the prose
of the modern world."[16]

Shelley too deploys the motif of temptation through the damnation to
which he consigns his characters at the end of both novels. But here it is
not that the multiple possibilities of the unsaid are repressed so that
literature "can achieve [its] own clarity" in "the prose of the modern
world"—a phrase in which Foucault echoes Hegel's account of the end of
Romanticism as the beginning of modernity and the "prose of actuality."[17] Rather, damnation, in the very act of bringing about the conflagration of other possibilities, also returns characters such as Zastrozzi and
Ginotti to the place where "do inhabit / The shadows of all forms that
think and live" (*PU*, 1.197–98). For the author of *The Necessity of Atheism*, damnation is both the conflagration of the archive necessary to produce the conventionally required plot and, as in Blake's *Marriage of
Heaven and Hell*, an apocalyptic parody of this conflagration, aimed at
unbinding its devils and angels from the plot positions assigned to them
in the present state of culture. Shelley will later call his lyrical drama
Prometheus Unbound, by which he refers not simply to the literal release
of Prometheus from his chains but also to the unbinding of writing from
the book in which it is bound. Peter Brooks, drawing on Freud, specifically relates this binding to plot, which he describes as a "binding of
textual energies that allows them to be mastered by putting them into
serviceable form, usable 'bundles' within the energetic economy of the
narrative."[18] In the Gothic novels, it is damnation that serves to dissolve,
defuse, and dissipate existing unifications so as to "recreate" them, as
Coleridge says of the imagination.[19] As the place where Shelley sends his
characters when they are finished with, damnation creates a space where
books are consigned, to be "taken up [again], fragmented, displaced,
combined." Once abjected into this space, the "phrases" and "phrase
regimes" from which these books are compiled become available for further thought, to evoke Lyotard's terms in *The Differend*, which I take up
in the final chapter. Here the fact that Shelley's novels are pastiche also
becomes significant. For pastiche, rather than creating organic unities,

breaks down its materials into a patchwork of phrases and ideas; it disintegrates them, making them available as junk for recycling.

As pastiche, the novels also deserve to be taken seriously as attempts to question both the cultural stereotypes in which they are caught and their own reinvention of these stereotypes.[20] For Shelley knows, with Žižek, that perversion occurs within the law—thus the novels can produce revolution only as perversion.[21] The seriousness of these texts is indicated by the way they seem in excess of what they are. Both novels are highly melodramatic and correspond to Peter Brooks' characterization of the melodramatic world as overburdened "by a weight of mysterious and grandiose reference beyond itself."[22] The titanic characters appear to be more than what they are, actors in some drama beyond their own. At the same time, this further meaning is never revealed, because the very flatness of melodrama, as a form whose characters have no interiority, impedes the emergence of such meaning. The novels do not convey a content so much as they suggest the form such a content might have. Their rapid pace and sudden reversals project a sense that they are dealing with something momentous. Their grandiose characters locate the intrapsychic conflicts dramatized in these tales of passion and murder within an action of world-historical significance. The characters are overdetermined, acting in different ways at different times. But instead of working these contradictions out as complexity or ambiguity, which would be to naturalize them, the texts leave them in suspension by stagily eliminating characters whose significance they are not ready to think through. In short, the conjunction of psychic turmoil with titanic characters asks us to read these texts in relation to some kind of political unconscious. But the abrupt endings of plots and the rapid accumulation of events unmediated by psychological or intellectual linkage also suggest Shelley's inability at this point to work through the content of history. Instead, like Blake's *Marriage of Heaven and Hell*, the novels cast their giant and parodic forms of male and female potentiality into the expanse, projecting and unworking them.

The novels do nevertheless introduce two key elements that return in the later drama. Both novels construct a form of closet literature in which reality has been replaced by hyperreality, and mimesis by the simulacrum. As examples of hyperrealism the novels are flamboyantly dramatic and completely unreal. In other words, their theatricality puts their credibility under erasure, detaining whatever designs they have upon us in the realm of writing. But at the same time they have a manic performativity, which is the condition of possibility for our rewriting them in the theater of our own minds. Functioning partly as a metadiscursive return to the first novel, *St. Irvyne* also introduces the *form* characteristic of the later work: a form composed of semiautonomous parts that do not add up to a whole, even as they remain haunted by the phantasm of an absent cause figured in Ginotti. As Kristeva says of her choice of *Jehan de Saintré*, the very crudeness of these novels manifests the "rules of structuration of the [narrative] genre," inventing an aesthetic and narratology *avant la lettre.*[23] But in *St. Irvyne* it is as if Shelley actually means to reflect on the form of his content. Moreover, if the parts of *St. Irvyne* unsettle each other, this is also the relationship that exists between the novels themselves. *St. Irvyne* is not a sequel, recantation, or paler repetition of *Zastrozzi*. Rather, the relation between the texts is mutually supplementary, with Zastrozzi functioning as the excess that survives his dismantling into his phantasmal remainder Ginotti.

I borrow the notion of overdetermined or nonsynchronous forms from Louis Althusser's extension of the Lacanian model of the unconscious to the historical process itself.[24] For Althusser in his rejection of an organic aesthetic of history—or aesthetic ideology—history is made up of semiautonomous parts, or "levels," that move at different speeds and in different directions, according to a "structural" rather than an "expressive" causality. The result, in his famous phrase, is that history becomes a "process without a *telos* or a subject." As Jameson explains the distinction in *The Political Unconscious,* a history (or narrative) organized in terms of expressive causality makes events the expression of an inner logic, wherein different levels are assimilated to one another, express one another, or are "modulations" of one and the same master narrative, as in the Aristotelian synchronization of plot and subplot. Each level (of the social system or aesthetic structure) is thus "folded into the next, thereby losing its constitutive autonomy and functioning as an expression of its homologues." By contrast, structural causality insists on the "semi-autonomy" or nonsynchronicity of these levels, with significant consequences for the "twin categories of narrative closure (*telos*) and of character."[25]

In Jameson's further development of Althusser the discrepancies between these parts make history the unconscious of the "imaginary" or "symbolic" resolutions we impose on its real contradictions, through narrativizations that omit intractable material.[26] The story that culminates in the marriage of Prometheus and Asia thus fails to take into account Demogorgon's violent overthrow of Jove, which in crudely Marxist terms manifests a discrepancy between base and superstructure, or in Hegelian terms cobbles together a Romantic aesthetic of ineffability with the awkwardness of the Symbolic. Likewise, the romance plot in *St. Irvyne* fails to "express" the Gothic level of the narrative, as the imaginary resolution of the lovers' marriage sidesteps the shadowy presence of Ginotti on the fringes of Eloise's story. This presence can be demystified if, like Radcliffe, we unmask Ginotti as nothing more than Nempere and accept the parodic homologies of the Conclusion. But the reduction of Ginotti to an empirically explicable character works only if we forget that Ginotti returns *after* Nempere's death and that he is also the phantasm of Zastrozzi, a figure for the haunting of this novel by its more transgressive precursor.

Overdetermined forms are by no means unique to Shelley. We find a similar use of form in Blake's revolutionary prophecies *Europe* and *America,* where the illustrations, main narrative, and preludia function as parts that cannot be synthesized because they inhabit different spaces, times, and discourses. In *America* the anagogic level of Blake's myth is crudely mapped onto the literal level of American history. Meanwhile the preludium, which recognizes the violent imposition of the myth as a rape—however ecstatic—and which ends (in two versions) with the Bard breaking his harp, stalls the seamless progress from inspiration to composition, proem to narrative. In *Europe,* the misogyny on which Blake's myth relies in the main prophecy in order to force the nightmare of history forward to its apocalyptic but ambiguous conclusion is also recognized in a preludium, which is spoken by a nameless shadowy female and cannot be neatly folded into the rest of the poem. As significantly, Enitharmon is asleep while eighteen hundred years of European history transpire. Though this is usually taken as her obliviousness to the nightmare she has caused, we can also ask how she can be blamed for events for which she seems conjured up as the absent cause. Once again, the disconnection of the mythic and historical levels may reflect the forced imposition of Blake's mythopoeic narrative on what is really a process without a subject or *telos.* The question of whether the visionary and the empirical mutually "express" each other is also raised by the cleavage between mythopoeic and Hogarthian plates. In the famous "Red limb'd angel," the plate itself is divided between two incomplete visual segments, which are spliced together and then overlaid on the text: one being a frontal view of the Orcian figure of a manacled prisoner, and the other a rear view of some kind of rough beast slouching away, perhaps the jailor or perhaps the prisoner himself.[27]

Nor is this use of Althusser to read the embeddedness of Romantic forms in history wholly anachronistic. For one thing, as Jameson points out, Hegelian phenomenology contains elements of what Althusser later calls structural causality within a model of the historical process that is still expressive and teleological.[28] Second, the notion of necessity so crucial to Godwin and Shelley is itself the locus of a conflict between organicist and mechanist notions of history, which provide the historical antecedents for Althusser's distinction between structural and expressive causality. That Demogorgon is amorphous and absent, that he resists representation and expression but is a "living spirit," and that spirits nevertheless have "inorganic" voices (*PU*, 1.135; 2.4.7) are all indications that Romantic historiography is consciously overdetermined by organicist and mechanist discourses, freedom, and determinism.

We can begin with the structurally simpler of the two novels. *Zastrozzi* opens in a rocky landscape, with the wimpish Verezzi, who has been kidnapped by Zastrozzi, chained in a cavern. Verezzi, who then manages to escape, is engaged to the beautiful Julia, who is too good to be true; but he is also loved by her dark counterpart, Matilda. Matilda has persuaded Zastrozzi to kill Julia and hand Verezzi over to her, so that she can work her wiles on him. As we further learn (but not till the very end), Zastrozzi has been willing to oblige her in order to avenge the wrong done by Verezzi's father to Zastrozzi's mother, whom he seduced and betrayed. In the course of the novel, several schemes are hatched for killing Julia, but long before even her presumed death Verezzi has begun to feel the power of Matilda's "arts" and blandishments" (87). On being told halfway through the novel that Julia has died, Verezzi falls into a fever and is "filled with irresistible disgust, as, recovering, he [finds] himself in Matilda's arms" (100). Nevertheless, he once again becomes fascinated with Matilda, whose "voice of celestial sweetness" as she draws "sounds of soul-touching melody from [her] harp" (113) enigmatically anticipates the seduction of the Poet by the veiled maid in *Alastor*. The fascination is cemented when a ruffian (Zastrozzi in disguise) pretends to attack Verezzi, and Matilda is wounded in saving him. They are married, but then, as they are in the process of fleeing Matilda's summons before the Inquisition, Verezzi suddenly sees Julia in Venice (136). He still confusedly swears loyalty to Matilda, but then Julia appears at Matilda's house, and Verezzi, stricken by remorse, plunges a dagger into his heart. Thereupon Matilda does indeed kill Julia, stabbing her "in a thousand places" (142). Finally, both Matilda and Zastrozzi are brought before the Inquisition, where Matilda recants and finds religion again, while Zastrozzi dies on the rack with a "smile of most disdainful scorn" and "a wild, convulsive laugh of exulting revenge" (156).

Although *Zastrozzi* contains only one plot and ends predictably with the defiant defeat of its hero, its effect on the reader is already overdetermined by the splitting of the villain into a male and female figure and by a disconnection between ideas, acts, and agents that allows the novel as writing and hypothesis to survive its dismantling as plot and mimesis. In contrast to *The Mysteries of Udolpho*, which can also be seen as closeted feminist Gothic, Shelley's male and female protagonists are allied, while Julia, the equivalent of Radcliffe's Emily, is relegated to the margins. A composite of Faust, the Jacobean revenge hero, and Beckford's Vathek, Zastrozzi himself embodies a defiance of existing norms that is conflictedly projected as Promethean and destructive, as he is torn (though we never see it) between "revenge" and "agonising remorse" (75). Zastrozzi's female conspirator, however, is motivated not just by revenge but also by desire. Shelley's heroine is, among other things, an intertextual development of a character with the same surname, Laurentini, who appears in *The Mysteries of Udolpho* as the silenced double and ancestor of that novel's more conventional heroine. Reduced by Radcliffe to a (hi)story told by others, she returns from the archive in *Zastrozzi* as Matilda de Laurentini, to rewrite the patriarchal encoding of women who seek control over their sexual and legal property within narratives that associate good with passivity and female will with evil. She is not exactly a rewriting of Wollstonecraft's Maria, but the otherwise eminently forgettable episode of Claudine in Shelley's novel, in which Matilda provides for the kind woman who has sheltered Verezzi, picks up and mocks the similarly tacked-on episode of Peggy in *The Wrongs of Woman*, where sentimental philanthropy is one of the phrase regimes used to compensate for and legitimize feminist transgression.

Matilda is passionately in love with Verezzi, and the fact that she has a "commanding countenance," while her rival Julia has a "mild, heavenly countenance" and "ethereal form" more or less prescribes the hopelessness of her passion (84, 88). The ease with which Verezzi transfers his affections to Matilda, however, indicates the arbitrariness of the social script within which his love for Julia, or rather her "image" (116), has been constructed. Indeed, despite the absolute contrast between the two women, Verezzi, we are told, "could not help observing a comparison between [Matilda] and Julia" (84). As if to highlight the exchangeability and polymorphous perversity of plot positions, the novel actually thematizes plots and plotting in the scene in which Matilda arranges with Zastrozzi to have Verezzi attacked so that she can then save him and win his gratitude (120–25). In staging this scene, Matilda constructs a plot that allows Verezzi to see her differently, by shifting the actantial positions assigned to characters within the stories into which society writes them. She replots her life so as to act it out beyond the constraints of a gendered semiotics. Yet Matilda's replotting of Verezzi's life and her own is not simply a deception, since on some deeper level she *is* risking her life for him, and she does ultimately die for the plot she stages (insofar as a paper character can die). On the one hand, as Žižek says, fantasy—Matilda's fantasy of killing Julia, Shelley's fantasy of adolescent transgression—"is a 'primordial lie,' a screen masking [its] fundamental *impossibility*."[29] On the other hand, this plot, in which Matilda appears as Verezzi's savior but is actually his seductress, is itself a disguise for the plot she does not know how to write or act within the narratology available to her. This is to say that winning Verezzi is merely an alibi for rewriting woman's position in the Symbolic: a rewriting with which Shelley also experiments in letting Matilda transgress the wrongs of woman through her incredibly easy access to wealth even after her marriage to Verezzi.

Put differently, the plot Matilda constructs performs what Žižek calls an "anamorphic reading" of things as they are: a distortion or perversion that makes us discern in the "positive figure" of the sentimental love object (Julia) a "mere positivization of a negative gesture." Žižek's example is Lacan's shift from "*le Nom-du-père* [to] *le Non-du-Père*" as a "theoretical anamorphosis" that produces a "traversal" of the "fantasm" of the

Father. Such reading, Žižek argues, is "the elementary procedure of the critique of ideology: the 'sublime object of ideology' is the spectral object which has no positive ontological consistency, but merely fills in the gap of a certain constitutive impossibility."[30] But the Gothic is a doubly and even triply anamorphic genre. Thus not only is the spectral object that is Julia negated by Matilda's mimicry of the sentimental plot, and not only is Matilda's fantasy of transgression thereby also negated by its perversity, Matilda's script is itself an anamorphosis of her desire, the distortion of which calls for rereading insofar as it *protects* what cannot be coherently posited within a seemingly negative gesture.

The splitting of the transgressor into a manipulative male and a female lamia, together with the resulting introduction of the gender issue, provides the space for this rereading by making transgression at once legitimate and cynical. As important, this splitting corresponds to a suspension of the text between acting and action that is characteristic of closet literature. Zastrozzi commits crimes, but until close to the end Matilda only imagines them. We are first introduced to Matilda through the "escritoire" at which she has been writing (76). For much of the novel, her outrageous violations of morality remain unreal because Julia's death, the event that allows her to replot Verezzi's life, has not really happened. At the end of chapter 6, when Zastrozzi tells Matilda that Julia is dead and Verezzi then falls into a fever, Julia is in fact not yet dead (93). In chapter 13 she is again described as having met a gory death, which has still not happened (132). For much of the novel, then, we are dealing with fantasy; and fantasy, as Žižek argues, is a form of transcendental schematism that teaches us how to desire rather than literally imagining the attainment of its object.[31] Indeed, Matilda is summoned before the Inquisition before she has actually done anything (133). When the fictional narrative is finally made real with the deaths of Julia and Verezzi, responsibility is again deferred away from Matilda by the introduction of Zastrozzi as the author of a plot into which her plotting has been fitted.[32] Enacting through Zastrozzi what he only imagines through Matilda, yet finally punishing him while he allows her to recant, Shelley is at once able to write and to withdraw a transgressive narrative, to recant and to withdraw his recantation. In other words, by rehabilitating Matilda while destroying Zastrozzi, he agrees not to perform his transgressive drama in the world and reclaims the right to write it in private. For Zastrozzi, after all, is punished for his "crimes" and not his ideas. His ideas, beyond a passing reference to atheism, have not been disclosed, let alone put on trial. Zastrozzi's heroic endurance supersedes Matilda's mandatory recantation and allows the "Idea" he represents, as the form rather than the content of that "Idea," to survive its inadequate embodiment in a juvenile antihero. Nor can Zastrozzi really be said to die. For he is not a living being with interiority, but a kind of humanoid or automaton, and as such he can only be disassembled, not destroyed.

Both the affinity between the novel and speculation, and the character of writing (in the Derridean sense of *écriture*) as a withholding of presence that is also possessed of performativity, can be linked to a certain semantic excess typical of closet literature. Or, put differently, this excess is what suspends the genre within the realm of writing, if by writing we imply something that is not ready to happen, something that is still being worked through: what Kristeva calls the semiotic, or the space between "word and drive,"[33] which she still associates with narrative in her early work (specifically *Le texte du roman,* on which "The Adolescent Novel" draws). Interestingly, in her later *Revolution in Poetic Language,* Kristeva subsumes narrative into the Novel as a form that has patriarchy embedded in its very structure, while she transfers the semiotic to poetry, thus implicitly recognizing poetry as the "idea" of the prose fiction that she had earlier analysed. In short, narrative as Kristeva earlier analyzes it discloses what Faflak calls the "radically chaotic moment" underlying the plots we construct and by which we are constructed. It does so, in Shelley's texts, by functioning as a form of "primary process." For "adolescent writing"—as a process inhabited by perversity, sexual ambiguity, and polynomia—discloses the "madness" underlying the articulation of a culture's discourses as fantasy.[34]

The word "madness" is Ross Woodman's, in his study of the relation between sanity, madness, and transformation in Romantic poetry: a project that can be extended to the analysis of Romantic culture and a modernity that needs to think culture Romantically rather than in the Habermasian and Foucaultian forms of much Cultural Studies. For Woodman this poetry consists in what we can call, following Friedrich Schelling, a "rotary motion," or an interminable dialectic among the three terms "sanity," "madness," and "transformation." In other words, poetry (or *poiesis*) is the site of a constant unbinding of the sanitizations—the social and critical institutions—created by a culture that struggles to transform a madness that is once again disclosed by the psychosis of these institutions. This psychosis is particularly clear in Shelley's novels, because they remove the barrier between the Symbolic and Real, which is part of the propriety of "mature" writing. Whereas the Real in more polished novels is "barred" in Lacan's sense, and while this barring constitutes the sanity of the Novel, in Shelley's novels we witness an irruption of the Real into the Symbolic in the texts' uninhibited murders and perversions. In Slavoj Žižek's terms these perversions manifest a Real that, far from being barred as an "external kernel which idealization/symbolization is unable to 'swallow,'" make explicit "the 'irrationality,' the unaccountable 'madness' of the very founding gesture" of culture, the confrontation with which creates a kind of clearing for this culture to be reimagined.[35]

If perversion and psychosis are the obvious instances of the texts' madness, at a structural level the disconnection between components and levels is a striking feature not only of these novels but also of closet texts in general. Ideas are voiced by characters without being grounded in a personality. These ideas then function in abstraction from their context and from the person who is their mouthpiece. For instance, at the end Zastrozzi, a thug rather than an intellectual, suddenly allies himself with an atheist materialism: while the philosophical position seems almost hypocritical as a justification of his actions, the idea of atheism leaves its impression on the text. Similarly, actions happen apart from their agents: someone is murdered, but the murderer seems more the vehicle than the agent of a crime that, in turn, is without emotional affect or effect. Because there is no determinate agency in closet literature, characters act without consequences; the characters produce powerful effects, but they are without psychological credibility, because they are signs for ideas melodramatically staged in the laboratory of a mental theater. Here closet literature shares something with fantasy. Just as closet literature is suspended between action and acting, so too fantasy is both productive and self-critical. Fantasy at once incites transgressive social desires, yet it also exposes the paranoid-schizoid structure of symbolic and imaginary constructions: the carnivorousness of the projective identifications that underlie both culture and the reimagining of culture.

The semiautonomy of actions and ideas in closet literature has two effects. It gives them a theoretical quality, thus withholding active commitment from them but also suspending their consequences so that the reader can entertain them as possibilities without being responsible for them. It also inscribes ideas, actions, and characters as signifiers, signs for a drive or desire rather than enactments of a specific ideology. Indeed, more than Zastrozzi, Wolfstein in the second novel is pure drive, a darkly cynical exposure of what lies at the basis of the libertine ideology more clearly developed in Nempere, but one could also say, an exposure of ideology itself as sheer drive. More exuberantly, yet also critically, Zastrozzi inscribes Shelley's desire for a contestation of social norms, but as a form for which he has still to find an appropriate content. Zastrozzi's transgression, even his desire to avenge his mother, is a vehicle with an incoherent tenor, a form for a content rather than the content itself, which is still to come. Kant sees this amorphousness as fundamental to the "idea," which he divides into aesthetic and rational ideas in the third *Critique*. An aesthetic idea is a " representation of the imagination which occasions much thinking though without it being possible for any determinate thought, i.e., *concept,* to be adequate to it." The "shapes" and dreams that Shelley deploys throughout *Prometheus Unbound* are aesthetic ideas. Conversely, "rational" ideas are concepts that have not been fleshed out,[36] like Zastrozzi's (or Shelley's own) atheism, which, as a signifier of revolution, has assumed a bad and untrue determinacy.

This disconnection between the shape and content of ideas, in turn, reflects the overdetermination of the social and psychic texts in which the narrative has its genesis. Closet writing thus resists closure, or it reaches an ending that is always premature. Shelley deals in two ways with the resulting sense of a text not yet ready for enactment, publication—the sphere of publicity, as Kant calls it. Whereas the staginess of the novels prevents what happens in them from really happening, *Prometheus Unbound* constructs a narrativization of history that it recognizes as a performance, and as we shall see, it provides us with the metanarrative tools to call this performance into question. Those tools, however, are ones that Shelley first stumbles across in his second novel. For unlike *Zastrozzi,* *St. Irvyne* is profoundly resistant to what Brooks calls reading for plot: a reading of the text in terms of its characters and events. Instead, it is Shelley's first metadiscursive text, in that it is about the functioning of the signifier. In that sense it is also a commentary on the form of *Zastrozzi,* on the problems in signification and emplotment that complicate the writing and reading of the texts we shape out of the political unconscious.

The second novel is more conspicuously disunified than the first one, although *Zastrozzi* had also omitted a chapter as a structural marker of its disconnection, anticipating Shelley's omission of the two chapters from *St. Irvyne.* In the Kleinian terms used by Kristeva and Hanna Segal, *Zastrozzi* is a product of the paranoid-schizoid phase whose underlying presence in culture the novel exposes. *St. Irvyne,* however, is a product of the depressive phase, which ensues when "separation from the object, ambivalence, guilt and loss" take over,[37] as a result of which projections are withdrawn and cathexes undone. Its less bombastic, more reflexive quality is accompanied by a shift of attention from theme to structure, from the signified to the signifier. For the theme of sexual transgression now seems almost beside the point, predictable and boring: gone is the perverse *jouissance* we accessed in *Zastrozzi* when the plot disposed of "good" characters such as Julia. Nor do we identify with the characters, who could as well have any other names than the ones they have. Now the focus is on the structural doubling of one plot as its other, reflected in the gloomy and depressing presence of Ginotti as Wolfstein's shadow and analyst. That Shelley, in returning to the genre of political Gothic, is detained at the level of structure and that structure takes precedence over character are problems with which he will grapple in *Prometheus Unbound.* For the later text can be read on both a narrative and a metadiscursive level, as staging an action in the form of a world-historical romance while giving us a framework in which to critique its emplotment of history. In *St. Irvyne,* by contrast, the narrative level is unreadable. Whatever Shelley is "saying" through his characters and the things that happen to them, it seems he must first negotiate the gaps in the unfolding of a plot whose real (as distinct from textual) closure is withheld by these very gaps. In considering the novel at a metanarrative level, I therefore focus on two things: the way Ginotti functions as a figure for deferred reference, and the double plot as a formal marker of a surplus—or lack—that was still unthematized in the earlier novel. I also suggest that in this early novel Shelley discovered certain semiotic shapes and structures that were formative for him and to which he consciously returned in *Prometheus Unbound.*

The first of these shapes is that of a narrative that works itself out in bits and pieces, so that the closure reached on one level is an imaginary resolution achieved by forgetting something else. Curiously enough, the two plots in *St. Irvyne* are not really as disconnected as Shelley makes them seem. In both, a recently orphaned and innocent virgin is abducted and then rescued. Megalena's character changes unaccountably, and she and Wolfstein seduce each other into evil; in Eloise's story, the roles of rescuer and seducer remain separate, as do the boundaries between good and evil, innocence and experience. Moreover, the two plots simplify and separate elements that were condensed into a single plot in *Zastrozzi*. Megalena's degeneration dehumanizes the more ambiguous character of Matilda, whereas the Eloise subplot idealizes subversion by constructing its erotic utopia upon the peaceful challenging of marital and other social conventions.

The gaps opened up by the double plot have to do with the relation between romantic love and Gothic power and between public and private spaces. Like the union of Prometheus and Asia, that of Eloise and Fitzeustace remains lyrically disconnected from the violence that proliferates in the rest of the novel, and that may even be the enabling condition of this love, which is predicated on libertine principles enunciated by Nempere.[38] This nonsynchronicity is figured in the later text by the two chariots that Asia sees after her dialogue with Demogorgon, one light and one dark, imaging a movement with different centers, which, like Yeats' gyres, may coincide only for a moment. As if to compromise this coincidence, *St. Irvyne* does not bring it into being by allowing the comic movement to succeed the anarchic overthrow of tyranny, in which "Heaven's . . . throne" is left "kingless" by the double deaths of Nempere and Mountjoy (*PU*, 2.4.149). Instead, the darker main plot reoccupies the foreground at the end, closeting the lovers in the narrative's past rather than its present or future. Thus the plot quite literally ends with a revolution, in the double sense of an overthrow and a cyclic return of the past that Shelley in *Prometheus Unbound* concedes only theoretically, when he allows that the Jovian age may return if "Eternity" at some point loses her grip on the "disentangled Doom" repressed into the abyss (4.565–79).

In freeing Eloise through a narrative convulsion that overthrows Nempere by bringing him back as Ginotti, Shelley inscribes the Gothic plot as the unconscious of a romance that is more nostalgic than subversive. For the gap between the plots is also a gap within Eloise's story, which is reopened by the closing paragraph. The cryptic equivalence, "Ginotti is Nempere. Eloise is the sister of Wolfstein" (252), gets rid of Ginotti by allowing him to recede into a story that is already over, but then raises doubts about Eloise by bringing her into a plot that is not yet over. The ending folds each plot into the other, reminding us of the kinship of Eloise with Wolfstein, who throughout the novel has been shadowed by a phantasm that De Quincey, in *Suspiria de Profundis*, calls the Dark Interpreter. Eloise never meets her darker double, since they are antithetically confined in separate spheres of the action. But by having her transit more rapidly the plot of kidnapping and seduction that proves Megalena's undoing, Shelley reminds us that Eloise's innocence is constituted on the text's forgetting the jeopardy in which it has so recently placed what it figures through her. That Eloise is connected to the dubious Wolfstein also reminds us of another curious detail. At the end of chapter 12 Eloise and Fitzeustace are about to go to England, leaving the dark continent of Europe, which is confusingly German, Italian, and French all at once.[39] Yet the story of Eloise has also been introduced to us as a retrospective narrative covering the five years before the moment when she returns to St. Irvyne, to find the place but not herself unchanged (209). The happy ending of chapter 12 is not the woeful story of seduction and abandonment we are told to expect in chapter 7, which leaves us unclear as to what Eloise's story actually is.

As the uncanny link between the two plots in which he has different names and functions, Ginotti/Nempere is the main locus of the nonidentity underlying the syntax of identification by which closure is imposed in the last paragraph. Moreover, because of his shadowy presence, he allows us to think of this nonidentity as a textual unconscious rather than just a gap or aporia: not an unconscious in any psychoanalytic sense, since the characters are without interiority, but more a *sign* for the unconscious. Ginotti is on one level a version of Zastrozzi. Both characters are "towering" and "preter-human" figures (*Zastrozzi*, 120; *St. Irvyne*, 183) and are possessed of unexplained power. Moreover, Ginotti plays the same role in relation to Wolfstein as Zastrozzi does in relation to Matilda, whom he manipulates while forwarding her destructive passion. Finally, both ground their conduct in the materialism of the philosophes, which is much more extensively developed in *St. Irvyne* as the absolute knowledge offered by "science," with the result that the second novel seems to reveal the metaphysical basis of the first, where there was nothing obviously supernatural about the title character or his ambitions. At the same time, unlike his precursor, Ginotti remains shadowy and absent. Despite his greater metaphysical seriousness, which makes him, as it were, the "principle" behind Zastrozzi, he seems a key to the plot's meaning that we are never given, a sign rather than a character. Whereas Zastrozzi's crimes are Gidean *actes gratuits,* which challenge moral absolutes, Ginotti, except for the account of his early years, which falls outside the *diegesis,* seems to have no motives. He does not really do anything, being no more than the condition of possibility for crimes that are actually committed by Wolfstein and Megalena. Instead he figures the absent cause that is "ideology," which is itself a patchwork of discrepant discourses that are "quilted" together, as Žižek argues.[40] As a disclosure of the serious yet incoherent philosophical basis of the Zastrozzi character, Ginotti then also becomes Nempere. Nempere–a curiously Lacanian name *avant la lettre*—is the name of the father from whose incestuous tyranny the young lovers must free themselves, a name for repression rather than transgression. But Ginotti cannot entirely be reduced to Nempere because Nempere himself seems to be more than, or other than, what he seems. As a sign that Nempere is more than his empirical character, and as the "mysterious disposer of the events of [Wolfstein's] existence" (223), Ginotti is the possibility that the crimes of the text's characters are not ordinary crimes but metaphysical acts, like those of Byron's Cain. But since Ginotti never discloses himself as Lucifer, this notion of crime as a signifier in a higher script also remains ungrounded, opening up the further possibility that history is simply a process without a subject, an action that only intermittently signifies.

The point is not to identify Ginotti but to recognize that as a gap in the plot's construction he functions as the text's unconscious, making all attempts at interpretation uneasily different from themselves. Moving one step beyond *Zastrozzi, St. Irvyne* discloses the hidden or metaphysical dimension behind surface events as a further text. In *Zastrozzi* the plot constructed by Matilda was written into a further plot designed by Zastrozzi, with the enfolding of plot within plot suggesting a mystery that is finally unfolded, although unsatisfyingly.[41] But Ginotti, who seems to know the script behind Wolfstein's life (195), is himself part of a plot he cannot read. Nor is the Faustian resolution of this plot anything but a stopgap, since Ginotti's promise to "appear in [his] real character" to Wolfstein is not fulfilled, and "time" does not "develope [sic]" his "unaccountable actions . . . in a far more complete manner" (195). As the locus of a deferral, Ginotti's abrupt death figures an absence already implicit in the death of his precursor, whose disclosure of his true motives and identity at the end is also unsatisfyingly incoherent. For the conclusion that feminist subversion in Matilda is the dupe of a masculine will to power in Zastrozzi unravels into the oddly contradictory information that Zastrozzi has made use of another woman to avenge the wrongs done to his mother by the patriarchy. The man who makes a woman his tool now turns out to be the tool of another woman, who is present only as a specter from beyond the grave, as part of the sedimented structure of the narratives underlying culture. To all this is added a description of Zastrozzi's defiant dignity in the face of death and a speech on "the non-existence of a Deity" (153), which seems thought up on the spur of the moment and yet is sufficiently important to return as a conceptual topos in *St. Irvyne*. Moreover, as if to prove Žižek's contention that ideology is "quilted" or patched together out of discrepant components, Zastrozzi, despite his atheism, draws on the very system of belief he repudiates to insist that, after the destruction of the "body," Verezzi's "soul" will be "hell-doomed to all eternity" (155).

While Zastrozzi may be too much of a stereotype for us to take him more seriously than the system he mocks, Ginotti is more "mysterious," a gaze that sees without being visible itself (193). Ginotti's sublimity, even if it is a contrivance, asks us to read him as one of the "gigantic shadows which futurity casts upon the present" and to read the text in which he participates as a distorted mimesis whose figures "express what they understand not" (*DP*, 535). Ginotti, in short, functions as a metanarrative figure for the political unconscious that Shelley later figures through Demogorgon. If the split structure of the novel reflects a sense that history and the histories we write are made of parts that do not cohere, the unconscious is the absent "cause" (193) that constantly promises and withholds coherence and that discloses the fundamental incoherence of ideology as something that is still in process. That is, the unconscious, as a depth that is not a depth, is the ambiguous possibility that overdetermination has some unreadable significance. That Ginotti dies and proves not to be supernatural certainly deconstructs this promise of a hidden meaning, but the fact that he dies twice as two characters reconstructs that possibility by allowing him to survive as an uncanny remainder. Although Ginotti remains curiously absent from the novel (this absence being what makes us read), it is important to recognize in him not simply absence but also possibility: the sense of something left over at the end of the novel, a certain narrativity that is the possibility of the characters being other than what they seem to be.

That Ginotti figures something unfinished, functioning as a remainder or a reminder, comes also from the fact that *St. Irvyne* evokes Godwin's *St. Leon,* which introduces into it an unfulfilled horizon of expectations. *St. Leon,* to which I return in the fifth chapter, treats with quixotic irony the hopes of eternal life that drive Ginotti and, some years later, Frankenstein. Having received the elixir of life from a mysterious stranger, St. Leon lives twice over, assuming quite different characters, first as a gambler interested only in the augmentation of his wealth and status and then as a behind-the-scenes reformer, the failed savior of Hungary. It is as if Godwin, like Shelley in *Alastor,* casts his giant form into the expanse twice over, hypothesizing two different stories for him, in this case clearly distinguished. *St. Irvyne,* by contrast, is a cynical deconstruction of the *sprezzatura* of *St. Leon,* in which Wolfstein becomes steadily more dissolute, as a means of dissolving and dissipating what Shelley is not yet ready to recreate. Since Wolfstein receives only the formula for, and not the benefits of, the elixir (238), he never becomes St. Leon and never even approaches the threshold of a gap between what he is and could be. Yet the concentration of allusions to Godwin towards the end of the novel runs against the grain of this depression of Enlightenment optimism. These allusions include Ginotti's excursus on his search for eternal life, Wolfstein's gambling, the sudden introduction of alchemy—which had not been previously mentioned—and the return to St. Irvyne as a missed encounter with the title of Godwin's novel. To be sure, the references to Godwin are inorganically "quilted" together. Yet together with a certain culturally prophetic Nietzschean quality in Ginotti's nihilism, these allusions revive the fantasy of revolutionary desire in the very moment of its dismantling.

From this perspective Ginotti's death does not end the narrative.

Rather, it returns the text's materials to the cultural unconscious, to a world inhabited by the "shadows of all forms that think and live," the phantasms and traces of other texts (*PU*, 1.198). It is this unconscious that Mary Shelley's Euthanasia also reenters when she is "lost" at sea rather than definitively drowned at the end of *Valperga*.[42] Ginotti is Percy Shelley's first experiment with the phantasm: a figure to which he returns in *Prometheus Unbound* but which is more fully developed in Byron's *Cain*. As Abraham and Torok have said, all "psychic activity which is not in direct contact with external objects can be described as fantasmatic."[43] Ginotti marks the phantasmatic, delusive character of all cultural production, which is haunted by what it disavows and yet survives as a disfigured potentiality. At the end of the *Defence* Shelley associates this profoundly deconstructive potentiality with poetry, which he sees not as an essence but as a negativity discernible only through the "gigantic shadows that futurity casts upon the present" (*DP*, 535), what Kierkegaard will later call irony as "infinite absolute negativity."[44]

In *Prometheus Unbound*, Shelley makes the phantasm one of the governing figures of a text whose "imagery" he describes as "drawn from the operations of the human mind, or from those external actions by which they are expressed" ("Preface," 133). When Prometheus tries vainly to recall his curse Earth tells him to visit the underworld and to "call at will" his "own ghost, or the ghost of Jupiter" (1.210–15), either of which will speak the desired words.

> For know there are two worlds of life and death:
> One that which thou beholdest, but the other
> Is underneath the grave, where do inhabit
> The shadows of all forms that think and live
> . . . .
> Dreams and the light imaginings of men
> And all that faith creates, or love desires,
> . . . .
> There thou art, and dost hang, a writhing shade
> 'Mid whirlwind-peopled mountains; all the Gods
> Are there, and all the Powers of nameless worlds,
> Vast, sceptred Phantoms; heroes, men, and beasts;
> And Demogorgon, a tremendous gloom. (1.195–207)

These lines are interesting in more than one way. To begin with, they distinguish two "worlds," or relations between life and death. The first is the empirical world, in which life and death are separate and where characters and the plots in which they act have a certain substantiality. But the second is a world of remainders, of the specter and the revenant, in which death as the finitude of human project(ion)s is throughout life as its unthought. Although Earth says that once the empirical being is returned to its image, death unites them and "they part no more" (1.199), this is clearly not true, since Prometheus can recall the phantasm of Jove and write him into a new plot. It would seem, then, that in reverting to its specter, the empirical being is depotentialized yet also returned to its potentiality. In the second act of *Cain,* Byron expands Shelley's figure, as Cain is led through the abyss of space, the repository of all previously discarded worlds. Shelley himself returns to this underworld in *The Triumph of Life,* where the "shadows of all forms that think and live" appear as the names of history who follow in the wake of the Car of Life. From this precession of simulacra the phantasm of Shelley as dreamer—like the Dreamer in Keats' *Fall* revisiting the Titans—calls up the phantasm of Rousseau so as to unbind him from the simple narrative of failure into which he has been written. For Byron, as for Shelley, the "phantoms" of these past worlds are "beings past" but also "shadows still to come" (*Cain,* 2.1.175). At this level characters, disconnected from their actantial positions and substantial identities, also become curiously interchangeable. For Prometheus, we are told, can attribute his curse either to Jupiter or to himself. As in Blake's *Marriage of Heaven and Hell,* where the same "history has been adopted by both parties" with opposite results (E, 34; 5), different characters can play the same role in a plot, or (like Ginotti) the same character can play different roles in different plots, thus allowing narrative to be a form of speculation rather than mimesis.

We can think of the realm of images that lies underneath the text as an "archive," to return to Foucault's figure in "Fantasia of the Library." Blake's "system" can similarly be thought of as an archive, rather than a developed conceptual structure with the architectonic completeness that Northrop Frye and Foster Damon attribute to it. The system, in structuralist terms, is a *langue* that precedes the *parole* of its differing narrativizations. These narrativizations occur through a process of selection and binding, along the two axes that narratology names the paradigmatic and the syntagmatic. Characters and plot positions are selected from a paradigmatic axis, which offers us a vocabulary with a choice of options, and they are then linked within the linear syntax of plot. As the most elaborate form in Romanticism of the archive that precedes this binding, Blake's system is a storehouse of characters, events, and concepts whose syntagmatic and paradigmatic relations are profoundly unsettled, such that any depth is an effect of experimental surface rearrangements, as Donald Ault argues in approaching *The Four Zoas* as "narrative unbound."[45] This archive, as the dismantled site of the elements bound together in particular stories, is the ground of the figures we construct through plot: the "disnarrated," whether traumatic or enabling, that Romantic narrative tries to access.[46]

As we have suggested, *St. Irvyne*, as a kind of spectral narrative, decomposes embodied narrative into the phrases, motifs, and "phrase regimes" out of which it is assembled. In its parodic yet almost deliberate crudeness, it is also what we might call an embedded narratology. As such, it exposes the rules of structuration and combination that govern the production of embodied narratives animated by an expressive causality: rules that reflect the current social or intellectual system—or any episteme with which one seeks to replace it. Blake's system is unusual in explicitly including, alongside the floating signifiers to be selected and linked (i.e., characters, events, and images), a number of these rules of formation—hence his characterization of it as a "system." Such rules of combination and hierarchization include the distinction between specter and emanation or the notion that contraries are to be absorbed into a "progression." In referring to an embedded narratology in *St. Irvyne*, I suggest that Shelley's archive, by implication, also contains these rules, but in a dis-organized form that more clearly marks their status as ideologemes.

Returning to this archive in *Prometheus Unbound*, Shelley replays *St. Irvyne* so as to emancipate Promethean romance from Jovian power according to a typically high Romantic plot. In so doing he attempts what Asia also does when, despite Demogorgon's refusal to provide any metaphysical grounding for her imaginings, she insists on making her heart its own oracle. Shelley, that is, creates a shape all light from something that has "neither form—nor outline," using language to impose an imaginary resolution on the "thoughts and forms," the floating signifiers "which else senseless and shapeless were" (2.4.7; 4.417). Shelley's narrativization in *Prometheus Unbound* of the archival materials he has at his disposal is as much an imaginary resolution as the Faustian endings of *Zastrozzi* and *St. Irvyne* are symbolic resolutions of those texts' underlying contradictions. But while *Prometheus* is a performance of things as they should be, it is also a metanarrative structure that defamiliarizes the processes by which it constructs its story—hence its form as a closet drama, which includes the process of its production. For the play is full of phantasmatic shapes—spirits, fauns, furies—that exist as what Blake calls "unnam'd forms" before being posited within a plot. Asia's dialogue with Panthea on dreams recognizes the purely speculative nature of this positing. Here Panthea cannot recall her dream about the renovation of Prometheus until she sees it mirrored in Asia's eyes. This mirroring or mirror-stage, moreover, constellates a projection in which what one sees in the other's eyes is no more than oneself, one's "own fairest shadow" (2.1.113). As for the Narrator of *Alastor,* however, "oneself" is by no means simple, presenting a labyrinth of possibilities, "Orb within orb, and line through line inwoven—" (2.1.117).

Crucial to the play's metanarrative dimension are two elements: a structural disconnection that consciously signifies the text's overdetermination, and a textual apparatus that shows how the action does not happen but rather is posited as happening through an act of interpretation. The play is conspicuously constructed from parts between which there are significant gaps. Critics have often pointed to the disjunction between the first three acts and the fourth, sometimes considered an afterthought. But in fact, the first three acts are equally unconnected, each being dominated by different characters. Act 1 supposedly accomplishes an inner revolution in which Prometheus is victorious over the Jovian elements within himself. Act 3 replays this revolution in the theater of history, where Demogorgon is the protagonist, while Prometheus retreats to a cave and utters only a few lines in the course of the entire act. Not only is the inner revolution externalized at a historical level solely through the awkward intervention of Demogorgon, who is so much a deus ex machina that he actually descends in a chariot, a vehicle for a tenor that remains imageless. This supposed inner transformation, prosthetically brought about by Prometheus' summoning of someone else's phantasm to recall his own curse, is also contradicted by the violence that Demogorgon—like the French revolutionaries—uses to overthrow Jove. Act 1 is likewise at cross-purposes with act 2, which opposes the cooperative feminist society of the sisters to a more agonistic and confrontational male psychology in act 1, where Prometheus, who proclaims himself "king over myself," still has recourse to hierarchical metaphors that are uncomfortably at odds with Shelley's antimonarchism (1.417). For most of the first three acts the sisters, as the vehicle for a dream of which Prometheus is the tenor, remain auxiliaries in a revolution that continues to be imagined in terms of heroic struggle. But Prometheus' disappearance after the first act and his demotion from agent to symbol in the third act allow the fourth act to substitute for a hero-centered drama a lyrical fluidity that, from another perspective, is still "pinnacled dim in the intense inane" (3.4.204). In short, the "quilting" together of different discourses of liberation exposes the extent to which freedom has yet to be worked through and is still only what Kant calls a rational idea. As in Althusser's model of history, which posits the semiautonomy of various sectors, ideology and its enactment, base and superstructure, inside and outside, move in different ways and speeds in different sectors of the text.

This semiautonomy of parts is recognized by the curious organization of the manuscript in the Bodleian Library: possibly one on which Shelley worked both before and after the text's publication.[47] This manuscript is "unbound" in a quite different and more uncanny way from the published text, arranged as it is in two columns and two voices, almost like Derrida's *Glas*. It begins with the fourth act on the right-hand side of the page, and after some four hundred lines, proceeds to alternate the first act on the left-hand side of the page with the remainder of the fourth on the right. It continues up to the middle of 2.2, then alternates part of 2.3 on the left side with the remainder of 2.3 on the right, finally placing the last part of 2.3 (the Song of the Spirits) on the left, alongside the crucial dialogue between Asia and Demogorgon (2.4).[48] Textual scholars have rationalized the state of the manuscript by focusing on the space Shelley had available in his notebook; they suggest that it is an intermediate draft in which he transcribed the first three acts, and then inserted the fourth as an afterthought, "wherever there happened to be a vacancy."[49] But this account does not explain why Shelley left several pages at the beginning of the notebook blank, if he was not already toying with the idea of putting something there. Nor does it explain why the unbinding of the play's linear narrative is continued through the disarrangement of the second act, even if Shelley then returns to transcribing the third act in a more straightforward way.

This bricolage, moreover, is not just random. Scenes are split and re-distributed between the two sides of the notebook at logical points, to create antiphonal effects. Thus, lyrical segments are in general separated from dramatic ones, although not always according to a division between left and right, which Shelley also puts under erasure. The period of Prometheus' enchainment appears alongside the cancellation of the Hours at the end of history, constructing and deconstructing the enfolding of the temporal within the eternal proclaimed by act 4. This enfolding or synchronicity of the finite and infinite is one of the tropes of a Romantic Ideology of Absolute Idealism, which Friedrich Schelling invokes when he writes that "the whole absolute is knowable" from the perspective of the infinite, "although appearing Nature produces only successively and in (for us) endless development, what in true Nature exists all at once and in an eternal fashion."[50] But in contrast to the early Schelling's idealism or to Blake's fourfold vision, Shelley makes the relation between the finite and infinite something uncanny. Thus Demogorgon's enthusiastic address to the Earth and the "happy dead" is set beside Earth's account of the realm of shadows, the implication of which may be that Demogorgon, as embodied agent, is himself no more than a phantasm. Similarly, the Song of the Spirits, with its movement beyond the veil of life and death, is set against the equivocal conversation between Asia and Demogorgon and displaced into the vacant pages used for corrections and afterthoughts. Altogether, the effect is that of a text that is quoting rather than performing itself, juxtaposing the imaginary world projected by desire against the complexities of the Symbolic order, and vice versa.

By re-citing the text in fragments, the manuscript reduces the play to the phrases from which it is assembled, thus putting its emplotment under erasure. For Paul Ricoeur plot or *mythos* is best understood as a process of emplotment or "configuration" (one could say mythmaking) that creates a "proposed world, a world that I might inhabit and wherein I might project my own most possibilities." This configurative activity, which causes the Narrator of *Alastor* so much difficulty, depends on "constru[ing] significant wholes out of scattered events." But it is precisely this "follow-ability" of the story that Shelley puts in question by making the plot of the play the very process of the plot's construal and production.[51] As important is the way in which the scenes that move the action forward double as part of a psychoanalytic apparatus that confronts expression with its own unconscious. I refer here to Asia's and Panthea's recollection of their dreams, the Magus Zoroaster's encounter with his own image, and Prometheus' recalling and repetition of his curse through the summoning of a phantasm. This last episode is on the one hand necessary to advance the play's action from the Jovian into the Promethean age. But on the other hand, its staging as a form of mental theater or ghost sonata also unworks the narrative work it performs. For the scene casts into relief the way Prometheus conquers his phantoms only through a projective repression of himself as Jove, and it further stages in miniature the phantasmatic quality of the entire action.[52]

The most striking component of the play's (psycho)analytic apparatus is of course the dialogue in the Cave between Asia and Demogorgon in act 2. Unlike the character who later overthrows Jove and presides over the Promethean age in act 4, Demogorgon at this point preexists any positing of his narrative identity and has neither "form—nor outline" (2.4.7). As I suggest elsewhere, he thus plays the role of, or rather has the effect of, a Lacanian analyst, repeatedly countering Asia's "light imaginings" (1.200) with answers that offer her only grammatical positions, which is to say, structural rather than expressive positions.[53] Asia, having asked who made the plenitude of creation and having received the answer "merciful God," wants to hear that Jove is responsible for the miseries of history. She wants a story that expresses her desire. But Demogorgon will only say that "He reigns," and will not "Utter [the] name" that the pronoun stands in place of (2.4.9–31). Frustrated by his refusal to divulge a "deep truth," Asia embarks on her own attempt to narrate the course of history as a phenomenology of the Promethean spirit. But, as in *Alastor,* the very extensiveness of narrative proves self-complicating, in ways elided by the lyric brevity of the play's songs and dreams.

Asia at first postulates a Saturnian age, followed by the Jovian age inaugurated when Prometheus "Gave wisdom, which is strength, to Jupiter" (2.4.44). The logical conclusion to this dialectic would be the Promethean age prophesied by the sisters' dreams, which would account for the Jovian age as a fortunate fall. Asia's narration, however, is rambling and is less a history than a chronicle, a series of episodes linked by "ands." Her story lacks what Ricoeur calls "followability" and only gropes towards a causal or teleological understanding of history. Having attributed Jove's power to Prometheus' necessary mistake when he "Gave wisdom, which is strength, to Jupiter," she repeats this segment of the plot in describing how Prometheus "Gave man speech, and speech created thought," thus resulting in a Promethean age, in which science and art conquer disease and death (2.4.72–99). It seems as if she is backtracking, repeating and telling the story differently, so that in one version knowledge leads to the ravages of power and in another to a new Promethean dispensation. Given that the Jovian and Promethean ages are thus interchangeable events on the paradigmatic axis rather than successive events on the syntagmatic axis of plot, there can be no guarantee that they are really distinct: that the Promethean age of art and science will lead to perfectibility and not bear traces of Jovian distortion. Also unclear is whether Prometheus himself—as in Mary Shelley's *Frankenstein,* subtitled *The Modern Prometheus*—brought about the present state of affairs by giving wisdom to Jove (2.4.43–49) or whether Prometheus was punished by an already powerful Jove for the "alleviations of his state" that he "gave to man" (2.4.97–100). This in turn leads to the question of whether the Promethean dispensation does not always exist within the Jovian, as a narcotic that "hide[s] with thin and rainbow wings/The shape of Death" (2.4.62–63). The fantasy of redemption, then, the fantasy that is the play, would do no more than "*bind*" temporarily "The disunited tendrils of that vine/That bears the wine of life" (2.4.63–65; emphasis mine).

Unbinding the strands of her story during her rumination in the Cave, Asia cannot bring it to a conclusion and returns to questioning Demogorgon. The play then performatively produces its conclusion, through a deliberate act of positing in which it binds its unnamed forms into a particular history. At the end of the scene the sisters are confronted by a procession of "Cars" in each of which a "wild-eyed charioteer" stands (2.4.130–32) and which, in narrative terms, present a number of possibilities on the paradigmatic axis. As with the summoning of the phantasm in act 1, through which Prometheus withdraws and reprojects his past self as Jove, the selection and identification of one of these options is left to Asia, as Demogorgon says: "These are the immortal Hours/Of which thou didst demand.—One waits for thee" (2.4.140–41). The choice Asia makes will decide the next step in a plot that she does not want to develop in the more traumatic way that Shelley does in returning to the figure of the Car in *The Triumph of Life*. Alarmingly, Asia selects a "dark chariot" containing a "Spirit with a dreadful countenance" (2.4.142–43). This Spirit does not obligingly echo back her "own words," thus failing to confirm her heart as its own "oracle" (1.190; 2.4.123). Instead, it tells Asia that it is the herald of a "Darkness" that will "wrap in lasting night Heaven's kingless throne" (2.4.148–49). The phrase ominously shrouds emancipation from monarchic rule in the more threatening vision of an utter vacancy at the heart of power as a process without a subject or *telos*.

Panthea then notices a second chariot guided by a "young Spirit" with "the dovelike eyes of hope " (2.4.159–60). Carlos Baker speaks for a long critical tradition when he identifies the two chariots selected from among the various "hours" as intended for the sisters and Demogorgon, respectively. The light chariot is supposed to convey Asia to her union with Prometheus, while Demogorgon is to descend in the dark chariot to overthrow Jupiter.[54] Baker's reading hierarchizes what may be independent, nonsynchronous movements in the historical process. It shifts the narrative from a structural to an expressive plane, in a process Shelley himself stages as metaphor: as the identification of the shapes in the various cars, the attribution of a tenor to a vehicle.[55] But as Demogorgon says, "The deep truth is imageless" (2.4.116), and the vehicle may well have no subject or *telos*. In fact, Asia initially attributes a different tenor to her vehicle when she assumes that the dark chariot is intended for her and asks "whither woulds't thou bear me?" (2.4.145). Although the Spirit in the ivory chariot beckons Asia to ascend with him (2.4.167), its "ghastly" brother has not actually denied her earlier assumption that she is to be swallowed up in his darkness. The first Spirit has only confirmed that he is the "shadow of a destiny / *More dread* than is my aspect" (2.4.146–47; emphasis mine). And as these lines ominously remind us, "the gigantic shadows which futurity casts upon the present" (*DP,* 508) may be unreadably, rather than predictively, prophetic.

After this scene, the play unfolds according to the scenario outlined by Baker. Its complex staging as mental theater, however, acknowledges that the plot is decided not by a set of events but by a form of secondary revision that produces interpretation as event. Or, in terms of the underlying metaphor of *St. Leon,* Asia, in gambling on the particular chariot she enters and then making this vehicle mean what she chooses it to mean, stubbornly represses the groundless, aleatory process of narrative as gambling that her choice exposes. After all, the "ghastly" Spirit's words could equally well portend a destiny like that which abruptly overtakes Ginotti and Wolfstein in *St. Irvyne* at the appointed "hour" of midnight (251). Thus the early novels, as mechanical, dis-organized assemblages of the ideas and *topoi* that recur in subsequent work, constitute this later work in relation to an archive of what has been de-selected: the shadows that haunt the attempt to produce futurity from the present. In this sense they ironically unravel poetry into the prose of the modern world that hovers on the edges of *Alastor* and *Adonais*. Yet not entirely, since this prose is not naturalized as realism but is de-formed as the Gothic, which is, as Jerrold Hogle argues, a "peculiar cultural space into which the horrors generated by early modern cultural changes . . . can be 'thrown off' or 'thrown down and under'—'abjected' in the senses emphasized by Julia Kristeva."[56] And also not entirely, since bits of the later texts are anomalously lodged in these novels as part-objects: for instance Ginotti's vision of the phantasm or Matilda playing a harp in *Zastrozzi* (113, 118), like the veiled maid in *Alastor*. Indeed, in contrast to *Zastrozzi*, *St. Irvyne* is itself punctuated by bits of poetry: epigraphs and inset poems in the form of lyrical ballads that physically, typographically, mark the abjected place of poetry in the prose of the world.[57] These cannibalized bits of poetry— bearing in mind Shelley's radical sense of poetry as a creative faculty rather than a genre—are abjects but also pro-jects. As such, they make prose as the narrative of particular facts an unsettled, heterogeneous genre open to poetry rather than part of the normalizing apparatus of modernity and the Novel.

CHAPTER THREE

Unbinding the Personal
Autonarration, Epistolarity, and Genotext
in Mary Hays's Memoirs of Emma Courtney

IN HER *Appeal to the Men of Great Britain in Behalf of Women* (1798), Mary Hays writes of the difficulty of positing women's identity. Women, she suggests, have been so constructed that they have lost "even the idea of what they might have been, or what they still might be":

> We must therefore endeavour, to describe them by negatives. As, perhaps, the only thing that can be advanced with certainty on the subject, is,—what they are *not*. For it is very clear, that they are not what they ought to be, that they are not what men would have them to be, and to finish the portrait, that they are not what they appear to be.[1]

In this chapter I use Hays's first novel, *Memoirs of Emma Courtney* (1797), to explore the work of the negative as a fundamental property of Romantic narrative. More specifically, I suggest that this work occurs between the events of Hays's life and their cathartic, speculative, sometimes aggressive transposition into the memoirs of her title character.

Emma Courtney's one-sided pursuit of Augustus Harley is infamously based on the story of Hays's unreturned passion for the Cambridge radical William Frend, author of the controversial pamphlet *Peace and Union Recommended* (1793), which contained an appendix justifying the execution of Louis XVI and which led to Frend's trial and expulsion from Cambridge.[2] Early female novelists such as Hays and Wollstonecraft were for a long time victims of a reduction of text to biography, and *Memoirs* has thus been seen as a monologic transfer of life into text. But Hays's novel is a textually self-conscious work, which draws on personal experience so as to expose the narratology we use to construct both life and text. As such it invents or at least crystallizes a larger Romantic intergenre, which I call autonarration. From Schiller's characterization of the sentimental or Romantic writer as being "in his work" whereas the classical writer "stands behind his work" "like divinity behind the world's structure,"[3] through Browning's distinction between subjective and objective poetry, the inmixing of the author in the text has been recognized as a characteristically Romantic move. But this mode, I suggest, should not be dismissed as narcissism or egotistical sublimity; rather, it makes the text the unfinished transcription of a subject still in process. For far from collapsing the boundary between life and text, Hays effects a series of "transpositions" (to borrow Kristeva's term) among life, fiction, and the institutions of ideology.[4] The transposition of experience into fiction recognizes that experience as discursively constructed. That Hays draws on her own experience is a way of authorizing what she does and reciprocally implicating the reader in the text. But it also puts the finality of the text under erasure, by suggesting that what it "does" or where it ends is limited by its genesis in the life of a conflicted historical subject.

If Browning's binary is really a distinction between Romantic poetry and a Victorian Novel that produced the dramatic monologue as the disciplined, closeted link to this poetry, autonarration is one form taken by the Romantic novel's attempt to access a poetry underlying prose as the genre with the emerging cultural capital that made it more obviously capable of challenging what Godwin calls "institution." Poetry in this sense is not verse, but what Joel Faflak, writing of the "discourses by which a society sustains itself," calls the "radically chaotic moment" of the "articulation" of a culture's discourses as "fantasy." Faflak here draws on Ross Woodman's seminal work on sanity, madness, and transformation. For Woodman, on the one hand, "madness" is the traumatic and creative core underlying culture, a Real (in Lacanian terms) that is barred from the codified, socialized sanity of the Symbolic, but which it is the work of poetry to transform. On the other hand, it also refers to "the strategies by which we struggle to transform [this madness]—strategies that largely describe what culture is" and that have "themselves become the victim of the madness culture is called to transform." Culture, in other words, is the sanitized form of a madness it represses, which it is the role of "poetry" to retrieve. Evoking Percy Shelley's understanding of poetry as an attitude rather than a genre—indeed, a faculty of perpetual deconstruction—Woodman therefore argues that society cannot afford to forget this "poetry"—a forgetting, I would argue, that is crystallized in the Novel.

For poetry, in Faflak's formulation, is the force that "might return the public sphere to its creative functioning" by dissolving and re-creating "the historical knowledge [that] becomes the dead weight of a culture threatening to bury itself . . . in its cultural life."[5] This dead weight is what Jean-Paul Sartre later calls the "practico-inert," or the matter in which past praxis is stuck by a "reifying sociality"; the result is "alienated *praxis*" and a "serial mode of co-existence."[6] Hays repeatedly refers to this cultural life—this "distemper'd civilization," as she says, quoting Godwin[7]—in her letters. These letters, as conscious epitexts for her novel,[8] also form part of the autonarrativity, and as I argue in the last section, the madness, that resists the closure of its plot.

Hays was for a long time remembered as Wollstonecraft's close friend, the person who introduced her to Godwin and the author of her obituary. But though she has consequently been identified with or dismissed as a more outrageous version of Wollstonecraft,[9] there are significant differences between the two. First, Hays's attitude to passion and the tradition of romance and sensibility was more positive than Wollstonecraft's. While she shared Wollstonecraft's sense that the Rousseauvian model of romance wrote women into a male script, Hays also discerned in *La Nouvelle Héloise* what Godwin in "Of Choice in Reading" called a "tendency" at odds with its "moral." Thus, in a scene reminiscent of Godwin's essay,[10] Emma Courtney is in the middle of reading Rousseau's novel when her father finds her and takes the book away, so that she reads about Julie's passion but not its correction. The resulting error produces a "long chain of consequences" (60) that are both disastrous and constitutive of her subjectivity.[11] Provoked by her father's insistence that she read history, Emma's interest in romance, unlike the sentimentalism of Wollstonecraft's Maria, thus cathects a subversive desire onto *imagos* that are part of the Symbolic order precisely to access the unstable moment of their articulation as fantasy. Second, *Memoirs* is the work of a woman who could not and then did not enter the marriage circuit, remaining single and singular. For although Wollstonecraft thought it would have been more appropriate for the novel to end with the death of the male protagonist and the unavoidable termination of Emma's love,[12] Hays has her heroine outlive the conventional ending of novels about women in death or marriage.[13] Hence, though The Wrongs of Woman is about much more than its love interest, whereas Memoirs of Emma

Courtney seems to be about nothing *but* romantic love, the terms of Emma's life are not really defined by that love. Rather, the novel is concerned with Emma writing and potentially reading her obsession with Augustus so as to understand women's representation in the Symbolic order.[14] It is worth noting that Hays (at Godwin's suggestion) had already begun to think of writing a novel based on her experience while still interested in Frend, that she may have written her letters partly with a wider audience in view, and that she began the novel only after her relationship with Frend had ended.[15]

Drawing on Hays's own letters to Frend and Godwin (who appears in the novel as Francis), the novel focuses on the one-sided correspondence between its title character and the man she chooses to love, Augustus Harley. Emma, like so many contemporaneous characters for whom the family is a failed structure, has lost her mother and aunt early in life, been brought up by an absent father, and transferred after his death to the care of an uncle. It is in her uncle's house that she meets the destructively passionate Montague, as well as the highly rational Francis, with whom she exchanges ideas and to whose not entirely sympathetic eyes she confides the story of her love. Her acquaintance with Augustus is preceded by her friendship with his mother, who takes the place of the female presences effaced from her own life. Augustus himself enters Emma's story by way of a violent coach accident, in which he saves her and Montague from death but is badly injured. Seeming to encourage her friendship at first, he later becomes evasive and refuses to answer her letters. His ostensible reason is his uncle's will, which stipulates that he will forfeit his legacy if he marries. Emma is never entirely convinced by the purely pecuniary motive, but her declarations of love and pleas for frankness are met by injunctions to be less selfish and to restrain her feelings within the bounds of propriety. Eventually it emerges that Augustus is married to a foreign woman he no longer loves and whose existence he has concealed for fear of losing his legacy (although he has also hinted at a prior entanglement).

This disclosure ends the relationship of Emma and Augustus, and Emma, now under financial pressure, marries Montague. She is a faithful wife and mother until a second accident outside her home brings Augustus back into her life. She learns that Augustus, having been reduced to poverty, has lost his wife and two of his children to illness. Emma nurses him until he dies and inherits the guardianship of his remaining son, also called Augustus. From then on her marriage deteriorates, culminating in Montague's murder of his illegitimate child and subsequent suicide. Emma tells her story partly through a series of letters: passionately rational letters to Augustus and rationally passionate ones to Francis, to whom she writes about the economic predicament of single women and the relationship between reason and passion. There are sixteen letters in all, not including those from Augustus, whose occasional letters are merely summarized. Of these, twelve are from Emma herself: seven to Augustus and five to Francis. Three of the remaining letters are from Francis and the last is Montague's suicide note. These letters, comprising about a third of the novel, are interspersed with an account of Emma's life in the form of a conventional plot-narrative to make up the memoirs of the title.

But the memoirs are also framed by four further letters to the now-adult son of Augustus: two at the beginning of the novel, one at the beginning of its second volume, and one at the end. This son, who is himself involved in a passionate relationship with "Joanna," occupies at the end of the text the narratological position occupied by Emma at the outset. His history repeats Emma's even to the point that he pursues a woman "whose heart was devoted to another object": a circumstance of which the woman has "frankly informed" him (*M*, 41), but one more enigmatically intimated by Augustus Sr. when he sulkily refers in a letter to Emma to "another prior attachment" (157).[16] Ostensibly Emma conveys her history as a cautionary exemplum to Augustus Jr., adopting the role she is assigned in the public sphere. Yet the epistolary form has crossed the bounds of private space, to say what cannot be said in public and to claim a certain immediacy and presence. In putting Emma's letters within her memoirs, rather than releasing her protagonist's memoirs into a larger narrativity as Wollstonecraft does in *The Wrongs of Woman,* Hays allows this radicalism of the adolescent present to be contained within the maturity of pastness. She yields, for the time being, to the dialectic of enlightenment, which allows Nicola Watson to see Hays's fetishizing of an ineffectual female sensibility as complicit with, and indeed as hastening, the death of the epistolary novel at the hands of "projects of recuperation [and] conversion" consolidated in the Regency novel.[17] But the framing of the memoirs themselves within a return to the epistolary form suspends this cautionary closure by once again transposing the question of passion from the past to the unresolved present. The frame, in short, both performs and questions our consent to a syntagm that requires the capitulation of "letter" to "plot" and the exigencies of the Novel.[18]

Crucial to Hays's novel is the concept of desire. Desire is part of the *Memoirs'* functioning or semiosis in ways to which I return. But it is also thematically central to a text that questions the opposition between reason and passion so as to reposition female (but more broadly Romantic) subjectivity within the psychosocial economy. Felicity Nussbaum has described how women's sexuality posed a threat to this economy in specifically material ways having to do with the inheritance of property and thus the maintenance of the class system.[19] Emma's aspirations are obviously subversive because of the social implications of a woman taking the initiative in love. But her desire has to do with much more than sexuality. As Hays suggests in a letter to Godwin, in which she justifies shifts that she made in lifestyle as part of her pursuit of Frend, these shifts, in which she gave up "the asylum of my youth" for a situation "less assured and more exposed," were all about an amorphous, unfocused *"change"* and "freedom" (L, 233–34).[20] Desire, as Lacan recognizes, is always in excess of its object, the object being only a partial representation of something beyond it and thus implicated in a chain of deferrals and transferences. Or as Emma herself puts it, "the mind must have an object," and the object she gives herself is a love-object (*M*, 149). In other words, *Memoirs* is not about Emma's desire for Augustus but about something else that is signified by that desire. For marriage to Augustus remains a signifier within the Symbolic order, while the further transference of Emma's desire to his son is still what Jameson calls a symbolic resolution. It allows Emma to be Augustus's mother, both the Symbolic mother who teaches and the Imaginary mother of his desire, and yet as mother in a paradoxical position of origination and subordination. As we have seen, Hays herself recognizes the substitutive nature of her project when she points in *An Appeal* to the difficulty of positing women's identity, given that women have been so constructed that "the only thing that can be advanced with certainty" is "what they are not."[21]

For Lacan, as is well known, desire transmits itself through a chain of transitional objects that are substitutes for the *Objet À,* which, in what de Man would describe as a catechresis, he calls the "phallus." But if the Lacanian connotations of desire let us approach *Memoirs* in terms of the negativity of the signifier, there are also limitations in his version of the concept. In tracing the history of desire from Jean Hyppolite's influential reading of Hegel through Jean-Paul Sartre to Lacan, Judith Butler comments on the attenuation that occurs as desire is transposed from a dialectical to a structural framework.[22] Not only does Lacan dissociate desire from a subject and convert it into a "purely geometrical, topological phenomenon,"[23] but he also denies that desire can be "materialized or concretized through language," whether directly or negatively. In this respect he moves sharply away from the still Romantic tradition of Hyppolite and Sartre, who continue to think of language expressively as "an object's further life, its necessary externalization,"[24] or its projection towards the future. Moreover, because he sees desire as endlessly metonymic and unsatisfiable, Lacan dispossesses the means by which it signifies itself of historical specificity or facilitating value, making the signifier no more than a position in a structural series.

In using the word "desire," then, I continue to have in mind Hyppolite's rereading of Hegel as part of a negative dialectic that is particularly (post)Romantic. Desire is the "very existence of man, 'who never is what he is,' who always exceeds himself," and who in that sense "has a future." As such, it is the power of the negative in experience—expressed for Hegel in the Symbolic and Romantic—as well as the reflexivity of a consciousness that must know itself partly as another and as existing for another.[25] Put in Lacan's terms, Emma's love is an articulation of the Imaginary within the Symbolic or of the subjective within the objective. Beginning as the idealism of a highly Romantic subject who resists being confined by things as they are, Emma's desire can express itself only in the socially prescribed form of heterosexual love. Her desire is doubly negative, in the sense that it resists her placement within the Symbolic order through an identification with the masculine that further sets it at odds with itself. Yet this negativity is dialectical, because desire makes the negative into "something to be labored upon and worked through."[26] For Emma this working through occurs in the epistolary format of the novel, which makes of self-consciousness an intersubjective process. Epistolarity, in other words, is part of the process advocated by both Godwin and Kant, of testing one's ideas by putting them *in process/on trial.*[27] For Hays this working through occurs when she takes up Godwin's challenge to write a novel about her experience. She puts her ideas on trial as part of a compact with Godwin: a compact whose full extent he did not anticipate, in which she also puts his ideas and his very *habitus* as a liberal intellectual on trial.[28]

To be sure, Emma's letters also fetishize desire, requiring of the reader what I describe in the next chapter as a "perverse identification" with a character who seems to enjoy her symptom. For Emma offends the propriety of readers brought up on Austen, who is sometimes thought to have based the eponymous heroine of her own *Emma* on Hays's character. Thus to give Emma the understanding she demands is to violate our own nervous normality. Freud discusses our identification with "pathological" characters and argues that its "precondition . . . is that the spectator should [herself] be a neurotic . . . who can derive pleasure" from the "recognition of a repressed impulse." In anyone who is not neurotic, Freud says, "this recognition will meet only with aversion." But for Freud, interestingly, this is only because in the "normal" person, repression has been more successful. Given that we constitute ourselves as normal, the writer's task, then, is to shake up an initial repression in the reader, since if the character is too removed from normality, the transference cannot operate. Thus Freud argues that to "induce the same illness" in the spectator as in the character is "especially necessary where the repression does not already exist in us" and must first "be set up."[29] Because the repression is *not* set up in the case of *Zastrozzi*'s Matilda, the perversity of our identification with Shelley's shorthand version of Emma is purely fantastic. The epistolary form of *Memoirs,* the typically novelistic account of Emma's family history, and realism's apparatus of diacritically differentiated characters are all means by which Hays sets up the space within which we experience and reconsider our own normality.

Emma's letters, in other words, ask us to recognize Hays's pursuit of Frend as what Žižek calls a *sinthome,* obsessionally reiterated as Emma's constancy to an "ideal object."[30] Raising the question of why, "in spite of its interpretation, the symptom [does] not dissolve itself," Žižek suggests that the Lacanian answer is enjoyment. He thus distinguishes between the symptom, a "particular, pathological, signifying formation" that "bind[s]" enjoyment, and the *sinthome,* a "certain signifier which is not enchained in a network but immediately filled, penetrated with enjoyment."[31] Emma's enjoyment of her symptom is not simply narcissism but is rather imbued with the passion of "the Real," with all the connotations of the term as Lacan and Žižek use it. Or as Hays herself wrote to Godwin: "My

MS was not written *merely* for the public eye—another latent, & perhaps stronger, motive lurked beneath– . . . my story is *too real*" (L, 254). That Emma makes romantic love into a fetish or *sinthome,* which provides an anamorphic access to the radically chaotic moment underlying her culture's neuroses, has to do with the way women have been constructed in the social text. She herself makes this point when she refuses to abandon her love of Augustus, referring to it as the mind's necessary "object" and "pursuit" and arguing, "I feel, that I am neither a philosopher, nor a heroine—but *a woman, to whom education has given a sexual character*" (*M,* 149). Thus, although Hays's critics found Emma's epistolary pursuit of Augustus unseemly and her concerns with her feelings narcissistic, to see the novel purely in these terms is to miss its point. *Memoirs* is contingently, circumstantially, rather than essentially about female sexuality. From the beginning Emma's desire is excessive: it exceeds the objective correlative it tries to find in Augustus, and even at the end it survives the dismantling of its object. At first Augustus encourages Emma "in the pursuit of learning and science" (102), so that her need for a relationship with him is also a desire for access to knowledge. Given women's exclusion from all but the domestic sphere, this love is also a desire for the enunciative position within the social order that a woman could have only in relation to a man. But as the convenient vagueness of the word "desire" suggests, it would be wrong to give it a precise referent. For when Emma does acquire the position afforded by marriage to Montague, it becomes an empty signifier that does not satisfy her, albeit one that she has to transit to become Augustus Jr.'s "mother" and thus gain the authority to write her memoirs.

Emma's desire is all the more difficult to characterize because in its emergence it is not even sexual; as she herself notes, it begins as a "transfer[ence]" of her affection for Augustus's mother (91), who takes the place of her own dead mother, though even this feminist scenario does not "solve" the "phenominon [sic]" of this desire (L, 243). Emma first becomes interested in listening to Mrs. Harley's accounts of Augustus because of his mother's affection for him, and she loves in *him* what he must inherit from *her.* What begins as a desire for everything effaced from her own upbringing in a patriarchal society is thus androgynously transcoded or displaced onto the masculine as the only sanctioned object of adult female love. It is significant that Emma's specifically sexual desire is set in motion before she actually meets him by Augustus's portrait (*M*, 91). This mobilizing of desire by an image that precedes its re-presentation in a real person anticipates texts such as Shelley's *Alastor*, in which the protagonist unites in an image "all of wonderful, or wise, or beautiful, which the poet, the philosopher, or the lover could depicture" (Preface to *Alastor*, 73), before he actually goes in search of his epispsyche. Figuring the precedence of the signifier over the signified, the portrait marks the fundamentally Romantic structure of desire, not simply as lack, but also as a form of imagination subversively knotted into the Symbolic structures of representation and the family.[32]

If the word "desire" suggests a noncoincidence of the subject with its object, we also need to set it beside Hays's own more positive term "passion" and to read desire and passion as glosses on each other. The frequent discussions of "passion" in *Memoirs* involve Emma's struggle to rethink the position of women in the Symbolic order by examining the identification of emotion as the site of feminine weakness. Hays's views on this subject are highly conflicted. On the one hand, in representing her memoirs as a warning against error, Emma purports to accept the dominant devaluation of passion and related terms such as "romanticism," "enthusiasm," and "imagination" (*M*, 116, 209). On the other hand, Hays differs from Wollstonecraft in arguing for passion as a form of strength. Writing to Francis, who is constantly chiding her for her emotional extravagance, and quoting one of Hays's own letters to Godwin (L, 239), Emma asks: "What are passions but another name for powers?" (*M*, 116). As distinct from a desire associated with lack, passions are thus connected with what Schelling and Novalis call potencies: with what Novalis further calls "romanticization" as the elevation of the lower into the higher through a process of *Potenzirung*, which discerns its occluded potential,[33] whether this potential, as Hays says, "is generated . . . upon a real or fancied foundation, of excellence" (L, 240). It is this Romantic rather than sensible understanding of her desire for which Emma pleads in her letters to Francis, and for which Hays pleads even more persistently in her letters to Godwin.

The questioning of the hierarchy between reason and passion links Hays to a reexamination of this opposition in Romantic thinking from Blake to Schopenhauer. But whereas Schopenhauer will argue that the representations produced by reason are no more than disguised expressions of the will, Hays's protagonist suggests that passion can be deeply rational. Writing to Francis, and again re-citing one of Hays's own letters (L, 239), Emma argues that reason and passion are not necessarily opposed, that reason begins in passion. "Do you not perceive," she asks, "that my reason was the auxiliary of my passion, or rather my passion the generative principle of my reason?" (M, 172). This statement significantly revises her earlier condemnation of herself on the grounds that "my reason was but an auxiliary to my passion" (93). If reason is originally the elaboration of passion in a series of general principles, the "bound or outward circumference of Energy," as Blake suggests in *The Marriage of Heaven and Hell* (E, 34), then passion and other "strong energies" (M, 174; L, 229) remain vitally necessary to a genealogy of morals that reconsiders what would otherwise congeal into law. For Emma's passion causes her to rethink the social and psychic structures or, in the term Hays takes from Godwin, "institutions" (M, 205), which condemn that passion as outrageous, and thus her desire also becomes the site of her emergence as a political subject. Or as she tells Francis, again repeating one of Hays's letters (L, 239): "Had not these contradictions, these oppositions, roused the energy of my mind, I might have domesticated, tamely, in the lap of indolence and apathy" (M, 172).

Hays's use of the term "passion" remains resentfully conflicted, for the active thrust of the word is continually negated by Emma's forced acceptance of its patriarchal encoding as something that one suffers and by which one is infected. However, a reading of the word in terms of lack does not convey the force of Hays's project. If desire does more than eroticize female powerlessness, that is because the discourse of desire is allied with the forms of autonarration and epistolarity. Linda Kauffman has provided a valuable account of how amorous discourse is elaborated through epistolarity, so that the text becomes a letter to the reader, thus putting desire in circulation. But a further untheorized element in her discussion is the auto-graphing of many of the texts she describes, which makes their stories "too *real*." *Jane Eyre* is curiously subtitled an autobiography, and Kauffman focuses on its correspondences with Charlotte Brontë's letters to Constantin Heger, the Belgian schoolmaster with whom Charlotte fell in love as a young woman. As interesting is the reception history of the *Letters of a Portuguese Nun*, which testifies to a compelling, if somewhat literal, desire to make the nun into a historical person.[34]

As Ruth Perry points out, eighteenth-century readers liked to see fictional characters as "real." This blurring of the line between fiction and reality potentially allowed readers to write themselves, to write revisionary sequels, or otherwise to pursue the trace of their desire through the text.[35]

Responding as such a reader to Godwin's texts, Hays in her letters implicitly formulates an aesthetic that extends the claim made by Godwin in "Of Choice in Reading," that the "tendency" of a text can be known only through its "effect," which cannot be fully known.[36] Hays describes the effect made on her by *Caleb Williams,* which excited in her "mind a sensibility almost convulsive," and she attributes "such convulsion" even to the "calm philosophical principles" of *Political Justice* (L, 224, 226). She thus sees reading as a transmission of intensities, the capacity to "receive forcible impressions" (229), to be disturbed, unsettled. Later she defends herself from Godwin's criticism of Emma Courtney, that a "person interested only in herself" is not interesting (255), by arguing that the effect made by Falkland or Caleb also comes from the narcissism of their suffering, which, by making us "wearied of this exhaustless theme" (246), communicates something in excess of itself. Clearly for Hays, in her letters to Godwin, defending her right to be miserable is something "filled, penetrated" by a perverse *jouissance,*[37] which allows her to claim her "malady" as a "proof of strength" (254). She is not able to be the "skilful physician" and diagnostician who can "retrace the causes, the symptoms [and] progress" of her "mind's disorders" (232), because to do so would be to bind her enjoyment. And this is because the aim of writing is to leave us disturbed: "Even now," Hays writes, "the affair, altogether, appears to me a sort of phenominon [sic] which I am unable to solve" (242).

This unsolvability of Hays's text has to do with the fact that its story "is too *real.*" *Memoirs of Emma Courtney* can be seen as an example of autonarration, a genre characterized by the way the text is filled, penetrated by the affect of the author's life. Autonarration formalizes a larger tendency of Romanticism, in which writers bring details from their personal lives into their texts, speaking in a voice that is recognizably their own or through a persona linked to the biographical author. Thus Coleridge's conversation poems are situated within his life through specific references to the time and place of their composition, to his ambivalent and unfinished relations with friends such as Wordsworth and Charles

Lamb, and to incidents from his domestic life such as the spilled skillet of milk that provided the occasion for "This Lime-Tree Bower, My Prison." Later poems continue, dejectedly and in a minimalist mode, the processing, through Coleridge's "life," of Wordsworth's texts and the desires that both Coleridge and Wordsworth projected onto "Wordsworth." Less literally Shelley, in *The Triumph of Life,* and Keats, in *The Fall of Hyperion,* inscribe in their texts sub-versions of themselves referred to by the pronoun "I," while the Byronic hero, though presented in the third person, is a figure for a public persona that is recognizably a mediated, fantasized projection of the author.

As I argue elsewhere, autonarration in its most ambitious form may also extend across an entire corpus or between corpuses that constitute a family of texts. Mary Shelley's fiction functions as a continuous autometaphoric record of her conflicted relation to Romanticism and the survival of her parents' unfinished legacies into the Regency and Victorian periods. In her complex mapping of real onto fictitious characters, Shelley divides and redistributes traits belonging to "real" persons between her fictional characters, so as to rethink Percy, Byron, and Godwin. She projects figures from her life as part-subjects or part-objects and puts them in different narratological positions. For example, she abjects Percy as the ineffectually angelic Woodville in *Mathilda,* then condenses him into her own self-representation as Euthanasia in *Valperga,* and brings him back as Adrian in *The Last Man.* This process further extends into a dialogue between her texts and Godwin's that connects his *Fleetwood* (1805), her *Mathilda* (1817), his *Deloraine* (1833), and her final novel, *Falkner* (1837). De-jecting Godwin as the nameless shadowy Father in *Mathilda,* Shelley thus conflates Byron and Godwin as the eponymous hero of her last novel: a character who alludes to Godwin's Falkland and his play *Faulkener*.[38] For in romanticizing Godwin as Byron, she promotes a perverse identification with the wounded masculine that both discloses the Byronic hero's indebtedness to Godwin and tries to recover the occluded potential of Godwinian misanthropy. In so doing, Shelley atones for what was done by and done *to* "Godwin" in *Mathilda,* in a complex reprocessing of their intertwined "lives" as texts that is bequeathed to the future— since Shelley's last novel is all about legacy.[39]

It is in this sense of a body of work in continuing autogenesis that Percy Shelley writes of the "poetic" faculty as producing "episodes" in a "poem, which all poets, like the co-operating thoughts of one great mind," are involved in "build[ing] up" (*DP,* 522). Shelley's statement, though couched as a Spinozist idealism about the many being modes of one substance, can also be read as assuming an archive that is "the chaos of a cyclic poem," from which different possibilities are generated (512). In Foucault's later return to the concept of the archive, he renames this chaos the "corpus," reserving the word "archive" for the "law of what can be said" or for "a practice that causes a multiplicity of statements to emerge as so many regular events." The corpus is thus what the archive had been in "Fantasia of the Library," namely, the "amorphous mass" of everything that has been or could be said, while the archive is now "the *langue* that defines the system of constructing possible sentences."[40] By returning characters and ideologemes to the corpus she shares with Shelley and Godwin, Mary Shelley's fiction, rather than repudiating Shelley's poetry from the perspective of a greater realism, also puts on trial the processes by which it generates itself provisionally through a series of part-characters and part-narratives.

Hays's novel provides a more concentrated case of this autonarration, which circulates an archive of practices—both conventional and resistant—between life and text. Criticism from Eliot to poststructuralism has taught us to exile the author from an ironic or a decentered text, and insofar as the Romantics deviate from this standard of impersonality, the author's presence in the text has been chastised as a form of egotistical sublimity. But the author's self-representation through a textual figure is quite different from her presence, and the Romantic author enters the text neither as absolute ego nor as the mature and completed subject referred to by Wayne Booth as the implied author but as a subject-in-process represented by a figure, sometimes a dis-figuration, of the self. On the one hand, then, the flagrant subjectivity of Romanticism offers the writer a speaking position that she is precluded from occupying by the aesthetic grammar of (neo)classicism and (post)modernism. As a subject who is not quite inside the space of the public, she can articulate desires that are different from (or that defer) the received genres of experience. On the other hand, these desires are textualized rather than literalized, so that the writer, in leaving life for text, ceases to be a transcendental ego and confesses her situatedness as a historical subject. Thus, if one of Hays's innovations, as Gina Luria Walker says, is "her discovery that female sexuality was a valid form of knowledge uniquely, if not exclusively, accessible to women,"[41] sexuality is not something in-itself but an anamorphic distortion that allows us to see women's construction within a narratological system that is itself a form of "institution." Yet it is not simply that life is made into text or ideology. For the historical as distinct from fictitious first-person position also embeds the textual within the Real, by marking its genesis in and continued urgency for a historical subject. "Sexuality" marks this urgency of the drive, in a psychoanalytic sense, even as it remains a constructed form of the drive. Or as Emma says to Augustus in a passage already quoted: "I feel, that I am neither a philosopher, nor a heroine—but *a woman to whom education has given a sexual character*" (M, 149).

As a specific form of the discourse of subjectivity, autonarration involves not simply the author's entry into the text through the first-person pronoun but also a sustained rewriting of events from the author's life. Autonarrations are not fictions, but they are not autobiographies. Hays's text is a highly fictionalized version of her life, in which the main character is writing her memoirs, thus inscribing the text itself as a sub-version and problematizing of the autobiographical project. I use the term "autonarration" rather than "autobiography" or "self-writing" deliberately. As a subset of biography, autobiography assumes a straightforward relation between representation and experience that allows the subject to tell her life story in the form of constative or performative utterance: either as it was or as it becomes through the act of rewriting. By contrast, self-writing extends beyond the formalism of autobiography and of genre, to what Lyotard calls "prose" as an "ungraded supply of phrases . . . from all genres" (D, 158), including diaries, journals, letters, etc. Autonarration, however, is a form of self-writing in which the author writes her life as a fictional narrative and thus consciously raises the question of the relationship between experience and its narrativization.

Although it is part of this discourse of subjectivity, Wollstonecraft's first novella, *Mary,* is not a full-fledged autonarration because it does no more than evoke the trace of the personal through the titular reference to the author's name. *The Wrongs of Woman,* by contrast, contains several parallels between Maria's life and Wollstonecraft's relationship with Gilbert Imlay. These parallels, moreover, are deliberately imperfect in that Maria's lover, Darnford, occupies the positions of both Imlay and Godwin. He resembles Imlay in being Maria's lover, but he also resembles

Godwin in being the father of her second child in the fragmentary endings (whose status, as I suggest in the last chapter, is itself problematic). That the author is and is not represented by her textual surrogate has significant consequences. Instead of generating a series of identifications in which the author recognizes her alter ego in the mirror of the text, the reading process involves a series of (mis)recognitions in which we cannot be quite sure of the relationship between text and reality. These misrecognitions generate a complex series of interrelations between what is and what could be, and among possibility, virtuality, and actuality. For instance, one of the pivotal events in Wollstonecraft's life was Imlay's betrayal of the desires that she symbolically invested in her love for him: desires that were social and political as well as romantic. That Darnford is both Imlay and Godwin narrates the possibility of a repetition that did not happen in quite that way in Wollstonecraft's life. At the same time, the transposition of this betrayal into the text is effected through its displacement into an ending that she did not integrate into her novel. This displacement suspends the inevitability of the "ending": it removes the betrayal from a climactic position in the text, and by re-citing it within a text, it also exposes this ending as a cliché, a discourse into which women are written and write themselves.

Autonarration thus puts under erasure the assumption made in autobiography that the subject can tell her own story. It is not autobiography because it is still fiction, but it is not just fiction because of its genesis in the life of a real individual. Crucial to the genre is the movement that occurs between the zones of life and fiction. But we should not think of the relation between these zones as being like that between story and discourse.[42] Story is a foundationalist concept, which implies that certain events happened in a certain order. By departing from the diary or journal and transposing their lives into fiction, writers such as Hays and Wollstonecraft recognize that their lives themselves take shape within a social text. Autonarration therefore involves a double textualization of both the narrative and the life on which it is based. At the same time, its genesis in experience complicates this textualization by inscribing the Real as what Jameson calls the "absent cause" of the narrative process.[43] In gesturing beyond the text to the author's experience, autonarration, while rendering the very term "experience" problematic, points us to something that cannot quite be represented in either the texts or the public life of the author. This something impels the author to articulate herself in the two different media of life and text, as if each requires the supplement of the other. Indeed, both Hays and Wollstonecraft use a third medium, the political tract, although it is the mixed genre of autonarration that sensitizes us to the intertextual and supplementary position of seemingly simpler signifying materials such as "life" and political prose.

But the term "life" itself needs to be further broken down: into Hays's public history and the autobiographical ground, for lack of a better word, that precedes her interpellation into a social script. This ground or matrix could be thought of as a provisional articulation of drives at the level of what Kristeva calls the "semiotic" R, 25). As such it finds no adequate objective correlative in the history of Mary Hays or her fictional counterpart but can only be sensed through a symptomatic reading of the differences between Hays's history and its further narrativization in Emma's memoirs. This provisional articulation involves desire: a desire that is at once metaphysical, political, and sexual. However, any expression of this desire is already a narrativization of the pre-text produced within the psychosocial structures of the family. In this narrative, desire attaches itself to an animus, or more properly, a masculine equivalent of what Shelley calls the epipsyche. We can note Hays's tendency to idealize men with radical political commitments, whether as mentors, in the case of Godwin and the preacher Robert Robinson, or as potential lovers, in the case of Frend. These men were her means of access to a sociopolitical order in which she could not easily participate, given the lack of professional avenues for women. Although Joseph Johnson published her *Appeal,* Emma Courtney recapitulates the position of a younger Mary Hays in having to express her views on the construction of gender in late-eighteenth-century society in a series of private letters to a male correspondent. Hays sought relationships with men because they were her means of access to knowledge and because the discourse of emotional relationships gave her a way of locating for herself an admittedly ambiguous enunciative position within the social text. And where her relationships with male mentors preserved the gender hierarchy that Emma struggles against in her correspondence with Francis, her more passionate relationships promised (at least ideally) a union with the male that would lead to a transcendence of hierarchy and difference— one could even say an incestuous union that is a union with the self.[44]

If Hays's public history already writes her desire in certain preset social forms, *Memoirs of Emma Courtney* tries to displace and defamiliarize this anterior social text. Central to this process are the differences between the novel and the "events" or "facts" that it symbolically transforms or anamorphically de-forms. These differences, rather than the events themselves or their fictional counterparts, are what allow us to sense the autobiographical pre-text misrepresented in Hays's public life. For it is not that she rewrites things as they are in her life into things as they should be in her novel: Emma's life is not resolved with any more outward success than Hays's affair with Frend. Rather, by enacting her relationship with Frend in two different signifying media, life and text, Hays dislodges the mimetic authority of either version and allows the reading process to operate in primarily negative ways to impede its premature closure. That the text does not exactly repeat Mary Hays's actual history opens up the possibility of a history that could have been different. On the other hand, the novel, as a deflected repetition of the life, is a deferral of that actual history that continues to haunt it and to reinscribe its utopian project in the structures of eighteenth-century society. It is also a difference from its own ending, which could be narrated differently if transposed into an alternative set of circumstances.

We shall focus only on the most significant of the divergences between life and text: Hays's representation of Augustus. Unlike Frend, Augustus is completely apolitical, though, like Frend, he has an incentive to remain a bachelor: a sordid rather than a respectable one, since Frend's motive for celibacy was that after being forced to leave Cambridge he was still entitled to receive the money from his fellowship at Jesus College if he followed the standard requirement of remaining unmarried.[45] Indeed, Augustus's own passion for the foreign wife he will not acknowledge makes him much closer to Emma than he admits, but utterly different from her in his hypocritical attitude to the feelings. Most significant of all is his secret marriage, given that Frend himself married only later, in 1808. This change is not only important because it makes Augustus unworthy of Emma's love, and because it hints that she could have had him if the plot of her life had been different, but also because that possibility destigmatizes her desire and frees the reader from having to judge it in terms of its failure, which may well be our only reason for condemning it.

At the same time it is crucial that we not rewrite the plot as it is worked out in the Symbolic order of Hays's history or that of Emma Courtney, by substituting for it an imaginary ending that discloses the marriage of Emma and Augustus as the text's hermeneutic secret. For this repositing of the subject within the existing social order is negated both by the displacement of the secret marriage onto a wife who is effaced from the text and by the disappearance of Emma's namesake daughter, whose early death prevents the marriage of Emma and Augustus from being consummated (even problematically, as in *Wuthering Heights*) in the second generation. The possibility of a marriage exists as no more than a trace that defers the outcome of Hays's life so as to make us think about it differently. But it is important that her desire should not succeed, because the nature of that desire is that it exceeds its articulation as sexual desire and cannot find itself in the object to which it is directed, who is, after all, unavailable. Augustus's unavailability also lets itself be phrased in more than one way. On the most straightforward level it is a rebuke to Emma's desire. But it also renders this desire innocent, not only of the failure that leads us to dismiss it, but also of the sexuality that cuts off the political radicalism of women's desire in the scandalous memoirs of writers like Charlotte Charke and Laetita Pilkington, perhaps alluded to in Hays's title.[46] The abjection of the foreign wife from the diegesis marks sexual passion as a failed position, a transposition. As important is the way the queer requirement imposed on Augustus, that he not marry, calls into question the normalization and institution of marriage. That the uncle is outside the diegesis and his demand so inexplicable makes his legacy all the more an enigma, which arrests the expediency of reading for plot.

The autobiographical pre-text, in other words, is not so much a ground as a zone of possibilities generated by the differences between Hays's and Emma's histories. As such it is like the archival or anarchic space figured by Shelley—an-archic in the sense of being before *arche*, or foundation—when he describes the restless place

> where do inhabit
> The shadows of all forms that think and live
> . . . .
> Dreams and the light imaginings of men,
> And all that faith creates, or love desires.   (*PU*, 1.197–201)

More precisely, we can describe this space as "anarchivic" in Derrida's word, before the practices that allow events to be archived in predictable ways.[47] This preoriginal or unbound space is not only the origin of the text but also the limbo to which its characters, events, and ideologemes return in order to be summoned back after the plot's conclusion in a missed encounter with itself. For Shelley this is the space of the poetry underlying culture, which Faflak evokes and which allows what is bound in a plot to be recomposed differently. In the novel this *poietic* potential emerges from its "genotext" as opposed to its "phenotext." I borrow these terms from Kristeva, who defines the phenotext as that which "communicates univocal information between two full-fledged subjects," while the genotext is a "process" or "*path*" that articulates ephemeral structures. The genotext can be "seen in language" but "is not linguistic (in the sense understood by structural or generative linguistics)" (*R*, 86–87). The phenotext, though not the same as Hays's public history, is its intratextual equivalent because both are produced within the Symbolic order. It includes the mimetic and pragmatic dimensions of the novel: its plot, and what Godwin would call its "moral," or its use of the letter as a way of forwarding the memoirs to their addressee as a cautionary tale. The genotext, according to Kristeva, is the unformulated part of the text, its "tendency," in Godwin's terms, evident for Kristeva in rhythm as that which exceeds statement. It is "a matter of topology, whereas the phenotext is one of algebra" (91). Associated with figures of space that differentiate it from the linear temporality of syntax, it is also conversely linked to temporal words such as "process," which inhibit us from placing it in space, making it visible.

Kristeva develops the notion of a genotext through Mallarmé and Lautréamont, thus with reference to a "poetic language" effectively confined to lyric. At least in *Revolution in Poetic Language,* she sets aside narrative as an oedipal form in which the "social organism . . . is viewed through the structure of the family," with the result that the "*matrix of enunciation*" centers in an "author" who is "a projection of the paternal role" (90).[48] Yet despite the connection of plot to the Symbolic order, writers such as Hays and Wollstonecraft choose subjective narrative rather than lyric because it provides them with access to the public sphere. Indeed, Wollstonecraft thematizes this choice in *The Wrongs of Woman* when she has Maria begin by writing rhapsodies descriptive of the state of her mind" but then has her turn to composing her memoirs (*W*, 82). One of my concerns is therefore to explore how there can be a genotext of narrative, opened up in this case through the dynamics of autonarration. As we have seen, the genotext exists partly as an intertext or a connective zone between the biographical and diegetic worlds, which is to say that it consists of the possibilities released by the negation of the various scripts into which the subject has been or could be written. But in addition the genotext is also between the text's syntagms. If the phenotext includes the plot and its characters as positive terms in a narrative syntax, the genotext is something the reader senses in the *form* taken by the content: in the rhythms and processes of emplotment and the spaces between characters and generic components. It is also important to remember that the drives produced in the semiotic *chora* reproduced in the genotext already bear the imprint of cultural structures. The genotext, as something that is not linguistic but that is seen in language, is the overdetermined place of an entanglement between dominant, residual, and emergent discourses. Insofar as it generates the gaps in which desire can emerge, this desire is produced within the Symbolic as an unsettling of its order.

Where the phenotext is positive in the sense that it communicates information or posits identity, the genotext can be conceived only as a negativity. As a form of negativity—which is a process, as distinct from negation, which is thetic and posits the negative as a fixed position (*R*, 109–13)—the genotext can be located first of all in the diacritical relations between generic components and characters. An obvious example is the way the affirmative element in Emma's passion emerges not from what she does but as something not quite stated and thus never confirmed in the difference between her behavior and the self-destructive passion of Montague. A far more complex version of this *différance*, which traverses the genotext, is the conspicuous doubling of the first generation protagonists of Hays's novel as the second generation, combined with a simultaneous maintenance *and* reversal of the symmetry that contains the doubling within the boundaries of gender. Emma is repeated as her daughter Emma and Augustus as his son Augustus, with a symmetry that seems at first to perpetuate the gender positions of the first generation. But then Augustus's death becomes the younger Emma's death, ex-terminating both the romance of failed sensibility and the plot of conventional domesticity as ideologemes of interpretive closure. Meanwhile, Augustus Jr. occupies the position in the plot occupied by Emma Sr., in that his own involvement in a passionate love affair provides the pretext for her to send him her memoirs. Put differently, the plot in the second generation does away with the woman and allows the man to survive, but only after his conduct has come to resemble Emma's more than that of his father. In a metaphoric sense the surviving Emma dies as the woman her child might have been, while her desire survives in the younger man, who, by occupying a female subject-position, allows Emma at last to occupy the same narratological subject-position as a man.

This complex rearrangement of the first generation in the second is genotextual in the sense that we must read it as a psychosocial text disorganized by certain rhythms. As important to this text as its characters are the processes by which gender and plot functions are mapped and remapped onto each other. For as the word "processes" implies, narrative (or at least subjective narrative of the kind written by the Romantics) is not simply the plot with its characters. It is an autogenerative mechanism, which produces and disposes of events and characters in such a way that its movements are themselves a symptomatic part of the text's content. Narrative, in other words, is the process by which plot and characters are produced, but only as transpositions that are worked through, set aside, (a)voided, or at times ex-terminated in an unresolved deconstruction of the ideological terms represented both by what the characters are and by what they could be. In the case of *Emma Courtney*'s generational plot as the conventional syntagmatic path out of the impasse of sensibility, the narrative begins by doubling its main characters along familial lines that preserve the separateness of male and female, by giving Emma a daughter and Augustus a son. But then it crosses these lines by partially reversing the roles played by the younger Emma and Augustus in the economy of the text. The chiasmus is incomplete, because while the younger Augustus clearly resembles his adoptive mother, Emma's daughter resembles Augustus Sr. only in one respect: they both die. It is, however, this incomplete turn, from the maintenance to the rearrangement of gender lines, that forms part of the genotext. The movements of the narrative are traces of something whose provisional articulation in the genotext is itself imprinted by the sexual structures of the Symbolic order. In other words, Hays's vicarious self-doubling of Emma as Augustus Jr. narrates her desire for a social order in which the division between reason and passion, male and female, will no longer obtain. This desire, however, is haunted by the possibility that Augustus may still be his father's son, that his future may not vindicate the rights of the woman who is no more than his metaphoric mother in a family that is an ideal rearrangement of his actual family. Finally, this desire is itself produced within the gendered economy against which it struggles. The symbolic resolution it projects, albeit tentatively, has Emma survive through her masculine counterpart at the cost of killing off the very female self she has sought to vindicate.

At the same time, this ambiguous transgression of the social order is connected to a (mis)identification with the role of mother that allows the death of Emma's namesake to function in more than one symbolic register. Emma Sr. survives as (the younger) Augustus's symbolic mother and can transmit her memoirs to a future reader only by assuming this role. It seems, moreover, that she can enter the Symbolic role only after transiting the literal function of motherhood. At the same time, she is not really Augustus's mother, and unlike Wollstonecraft's Maria, she occupies the role of literal mother only briefly. Even as it marks the loss of what she wants to preserve, the younger Emma's death is what enables motherhood to be no more than a rite of passage for Emma. It marks her reinscription into the structures of genre and family as the uneasy assumption of a position rather than of an identity, as Symbolic rather than Imaginary in Lacan's sense.[49] Implicated as it is in more than one signifying path, the younger Emma's death exemplifies the functioning of the genotext as process rather than as thesis, as a conflictual flux that is simplified by any attempt at paraphrase.

If the genotext emerges in the spaces between characters and between characters and their roles, it can also be seen in the structuring of the plot. As distinct from "structure," a concept that codifies a mimetic reading of the plot in terms of what happens in it or in terms of a network of social-structural relations stabilized by the plot, what we can call "structuring" or "emplotment" are concepts that call for a symptomatic reading of plot in terms of the pathology of its de(form)ation: a pathology that discloses plot as culture's crustacean enclosure of its own madness. The most crucial example here is the novel's emplotment through what is itself a highly charged signifier: the mechanism of repetition as a symptom not only of the characters' repetition compulsion but also of what Žižek calls the "blind automatism" of the structures that the Symbolic order imposes on them.[50] Emma and Augustus first meet through an accident in which the coach in which she is traveling with Montague overturns and they are rescued by Augustus, with both men being badly injured. The plot ends with an uncanny recurrence of this accident only six weeks after the birth of Emma's daughter, in which Augustus, who just happens to be riding past Montague's house, is thrown from his horse and dies of an "internal injury" (*M*, 200), with equally fatal consequences for Emma's marriage.

The framing of Emma's passion in terms of violent accidents is a conspicuous departure from Hays's life, for both she and Frend lived on into their eighties. The accident inscribes the end of the affair in highly conflicted ways. On one level, the association of passion with violence and death signifies its destructiveness. But such a conclusion in no ways sums up the complexity of the relations between characters. Throughout the novel Emma's passion has been distinguished from the ultimately murderous passion of Montague. Though she seems destined to meet Augustus, that meeting could just as easily have occurred at his mother's house. That her love for him is associated with scenes of destructiveness is thus accidental. Or, at the level of the genotext, the accident is itself a figure for the way passion and death are associated in the symbolism of the social text. It comments on the inscription of "passion" within the Symbolic order by marking this association as accidental, the result of a metonymic proximity. We can sense the disturbance of the phenotext in the symmetrical neatness of the plot, which deflects our attention from the text as mimesis to the processes that produce figures mimetically as truths whose rigidity is symptomatically registered in this symmetry. Moreover, within this circular containment of the plot as returning to the scene of the accident there is also a hysterical and uncontained piling up of events. As Nicola Watson notes:

> In stark contrast to the main part of the novel, in which frustrated emotion takes the place of action, in the coda which ensues . . . action proliferates uncontrollably and melodramatically. . . . [In twenty eight pages] Emma takes in Harley's orphaned son, hires a nurse for him whom her husband seduces and impregnates, is beaten by her husband . . . - discovers that the nurse has given birth and that Montague has murdered the child, witnesses his suicide, and eighteen years later is mourning the death of her daughter, Emma Montague, who was to have married her adopted son.[51]

This second reading of the accident is genotextual in focusing on the text as a body of affects rather than as simple mimesis: in focusing not on what the text says, but on what it does not say through its resistance to the conventional skeleton of the plot. As important is the simultaneously structural and psychic mechanism by which the ending is produced. For the recurrence of the accident should not be read as simply another stage in the plot but also in terms of what Jameson calls the form of content,[52] or in terms of a deformation of content that shifts attention from the event itself in the phenotext to its *structuring* as return or repetition. The event itself, Augustus's death, is not particularly surprising. If we think of an ending as a text's self-conscious recognition of what has already happened emotionally, Augustus's death is simply the plot's delayed reaction to his departure from Emma's life some years before. What is shocking is the way the story ends, with an uncanny repetition that foregrounds structure so as to make form as symptom take the place of content. In marking its structural mechanisms in this way, the narrative knots the signified within the signifier, so that one must attend not only to what the text says but also to the form in which the abortion of Emma's passion is communicated—an abortion literalized in Montague's murder of his child. This mechanism is all the more conspicuous because it involves a rewriting of the novel's pre-text, in which the circumstances of Hays's meeting with Frend and the eventual dissolution of their relationship are much less remarkable.

As a signifier, the mechanism of repetition is highly overdetermined. On one level, the fact that Augustus departs from Emma's life in the same way he entered it brings the plot full circle. This circularity has the function of purgation as well as closure: the end returns to the beginning to correct it, by disposing of Augustus and correcting Emma's initial error. But on another level this confusion of beginnings and endings within the motif of the return undoes the entire project of ending. It is not simply that the second accident reawakens Emma's passion for Augustus, contaminating the present with the past. It also reopens the whole issue of passion as the material site of women's struggles. For does Emma's "error" consist in choosing sensibility over sense, or is it in the fact that the Idea, as Hegel calls it, has not found an adequate embodiment in Augustus or in the social form or the disavowal that he signifies? As the locus of something unfinished, the repetition of the accident is connected to other forms of repetition: to the novel itself as memoir or return, and to autonarration as the author's return to her past. Repetition is most obviously a form of obsession: a return to something that cannot be disposed of because it has not yet been worked through. But it is also an occasion for revision, and in this sense it is linked to another instance of repetition in the novel, the repetition of the first generation in the second. This figure, which was to become increasingly common in nineteenth-century narrative, often signifies the taming and attenuation of the past in the present, as in Frankenstein's repetition as Walton or in the return of Heathcliff and Cathy as their Victorian children.[53] The repetition of Emma's letters as her memoirs purports on one level to be just such an act of self-taming. But given the curious reversal by which it is the present that functions as a shadowy type of the past in these texts and not vice versa, the typological drive that mobilizes repetition remains curiously unfulfilled, making the figure the site of a lack. As a moment of irresolution and unfulfillment, repetition figures the survival of desire within the asceticism imposed by the symbolic order, infecting or affecting the reader with this desire, by making reading into another form of repetition. The link between repetition as a motif in the plot and the functioning of the figure on a hermeneutic and narrative level is explicitly made through Emma's forwarding of her memoirs to Augustus Jr., who, as inscribed reader, embodies the potential for repetition as re-vision and, as Emma's male surrogate, embodies repetition as the impossibility of progress.

Central to autonarration is its implication of the reader in the continuation of its semiosis. The genre is thus part of Romanticism's construction of itself as incomplete, *à venir*, a legacy to the future formed and deformed in history and rethought through its reading. The question of reading is in the forefront of Hays's novel because of its semiepistolary format. Emma conveys the story of her passion as opposed to her official history through letters; indeed, passion and rationality are divided between letters and plot. Epistolarity as a form has been much discussed over the years. It is seen by Kauffman as a discourse of desire. It is commonly associated with dissenting groups and with a transgression of the boundary between public and private that allows what cannot be said in public to be voiced, though not quite in public.[54] In this sense it takes issue with the Enlightenment public sphere's assumption, made explicit by Habermas, that even private feelings exist for the convenience of the public.[55] While the epistolary mode is thus endowed with a sense of agency, it is also often seen as a form of solipsistic powerlessness or is approached through a vocabulary of presence and absence that emphasizes the textuality and supplementary status of the letter.[56]

To be sure, Emma's letters reflect and confirm her marginality and ineffectuality. They also say what the proper lady is not supposed to say and thus seek to renegotiate the terms of the social contract. Emma herself draws attention both to the precariousness of her position and the advantages of the letter when she says of her correspondence with Francis that she can express herself "with more freedom on paper" (73). For her meetings with Francis are in the company of others, and even her few private walks with him are constrained by an uncertainty about his relationship to the existing social order. Writing to him without these constraints, she can write to a subject dialectically split between the real and the ideal, between what he is and what he could be. Moreover, letters were not necessarily read only by the person to whom they were addressed, and for women they occupied a space midway between the private and public in the information network.[57] Hays kept drafts of some letters. She not only wrote to Frend but also wrote about her relationship with him in letters to Godwin, who was not just a friend but also the author of *Political Justice*. As such Godwin occupied a position whose ambiguity blurred the boundary between personal and public, thus allowing his correspondent a strategic enunciative position on that boundary. Moreover, Hays's letters may also have been read by Wollstonecraft, who read her novel and at times criticized Godwin for his masculine response to Hays.[58] In publishing the novel Hays formalized what had already happened in her writing of the letters; she placed her situation and her responses to it within a communicative circuit that was not confined to the addressees of the letters or the designated reader(s) of the novel.

But this circuit is not simply an external, phenotextual circuit involving full-fledged subjects, which aims at a pragmatic effect such as the creation of a female public sphere. It is also an intrapsychic, genotextual circuit involved in the work of the negative. Taking up the original version of this chapter, which focuses on autonarration as the transference of desire to a reader who is required to be as implicated in the text as the writer, Mary Jacobus asks "just what kind of transposition" the "epistolary and novelistic transfer involve[s]." She suggests that the epistolary form sets up a psychoanalysis that is both analogous to an "Enlightenment practice of self-analysis" and (more troubling) to a circulation of fantasies that broaches the limits of this enlightenment. In other words, for Jacobus the analyst-analysand dyad of Hays's correspondence with Godwin, mapped onto "the in-between form of the memoir and the letter-novel," opens up the text as itself an "intermediate state" or "in-between world": a "potential space" as D. W. Winnicott terms it in "Transitional Objects and Transitional Phenomena." As Jacobus suggests, this in-betweenness of the epistolary form "redefines the relation between actual and possible worlds as the space of the literary,"[59] of *poiesis* as the chaotic or unbound potentiality covered over by culture. This potential space, as Winnicott goes on to describe it, is an "intermediate territory between 'inner psychic reality' and 'the external world as perceived by two persons in common,'" two fully formed phenotextual subjects. It is "not *inside,*" but neither "is it *outside,* that is to say it is not a part of the repudiated world, the not-me, that which the individual has decided to recognize (with whatever difficulty and even pain) as truly external."[60] Hays herself acknowledges the deliberate in-betweenness of the "delirious" and "insane" state (L, 239)—the resistance to reality testing—unleashed in her letters, when she insists that it is irrelevant whether the object of love "be generated" upon "a real or fancied, foundation" (240). And when she insists that it does not matter "whether abstractedly consider'd . . . a misfortune be worthy of the names, substantial and real, if the consequences are the same" (238). For at some level the body, as Foucault says, is "the inscribed surface of events . . . totally imprinted by history and the process of history's destruction of the body,"[61] which is to say that the body, impressed as it is with the biopower of the "distemper'd civilization" against which Hays chafes in her letters (239), is an archive of experiences that one is driven to have, neurotically, imaginatively, even when they lack an adequate objective correlative, and because the paranoia of sensibility has a cognitive value.

Interestingly, Winnicott identifies what he calls potential space—which, I suggest, is a space not only of possibility but also of trauma and the potentiality of trauma—with the "whole cultural field." It is thus "the paradoxical location" both of culture and the "madness" that culture is and creates when "an adult puts too powerful a claim on the credulity of others, forcing them to acknowledge a sharing of illusion that is not their own." For Winnicott this madness "simply means a *break up* of whatever may exist at the time of *a personal continuity of existence.*"[62] Francis also uses the word "madness" of Emma (*M.* 169), as does Hays of herself, acceding to the way others see her "in the 18th century" (L, 240). But Hays's claim, in the context of an autonarration whose author is "ever talking of myself" (246), is that hers is a "madness" we must fictionally accept as ours: "With the apostle Paul, permit me to say—'I am not mad, but speak the words of truth & soberness'" (244). Hays's "madness" is the anamorphic disclosure of the madness of culture. Yielding to this madness in her letters, Emma/Hays is allowed to become a part-subject: she becomes a specialist in just one thing, which she practices almost as a profession. For as Hays writes to Godwin, provocatively paralleling her pursuit of Frend with his writing of *Political Justice:* "My pursuit, being ardent, has call'd forth energies & talents suitable to it—yours has done the same. They are streams, rising from the same fountain, but parting at their source & winding different ways" (248). As she also insists, arguing against Godwin's dismissal of her heroine's narcissism, "a hopeless, per-severing, & unrequited, attachment" is not in itself "uninteresting" but is proof of a "lively & strong imagination . . . an unconquerable spirit" (251). We can call this spirit "fanaticism" (251), but for Hays *poiesis* and fanaticism are not so easily separated as Keats claims at the beginning of *The Fall of Hyperion,* before his distinction between poets and dreamers/fanatics begins to collapse.[63]

For Winnicott the borderline space between imagination and fanaticism opened up in Emma's letters is navigated by "play"—which, I would further suggest, includes playing with one's misery—a word Keats also uses of his dreamer (*Fall of Hyperion,* 1.149). Describing play as something observable in childhood but by no means confined to it, Winnicott sees it as a form of *poiesis* without which "the child is unable to see the world creatively" and is "thrown back on compliance and a sense of futility." If the intimate letter dis-integrates the fully fledged subject in a way that Francis resists (and with which he can deal only by disappearing at key points),[64] narrative puts in play the materials that are thereby un-bound. Importantly play is not innocent but involves "aggression and destructiveness": Emma's insistent thrusting of her obsessions onto Fran-cis, her readers, and even herself; or Hays's substitute killing of Augustus, Montague, his child, and her own child. In play an object (or a character) can be "destroyed and restored"; "hurt and mended": "given away" as unsatisfactory (like Francis), yet also "kept" in reserve; or "killed and brought alive,"[65] like Augustus Sr., who is (both nostalgically and sadistically) revived as Augustus Jr. Following Winnicott I suggest that narrative as an autogenerative mechanism puts in play the traits, positions, and syntagms that narratology reifies as a *langue*. Interestingly, the second term in Winnicott's descriptions of play is always affirmative, which speaks to a certain utopianism in what he notes as the "destructiveness" of play and in what psychoanalysis after Klein refers to as "bad feelings."[66] But whereas for Winnicott, as for Klein, the construction of others as part-objects is always transitional to their reapprehension as whole objects, the aggression of narrative serves as a form of deconstruction that remains fundamentally unfinished.

It is likewise with the characters figured as intratextual readers and with whom the text plays as a focus of transference. For a discussion of *Memoirs* as a letter to the reader that breaches our enlightenment must begin with a curious anomaly about the readers inscribed *in* the text. The novel in so many ways calls for a female reader. But while Maria in Wollstonecraft's *Wrongs* writes her memoirs for her daughter and then redirects them to both Darnford and Jemima, Emma's readers are exclusively male. And Wollstonecraft was critical of Hays at the beginning of her career for her "fawning dependence" on men.[67] However, the turn to Augustus Jr. should not be read phenotextually, as the positing of an actual addressee, but rather tropologically, as a turning away or an "aversion," whose role in the work of the negative I analyze in the next chapter. For in writing to her daughter, Wollstonecraft's Maria turns to the future, but she also returns sentimentally and traumatically to someone whose fate may repeat her own and who never becomes present in the diegesis even to the point of acquiring a name. Recognizing this aporia, the narrative of *Wrongs* plays with the possibility of disposing of the daughter, albeit in the form of a disavowal that conventionally mourns her loss.[68] More decisively but no less ambivalently than Wollstonecraft, Hays turns against the disempowerment imposed by domesticity by killing off Emma's daughter and ending this episode of her life with a perfunctory sentimentalization of motherhood. Yet in so doing she does not turn to the male reader, be it the liberal male reader figured as Francis or the future reader figured as Augustus Jr. Rather, she turns to the wounded masculine in herself: to that part of herself that cannot survive except by figuring itself as male.[69] To evoke a line that Hays quotes from Christina, Queen of Sweden: "I would become a *man*," "but it is not that I love men because they are men, but merely that they are not women."[70]

This is to say that the recourse to a male reader must also be taken in conjunction with the fact that the novel's three male protagonists are all hurt but not mended, destroyed but not yet restored. These failures displace Emma's investment in the masculine to the level of a temporary and uncertain signifier. Of the three Francis is the most salvageable. Because Francis (unlike Augustus Sr.) is given epistolary voice in the text and because he does not die but (dis)appears, the Godwinian position is kept in reserve as itself open to changes that we do in fact see after 1798. Significantly, in her responses to the real Godwin's criticisms, Hays continues to appeal to the unfinished narrativity, the "strong feelings" (L, 229), or bad feelings, of *Caleb Williams*.[71] On the other hand, the dismissal of Francis, once he has served his purpose as a stimulus for Emma's ideas, intimates that the male reader is less the text's designated reader than a trans-position that is still being worked out. In short, by gendering her addressee as male Emma allows *herself* a trans-position from which she can be heard. Both positions (those of the addressee and the writer) fluctuate even within the space of the novel, with the ambiguous supplementation of Francis by Augustus Jr. For Francis is characterized in sufficient detail to limit what Emma can say to him. Although she pushes against those limits by pleading her passion as well as discussing it rationally, Francis, as he is "*pro tempore*" in 1797,[72] cannot really hear Emma. Yet perhaps Godwin does hear Hays a year later in publishing as part of Wollstonecraft's posthumous works a correspondence with Imlay that resembles Hays/Emma's correspondence with Augustus/Frend, thus putting into question the representation of Wollstonecraft as a rational Female Philosopher less prone to sensibility than Hays. Unlike Francis, Augustus Jr. takes no significant part in the novel's action, and we have no way of guessing his responses. For a moment, then, his extradiegetic status lets him figure the possibility of a reading not constrained by things as they are. Yet at the same time the haunting of this extradiegetic reader by the name of his father means that what the turn to her adopted son allows Emma to do is painfully—and consciously—knotted into what it disables her from doing. For this reader requires Emma to survive in a space that remains Symbolic because it must still accept or, more precisely, adopt the syntax of kinship and family structures. The (re)turn to Augustus, in other words, is itself tropological: a narrative syntagm that Emma/Hays is backed into using as a way of preserving a desire that the plot has invalidated. And Emma's frustration with this stratagem makes itself felt in an anger towards this "rash young man" (*M*, 41) that is by no means explained by her chagrin over his futile desire for a woman pledged to another man.

It is therefore important to remember that Augustus Jr. is only the temporary addressee of the memoirs. The memoirs forwarded to him are "extracted" from "preceding materials" requested by Francis, in which Emma had both "dr[awn] up a sketch of events" of her "past life" and "unfolded a history of the sentiments of [her] mind." They are not in the first case written for Augustus, the very repetition of whose paternal name marks the name as a placeholder. Nor can we assume that the earlier "manuscript" (168) took the composed form of memoirs. But whatever it may have been, in its transmission both to Francis and to Augustus Jr. the original text's "close-twisted . . . associations" have been "torn" from Emma (167, 41; cf. L, 239), deformed by the phrase regimes to which they have had to submit. Hays draws attention to this process of phrasing, to which we shall return in the last chapter, by her very compositional technique, wherein she literally cuts and pastes sentences from her real letters into the letters written by her fictional character. In so doing she links her novel back to an archive, the deepest layer of which remains invisible, like the earliest, anarchival "manuscript" of her text, which is the primal scene of her autonarration. An archive in the sense explored by Derrida, who says that despite the absence of a clear "concept" for this archive, in the wake of Freudian psychoanalysis we can no longer conceive of archivization as we previously did, according to a purely "economic principle" of the "accumulation and capitalization of memory." For after Freud, the archive is marked by what Derrida calls the "Freudian impression," in the triple sense of the impression made by Freud and psychoanalysis on "the concept of the archive and of archivization"; the impression "*left*" by the subject—Freud for example—which includes "the impression *left* in him"; and impression as a form of printing or imprinting, which makes the body and the sedimented traces impressed on it part of an archive that includes the body, the texts that write it, and the forms by which it imprints itself back on culture.[73]

It is in these last two senses that Hays also repeatedly uses the word "impression" in evoking a Godwinian account of the "outward impressions" or circumstances that leave their "unavoidable" imprint on the subject (L, 244). For in Godwin's understanding of character as the impression of circumstances, the *mechanical* aspect both of the imprinting of culture on the body and the body's resistance to this biopower, which Godwin draws from associationist psychology and which Hays calls "the stubborn mechanism of the mind" (L, 239), is analogous to the *typographical* aspect of Derrida's theory of the Freudian impression. Godwin's empiricist account of the mind as mechanism, in other words, functions as a figure for archival effects in excess of any discourse of perfectibility that aims to liberate us from our mind-forged manacles. Printing her text so as to imprint it on the reader's psyche, Hays allows narrative to be the site of what Derrida calls a "general archiviology" of these effects.[74] They are not, she suggests, limited to the impression of culture onto the subject, as "without such impression," Hays asks, "shou'd we be anything?" For impression, as Hays sees it, is not simply a form of determinism, the disciplining of the docile body. It is also a "capabilit[y] of receiving forcible impressions," of "*receiving* sensation" and responding to it. "Into what channels this shall be directed, depends not on ourselves." But even if these channels are unpredictable, the process is productive of "strong feelings & strong energies" and is thus the site of a certain invention (229, 244; emphasis mine). Yet invention risks ossifying into institution if, as Percy Shelley says, "no new poets should arise to create afresh the associations" that have become "disorganized" (*DP,* 512). For Hays, then, her autonarrative work as the protection of those "close-twisted . . . associations" that are regimented by plot (*M,* 167; cf. L, 239), is part of a care of the self that, even as it is in excess of itself, is aimed at an unworking of institution. This care or "self-exercise," according to Foucault, "involve[s] taking notes on oneself to be reread, writing treatises and letters to friends . . . and keeping notebooks to reactivate for oneself the truths one need[s]."[75] For Hays it involves an archivization of both her text and her letters as the record of the impressions imprinted on her body and the imprinting of that body on the text. As Derrida says, this archivization includes "'repression' and 'suppression.'" But it also involves a "movement of the promise and of the future no less than of recording the past" and therefore "carries an unknowable weight," which does not "weigh only as a negative charge."[76]

As an alibi for Emma to archive and pass on her text, the younger Augustus is also "the sacred deposit" of "an adored and lost friend" and of Emma's own past (M, 41). "Deposit" means both that this past is preserved yet somehow (de)posited in Augustus's son and that Emma deposits in him the archiviological project that impels narrative. Through the younger Augustus, then, Emma opens a space for further reading in this complex sense that entwines memory and promise. But she also disengages us from identifying with the novel's intratextual readers, using them only to create a certain readability, a reading-function within the text, but discarding her actual addressees. For at the risk of stating the obvious, *Memoirs* is a *text*. And as Kristeva says of the text, it retains the "analytic situation's requirement that the process of the subject be realized in language," with the result that its "designated addressees . . . are often its focus of transference, its objects of seduction and *aggression*" (emphasis mine). But "the absence of a *represented* focal point of transference," such as the flesh-and-blood analyst, "prevents this process from becoming locked into an identification that can do no more than adapt the subject to social and family structures" (R, 209). To be sure, Emma claims a position from which she can be heard by figuring her addressee as male and transmitting her desire to "Augustus," whose story has come full circle, insofar as the narrative has conveniently moved the son into the position the father had disavowed. By passing on her story to Augustus Jr., Emma vindicates her rights as a desiring subject. But vindication, as Janet Gezari points out with regard to Charlotte Brontë, also involves a certain vindictiveness, which bespeaks the unfinishedness of its project:

> "Vindicate" has its roots in the Latin "vindicare," which means both
> to liberate and to avenge or punish. The Latin "vindicta," which is
> the root of "vindictive," literally refers to the rod with which the
> praetor touched the slave who was to be freed and can mean deliverance
> from something as well as vengeance of punishment. Although
> acts of vindication may be undertaken without punitiveness, our word

"vindictive" is properly applied only to punitive actions. But vindication, and especially self-vindication, is as easily charged with vindictiveness as self-defence is with defensiveness.[77]

This vindictiveness in *Memoirs* is not just towards the dead Augustus. Nor is it only towards the second Augustus, whom Emma does nothing but scold, perhaps because he does *not* understand her desire and can only blindly repeat it, because his passion for Joanna is on some level disappointing, like his father's sordid interlude with a foreign woman barred, like Joanna, from the text's potential space. Beyond her aggression towards "Augustus," Emma's vindication of her desire also entails a violence towards herself, which dis-figures what promises to be its triumphal transmission to her adopted son. The narrating of Emma's vindication, in short, brings out what is masked by the positivity of politics, what Godwin also discloses in juxtaposing the "wrongs" of woman against the title of the collection in which he includes Wollstonecraft's text: *Posthumous Works of the Author of "A Vindication of the Rights of Woman."* These wrongs are felt in what Peter Melville Logan calls a "complex incarcerated voice, which can only indicate itself by turning on itself" in a form of "self-violence."[78] The violence that unworks simply productive readings of the text—whether feminist and emancipatory or moral and didactic—is literalized in an ending riddled with collateral damage: the dead bodies of Augustus, Emma Jr., Rachel, Montague, and their child, figuring the ex-termination of all the scenarios that might close the text one way or another. Writing about Brontë and Austen, Virginia Woolf suggests that Austen got "infinitely more said" because she wrote "without hate, without bitterness . . . without protest, without preaching," all of which "deformed and twisted" Charlotte Brontë's work.[79] Hays, vindicating herself against similar charges from Godwin (L, 244, 250–56) allows that she has "spoiled [her] story" but will not rewrite it (254), for this very dis-figuration is what links it to an archive that demands further reading.

CHAPTER FOUR

The Scene of Judgment

Trial and Confession in Godwin's Caleb Williams *and Other Fiction*

WHAT DOES POLITICAL JUSTICE MEAN, when the text by this name insists that we think justice beyond institutions and so beyond or before the political? And how does narrative allow us to think before the universality of institution? Though Godwin's *Enquiry Concerning Political Justice* deals extensively with the ideological and repressive state apparatuses that are part of the limited realm of objective spirit in Hegel's analysis of civil society, for Godwin the political must constantly be made responsible to individual reason and conscience, which is to say ethics, or "spirit" in a more expansive sense. Refusing to separate political and moral science,[1] Godwin unworks all categorical imperatives by emphasizing the differences that impede judging even similar cases uniformly. "No two crimes," he insists, "were ever alike; and therefore the reducing them . . . to general classes, which the very idea of example implies, is absurd" (*PJ*, 2.347). To judge a crime by the act is simple enough. Yet as Godwin insists, in dissociating exteriority as mechanism from an unknowable interiority, "Man, like every other machine the operations of which can be made the object of our senses, may, in a certain sense, be affirmed to consist of two parts, the external and the internal. The form which his actions assume is one thing; the principle from which they flow is another. With the former it is possible we should be acquainted; respecting the latter there is no species of evidence that can adequately inform us" (2.348).

If we judge a man by his actions, we fail to take into account his intentions, but if we base our judgment on intention our analysis becomes, and must become, "unlimited" (2.350). The only categorical imperative that survives this analysis is the dissolution of government, of institutions. But institution ultimately means not just social and political structures but also anything that has been instituted, including concepts with public and collective authority. Indeed, Godwin often uses "institution" in the singular to connote the activity as well as products of normalization: "positive institution" is the process by which obedience is compelled, sometimes through "positive law" but sometimes in more invisible ways (1.175–78). As such, positive institution is not unlike what Michel Foucault calls discourse. Given this broad use of the term, a theory of the dissolution of institutions can found political theory only as the most radical, unlimited form of deconstruction. Or in Godwin's words, if "government" goes beyond the "public institutions" to which we commonly attach its effects and power, and "insinuates itself" into the arts and even into "our personal dispositions" and "most secret retirements," if government is an attitude, who "shall define the extent of its operation" (1.4–6) and thus the work of dissolving what Foucault calls "governmentality"?[2]

First published just three years after Immanuel Kant's *Critique of Judgment* (1790), Godwin's *Enquiry Concerning Political Justice* has much in common with the Kantian project of critique, as Henry Crabb Robinson already recognized in 1802, and as Franz Von Baader, who visited Scotland, also saw.[3] For it is not so much a key work of liberal evolutionism as a critique of judgment at the site of practical reason in its intersection with institutional rationality. Godwin shares Kant's extension of the term "judgment" to the very *habitus* of thought as the relating of particular cases to universal rules.[4] Of course, Kant uses "judgment" philosophically while Godwin, as a political theorist, focuses on government, including the law. But this should not obscure the fact that for Godwin too the judicial system merely crystallizes a larger process of "judgment," which is at work throughout public and private life. And Godwin, unlike Kant, does not separate public and private. Repudiating the view that "positive institutions ought to leave me free in matters of conscience, but may properly interfere with my conduct in civil concerns" (*PJ*, 1.175), Godwin takes a very different view from Kant's notion of "enlightenment" as freedom of thought but not necessarily freedom of conduct.[5] Godwin's use of the term "judgment" extends to education, not to mention literature. Arguing against a system of national education that would institutionalize current opinion, he insists that "no vice can be more destructive than that which teaches us to regard any judgment as final" (2.300). Judgment must always be individual and infinitely self-differing. Democracy, the judgment of the people, is the tyranny of the majority. Thus Godwin criticizes "national assemblies" because of the uniformity of opinion they impose in finally bringing things to a vote phrased in some way that suppresses differences: "A multitude of men, after all our ingenuity, will still remain a multitude of men" (2.204–5). For Godwin, who thus anticipates Jean-Luc Nancy's critique of "society" as distinct from "community,"[6] any collectivity, party, or group interferes with the individual's relation to his own conscience (2.203). Juries are collectives that are at least more local than national assemblies, and Godwin does indeed prefer judgment by "juries" to the decisions by a magistrate that occur in *Caleb Williams*. But even juries are flawed because they must finally reach a decision: the ideal jury for Godwin would be one that "invite[s]" rather than "decide[s]," that "recommend[s] a certain mode of adjusting controversies, without assuming the prerogative of dictating that adjustment" (2.211).

Godwin's reservations about "decision" are pursued in a more purely philosophic way by Kant. Kant rethought the finality of judgments by distinguishing between determinant judgment, which subsumes particular cases under established rules, and reflective judgment, in which "only the particular is given, for which the universal is to be found" (*CJ*, 67). The absence of this universal means that judgment is not bound to things as they are. On the other hand, for the ever-cautious Kant it also means that such judgments cannot be grounded: the reflective judgment operates by a "transcendental" principle that it can "only give itself . . . as a law, and cannot derive . . . from anywhere else" (67). Godwin, too, faced this dilemma at the very heart of a Dissenting tradition that included Rational Dissenters and sectarian fanatics: namely, that if individuals must judge according to their own conscience through the law that Reason gives itself, then Reason risks being a form of autoaffection. But for Godwin more than Kant, who is still uneasy with not privileging determination, judgment must always be reflective if thought is not to be determined by prejudice. One cannot separate public "conduct" from "conscience" or "private judgment," to which public conduct is always answerable (*PJ*, 1.175). Reason can nevertheless avoid autoaffection, but only by making (self)reflection "unlimited" (2.350).

Kant's separation of reflective from determinant judgment corresponds to a further distinction he makes between ideas of Reason and concepts of the understanding, in which concepts determine thought in terms of what we already know, while ideas (such as the "idea(l)" of freedom) lack this specificity and are a basis for future reflection. Kant's example of an idea in *The Critique of Pure Reason* is Plato's Republic, which is an idea inasmuch as "in experience nothing perfectly corresponding to [it] could be found."[7] Among Kant's own utopian ideas are the ideals of cosmopolitan history and the "league of peace," which later became the basis for the League of Nations: ideas developed in his political essays, some of which were translated by John Richardson in 1798–99,[8] leading the *Anti-Jacobin* to see Kant as a dangerous radical. These ideas, and the very notion of the idea, form a further ground of affinity with Godwin, as political justice is also an "Idea" of Reason, not to be limited by established concepts or institutions. The Kantian idea, as something "to come," has been important for a continental tradition of thinking about justice that includes Jacques Derrida and Jean-François Lyotard. For Derrida, the Kantian idea is nevertheless limited by being the infinite abstraction into the future of an ideal, such as cosmopolitan history, whose content cannot or need not be worked on now but whose contours we already know. Derrida thus complains that the idea is both "too futural," in not "think[ing] the deferral of difference in terms of 'now,'" and it is not futural enough," in already knowing "what tomorrow should be."[9] Derrida in effect criticizes Kant for putting off into the infinite future the task of thinking through the inadequacies of the idea, while already deciding what the idea presently is and thus predetermining this future.

Regardless of whether Derrida is correct,[10] Godwin too would fall into this bad infinity as premature utopianism if we literalized his idea of the dissolution of government as the disappearance of all civil structures. This anarchism (a notion about which Godwin is ambivalent) would then be a position determined in advance of all reflection, even if its arrival is infinitely deferred; it would be its own form of institution.[11] Yet political justice, I suggest, is the process rather than the product of reflective judgment. It is not a position but the ongoing work of unworking that which, in the very taking of positions, fails to do justice to the other, through a sceptical sifting of all positions in terms of their discursive exclusions. The dissolution of government is in this sense a kind of *poiesis*, as Shelley was to suggest in evoking Christ and Plato as poets (*DP*, 524–25). If Godwin's text does sometimes seem to urge an actual dissolution of government, this projection knows itself to be a form of romance. For as Derrida also concedes, one cannot entirely dispense with the Kantian idea,[12] nor can one do without the romance of a just future as provocation and inspiration.

Indeed, in his intricately deconstructive essay "Of History and Romance," written for a second edition of the *Enquirer* in the year he revised *Political Justice* but never published, Godwin provocatively claims that the romance writer is the true historian. He promotes a romance dedicated to ideas over a history organized by concepts, only to then turn round and make the "bold outlines" of romance accountable to the minute shades of particular situations and characters.[13] In effect, if romance is the poetry in history, Godwin also finds in the realism at the heart of prose a texture that thwarts the structural discipline of the Novel and makes poetry as negative capability the "Idea" of prose. It is thus fiction or narrative, in its exploration of these minute, realistic particulars, that Godwin sees as forcing us to confront the problem of political *justice*, of institutions that are just, in the present. At the same time justice "now" will always seem impossible, since the political or moral is always a position, that is to say, an imposition. Thus we need the romance of theory in *Political Justice* as a horizon against which to think the aporia of the term "political" justice within a negative dialectic: all the more so in the deeply pessimistic later fiction. Indeed, Godwin still speaks of *Political Justice* as his "favourite work" years later when he had profoundly qualified its theoretical fantasies.[14] These fantasies or romances should not be seen as ones that Godwin literally imagined attaining. For fantasy, as Slavoj Žižek argues, is a form of "Kantian transcendental schematism in that it merely "constitutes our desire, provides its coordinates," and "teaches us how to desire."[15]

Through their use of the tropes of trial and confession, Godwin's novels all foreground the aporia between the political or morality (as distinct from ethics) and justice, between passing judgment and truly doing justice to the other. This difference can also be seen as one between the Novel as a form of Hegelian objective spirit and narrative as answerable to the subject. For in what follows I argue that Godwin puts on trial the very genre of the Novel as judgment: the very reaching of a moral decision formalized by "deciding" or resolving the plot. In the process he also submits our own ability to constitute ourselves as whole subjects through the power of judgment to a kind of "madness," to evoke Ross Woodman's term. Godwin's novels are often significantly unended. *Mandeville,* which deals with the confused history of the Cromwellian period, positions itself as written at the end of the protagonist's life, from a position of mature repentance. But it breaks off traumatically in the aftermath of Charles Mandeville's assault on the triumphal marriage coach carrying his sister Henrietta and his rival, Clifford, on the threshold of the Restoration. Godwin had planned four volumes, but the novel, as one nineteenth-century reader put it, "instead of *ending . . .* breaks off in the middle,"[16] with the defacement of Charles's face in the assault. *Fleetwood,* Godwin's earlier novel about misogynistic domestic relations, ends disappointingly by promising and withdrawing a reconciliation between Fleetwood and his wife, Mary. And finally *Caleb Williams,* even as it seems committed to the "decisiveness of a trial,"[17] has two endings. These refusals of a definitive ending make it difficult to use the concluding of the plot as a way of drawing conclusions. A political criticism, a literary criticism that reads for political conclusions either by identifying Godwin with some form of critique or subjecting him *to* a critique, is also at issue here, since such criticism is a form of institution. In *Political Justice* Godwin raises the question of literature as the dissolution of juridical institutions, in terms that recall his own use of narrative in his first novel, *Things as They Are; or, The Adventures of Caleb Williams.* Insisting that judgment must be the right of judgment we exercise over judgment itself, Godwin writes of the judgment elicited by the difference between the "narratives" of condemned criminals and the "construction that was put upon them by their judges" (*PJ,* 2.276, 354). He thus gives literature the role of a critique of judgment. But the burden of his fiction, I suggest, is that the critique so generated, the critique we judge literature to have produced, is itself inscribed in the very work it institutes: that of narrative as a genealogy, even archiviology, of morals and a process of unlimited reflection.

Issues of law, libel, and punishment raised in *Political Justice* are pursued throughout *Caleb Williams,* which is concerned with the stories we construct about others and ourselves, with the self-interest of interpretation, and with judgment and justice. There are two stories in play, Caleb's and Falkland's, the latter also largely conveyed by Caleb who says, somewhat ingenuously, that to " avoid confusion . . . I shall drop the person of Collins, and assume myself to be the historian of our patron" (*CW,*

66).[18] But here it might be useful to distinguish between stories within the text and narrative as its overall mode. I use the term "narrative" to suggest something more complex than a story: the process by which this story is produced, which puts the story itself, in Julia Kristeva's phrase, *en procès:* in process/on trial. A story according to Godwin is a form of rhetoric, told "with great artifice and appearance of consistency" (437). The stories of Caleb and Falkland are fictionalized arguments, which aim at a vindication of their authors; they are speech acts, and Godwin, as Angela Esterhammer has shown, was highly suspicious of speech acts.[19] By contrast, narrative, according to Lyotard, "recounts a differend or differends." Lyotard's comments on narrative occur in the course of his larger discussion of the differend as the catalyst for an (im)possible justice foreclosed by the institutions of the public sphere. The paradigmatic structure for this foreclosure is the binarism of the law, even when it operates by what Godwin calls the enlightened "maxim of hearing both sides" (*CW,* 403). For a differend occurs when there is "a case of conflict, between (at least) two parties," that "cannot be equitably resolved" within the law "for lack of a judgment applicable to both arguments." A differend is something that cannot be put into "phrases" because the parties lack a shared language in which their claims can be adjudicated.[20] The differend, I suggest, occurs with particular intensity in narrative, because of what Lyotard calls an "unleashing of the now" (*D,* 151–52), wherein the "event," in its sheer affective and motivational complexity, exceeds its syntagmatic reduction within the plot. Or as Godwin says, in elaborating on the way his novels unfold as analyses of "the private and internal operations of the mind," the "folds of the human heart" and "the endless intermixture of motive with motive, make it difficult to determine "which of these has the greatest effect in producing" a given outcome that would reduce "event" to summarizable "action."[21]

In the end Lyotard sees narrative as an institution of the public sphere that closes down the differend, because he does not associate the event with the logic of the narrative genre. Rather, he equates the epistemology of narrative with a reading for plot in which "the occurrence, with its potentiality [*puissance*] of differends . . . is domesticated by the recurrence of the before/after" (152). The event, in other words, is absorbed by a sequencing and causality that selectively reduces the emotionally charged and overdetermined impact of the "now."[22] Godwin too is aware of "the diachronic operator, or operator of successivity" (152), which results in "incident follow[ing] upon incident, in a kind of breathless succession" (*CW*, 210) that "'swallows up' the event and the differends carried along by the event" (*D*, 152). Nevertheless, for Godwin literature is a medium in which we move beyond this considering of "every incident in its obvious sense," to turn the story "a thousand ways, and examine it in every point of view," so that what begins as "distinct and satisfactory" gradually becomes "mysterious" (*CW*, 179–80). The words are Caleb's as he describes his response to Collins' history of Falkland. But they apply equally to Caleb's own story or to whatever story we construct from Godwin's narrative. In Godwin's account, then, literature is a form of intension that makes the "*enjambement*" we found in poetry part of the legacy of prose: a legacy paradoxically inscribed in the very realism and sobriety of the novel. The process Godwin describes is the reverse of the one projected by Shlomith Rimmon-Kenan when she writes: "Just as any single event may be decomposed into a series of mini-events and intermediary states, so—conversely—a vast number of events may be subsumed under a single event-label."[23] For Godwin, by contrast, narrative calls into question the institution of interpretation by decomposing the event into the minute "particulars"—or in Hays's terms, "the close-twisted associations"—that unsettle the event-label that facilitates the absorption of texture into structure (HR, 458).

If stories subordinate the event to a structure, or "moral" as Godwin call it in "Of Choice in Reading," it is the *reading* of stories, foregrounded by the way the novel thematizes their mediation and transmission, that reactivates the differend closed down by the plot. Hence Godwin's theorization of an "individual" (rather than a general) reading anchored in private judgment as a magnetic field of unstable elective affinities that opens up the "event": "We go forth into the world . . . and when we return home and engage in the solemn act of self-investigation, our must useful employment is to produce the materials we have collected abroad, and, by a sort of magnetism, cause those particulars to start out to view in ourselves, which might otherwise have lain forever undetected" (HR, 455).The *stories* of Caleb and Falkland each claim to tell the whole truth and nothing but the truth. But because it contains so many different stories, the *narrative*, though told by Caleb, becomes a magnetic field of interactions between characters, and characters and readers, that is in excess of Caleb's actual story. By the end, then, the "plain and unadulterated tale" that Caleb promises has become a "half-told and mangled tale," which must be repeatedly discarded and rewritten, to the point that the very ending of the story is written and then crossed out (*CW*, 431, 434). The problem of doing justice has to do with this difference, or differend, between "tale" or "story"—terms that Godwin repeatedly foregrounds[24]—and the more complex chemistry of a narrative that puts them in process/on trial. And the figure for this process is the trunk that is never opened, which makes the ex-tension of the story a perpetual supplement to the in-tension of narrative. Indeed, Caleb concedes this supplementarity when he claims that if the "narrative" in the trunk "never see[s] the light," this "*story* of mine may amply, *severely* perhaps, supply its place" (423, emphasis mine).

Caleb's claim is made without any trace of irony. But Godwin's suspicion of stories is tied up with his profound distrust of any form of institution, any public declaration of a truth. A tale or story, for Godwin, seeks to be "plausible" (235) by seeming "consistent and complete" (254). But this completeness is achieved by entering "with minuteness" only into "some parts of the story" (436). Inasmuch as a story, to adapt Lyotard, is a legal "demonstration, by means of well-formed phrases and of procedures for establishing the existence of their referent" (*D*, 8), it is the phrases and procedures that establish the referent, these procedures being "consistency," "progress," and "probability" (*CW*, 179, 436). A story is thus not a recording of events but a performance that posits or imposes itself at the cost of a certain violence towards what it leaves out. Likewise, with the concept of "character" as a principle of predictability and totalization, which Godwin deconstructs when he has Caleb confess: "I have now no character" (434).[25] Both character and story have the same structure of institution as the various other linguistic or speech acts that Godwin distrusts as forms of imposition that curtail the free use of reason: namely, oaths, declarations, contracts, constitutions. Yet it is not the case that Godwin's suspicion of stories for being too well-made implies a truth above rhetoric that frustratingly eludes him in his fiction.[26] Rather, it is through the conflict of stories that we sense truth as the differend, the desire for justice, produced by its very misrepresentation.

The third volume of *Caleb Williams* might well seem to imply a clear truth beyond the (mis)representations of language. Here Caleb, as he flees the persecution of Falkland and Forrester, becomes the subject of the most preposterous stories, which the reader can easily reverse to produce the truth. In *Political Justice* Godwin seems to uphold precisely this simplicity of "the truth" when he argues against the censoring of libelous stories on the grounds that Reason will always find its way to truth (2.270, 274–76). But this argument must be read alongside his rebuttal of censorship in "Of Choice in Reading," wherein he claims that a text's meaning consists in its "tendency" rather than its "moral," thus suggesting that truth is by no means simple. The moral, according to Godwin, "may be defined to be that ethical sentence to the illustration of which the work may most aptly applied," but as in "the regular moral frequently annexed" to Aesop's fables, we generally find that this "lesson set down at foot of [the text], is one of the last inferences that would have occurred" to us. The tendency, by contrast, "is the actual effect . . . produce[d] upon the reader," and it "cannot be completely ascertained but by the experiment," since it will vary "according to the various tempers and habits of the persons by whom the work is considered." Restricting a text's circulation because of its moral or intention is futile because there is no correlation between moral and tendency: a pernicious work may have salutary effects and vice versa.[27] If a text is not what it says but what it does, a "praxis upon the nature of man" (HR, 461), then truth itself must be radically rethought. Truth cannot be something known in advance; it is rather the totality of a text's effects and the attempt to understand them, bearing in mind that even the most egregious misrepresentations may contain a grain of truth or produce some aspect of truth as their effect (*PJ,* 2.274).

From this perspective the third volume of *Caleb Williams* is not a demonstration *a contrario* that a firm truth exists. Nor is the choice between Caleb's own story and the falsehoods spread about him intended analogically to guide a choice between the stories of Caleb and those of Falkland. Rather, the proliferation of assumed identities, forgeries, and calumnies foregrounds the constant danger of misjudgment, the way judgment is never in-itself but is always tropologically constituted by a turning away or an aversion that becomes a turning towards or sympathy. Judgment is an effect, and it is only by rigorously scrutinizing the genealogy of such effects that we can arrive at truth as a tropological and contingent process: a differend. That truth is tropological, in the sense of trope as "turning," is an important point to stress. Thus the vindication of Caleb in the reader's mind, which occurs in the third volume, is produced by a turning away from, an aversion to the stories about him, rather than being based on the absolute justice of his conduct towards Falkland. Similarly, our judgment in Caleb's favor in the middle of the novel is tropologically produced by an aversion to Falkland's abuse of the judicial system. But this requires that we judge Falkland only by his actions rather than also by how these actions came about. And as Godwin suggests in his Preface to *Cloudesley:* "The folds of the human heart, the endless intermixture of motive with motive, and the difficulty of assigning which of these had the greatest effect in producing a given action . . . all render the attempt to pass a sound judgment upon the characters of men to a great degree impossible."[28] Thus, as we remember and work through to the beginnings of this narrative, we cannot avoid some sympathy for Falkland, based on the injustice of holding him responsible for the murder of someone who was so monstrously unjust, not only to him but to others for whom he was concerned. Yet this turning towards Falkland is itself unstably produced by a turning away from Caleb's overcharged curiosity: a curiosity we share, one that is not wholly without justice.

The resolution of reading in a judgment through bringing the plot to a decision is further complicated by the novel's genesis, which Godwin made part of its context. As he explains in his Preface to the standard edition of *Fleetwood* thirty-eight years later, though he wrote *Caleb Williams* in linear fashion, starting with the first volume, he imagined and first sketched it in reverse, proceeding from the third to the first volume. The third volume was conceived as a "series of adventures of flight and pursuit," built around the narratological dyad of "pursuer" and "victim" and oriented to plot and action. But in the second volume Godwin had to come up with a "dramatic and impressive situation adequate to account for" the pursuer's behavior, while in the first he employed his "metaphysical dissecting knife in tracing and laying bare the involutions of motive" behind this situation.[29] The work Godwin constructs in moving the plot forward to its conclusion thus contains its own deconstruction in the form of a pre-text, or "*avant-texte,*" the term that the editorial theorist Jean Bellemin-Noel coined, in his theory of genetic criticism, for the drafts and sketches that precede and underlie the text.[30] This *avant-texte* works back from a suspense story completely contained by the diegesis, and entirely under the sign of the diachronic operator, to a receding origin: the intricacies of Caleb's and Falkland's early relationship and beyond that, Falkland's history before the time of narration. Or, to evoke the terms Godwin will introduce in "Of History and Romance," the archeology set up by this *avant-texte* moves from a "general history" of the operations of power and political injustice in the third volume, to an "individual history," which follows each protagonist into his separate "closet" (453–55, 458). This archeology unravels the "external" mechanisms of the narrative and its ex-tension as story into the fundamental obscurity and in-tension of the characters' motives, about which "no species of evidence . . . can adequately inform us" (*PJ*, 2.348).

Moreover, it is not only a question of the "two or three sheets of demy writing-paper" assembled in reverse order to the text.[31] We would know nothing of this earlier compositional stage without Godwin's later account of the text' genesis. The *avant-texte* is therefore also an *après-texte*. This *après-texte*, or afterthought, decomposes the text, preventing it from being in-itself. It discloses a difference between the text's execution and conception, perhaps a difference within its very conception, and certainly a difference within the rules of structuration and formation that inform narrative. Thus, Godwin on the one hand takes credit for a consummately well-made story, which he describes at the level of its ex-tension. He claims a "great advantage in thus carrying back" his "invention from the ultimate conclusion to the first commencement" of his story. Knowing the end before the beginning, he suggests, allows him to construct "an entire unity of plot" as the "infallible result" of a cause-and-effect sequence culminating in a moral or ethical "sentence"—a word that brings together the moral and juridical aspects of interpretation.[32] On the other hand, Godwin confesses that the cause was invented after the effect and thus that the narrative arose as a process of supplementation in which a second volume had to be conceived to explain the third, and a first to explain the second. Not only does the structurality of the text's structure suggests a Humean *in*adequacy of cause to effect; our knowledge of the text's history also impedes any straightforward reading, compelling us to read forwards to a judgment to be arrived at in the concluding trial scene, and backwards to the psychological in-tensities of the protagonists' histories, which persist throughout the text as a ground of indecision about this judgment. This knowledge, in other words, impels us to read between the lines of the text, so as to turn the story around in "a thousand ways, and examine it in every point of view" (*CW*, 179).

The problem of judgment and justice comes to a head in the reflective process Godwin set in motion by concluding *Caleb Williams* and then completely changing the ending four days later. This reversal, which makes revision the engine of narrativity, reflects the way the text's writing has become for Godwin a form of self-reading that is known "only in the experiment." For if the original ending, which vindicates Caleb in the mode of defeat, is where the idea of the text had its inception, in writing towards this ending, Godwin finds that he cannot carry "back [his] invention from its ultimate conclusion to its commencement." Instead, the commencement renders the conclusion problematic, thus putting in jeopardy "the decisiveness of a trial" (169) and making it necessary to commence again from the end.

That both versions of the novel culminate in a trial because of Caleb's capital accusation against Falkland makes explicit an imperative built into all narrative, to resolve the plot, to reach a decision. But there is a curious redundancy in joining the textual to a legal decision, since we already know that Falkland is guilty of Tyrrell's murder. Why arrive at a conclusion at which we have already arrived? The decision demanded of the reader must therefore be of another kind: an ethical rather than a legal decision. This decision, however, is more difficult, since the ethical is the awareness of judgment as tropological and is a dis-integration of the subject constituted by judgment. For Caleb's need to proclaim Falkland's guilt publicly stands in place of, and is a supplement for, Caleb's innocence about which we, and even he, are less sure. However, were we to condemn Caleb for his excessive curiosity, this judgment too would simply turn away from the difficulty of excusing Falkland for letting the Hawkinses die for Tyrrel's murder, even if we understand, or forget, Falkland's murder of Tyrel. In concluding only to abruptly unravel his conclusion, Godwin therefore calls into question the very morality of the novel as a juridical form that enjoins its readers to reach a verdict.

This incommensurability of the ethical and the legal is not yet present in the original ending, which is still a critique of civil institutions, not of "institution" in general. Based on the original ending we can still treat the text as a "general history," focused on an individual *story* to be sure, but as an example or illustration of the "causes that operate universally upon masses of men" (HR, 454). The example, as Agamben argues, is "one singularity among others which, however, stands for each of them and serves for all," thus ultimately forgoing its "particularity."[33] In the original ending, which culminates a history of political injustice, Caleb is denied justice at the trial, is imprisoned, and sinks into despair and madness. Doing justice, for the reader, is a matter of reversing the law's injustice. Political justice, even if unattainable now, is something definite: the dissolution, literally or through critique, of the existing judicial and class system. Political justice in this ending can be decided within a discourse of rights that assumes damages rather than wrongs. Damages, as Lyotard explains, result from an injury done by one party to another within a shared discourse, and they can be repaired within the rules of that discourse (D, xi). The damage done to Caleb would thus be repaired by a public finding of Falkland's guilt, as Caleb assumes. But a wrong results from the differend that occurs when the two parties do not speak the same language or when the discourse in which the judgment is passed is not that of one of the parties (5), as would have been the case if Falkland had originally been convicted of Tyrrel's murder. Most importantly, though Lyotard does not say it, a wrong results when one is oneself an inhabitant of incommensurable "phrase regimens" (xii). A wrong is a wrong done to oneself and not just a wrong one suffers.

The wrongs involved in the dispute between Caleb and Falkland are multiple, and all the more so because we will inevitably translate them into the wrong phrases. "Wrongs," the word Godwin used in pairing Wollstonecraft's unfinished *Wrongs of Woman* with what he saw as her far less daring *Vindication of the Rights of Woman*,[34] cannot be the subject of a litigation within the public sphere because they cannot, or cannot yet, be redressed through rights. Falkland points to a wrong done when he asks, in response to Caleb's insistence on exposing his past, if "barren truth" is "entitled to adoration for its own sake, and not for the sake of the happiness it is calculated to produce" (CW, 384). One can dismiss Falkland's utilitarian argument as sophistry and his attachment to his reputation as shallow. But is reputation really the issue? "Reputation," to be sure, is the word Falkland uses to justify his conduct, and the term used by commentators to phrase Godwin's novel as a critique of the ancien régime. But reputation is simply an outward simulacrum for some part of truth that is lost if we "reduce" (330) Falkland to being only a murderer. At the same time, the wrong done to Caleb's concept of "truth" by Falkland's acquittal is as inestimable as the wrong done to Falkland in destroying his reputation. "Truth" too is a figure for the multiple losses that would result from leaving the case of Falkland alone, including the political loss of countenancing wrongs that could not occur if men such as Falkland did not hold absolute power. And yet Caleb betrays the extent to which truth for him is also an institution tied up with his reputation or self-representation, in the Freudian slip that leads him to ask Falkland why he, Caleb, "should sign away my own reputation for the better maintaining of yours" (385).

The revised ending thus presses beyond the formalities of the legal hearing to put Caleb and Falkland in a face-to-face relationship, also removing the agents of "administrative justice" present in the more polemically angry first ending (438).[35] In the new ending, confronted with an appallingly emaciated Falkland, Caleb, in a moment of radical generosity, claims to make himself responsible for Falkland's suffering and conduct, moving Falkland to withdraw his resistance to Caleb's charges. Pamela Clemit describes the revised ending as a "counter-proposition to the cycle of revolution and tyranny," which replaces Caleb's "rebellious zeal" with a no less "revolutionary change of heart."[36] But just as the decision of guilt and innocence in the case of Williams versus Falkland had proved undecidable, one cannot decide how to respond to this incredible embrace of confessions. Do we, as readers, give back to Caleb the claim to justness that he concedes, as Falkland with equal generosity proceeds to do? Or is confession a form of bad faith, which takes back what it gives in self-congratulation and thereby forfeits what it reclaims? Perhaps Caleb's confession and entire tale, as Falkland insists in the original ending (437), is a form of sophistry that produces truth as the autoaffection of one's own voice. For even in their most heartfelt professions of sincerity the characters speak too well—so well that we suspect that their positions are produced purely in language, like the too-seamless causality of the novel itself, which Godwin marks in his Preface to *Fleetwood*.

The idealism of the revised ending is in one sense simply the reverse of the paranoia that has hitherto dominated Caleb's and Falkland's relationship, and it bears the impression of this paranoia. Commenting on emotion as an agitated, volatile form of cognition (which is thus possessed of a certain narrativity), Thomas Pfau notes the doubly deconstructive structure of the paranoia of the 1790s, or we could say the paranoia of ideology. Paranoia, he suggests, is "an urgent, counterfactual narrative bent on stripping the real of its deceptive symbolic veneer." As a hysterical critique that has an "emphatically *analytic* quality" at its core, paranoia pushes the facts to an extreme so as to expose the fantasies of the symbolic order, while simultaneously exposing its own fantasized nature. In other words, paranoia, in Žižek's terms, involves a double "traversal of the fantasm" and thus a continual deconstruction of any narrative that is posited.

But it would not be right to allow the idealism of the revised ending to be swallowed up in a vertiginously self-canceling hermeneutics of suspicion, even granting Godwin's caution about the seductive performativity of rhetoric. Nor would it be convincing to see the text as projecting a utopian reconciliation such as Shelley imagines for Prometheus and Jove in a scene clearly modeled on this one. Such a synthesis in mutual forgiveness is belied by the manipulative complexities of Caleb's and Falkland's previous relationship and the realities of the situation. After all, Caleb does not entirely yield the case to Falkland; on the contrary, much of his speech is concerned with the way *Falkland* has missed opportunities to resolve the issue between them (429–30). On the one hand, then, Caleb's back-handed generosity betrays the fact that he still craves vindication. On the other hand, an unconditional generosity would indeed carry the imposture of idealism too far. Thus the concluding scene does not bring things to a decision, but rather stages an irresolvable ethical moment in excess of any judgment: be it in favor of one of the parties or in favor of the resolution of the dispute in an impulsive, unsustainable reconciliation that achieves justice now.

The concluding scene is a further counterfactual narrative. As such it is not the resolution of the plot but a form of what Lyotard calls *Begebenheit*: "an event or act of . . . deliverance" that "delivers itself into human history" (*D*, 164). Lyotard is commenting on Kant's "fourth critique," the critique of political reason that Kant never wrote but that exists throughout his work "in phrases," which, as such, cannot be institutionalized.[37] Rather than being limited to what is given—a *Gegebene*, "which can never do anything more than validate the phrase that describes it" (164), a *Begebenheit*, we could say, is an opening within narrative—at once generous and traumatic—an event that gives itself to the future. It is something so unexpected that it breaks out of the closure that narrative as plot uses to suppress the differend. But the event in question does not literally occur; rather, it occurs as "an index" or sign (of itself): "This event would merely indicate and not prove that humanity is capable of being" both the cause of its problems and the "author of its progress" (164). Lyotard is discussing Kant's famous comments on the French Revolution, which, as the problem of whether change is possible at all, is also in the background of *Caleb Williams*.[38] Lyotard takes up the issue of how Kant can approach the French Revolution in such a way that his (romantic) enthusiasm about it can be consistent with his rigorously critical attitude. From a strictly critical perspective, "revolutionary politics," including the revolution in feeling that Godwin stages at the end of *Caleb Williams*, "rests upon a transcendental illusion," which confuses "what is presentable as an object for a cognitive phrase" with the object of "a speculative and/or ethical phrase" (162). Yet Kant's sympathy for the French Revolution suggests that he could see a "passage" from the cognitive phrase, which deals with things as they are, to the speculative phrase, "which awaits the progress of freedom" (163). He could see the same "referent—say a phenomenon grasped in the field of human history" as presenting "qua example . . . the object of a discourse of despair," while as "guiding thread" it presents a metaphor for "the discourse of emancipation" (163–64).

However, this passage is, precisely, speculative. Moreover, it is a passage from one phrase regime to another and not from one actuality to another, the point of a second ending not being to accomplish a revolution but simply to show the possibility of changing phrases. Changing phrases allows us to conceive of a new ending for history, yet "not according to the rule of direct presentation proper to cognitives but according to the free, analogical presentation" of dialectic (163). Indeed, the narrative based on such a change deconstructs itself in the moment of its positing. Hence the incredible quality of Godwin's new ending, which is the "most inconsistent possible 'passage,' the impasse as 'passage'" (166), or the idea produced by the very impossibility of passage. The revised ending of *Caleb Williams* does not happen mimetically, cognitively, but hypothetically. It is a form of enthusiasm, which Kant carefully distinguishes from *Schwärmerei*. Whereas the latter proceeds to a "noncritical passage," enthusiasm provides a "supremely paradoxical presentation, which Kant calls a 'mere negative presentation' that "sees nothing, or rather sees that what can be seen is nothing" (166). On closer scrutiny, in the dialectic of romance and history necessary if we are to think justice "now" and not only in the future, this scene's resolution of the impasse will still turn out to be phrased in the wrong ways. For a phrase regime is always, for Godwin too, a false reduction of a certain "chaos" of thought and perception "into a grammatical and intelligible form" (*PJ*, 2. 204). Nevertheless, as Lyotard argues with reference to Kant, the sign of history is not groundless. For if we limit ourselves to "immediate, intuitive data" and ascertain on the basis of things as they are that "political history is chaos," the "disappointment accompanying the ascertainment is in itself a sign" that we desire something more (*D*, 163). The disappointment produced in *Caleb Williams* by the original ending, a cognitive that knows things as they are, is the sign that causes Godwin to write another ending, but as what Kant calls a paralogism or hypotyposis: a figure for a concept that has no figure.[39]

If the two endings perform the difference between judgment and justice, this process is the prototype for reading all Godwin's novels as trials of judgment. For these novels, even though they do not deal directly with the judicial system, contain scenes of flagrant misjudgment, such as the verdict against Mandeville in the schoolboy trial that finds him guilty of hiding antimonarchist cartoons, or Fleetwood's Othello-like conviction that his wife Mary is guilty of adultery (in the doubly mental and juridical senses of the word "conviction"). More important, the novels all continue from *Caleb Williams* in the use they make of the related form of confession and in the way they extend Godwin's emphasis on the responsibility of private judgment in *Political Justice*.

Pointing to the seminality of his first novel for his later fiction, Godwin in the 1832 Preface to *Fleetwood* tells us that he began *Caleb Williams* "as is the more usual way, in the third person," but grew dissatisfied with a heterodiegetic narration and made "the hero of [the] tale his own historian"; in "this mode I persisted in all my subsequent . . . fiction."[40] Given Godwin's distrust of stories, we can ask why he allowed his heroes the privilege of homodiegesis, though in the complex form of confession, as a story that disavows itself. It is not that he saw confession as a form of transparent communication, since *Fleetwood* (1805) and *St. Leon*

(1798) are the narratives of a confession and not the stories confession institutes. But we should not simply be sceptical of Fleetwood's and St. Leon's stories, as critics assume in treating confession as a form whose truth is rhetorically produced through the false sincerity of a turning upon oneself. Such readings constitute *St. Leon* as a critique of masculine ambition or *Fleetwood* as a critique of Rousseauvian education and the misogyny at the heart of political idealism from the Enlightenment to the Jacobinism of Godwin's own time. The critique may be Godwin's critique of his character, or it may be our critique of his complicity with his hero from a more enlightened contemporary perspective. But as Derrida says, such "critique always operates in view of the decision after or by means of a judgment," and "the authority of judgment or of the critical evaluation" cannot be "the final authority" for justice.[41] Or as Foucault concedes, although only in passing, critique is itself "a line of development of the arts of governing,"[42] and thus a form of institution.

To be sure, St. Leon, in seeking to win our sympathy by confessing his errors, might be trying to profit from them, like the felon who sells his memoirs to the media. But if we judge him purely by his wife Marguerite's standards of female care and middle-class thrift, we ignore the political imagination at work in his reconstruction of Hungary, and we are guilty of a sanctimony he avoids by at least putting his being at risk in the world of gambling, prodigality, and political desire. As Sartre argues in discussing bad faith, good faith—the belief that one's own character is not also tropologically produced by a turning away from the other—is the worst form of false consciousness. In Sartre's example, the homosexual who will not admit his disposition would be even more in bad faith if he confessed "what he is," since he is not simply a legal or moral category. His bad faith is in some sense forced on him, as Caleb too discovers when he assumes false identities to protect the "truth" of what he is. Indeed, we who make the other confess are worse instances of bad faith, since bad faith reflects the very structure of the human as being other than what it is: as "being what it is not, and not being what it is."[43] On the one hand, confession would then seem to be the prime example of what Joel Faflak calls the "pornography of the talking cure," wherein the perpetuation of talk even as (psycho)analysis "economizes" the dis-ease it discloses within an established, even hypocritical, social circuitry. This complicity of confession with what Faflak calls "moral management" is all the more powerful on one level because, by "telling all," as Foucault argues, the subject is normalized, thus analogically procuring the confessions and normalization of his readers.[44] On the other hand, Godwin, I would argue, evokes the form of confession precisely to remind us of the interpellations at work in the penitential apparatus. Nowhere is this more apparent than in *Mandeville,* whose protagonist's refusal to be cured breaks open the institution of confession so as to expose the pathology of normalization.[45]

In making his heroes their own historians, Godwin goes beyond morality to an ethics that insists on reading as a responsibility to this excess within the subject. For the very form of the first person requires an identification with the narrator, which is intensified by the double way that confession constitutes him as both a legal subject who must be the object of a judgment and a spiritual subject in search of understanding. This identification may be deeply "perverse," even to the point of doing a wrong to ourselves. Godwin first thematizes the perversity of identifications in the psychotic interlude, modeled on the mousetrap scene in *Hamlet,* where Caleb and Falkland are discussing Alexander the Great (*CW,* 183–87). Falkland obstinately identifies with Alexander in the face of Caleb's more enlightened critique of his brutality and megalomania. Caleb is of course morally correct, and he says what "we ourselves" would say. So if we still identify with Falkland, it is not because we agree with him but because we are disturbed at the unnerving "pleasure" that Caleb takes in manipulating him into "the situation of a fish that plays with the bait employed to entrap him" (180, 182). But as the phrase suggests, Falkland's praise for Alexander is itself of a particular and perverse kind, a *sinthome,* in Lacan's terms. It is a way of resisting Caleb's game, while playing with and playing into Caleb's caricature of him to disclose a certain madness underlying the rationality of judgment that is the goal of Caleb's attempt to produce Falkland's confession. As a Hitchcockian psychoanalysis of this psychosis of judgment, the scene models in Falkland's affinity with Alexander or Caleb's own "magnetical sympathy" with his patron (186), a weird quasi-identification in which "particulars" "start out to view in ourselves, which might otherwise [lie] undetected" (HR, 455). For the point of Godwin's later account of the magnetic field of reading and renarration is that the affinities it describes are not between whole subjects, but involve part-objects and parts of subjects unbound from the wholes in which they are found. These affinities are beyond good and evil and, if unleashed, produce a kind of madness, as happens in the scene with Falkland. This madness is what Faflak, following Woodman, calls the "radically chaotic" or anarchic moment—anarchic in the sense of being before *arche,* or foundation—which underlies a culture's articulation of its discourses as fantasy, whether this culture is that of things as they are or things as they should be. And when "we return home and engage in the solemn act of self-investigation" (455), the minute particulars thus unleashed become the object of an unlimited analysis of the transference and counter-transference involved in the process of judgment whereby we constitute ourselves as "whole" subjects.

The mousetrap scene is the prototype for the trial of judgment in which the voyeurism of confession forces us to engage in all Godwin's subsequent novels. In the same way that we identify with Falkland's part-identification with Alexander, there is a magnetical sympathy or elective affinity between the reader and Fleetwood that instinctively grasps the differend foreclosed by a more straightforward judgment. Commenting on the chemistry of elective affinities, Goethe links affinity to substances that are *antithetical* and that "perhaps precisely because they are so . . . seek and embrace one another, modify one another and together form a new substance."[46] Fleetwood, then, draws in the reader through an unstable compound of attraction and repulsion, wherein his marriage to Mary operates as a kind of free radical, a diseased radicalism, which cannot be bound within any obvious story about the incestuous structure of patriarchy.

Hence it would be wrong to reduce Fleetwood, who is a broken man at the end, to the misogyny betrayed by his treatment of Mary. Rather, he is drawn to her by a profound restlessness with social structures, which requires us to read his story anamorphically rather than as a mere negative example. While Mary's father, MacNeil, suggests marriage to a much older man as an experiment to cure his friend's ennui, Fleetwood himself is drawn to Mary by something more profound: her melancholia after her parents' death by drowning. He discerns in this death a "suicide," as if the idea they represent, the idea of radicalism, has failed.[47] But this idea is itself incoherent, in ways that uncannily foretell the contradictions between Godwin's own ideals and behavior in the 1790s and his treatment of his daughter years after writing *Fleetwood.*[48] For MacNeil, having gone against social conventions in his own marriage to protect the rights of woman, and despite being critical of Rousseau's ideas on the education of women, thinks nothing of making his daughter a toy to satisfy his middle-aged friend. Reaching towards a restlessness of the negative that MacNeil covers over but of which his death is the symptom, Fleetwood is drawn to the trace of this death in Mary's melancholia, but he in turn uses woman as a mere fetish for his own restlessness. He is then impelled, as if plagiarizing Othello, to destroy a marriage that has always been in bad faith.

But this behavior, which successively consumes the narratological positions into which Fleetwood is written by the second-rate scripts and fragments of scripts available to him, is not mere self-indulgence. His compulsion to destroy the attachments he has created as a way of destroying what is flawed in himself acts as a form of death-drive. The Romantic name for this death-drive is irony or infinite absolute negativity: the negation of the real from the viewpoint of the ideal and of the ideal from that of the real. Irony, as Kierkegaard defines it, is a radical aversion, in which particular phenomena are negated only as alibis, like the *objet petit à*, for the way all "existence has become alien to the ironic subject."[49] Paradoxically, Fleetwood can express this aversion against any form of institution only as a violence towards the other that is, like the trauma that literally concludes *Mandeville*, a form of automutilation. Yet as Baudrillard says, despite being aimed against eros the death drive is deeply idealistic: it "dissolves assemblages . . . and undoes Eros' organic discourse by returning things to an inorganic, *ungebunden,* state, in a certain sense to utopia as opposed to the articulate and constructive topics of Eros,"[50] of institutions. It dissolves and dissipates existing structures so as to force them towards the radically chaotic potentiality underlying the social, yet without the assurance we have in *Emma Courtney* of a future, a constructive moment.[51]

To do justice in these terms to the potential *poiesis* in this frustratingly antisocial text is by no means easy. For the female or enlightened reader must identify against the grain with a character who is sordidly, not even Byronically, disturbing. Similarly, in *Mandeville* (1817), sympathy with the deeply wounded, misanthropic Charles Mandeville requires that we perversely turn against his rival, Clifford, who seems the very embodiment of generosity and reason. For his part Mandeville, whose hatred of Clifford only increases when he becomes engaged to Charles's sister Henrietta, is a classic case of male envy, an example—or helpless symptom—

of a society that exchanges women as commodities. Thus, in identifying with Mandeville, we do not simply refuse the good as conventional. The female reader also renounces, or at least defers, the desires of the only female character in the text, even if she thereby becomes the surrogate for Henrietta's failed and (im)possible desire to love her brother as well as her future husband.

Such identifications, uneasy as they are, profoundly disturb our ability to constitute ourselves as whole subjects through the power of judgment, which Godwin, going well beyond Kant, dis-integrates. Moreover, it is the aesthetic, and specifically narrative as an unbinding of the particulars concentrated in the event, that allows for such perverse identifications; it is not likely that we would identify in the same way with Mandeville in real life. Perhaps we identify with him fictitiously because we find him more interesting than Clifford. The question that then arises is whether the aesthetic is a form of irresponsibility or the space for a different kind of judgment and an ethics beyond morality. Yet because the ethical relation to the other can involve a wrong to oneself, narrative justice as responsibility to a subject is not anything so simple as identifying with the narrators of these homosocial, homodiegetic histories. It is rather a responsibility to the subject we become by (not) identifying with these subjects, a dis-integration of the power of judgment. For a wrong is done both if we vindicate the hero by allowing him to be the only speaker in a narrative that includes others and also if we judge him in an idiom that is not the one in which he presents his case.

Moreover, the very act of identification, as a sympathetic turning towards an other and/or a perverse turning against oneself, is deeply tropological and re-turns on itself. It is too ingenuous to say that in empathizing with Godwin's misanthropes we engage in a self-sacrificing ethics. On some level, we also realize our own desire by identifying as part-subjects with characters we should critique, in a fantasy of transgression that allows us to experience Caleb's much-vaunted "truth" psychoanalytically rather than morally. Such is the case in the self-destruction that concludes Mandeville's history as a traumatic return to the scene of his psychic birth in the violence of the novel's opening in Ireland. For in *Mandeville,* the union between the Presbyterian Henrietta and the Royalist Clifford, a late convert to Catholicism, is the very epitome of "institution": an inscription of the political on the domestic that recalls Scott's masculine imposition of the rule of history on romance in the recently published *Waverley* (1814), where the marriage of Edward and Rose confirms the Act of Union. Charles's futile assault on the marriage coach, which announces the impending event of the Restoration, figures our frustration with this accommodation, yet only as a fantasy, which is to say, at a certain distance. This desperate gesture also unreasonably destroys all forms of reconciliation, all hopes of phrasing things differently, which are cathected with the figure of Henrietta, yet also abjected by her overidealization.[52] As a process in which we are affectively displaced between characters, as a form that consists in this displacement rather than the establishment of structure, narrative thus continuously puts the positions it reaches on trial/in process.

The analysis provoked by narrative as a setting in motion of this force of displacement is necessarily "unlimited," given the profound incoherence that Godwin sees at the heart of "character" as a circumstantial, contingent aggregation of impulses that the narratological apparatus of culture falsifies into a principle of totalization (*PJ*, 1.47, 370). It is this incoherence that leads St. Leon to describe himself as an "equivocal character, assuming different names,"[53] and that leads Caleb to conclude by saying that he now has "no character" to vindicate (*CW*, 434). This autodestruction of its main characters is the death drive that impels all Godwin's major novels towards their unconcluded endings. While Godwin's earlier protagonists manage to assume a character through the imposition of a rhetoric (of "reputation" or "truth") on something more amorphous, Mandeville is entirely without a center, unable to take up a coherent political position in what purports to be a political novel. The novel begins with his memory of his traumatic delivery from his parents' death in the Irish Uprising of 1641, into the hands of a warped Calvinist priest and later a misanthropic and melancholic uncle. As the primal scene of his psychic birth, the slaughter in Ireland brings the infant Charles into being as a *corps morcelé*, a paranoid-schizoid body in bits and pieces rather than an integrated subject. Thereafter, as Scott's biographer John Gibson Lockhart complained, there is no reason for anything Mandeville does: "a causeless aversion preys upon his soul."[54] Since his character is pure aversion, Mandeville cannot be judged as "homosocial" or "misanthropic." These pathologies, including his incestuously possessive attachment to his sister, are tropes; they are the form taken by his turning away from things as they are. And because we receive Mandeville's confession within the analytic scene of narrative, it is our responsibility to imagine what this turning away cannot turn towards.

The political backdrop of *Mandeville* is similarly decentered, in ways that make politics, like character, a scarred and defaced project. The novel is set in the Cromwellian period: the site for Godwin of what Jon Klancher calls "the unavailability to modern Britain of its own revolutionary moment."[55] It is a historical novel in which, paradoxically, Mandeville's psychic history usurps the foreground, while the clash of religious and political factions provides the background. But this clash cannot be mapped in terms of dialectically meaningful differences, since Godwin does not follow Scott in focalizing events through an epic contest of opposed sides.[56] As Slavoj Žižek argues, the ideological field is normally made up of a "multitude of 'floating signifiers'" whose "identity is 'open'" until they are structured into a unified field "through the intervention of a certain 'nodal point.'" This *point de capiton,* an issue such as the conflict of Cromwell and Charles II, "'quilts' them, stops their sliding and fixes their meaning." In *Mandeville* this *point de capiton,*[57] which would give shape to the novel's animosities, has disappeared. Instead the narrative breaks down into a series of power struggles on the Royalist side, while the other side, the Republican, is oddly absent from the diegesis. More than any identifiable conflict, the novel manifests what Žižek calls the "Real of antagonism," for which factions or class struggle are simply a "name." As Žižek argues, antagonism, far from being "the ultimate referent which anchors and limits the unending drift of the signifiers," is "the very force of their constant displacement." This is why in Godwin's novel the specifics of political oppositions—what it means to be Catholic or Presbyterian, or a Presbyterian supporting the Royalists, or a Presbyterian turned Catholic—scarcely matter. Such antagonisms function, in this Hobbesian political universe, simply as "operator[s] of dislocation." Political (or religious or sexual) difference, rather than providing the meaning of the text, is a symptom: "that which 'skews' the discursive universe, . . . that on account of which every *symbolization* of . . . difference is unstable and displaced with regard to itself."[58] Sheer antagonism rather than ideologically legible differences forms the traumatic core of this novel.

It is against this backdrop that Mandeville's confession bequeaths to us the task of finding the creative residue, the *poiesis,* in pathology, given a subject whose desire is skewed by the perversion of institutions. Godwin's novels all reduce their subjects to their underlying paranoid origins, so as to disclose, through character as a symptom of the social, what Žižek calls the gap between "the explicit symbolic texture and its phantasmic background." They break down the "public text" of politics (in *Mandeville*), truth and justice (in *Caleb Williams*), or the domestic politics of Jacobinism (in *Fleetwood*) into the "obscene libidinal foundation[s]" that are its "phantasmic support."[59] In *Mandeville*, in particular, this disintegration of characters and the stories they tell goes hand in hand with a radical destructuration of the ideological field itself. This destructuration is the dark side of what *Political Justice* had attempted before Godwin confronted the madness of culture: a deconstruction of institutions that is necessary if we are to bring forth what cannot be phrased in the articulate and constructive topics of ideology.

Godwin's later novels certainly leave us with little reason for optimism "now." While Caleb and Falkland undergo a revolution in feeling that may or may not be convincing, as Gary Handwerk argues, Mandeville (and also Fleetwood) remains stubbornly attached to the repetition of his traumas.[60] In these novels, therefore, Godwin does not repeat the reconciliation fantasized in *Caleb Williams*, if only as a transcendental schematism. Rather, he submits the romance of justice to the particularities of history: the intricate entwinement of political, social, psychic, and domestic history. *Fleetwood* promises a reunion between Fleetwood and Mary only to withdraw this reparation as a worse wrong: the wrong that occurs when novels on the wrongs of woman end with marriage or the forgiveness of these wrongs. In *Mandeville* the clash between the protagonists antithetically mimics the face-to-face encounter of Caleb and Falkland, even to the point of the scarring of Mandeville's face. As for the promise of the novel's setting in the Cromwellian period, the historical backdrop of the novel is the scene of a lost Republican moment that never materializes because, disappointingly, there are no Republican heroes in the text.

Yet political justice is, throughout, the absent cause of a historical scene so chaotic that one cannot tell left from right, right from wrong, or one side from another in a novel in which each side seems to divide into further sides. Political justice, as the imperative to go beyond the mere rearrangement of the characters inhabiting the power structure to discern the psychic wrongs done by the very institution of "politics," enters the text through the distance between then and now. This distance further opens into the distance between "now" for Godwin and the now of our own reading. History thus functions as a negative *Begebenheit,* a space in which trauma can become a gift that "gives itself" to the future, provoking us to phrase things differently. Indeed, Godwin's well-known "necessitarianism," his insistence that man is originally a tabula rasa, and that human beings are purely products of circumstances, is nothing but a belief that things could be phrased differently. The "sign" that there could be something other than the unrelieved darkness of the "now" is our disappointment that the Republican revolution produces nothing but conflict; that this novel about the psychic history of a traumatized individual never becomes the historical novel it promises to be; that there is not even a Republican hero in this novel by the author of *Political Justice,* but only a character who takes political sides out of the most personal aversions. Disappointment is fundamentally messianic, as Percy Shelley recognized when he wrote of how hope "creates/From its own wreck the thing it contemplates" (*PU,* 4.573–74). The reconciliation imagined in *Caleb Williams,* though (im)possible here, remains the horizon within which we can approach these novels speculatively and beyond their cognitive phrasing of the impasses with which their plots end.

CHAPTER FIVE

Gambling, Alchemy, Speculation

Godwin's Critique of Pure Reason in St. Leon

T HE SPECULATIVE PHRASE is the very genre of *St Leon:* a text as playful as Godwin's other novels are traumatic but in which narrativity is similarly a principle of antieconomy. Godwin's second novel makes narrative the space of the (im)possible by using alchemy and gambling as its operative metaphors, not just subjects of the text but also ways of producing and critiquing its narrative: as speculation, as the (in)credible transformation of one phrase into another, and as an (un)willing suspension of disbelief. *St. Leon* is the story of a sixteenth-century French aristocrat who loses his fortune in gaming and regains it in Switzerland after receiving the philosopher's stone from a dying stranger. After many vicissitudes, St. Leon ends his history in Hungary, as a man younger than his own son: a situation that so confounds logic as to be both a source of irony and of speculative possibility. In the meantime, he has been estranged from his family by his unexplained wealth and his oath of secrecy to the stranger. Thus, in the second stage of his "experiment," rejected by his son, rebuked by his wife's death, and having left his two surviving daughters well settled in life, St. Leon is a last man, "the outcast of [his] species" (368, 366).[1] Yet as such he is also a free agent, as the text unfolds into Godwin's own experiment with undoing the institutions of nation and family, of promising and credibility, embedded in the very protocols of the realist Novel.

Gambling functions in *St. Leon* both as an object of judgment and as a way of producing Godwin's text as a gamble subject to a critique that depends on how one judges gambling. St. Leon's career is a continuous gamble, first literally, when he takes up gaming, and then metaphorically, when he gambles on rebuilding Hungary by investing his imaginary money in its war-torn economy. Yet St. Leon, an "equivocal character, assuming different names" (475), is by no means one character. In Switzerland, where he flees on losing his fortune, the stranger's gift unbinds him from the frugality of domestic pastoral, and he returns to France to educate his son. In this first phase of his career, St. Leon uses his secret ostentatiously for private aggrandizement. Godwin abhorred promises and contracts because "they depose us . . . from the use of our own understanding" (*PJ*, 1.202), and he seems to judge his protagonist harshly for the damage caused to St. Leon's family by his oath of secrecy to the stranger. One is not surprised, then, that St. Leon suffers the consequences: distrusted by his family, he also becomes an object of public mistrust because of his mysterious wealth; he is jailed on his return to Constance on suspicion of murdering the stranger, released, and then imprisoned again by the Inquisition. But on escaping again, St. Leon, who has reached the age of eighty-six when he tells his story, takes the elixir of life and enters Hungary as Chatillon, a man of twenty-two. He is now free of a different contract, that of marriage: the contract to the discourse of the family, the promise of absolute frankness even when secrecy is necessary, as Kant, who also opposed secrecy, recognized it sometimes is.[2]

In this second phase of his career, St. Leon, no longer bound to provide for his family or for its reputation through his son, turns his powers to the rebuilding of Hungary, despite "the unruliness of those for whose benefit" he plans (*St.L*, 382). The Hungarian experiment partly responds to political injustices St. Leon himself had suffered in Switzerland, which was seen as a Republican utopia by contemporaries such as Helen Maria Williams, in her *Tour of Switzerland* (1798), but not by Godwin himself. For although Godwin describes the government of Switzerland as "simple and moderate" (123), as foreigners the St. Leon family, when they lose everything in a storm, are not given access to the compensation provided by the government; they suffer under the "coercive regulations" of government as they are forced into a "second emigration" (96–97), their property is confiscated, and St. Leon is falsely imprisoned, even though he does ultimately obtain redress (122–23). Facing a similar scene of economic ruin and the selfishness it unleashes in people in Hungary, St. Leon now has the wealth to address the situation. It is true that he initially wants to make a show of his philanthropy: "to pour the entire stream" of his "riches like a mighty river, to fertilise [Hungary's] wasted plains" (369). But he soon realizes that he must operate "with the least practicable violence upon the inclinations and freedom of the inhabitants" and by using his money simply to give "new alacrity" to materials already at hand (373).

Moving from the venial to the altruistic use of his powers, St. Leon has undergone that improvement that divides the fake from the genuine alchemist in justifications of alchemy and that later led Jung to see the *opus maximum* as a metaphor for psychoanalysis.[3] St. Leon, to be sure, is very much a figure of the Enlightenment, both in its more benevolent aspects and in those critiqued by Theodor Adorno and Max Horkheimer in their *Dialectic of Enlightenment.* It is because of his "daily efforts for the dissemination of happiness," his desire to be "the parent and benefactor of mankind," that he is hated by Bethlem Gabor (401, 416), the misanthrope whom he befriends and who reduces St. Leon's project to ruins by kidnapping and imprisoning him. Bethlem Gabor is one in a series of characters, beginning with Tyrrel in *Caleb Williams,* through whom Godwin attempts to confront the dark forces in public and psychic history, which he will thoroughly explore in *Mandeville.* St. Leon describes in alchemical language his efforts to refine this base creature, whose complexion was "universally dun or black" (396), and to bring him back into the human species (402, 427). But Godwin's ironic sense of the limits of enlightenment is evident in the way St. Leon can deal with what Blake calls the specter only prosthetically, as something completely outside the self, only as a negation and not as negativity. In this case there is no magnetical sympathy or elective affinity between opposites, such as exists between Caleb and Falkland. Thus St. Leon represents a certain complacency of the Enlightenment, an inability to grasp the limits of optimism. Yet his son Charles, who resurfaces in the last episode of the novel, is hardly an alternative moral center. For Charles, the Crusader who excoriates his father for having saved Hungary from a famine that would have delivered it into the hands of the Christians (436), surely represents the most extreme form of the racism from which his own family had suffered in Switzerland.

Just as St. Leon is not a simple character, gambling, which in novels such as Radcliffe's *The Mysteries of Udolpho* is associated with disreputable "French" modes of behavior, is by no means to be dismissed. For St. Leon's travels take him through time as well as space: from his native France at the end of the chivalric age; to a Switzerland that anachronistically represents yet fails to be the Republican utopia of Dissenters like Helen Maria Williams,[4] and finally to Hungary, after it had been overrun by the Turks. These wanderings bring into play different chronotopes of value. France under the ancien régime, as Thomas Kavanagh has argued, was an aristocratic culture in which gambling was a form of potlatch. Gambling formed one of a number of social practices, like dueling, that were "substitute affirmations of nobility," whereby the aristocracy proclaimed their "ultimately impossible superiority . . . to the force of money" and their commitment to a code of honor and risk rather than self-protection.[5] In Switzerland, where St. Leon's history is dominated by his wife, Marguerite, and Godwin's own emergent middle-class culture of thrift and self-reliance, the ideal is "a small portion of land . . . sufficient with economy for the support of [the] family" (90). Here gambling is the vice that Radcliffe saw it as being. Yet finally in Hungary, St. Leon engages in an early form of deficit-financing, which anticipates the economic legitimation of gambling as credit. By the early eighteenth century, moreover, there were those who held that lotteries were justified if they raised money for the poor and that there is a difference between "unproductive" and "productive" gambling, which included lotteries and insurance contracts.[6]

St. Leon's career in Hungary bears an intriguing resemblance to that of the Scotsman John Law, a "projector" whose "System" Kavanagh describes as "the single most important economic event in eighteenth-century France" prior to the Revolution. Law wrote *Money and Trade Considered with a Proposal for Supplying the Nation with Money* in 1705, when he tried unsuccessfully to get his proposals for economic justice accepted in Scotland. He came to France in 1715 with a fortune made in gaming, at a time when the country was almost bankrupt, but left five years later, virtually penniless, having been done in by his enemies and a collective panic. While he had the trust of the Regent, he infused large sums of money into the economy, by backing his paper currency with the promise of land in America, a form of credit that he saw as more secure than printing money or increasing the supply of metal.[7] Yet Law was not out to make his fortune: he complained that "a small portion of the people lived on wealth drawn from loans made to others whom they ruined," and he believed that the "evils brought about by the System" finally came down only to "having diminished the wealth of high-interest moneylenders and *rentiers*."[8] Like St. Leon, who is aware that "money is not wealth" and that its value lies in the way the "continual influx" of precious metals "into the market" might "stimulate and revive the industry of the nation" (*St.L*, 372–73), Law believed that money has no intrinsic value. It is only as it "moves from hand to hand" that it "increas[es] the value of everything it touches." For money, according to Law, increases employment, manufacture, and trade, puts houses and farms to use, and relieves debt, thus increasing "Wealth and Power."[9] Since money is what it does, why not increase the supply? Thus Law writes, in terms echoed by Godwin, "should someone once dare to introduce credit and make it the equivalent of money, men's work, industry, and commerce will be reborn."[10] The System, after an initial success, backfired, in part because people prematurely lost faith in it. The inflationary aftermath of its collapse so traumatized the French that they could neither renounce deficit-financing nor build up the necessary credit mechanisms to make it work, as Law had tried to do.

Law's System is nevertheless a crucial part of the genealogy of the French Revolution, both in positive terms—because of its democratizing aims—and because the chaos precipitated by its curtailment made a revolution all the more inevitable. Alluding to Law, Edmund Burke thus sees the beginnings of the Revolution in the fact that the French, even under the ancien régime, were already "open, with a censurable degree of facility, to all sorts of projects and projectors." France, he complains, has "founded a commonwealth upon gaming" and made "speculation as extensive as life."[11] As Kavanagh writes, there is something "immensely sad" about Law's "gamble": "Looking back on it from the 1990s with our experience of Keynesian theory, supply-side economics, mortgage debt, and junk bonds, we know there was no intrinsic reason why it was doomed to failure. If anything, it too abruptly anticipated an understanding of economic structures that would take more than two centuries to gain general currency."[12]

St. Leon, too, may simply be ahead of his time. Like Law, Godwin's protagonist is a "projector" who commits "the fault, so common to projectors, of looking only to ultimate objects and great resting places, and neglecting to consider the steps between" (*St.L*, 169). The term "projector," associated with "theory" as opposed to common sense, is also a term connected with alchemy, where "projection" designates the final and riskiest phase in the alchemical process, in which the powder (or philosopher's stone) is thrown onto the molten metal to produce gold. Burke, for instance, associates "projector[s]" and "alchymist[s]" with the ethos that led to the French Revolution.[13] As in *St. Leon,* alchemy, the manufacture of coins not backed by real wealth, is a metaphor for credit. Credit scared both the nobility, because it untied wealth from land and inheritance, and the middle and working classes, because it called in question the value of honest work. The humble life St. Leon leads in Constance, that of a middle-class family always on the verge of being part of the working poor, grounds value in something already possessed. As inherited privilege had been backed by land, so middle-class moral privilege is guaranteed by work invested in property, be it a limited stock of possessions or a house on a small piece of land. The middle class differs from the aristocracy in its attachment to property only in not living beyond its means, but for this reason it is perhaps even more bound than the nobility to things as they are. Hence, for example, Mary Wollstonecraft's anxiety throughout *The Wrongs of Woman* about notions such as "imagination," which were to be central to the discourse of Romanticism. Hence also St. Leon's perverse discontent with his wife, as he admits that, instead of "being weaned, by the presence of this admirable woman," from his "passion for gaming, it became stronger than ever" (66).

By contrast, gaming, as St. Leon writes, "subverts all order, and forces every avocation" or institution "from the place assigned it" (60). Gambling is either a sordid activity or a revolutionary force, depending on how one judges it. Thus *St. Leon* is at once Godwin's critique of his own political idealism and his gamble with the future of this idealism, which he projects through a character who lives beyond himself into the future. "Gambling" shifts the text between the moral phrase, by which critics generally judge St. Leon from the perspective of his wife's middle-class virtue, and the speculative phrase, which experiments with judging his "communication on [its] own terms" (214). For "speculation," also the name of a card game, had the connotation of playing with money as early as 1774,[14] and it is used in this sense by Burke. As speculation's primary meaning involves taking risks with thought, the debate around gambling also stages a debate, or rather a differend, between two forms of thought: the Common Sense philosophy, on the one hand, and speculation, or "theory," on the other.

These two discourses provide two radically different ways of phrasing St. Leon's history. The ethos of common sense now dominant in nineteenth-century studies would see his life as an example of Romantic imagination, which violates the values of care and thrift at the heart of the family. That of speculation would read Godwin's novel as a gamble with new ideas, which are cast in the virtual reality of fiction so that they can be both elaborated and critiqued. This process, I argue, has much in common with the affirmative (de)construction that also occurs between Kant's *Critiques* and his utopian political essays. Speculation, according to Samuel Johnson, is a "mental scheme not reduced to practice" and is more or less synonymous with "theory." Johnson defines the latter as "speculation, not practice; scheme; plan or system yet subsisting only in the mind," and he similarly characterizes a projector as "one who forms wild impracticable schemes," and he uses "chymists," "quacks," and "lawyers" (presumably because of their use of sophistical logic) as examples.[15] "Theory," or "ideas," as David Simpson has argued, was widely blamed for the French Revolution by Burke, Arthur Young, and others.[16] Projectors, alchemists, and speculators, in the double sense of gamblers and theorists, are all connected, in a British Common Sense discourse sceptical of radical ideas that are not grounded in experience and associated with "enthusiasm." As Burke's extensive analysis of the monetary crisis in pre-Revolutionary France symptomatically suggests, the operation of these ideas also has much to do with credit as a new semiology, one that legitimizes what was previously considered sophistry. For in the century preceding 1789, huge amounts of gold and silver coins were minted without being backed, according to Burke, by an increase in GDP. What Burke chooses to phrase as a deficit could also be seen as credit:[17] a borrowing against the future that recasts not only monetary signs but signs in general. Law's system, according to Kavanagh, was "an early and unrecognized champion of signifier over signified": "The traditional economists of Law's day insisted that every credit instrument . . . retained its value only to the extent that it was backed by and rooted in the past of the issuing authority's actual holdings in gold or silver. Law reversed that temporality. First there would be money and then, as a result of its circulation, there would be gold and silver."[18] The credit system, as Terry Mulcaire argues, does not simply present problems for "epistemology" but also offers "new resources . . . for desire" and analogies for imagination. Indeed, Defoe even describes credit as the "best philosopher's stone in the world."[19]

৵

Credit has significant consequences for the economy of fiction, given the Novel's middle-class anxiety about not living beyond its means, evident in the fear of debt and bankruptcy we see in Dickens' novels. Suffice it to say for now that credit, as a willingness to deploy monetary instruments whose value is unproven, has much to do with speculation as a willingness to entertain ideas that cannot yet be empirically established. "Speculation" is, of course, the term generally associated with (post)Kantian idealism, from the 1790s (when F. A. Nitsch and A. W. Willich published the first introductions to Kant in English) to Coleridge's *Biographia Literaria,* in 1817. And Godwin, as suggested in the previous chapter, resembles Kant both in his commitment to "ideas" and in the criticism to which he subjects them. (Post)Kantian Idealism is distinguished from the empiricism of the British by being "speculative," not grounded in experience, but by the same token not limited by it. Kant could therefore speculate on perpetual peace, while Godwin could imagine a euthanasia of government and the achievement of immortality. Speculation, not bound by the rules of the understanding, is the thought undertaken by Reason, which Kant says, in evoking Plato's *Republic,* "raises itself to cognitions far too elevated to admit . . . of an object given by experience corresponding to them" (*CPR,* 219–20). In other words, the "conceptions of Reason" are "transcendental ideas" such as peace and freedom, whereas those of the understanding are "categories" that are used to arrange phenomena (218). It is in this sense that Godwin, also evoking Plato, uses the word "speculation" in linking *St. Leon* to the project of political justice: "In the early ages of antiquity, one of the favourite topics of speculation was a perfect system of civil policy" (*St.L,* 1). "Reason" is a term that recurs in *Political Justice* (e.g., 2.210–11) and is best understood, not as a synonym for rationality, but in the Kantian sense, accepted by Coleridge, of a faculty higher than the mere understanding of Common Sense philosophy. Reason is "the *faculty of principles,*" where understanding is the "faculty of rules" (*CPR,* 211). Thus, as Karl Jaspers puts it, "reason makes things too big for the understanding," while understanding "make[s] them too little for reason."[20] *St. Leon* can be seen as Godwin's critique, in the double sense of Kant's title, of this deeply quixotic faculty of Reason, which is sometimes closer to imagination. For the genitive of Kant's title suggests, on the one hand, the critique devoted to Reason, as *The Critique of Judgment* is about judgment. But it also suggests a criticism *of* Reason and the "irresistible illusions" of which Reason is the "parent," when it tempts us to go beyond the positivism of "experience," which for its part is equally "the parent of illusion" and convention (*CPR*, 221). The two are related, since the criticism of Reason is the condition of possibility for a critique, in the sense of an exposition, of Reason's possibilities.

Speculation has been the site of a deep division between British and continental thought, from the Common Sense philosophy of Kant's own time to a subsequent analytic tradition. In 1798 Schlegel already comments that the "few attacks against Kantian philosophy . . . are the most important documents for a pathological history of common sense," adding that this "epidemic, which started in England, even threatened for a while to infect German philosophy."[21] Yet Kant has been claimed by both traditions, and as if to prove Schlegel's point, he himself claims that his roots were to be found in Scotland.[22] Kant is on both sides of a debate over "metaphysics," "spirit," and "enthusiasm"—all terms having to do with knowledge of what Nitsch calls "the existencies of immaterial objects" and ungrounded hopes and intuitions.[23] Thus Kant's emphasis on the *sensus communis* is an attempt at a transvaluation of "common sense." From this perspective, he criticizes "exaltation" (*Schwärmerei*) in his "On a Newly Arisen Superior Tone in Philosophy" (1796), which takes aim at philosophies that claim secret or esoteric insights, which he interestingly figures as forms of alchemy. In the same essay Kant makes Plato "the father of all exaltation in *philosophy*," and he insists that "philosophy" should be "prosaic," even comparing the philosopher to a businessman.[24] Yet despite this attack on the "Plato- enthusiasm" of the 1790s,[25] in the first *Critique* Kant had spoken favorably of Plato (*CPR*, 219), and in 1798 he will praise the "enthusiasm" inspired by the French Revolution even if it is "fraught with danger."[26] Similarly, as Gregory Johnson argues, in *Dreams of a Spirit-Seer* (1766) and related work Kant is ambivalent about and not simply dismissive of Swedenborg. Indeed, "the speculations that Kant presents as his own" are similar to Swedenborg's but "purged of certain 'enthusiastic' excesses" and of the superior tone that hypostatizes speculation as vision.[27] For Kant is not hostile to spirit, and he later writes that by means "of reason, the human soul is endowed with spirit (*mens, nous*)," which makes man more than "a mere mechanism of nature."[28] It is this double-voicedness in Kant's work that makes it particularly appropriate to read the author of *Lives of the Necromancers* alongside the author of *Dreams of a Spirit-Seer,* and even to reread Kant through Godwin, as a way of rereading Kant's "critique" of Reason through his practice of Reason in the essays translated in the 1790s, which include such utopian pieces as "To Perpetual Peace" and "Idea for a Universal History from a Cosmopolitan Point of View."[29]

Among contemporaneous commentators, Willich stresses Kant's caution about "pure" Reason and his greater commitment to the "practical" sphere of ethics. The ideas of Reason, as Nitsch puts it, "are not derived from experience"; they are "ideas a priori [and] the roots from which they shoot up lie in . . . *pure* reason." Recognizing that we can conceive but cannot know ideas such as "*God, Liberty, Immortality,*" which "rise above the world of sense, and, which we consider as the most sublime," Willich sees Kant as more modestly claiming "a practical and subjective knowledge" of man's "relations" to these ideas. "Though our views of the nature of these objects be not thereby enlarged," Kant therefore takes consolation in the fact that the knowledge of practical reason "affords us sufficient grounds, upon which we may safely establish rules for our conduct."[30]

Willich's reading seems to be borne out by Kant himself. On one level, Kant's first *Critique* actually seems an exposition of the *understanding:* an attempt to curb Reason's ambitions from the more cautious perspective of what post-Kantians such as Coleridge and Hegel saw as a lower faculty.[31] Kant repeatedly insists on "discipline" and on the "*negative* element in knowledge" (*CPR*, 407). He fears that if Reason is neither "held in a plain track" by "experience" nor concerned with "pure intuition" (as in mathematics), if instead it is allowed to operate in that mixed field, where "pure conceptions" are projected into experience and the transcendental is confused with the empirical (408), its ideas will become the "parents of irresistible illusions" (373). Such illusions are indeed the cause of St. Leon's troubles both in Switzerland and in Hungary. Kant further distinguishes between the part of his text that is an analytic, or "logic of truth," and the part that is a dialectic, or critique of "illusion." He provides an analytic of the understanding as a firm basis for knowledge, but he makes Reason the object of a "dialectic." This dialectic cautions against what will become dialectic in the Hegelian rather than the Socratic sense, where ideas are actually transposed into history under the "sophistical delusion" that we can enlarge "our cognitions by" "means of transcendental principles," which the mind invents for itself (68–70).

But unlike Willich, Nitsch sees Kant as arguing that "speculative philosophy is [as] susceptible of universal evidence" as logic. Critique is therefore not a renunciation of pure for practical reason, of principles for rules, but a way of making speculation more credible. Coleridge writes in stronger terms when he says "I could never believe, it was possible for [Kant] to have meant no more by his Noumenon, or THING IN ITSELF, than his mere words express." Coleridge introduces Kant in the chapter of the *Biographia Literaria* that begins with his own debt to Boehme, whom he describes as an "enthusiast," a term he is careful to distinguish from "fanaticism" or "*Schwärmerei*." Coleridge therefore implicitly associates Kant with enthusiasm and spirit, noting that the dryness of the first *Critique* may be due to a censorship internalized as prudence or may have come about because Kant felt it appropriate to leave behind his enthusiasms "in a pure analysis, not of human nature in toto, but of the speculative intellect alone."[32] Indeed, despite Kant's cautiousness in the first *Critique*, which Coleridge reminds us was not his only work, in the 1790s Kant was seen in some English circles as dangerously radical. As David Simpson argues, Kant was associated with "theory": a "speculative or hypothetical mental projection"that, if it did not quite have its present meaning, was blamed for the French Revolution and was already the object of a British resistance to theory.[33] Kant, according to correspondents in the *Anti-Jacobin*, expressed "too great confidence in an unlimited perfectibility of the human mind," paving the way for "the sublimest flights of *the newly deified intellect of man*."[34] Moreover, as Simpson suggests, the very term "pure reason" would have aroused the suspicions of conservative readers, given that Gerrard Winstanley, the Digger leader (from a period that deeply interested Godwin) "had spoken of a ' "pure reason' as the authority for his radically remade world" (30–31, 95).[35] To associate Kant with the Levellers and Diggers of the Cromwellian period reviled by Burke is an exaggeration, But Kant's use of critique as a form of irony or double negation—a critique that questions critique itself—leaves space for the Reason whose pretensions he criticizes to return, albeit only by default and as a claim that is disavowed as soon as it is made. Put differently, when Kant criticizes mysticism and enthusiasm, it may be that he is criticizing, not speculation per se, but a "superior tone" in philosophy that occurs when "reason raises its voice,"[36] so as to render dogmatic what should remain hypothetical and open to further speculation.

What, therefore, would be a "Kantian" reading of Godwin's novel? From one perspective, Kant wants to stay away from any rhetoric that associates philosophy with expansion, wealth-creation, or "additions to the sum of our knowledge" as opposed to the regulation of the knowledge we already possess (*CPR*, 407). He distrusts credit, which he sees as debt.[37] Correspondingly, he does not believe in anticipating what we do not yet have through "intuition," which he describes as "seeing something extravagantly great" where there may be "nothing" at all. Like the projector who leaves out the intervening steps, "intuition would immediately present the object and grasp it all at once," whereas understanding must "climb many difficult steps in order to make progress in knowledge." While the enabling structure of intuition is credit, that of the understanding is work, and Kant's essay on the tone of philosophy is pervaded by the rhetoric of work and a correspondingly middle-class tone. Thus "the philosophy of *Aristotle* is . . . work," while Pythagoras and Plato neglect the "law . . . whereby one must work to acquire a possession."[38]

From this perspective, a "Kantian" reading of Godwin's novel would be a Common Sense reading, which critiques St. Leon's neglect of family values and his exalted ambition. "In exaltation," Kant says, "human beings raise themselves above humanity."[39] Thus Godwin, we can argue, repeatedly exposes the superior tone assumed by his protagonist: the tone of the mystagogue, the alchemist, or the possessor of secrets, all of whom Kant so often criticizes. As significant as St. Leon's moral *hybris* is his epistemological overreaching, and here too Kant proves useful. St. Leon is continuously guilty of what Kant calls "errors of *subreptio*," whereby an idea "is applied to," or one could say projected onto, "an object falsely believed to be adequate with and to correspond to it" (*CPR*, 373), whether the object be personal wealth or the political renovation of Hungary. Moreover, as part of his critique of the process by which "pure conceptions" insensibly assume an empirical reality and "signs" are "confuse[d]" with "things,"[40] Kant at key points in his *Critiques* takes up figures of speech and thought, such as paralogism and hypotyposis, that rhetorically cover over the positing of presuppositions that are groundless. Hypotyposis is the "presentation" or "making . . . sensible" of an intuition that cannot be proven: a symbolic hypotyposis thus provides a figure for a "concept which only reason can think, and to which no sensible intuition can be adequate" (*CJ*, 225). The "body politic," with its assumption that social relations are organically integrated and purposive, is such a hypotyposis, and its mode is purely analogical. But we tend to forget that language "is full of such indirect presentations, in accordance with an analogy, where the expression does not contain the actual schema for the concept, but only a symbol for reflection" (226). Through these sleights-of-hand, ideas, instead of remaining "regulative" and "hypothetical," become "constitutive" and pass themselves off as "conceptions of actual things" (*CPR*, 373).

In *St. Leon*, alchemy is nothing but a sublime hypotyposis for political justice, which itself may be a hypotyposis. St. Leon's entire history is also an example of a transcendental paralogism, which is to say that it unfolds logically at the level of mimesis, if we accept his "communication" on its "own terms" (*St.L*, 214), but it is based on an illogical presupposition. Kant defines a logical paralogism as occurring when an argument is false in form, "be the content what it may." In a transcendental paralogism, though "the form is correct and unexceptionable," the argument "concludes falsely" because of the inference of an antecedent from a consequent condition: thus B is used to ground the antecedent premise A, which B needs to ground itself in the first place (*CPR*, 233). As we have already seen, "character," which for Godwin depends on this circular logic, is an example of a specifically "transcendental" paralogism because it has to do with the categories through which we experience the world, the laws that the mind gives itself. Whereas the paralogism of character in *Caleb Williams* emerges only after much critical thought, no attempt is made in *St. Leon* to disguise the fact that the entire plot is based on the positing of a presupposition that may be groundless. Why should one believe that there is a stranger, when this stranger himself is not possessed of the wealth or immortality whose secret he supposedly imparts to St. Leon? St. Leon himself raises this question (*St.L*, 143). How can one believe that the stranger really is able to communicate a complex process requiring "methodical and orderly discourse" (157) after three paralytic strokes?

Moreover, until close to the end, there is no reference to the tools St. Leon uses to manufacture gold and no use of even a single technical term from alchemy, so that a certain incredulity attends everything that he does. That St. Leon does explicitly call for his alchemical chest when trying to bribe Bethlem Gabor to release him (418–20) renders his escape from his first prison, without any reference to his tools, all the more unbelievable. Perhaps he initially avoids referring to the mysterious chest because he must not only "hide" his "secrets" but "conceal" that he has "any to hide" (161). But then ceasing to hide his secret, especially in the light of Bethlem Gabor's contemptuous reaction to the contents of the toolbox, suggests that there was nothing to conceal in the first place: that the philosopher's stone or the ideological secret it signifies promise something extravagantly great that amounts to nothing.

Such a reading, which is obvious enough, would make *St. Leon* a work of what Kant calls pragmatic anthropology, which is where Kant, in his *Anthropology from a Pragmatic Point of View* (1798), does indeed place novels, alongside travel and biographies, as providing "knowledge of the world." Pragmatic anthropology focuses on what "man makes, can, or should make of himself as a freely acting being" and thus on "rules of conduct" for the practice of everyday life. As a discipline of the "understanding," it is not concerned with the phenomena of sensibility, at one end, or Reason and the supersensible, at the other, with "physiological anthropology," on the one hand, or "metaphysics," on the other.[41] Or rather, Kant does take up these phenomena extensively in terms of the divisions between sensibility, understanding, and reason already developed in the first *Critique*. But the *Anthropology* as Kant's equivalent for the novel of manners wants to regulate human behavior in relation to aberrations of sensibility or reason for which novels are invaluable source books: aberrations that range from drug taking and drinking to dreaming or claiming to foresee the future. At issue, then, in reading Godwin with the anthropological Kant, is the kind of knowledge novels are assumed to produce. I return in the last section to *St. Leon* as a fiction about fiction and thus to Godwin's relation to the institution of the Novel as pragmatic anthropology. Suffice it to say that, rather than "enlarging" our views, as Willich puts it,[42] the knowledge Kant associates with novels is that of pragmatic containment. Kant shared the prevailing Common Sense view of novels expressed by Wordsworth and others. Thus Wordsworth himself refers to "frantic novels" and "sickly . . . German tragedies," which apply "gross and violent stimulants" to the mind, while Coleridge attacks Rousseau as a "dreamer of lovesick Tales" and criticizes novels for "painfully" affecting the "feelings" and exciting "curiosity and sensibility."[43] This view was instrumental in the formation of the novel of manners and the institution of the nineteenth-century Novel as an ideological apparatus for managing the errors with which novels and novel-reading were associated in the eighteenth century. Kant therefore included novels in the section of his *Anthropology* "On the Soul's Weaknesses and Illnesses with Respect to Its Cognitive Faculty." He complained that "reading novels, in addition to causing many other mental discords, has also the consequence that it makes distraction habitual." Not only do novels contain distractions, which are dangerous because of the unpredictable (or Godwin would say "magnetic") affinities they arouse in their readers; they also cause one to "invent digressions" and "further fictional occurrences" and thus to become even more distracted from the path of understanding "during the reading."[44] Novels are, in effect, a form of speculation.

In short, novels, which in the late eighteenth century were not yet clearly separated from romance, are fertile territory for hypotyposes and paralogisms. Yet such deviations from the new economy of "evidence" are not necessarily to be dismissed.[45] As Lyotard argues, paralogism may be the breach in logic that makes genuine science possible.[46] And in his political essays, translated into English in the 1790s, Kant himself indulges in paralogisms, hypotyposes, and hypotheses. Most notable among these are his ideas of a "league of peace" and a "universal *cosmopolitan state*." Not only are these notions themselves hypotyposes; they are also based on ideas of perfectibility and purposiveness in human history that are entirely paralogical and presumptive. For example, faced with the "senseless course" of history and the Hobbesian reality that "man's natural state is one of war," Kant argues that human beings *will* see the disadvantages of war because they *should*.[47] He converts desired effects into grounding causes, in what Slavoj Žižek calls a positing of the very presuppositions that make positing possible in the first place.[48]

This circular logic is what Kant himself describes as "*insert*[ing] speculations into the *progression* of a history in order to fill out gaps" between cause and effect. Kant famously continues: "To produce a history entirely from speculations alone is no better than to sketch a romance." Yet the

"Speculative Beginning of Human History" (1786), where he makes these statements,[49] sketches just such a history, in a confounding of fiction and history that ironically plays on Scottish conjectural history's standards of probability and that curiously foreshadows Godwin's "Of History and Romance" (1798). Kant himself concedes that his utopian histories in "Speculative Beginning," "To Perpetual Peace" (1795), and "Idea for a Universal History" (1784) are "philosophical" and not "empirical": led as they are by an "*a priori* guiding thread," they are "projects" of "reason" or "imagination in the company of reason" and are thus a form of "romance." But like Godwin, Kant in this essay uses the methods of sophistry to cut through a dialectical impasse between Reason and understanding, by confounding history and fiction, evidence and fantasy, so as to deconstruct such limiting oppositions. Thus, having insisted in the "Speculative Beginning" that "speculation need not be fictional, but can instead be based on experience," Kant proceeds to base this so-called experience on *Genesis*. He calls *Genesis* a "historical document" but describes its initial assumption of a single human pair as "something that human reason is utterly incapable of deriving from any previous natural causes." Everything else follows from this presupposition: because there are two people the human race can come into being, because there is "*only a single pair* . . . war does not arise," and so on.[50] But the grounding proposition is unhistorical. By thus intimating that what passes for history is fancy, Kant by default claims the status of history for his own "flight of fancy," not unlike Godwin, who in "Of History and Romance" similarly undoes the opposition between the two genres, in ways that are at once sophistical and imaginative.

To be sure, Kant's utopian claims are hedged with irony, which keeps them in the realm of hypothesis. As Hannah Arendt argues, Kant's attitude to radical political action was that of a "spectator,"[51] which allowed him to stay on the safe side of the boundary between the empirical and the transcendental. Conventionally, it is Hegel whom we associate with Reason as a "positive" rather than "negative" faculty, and so with the "transformation of what Kant calls dialectics with purely negative" or critical "connotations into dialectics as a method for the discovery of the truth and simultaneously as truth revealing itself."[52] For Hegel dialectic is no longer just a form of logic but constitutes history as the process of the Idea working itself out through trial and error. St. Leon, then, seems more a Hegelian than a Kantian, especially given his exaltation into a world-historical spirit of unusual longevity: an idea for which Kant showed less enthusiasm than Godwin.[53] St. Leon, as we have seen, constantly projects ideas into history, with unfortunate consequences. Yet Kant's fantasy of a League of Peace did indeed assume historical form in the League of Nations, and in the end it is not clear that he was opposed to implementing ideas, except insofar as doing so foreclosed further debate on these ideas. As Susan Shell suggests, referring to "An Old Question Newly Raised: Is the Human Race Constantly Progressing?" (1798), which contains Kant's thoughts on the French Revolution, Kant believed that an "idea" is distinguished from a "romance" by the fact that "an idea, to the extent it is propagated, can become a self-fulfilling prophecy."[54] Clearly, the embodiment of Reason can proceed only uncertainly through imaginary or symbolic resolutions of underlying contradictions. Yet as the history of Kant's ideas shows, it is only if one takes risks with an idea that even this uncertain, "abderitic" form of progress is possible.[55]

In the third *Critique,* Kant comes close to a version of dialectic that more cautiously converges with Hegel's. Whereas in the first *Critique* dialectic is simply the exposure of illusion (*CPR,* 69–70), in the third it has the more constructive role of negotiating a conflict, dispute, or contest (*CJ,* 214) so as to move beyond it, by showing that "two apparently conflicting propositions . . . can be compatible with each other, even though the explanation of the possibility of their concept exceeds our faculty of cognition" (216). Dialectic, in Kant's later version of it, is therefore in the service of Reason and not just of its critique from the viewpoint of the understanding. An example of the kind of antinomy or aporia, which dialectic tries to resolve, is the impasse Kant sees in "An Old Question" between the "chiliastic" or progressive view of history and the "abderitic" view, that for every step forward there is a step backward. Kant does not see these two notions as contradictory but defers their resolution to a future point in history. Here, as also "in the Critique of Practical Reason," Kant writes, "the resolution of the antinomies" compels one, "against one's will, to look beyond the sensible and to seek the unifying point of all our faculties in the supersensible"(*CJ,* 217).

In the third *Critique,* which deals only with taste, the resolution of antinomies or aporias is still a logical problem, which is not invested in history. Yet history is strongly present in Kant's political essays, both as the object and the medium of dialectical *thought*. It is then only a short step to history as the actual medium for a self-critical positing of presuppositions. The (post)Kantian historical dialectic is made possible by credit as a way of borrowing against the future. Kant did not favor credit, which he saw within a more conservative phrase regime as a form of debt, though he also saw, as John Law did, that the repayment of debt could "be forestalled indefinitely by the economic stimulus that derives from credit's influence on industry and influence." Still, for Kant, credit was the "ingenious invention of a commercial people [England] during this century."[56] It was one of those paralogisms that Kant saw as sophistical: first there was money, and then as a result of its circulation, there was wealth. Yet Kant's notion of ideas as self-fulfilling prophecies is nothing if not a paralogism and a form of credit. And credit, as the promise of what is not-yet, is linked at a deep-structural level to Romanticism and Idealism as economies of the future. Analogically, credit created an environment for expansion and the coining of new ideas. In the definitions of Romanticism provided by the Schlegels, Classicism is content with things as they are whereas Romanticism is the production of the new within a striving for the infinite. The two modes also correspond to completely different cognitive economies, which Kant distinguished as understanding and Reason: thus for Hegel Classicism is the "adequate embodiment" of an idea that we already understand, whereas Symbolic and Romantic art put forth ideas that have yet to find their ground in actuality (*A*, 1.77–79). For Hegel, as we shall see, the novel was the end of Romanticism, despite having developed from romance; it was already in the process of becoming the Novel. But for Friedrich Schlegel the novel was the very epitome of Romanticism: as in his famous equation of the novel, or *roman*, with "*romantische Poesie*" and his description of it as "*ein Romantisches Buch*."[57] For Hegel two decades later, the end of this Romanticism was also the end of art, which he felt obliged to approve from the perspective of common sense. But Godwin in the 1790s sees the relation between Romanticism, Idealism, and fiction somewhat differently.

As befits someone writing within what Kant and Hegel criticized as commercial culture, Godwin focalizes the relation between Romanticism and the Novel through the highly ambiguous metaphor of credit. Godwin turns the economic underpinnings of the Novel's pragmatism inside out by making money a vehicle for Romanticism, while also raising the question of whether Romanticism is credible. For *St. Leon* is built around questions of credit, credibility, and fiction itself as a form of credit, inflected by new monetary forms that, incredibly, recast the relation between signifier and signified, imagination and actuality. St. Leon is born at the end of an age that grounds wealth in land. But he ends by using the manufacture of gold—the very metal that was the bedrock of the gold standard—as a hypotyposis for printing money: a scheme unimaginable in the sixteenth century except through metaphors like alchemy, yet certainly possible by Godwin's time. In experimenting, before his time, with a New Deal for Hungary, St. Leon invents a form of credit that brings with it new ways of phrasing the problem of belief. Or more precisely, St. Leon does not literally use credit as a monetary form, since the money he uses *is* gold. But whether we believe that he has this gold, that he can manufacture gold, depends on whether we credit Godwin's fiction. The antinomy of belief, as Kant might call it, emerges as an aporia that demands a new resolution because of a narrative temporality that eludes linear thought. Within this temporality we can believe *and* disbelieve Godwin's fiction. For Godwin invents himself as a character ahead of his own time in the sixteenth century but involved in practices that have grown discredited two centuries later. And yet this character might still outlive his author, since St. Leon, unlike the stranger, is not shown as dying: he does not quite submit to the terms of the Faustian wager, in which, contrary to the economics of credit, what one gains is always lost because one never really had it. St. Leon, moreover, writes his history in 1590, thirty years after the end of the story, at what may be roughly the age of eighty-five.[58] But since the stranger has enjoined him not to divulge any particulars of the stranger's story until a century after the latter's death (126), it is unclear when we are reading the story. If we imagine ourselves as reading it when it was written, St. Leon must have violated his compact with the stranger, and then we cannot trust what we are reading. Only on condition of reading the narrative as if we were in the future can we believe what we cannot, by the very "terms" of St. Leon's own "communication" (214), believe in the present.

St. Leon's situation allegorizes that of Godwin. For credit or credibility is also the issue facing Godwin, whose ideas of political justice had been discredited, perhaps because they were before their time. As Mark Philp has shown, Godwin's beliefs did once have currency among Radical Dissenters. These ideas, at their most "far-fetched," included his hope for a longevity that would make propagation unnecessary,[59] as human beings grew "immortal" and the earth became a place "of men, and not of children," where there is "no war, no crimes, . . . no government" (*PJ*, 2.528). But as Paul Hamilton has recently argued, Godwin wrote his second novel at a time when events (including the English reaction to the French Revolution) had deprived radical discourse of public support.[60] How then to make these ideas credible, even to oneself, without a community of believers? Despite his greater emphasis on private judgment, Godwin was committed to what Kant calls "publicity": the principle that "private maxims must be subjected to an examination by which" one finds out whether one "can declare them publicly": whether they can be made to count but also whether they can withstand public discussion and rational proof. Kant disliked secrets and mysteries and felt that "Reason is not made 'to isolate itself but to get into community with others.'"[61] That the stranger craves "oblivion" (126) but St. Leon *writes* his story marks Godwin's enlightened belief in the "freedom" and the responsibility "not just to think but to publish—'the freedom of the pen.'"[62] Yet publicness does not ensure and might indeed impede freedom of thought. Kant, who himself suffered overt and internalized censorship, cannot have been unaware of the fine line between his ideal of publicness and the tyranny of public opinion. Publication and the public sphere constituted by the explosion of print culture both facilitated and constricted the "choice in reading" that Godwin advocated. For public opinion might retrodetermine what was written and limit how it was read. And Godwin's novels, particularly *Caleb Williams,* are full of scenes that thematize the limitations of "publicity" through the impossibility of making what one privately knows to be true publicly credible.

St. Leon crystallizes this problem of conveying private judgment into the public sphere, as the aporia produced when Godwin, who espouses Enlightenment values of frankness and public discussion, uses a character like St. Leon to convey his ideas. Because St. Leon has sworn an oath of secrecy to the stranger, the proof that he can do what he claims to do, that he is not lying when he denies murdering the stranger—indeed, the entire empirical and factual basis for his story—must be taken on faith. He cannot tell "the plain and unanswerable tale" required by his son and can only "utter a forged and inconsistent tale" (*St.L*, 188, 193). As St. Leon declares, "the pivot upon which the history I am composing turns, is a mystery. If [readers] will not accept of my communication upon my own terms, they must lay aside my book" (214). Like Kant, Godwin too did not believe in such "mystery" and "mysticism." One of the developments that led to the modernization of alchemy as chemistry was print culture, which "created the category of the public" and the idea that knowledge must be "more widely and exoterically disseminated."[63] Yet what to do when one's ideas have been exploded, like the erstwhile "science" of alchemy, even though these ideas may be ahead of their time, like St. Leon's proto-Keynsian economics?

The historical situation of alchemy in the late eighteenth century aptly embodies the paradox of a pure Reason that cannot be made public. St. Leon cannot divulge his secret, but if he did, nobody would believe him anyway, since no one in an age of paper money believes that a man can manufacture gold. As we have seen, Godwin deals with the incredulity that is likely to greet his text by constructing its transmission around this very (im)possibility. As Paul Hamilton has also argued, the very mode of the text is "duplicitous";[64] or perhaps we should say, putting it more positively, that it is paradoxical. St. Leon is debarred from publishing his story and insists that his "pages shall never be surveyed by other eyes than mine" (162). It would seem, then, that the only way we can read Godwin's novel is to read it as not having been written, as not claiming what it claims. Yet the pages have been not only written but transferred into the public sphere, so the text must in some sense claim what it disclaims and be able to do what it cannot do. This paradoxical mode of publication as an allegory of Godwin's own relation to the sphere of publicity functions very much like the ironies and double negations that keep the Kantian critique in motion. For Kant faced a similar problem of credibility in admitting his interest in Swedenborg, which might well have jeopardized his search for a university position. Swedenborg was seen as a heretic and an enthusiast, even though as we now know, Newton, the very exemplar of the scientific Enlightenment, had done extensive work on alchemy. Newton may even have seen his alchemical work, which, curiously enough was rediscovered in our own time by Keynes, as his true achievement.[65] Raising the question of whether one can believe in spirit(s) in the age of the Enlightenment, Kant makes a place for spirit on the grounds that dismissing it would itself be dogmatic and uncritical: "It is just as much a foolish prejudice to believe without reason *none* of the many things that are recounted with some semblance of truth, as to believe *all* that is spread by popular rumor without proof; hence the author of this work, in order to avoid the former prejudice, has allowed himself to be in part carried away by the latter."[66] To be sure, the rhetorical figure underlying Kant's (dis)claimer is litotes, whereas Godwin's mode is paradox: Kant does *not* make a claim that he nevertheless makes, whereas Godwin *makes* a claim that he does not make. Yet the effect is similar to that of the Kantian critique, which is not a dismantling of the claims of Reason, but a critique so thoroughgoing as to generate a continual disbelief, even in disbelief.

By this logic, might not St. Leon's story and Godwin's ideas possibly be true? These ideas, as Lyotard and Jean-Loup Thébaud say of the Kantian "idea," rest "upon something like the future of further enquiry."[67] After all, we are not speaking of the ideas literally put forth in the text—preposterous claims of immortality and making gold—but of ones not fully divulged for which they are metaphors. Kant too could not "really" have been a follower of Swedenborg, whom at times he parodically calls Schwedenberg. His interest in the spirit-world is a figure for the possibility of some process at work in history that we cannot conceive: a process like Hegel's Spirit, which might bring into being far-fetched notions such as perpetual peace and the League of Nations. The proof that Kant was not wrong is that these notions have become more credible since his time, if no less impossible. Godwin makes alchemy a metaphor for his ideas not only because it raises the problem of what can and cannot be communicated exoterically but also because alchemy, which "mixed rational endeavour with speculation," existed on the border between "the possible and the impossible, the real and the fictitious."[68] Moreover, Godwin is not interested in alchemy as a way of making a metaphysical claim, but rather in the thought experiments it makes possible. As St. Leon writes: "My design in writing this narrative . . . is not to teach the art of which I am in possession, but to describe the adventures it produced to me" (160). Insofar as this "art" is to be conceived as the effects it produces, alchemy is like money in Law's system, or even money for Kant, who, despite his comments on credit, also sees money as a way of stimulating industry. For Kant, who is not interested in money per se, the "intellectual concept under which the empirical concept of money falls" is that of "circulation": circulation, as the idea was reinvented outside of physiology by the new sciences of wealth, stimulates "industry" not just in an economic sense but also in the "sciences . . . insofar as they would not otherwise be taught to others."[69] In this sense alchemy and money, in the effects they produce, are also like literature. For literature, according to Godwin, is its circulation or, better still, its dissemination. The work of art does not contain a meaning but is the "effect it . . . produce[s] upon the reader," which "cannot be completely ascertained except by the experiment" (136). "Experiment" is also a word Godwin often uses in *St. Leon* (117, 199–200, 230, 232, 368), and it explains how alchemy, far from being a form of mystery or dogma, is part of the conceptual matrix by which Godwin configures the economy of fiction as one of speculation.

❧

Ben Jonson portrays the alchemist as what Marguerite in *St. Leon* calls a "low character" (*St.L*, 210), and Johnson's *Dictionary* and the *Encyclopedia Britannica* also cast aspersions on alchemy.[70] But the author of the entry on alchemy in the *Encyclopédie* sees alchemy as an experimental chemistry that simply "executes more quickly" what nature "takes centuries to produce." Moreover, once its operations become "more known," they will take their place in "ordinary chemistry," suggesting that alchemy may be only strategically esoteric.[71] This ambiguous relation to print culture may explain why the stranger wants to transmit his knowledge only to a single adept and yet does not rule out a wider dissemination in the future (158, 126). Given these opposing views, how we judge alchemy, gambling, or even fiction may have much to do with nationality, and in *St. Leon* Godwin experiments with a character liberated from the very institution of nationality. For St. Leon does not simply leave his native land and return, like Wordsworth in *The Prelude* or Emily in *The Mysteries of Udolpho*. He is a kind of postcolonial who migrates from place to place, even leaving Western Europe entirely and in the process deterritorializing the very bases of judgment.

England is one country St. Leon omits in his travels through Switzerland, Germany, Italy, Spain, Hungary, and, sartorially at least, Armenia (359). But England (or a still tenuously "United" Kingdom) is implicitly present insofar as all Godwin's novels are about the emerging ideological apparatus of the Novel and its related institutions of the family and public opinion. For the Novel is part of the discourse network of the public sphere, whose inception Habermas traces to "Great Britain at the turn of the eighteenth century."[72] The Novel defines itself as a critical category against "romance," the word still used for novels in Germany, which for Friedrich Schlegel is etymologically continuous with Romanticism. Summing up this opposition, Clara Reeve in *The Progress of Romance* describes the romance as concerned with "fabulous persons and things," while the "Novel is a picture of real life and manners" and "the times in which it is written."[73] What Reeve distinguishes as romance versus novel, Kavanagh describes in France as a turn from the adventure-novel to realism, marked by a terminological shift from *roman* to *histoire*. For Kavanagh, the history of fiction is part of a genealogy of gambling that culminates in a "taming of chance," as probability replaces possibility. Within this double history, the demise of the adventure-novel is homologous with the emergence of the new discipline of statistics, which introduced expectations of predictability and normativity. An emphasis on "evidence" dissociated literature from the showing of the extraordinary.[74] An emphasis on the statistical mean placed the "*homme moyen*" and his values at the center of the genre's target audience, thus making the novel a "didactic analysis of character within an ultimately rational world,"[75] resulting also in what Browning calls "objective" poetry. In Britain this triumph of probability as normativity has been marked by the prominence given in current histories of the Romantic novel to just two novelists: Scott, who recontains romance in a historical novel focalized through a "mediocre, prosaic hero," and Austen, who develops the novel of manners as the sphere of female governmentality.[76]

Hegel, too, has things to say about the Novel, this time in the context of Romanticism. Discussing in his *Aesthetics* the art leading up to his own time, Hegel sees this period as typified by two forms: Dutch "genre painting" and what we would now call the Novel, the world of prose and objectivity confronted by the Narrator in *Alastor*. Both are bourgeois forms produced by commercial cultures (*A*, 1.595) and epitomizing the "prose of actuality" produced by the "imitation of nature": "i.e. man's daily active pursuits in his natural necessities and comfortable satisfaction, . . . the activities of family life and civil society business" (1.592, 595). Dutch "satisfaction in present-day life" and attention to "what is useful and necessary" "even in the commonest and smallest things" (1.597) amounts to a kind of mediocrity.[77] The situation with novels is more complex, as indicated by Hegel's description of them as the "modern" form of romance (1.592). Here it seems the idealism of earlier romance, with its knights-errant, is displaced into narratives of youthful transgression and resistance to civil society, attempts to "change the world" and "improve it." But unlike Kristeva, for whom the very essence of the novel is its adolescence, Hegel emphasizes the necessity of growing up, which produces the *Bildungsroman* as the product of civil society, with its disciplinary mechanisms of "police, law courts, . . . political government" (1.592–93). Although Hegel, as a man of his times, feels obliged to accept this development from romance to novel, it is notable that the triumph of prose at the end of history is also the end of art. Hegel's apparent celebration of the demise of art and its replacement by a "philosophy" more consistent with the aims of modernity thus masks a profound melancholia. The symptom of this melancholia is the *typological* category of Romanticism, as a resistance between spirit and matter that cannot find adequate expression in the art produced in the *chronological* period of Romanticism, whether it be "romantic" or everyday art.

Yet it is by no means clear how definitive the turn to realism was in this period. Kavanagh locates the end of the adventure-novel at the beginning of the eighteenth century, when Law, who was very much an adventurer, arrived in France. Similarly, whatever theoretical shifts were under way,[78] in Godwin's time the division of novels from romances had not yet been successfully instituted. Even by the 1830s Mary Shelley has heard of Austen, but she does not present the "Miss Austen view of domestic life" as normative. Shelley also uses the term "novel" synonymously with "romance," even though she distinguishes them when she says "the Italians have no novels," which she glosses as "tales relating to the present day, and detailing events and sentiments such as would find counterparts in the histories and minds of themselves and their friends."[79] Thus Godwin's "Of History and Romance" and its fictional companion *St. Leon* could both be seen as attempts to find a more viable place for what Hegel calls Romanticism as the differend between *roman* and *histoire*.

Reeve's staging of the debate over fiction through a dialogue among conversants of different sexes—a form she borrows from Bernard de Fontenelle's *Plurality of Worlds*—also aims at unsettling a too easy distinction between romances and novels, which would mark the end of

"Romanticism." Ideally, according to the public opinion she re-cites, romances arouse extravagant desires while novels provide "examples of virtue rewarded and vice punished."[80] Yet Reeve unsettles this seeming valorization of the Novel by exposing the gendered mechanisms of a discourse that both implicates women as rebellious subjects and offers them a palliative interpellation as educators of youth and writers of conduct books. Indeed, her use of the conversation, the form par excellence of the public sphere, puts on trial this middle-class public "opinion" that, as Habermas argues, had only recently been elevated from prejudice to consensus.[81] By ironically placing her history of prose fiction in the Enlightenment genre of "progress," while constructing a genealogy in which novels and romances symptomatically overlap, Reeve shows that the Novel is a purely disciplinary and not an empirical category. Actual novels are troublesome: a trouble connected with women, circulating libraries, and the "effects" that literature, regardless of its author's "intention," might have on readers. The Novel must therefore comprise "books, which though published under the title of Novels, are designed as an antidote to the bad effects of" novels.[82] Reeve thus allows us to see how the institution of the Novel not only is produced by but also serves as an agent of public opinion. Her extensive references to romances imported from Europe, which in turn came from the Orient, further implicates British ideas about literature in a larger cosmopolitan public sphere, in which the identity of fiction is by no means settled.

St. Leon has generally been read as a Novel by those who see it as condemning Romantic ambition and make Marguerite Godwin's touchstone by identifying her with Wollstonecraft.[83] But as a text provocatively built around a fabrication—the philosopher's stone—*St. Leon* should rather be seen as inhabiting the debatable land between fiction as possibility and the empirical and moral realism of the Novel. At the heart of a reading of Godwin's text within the institution of the Novel is the discourse of the family, which, by a deliberate anachronism that reduces the family itself to a hypothesis, is the nuclear bourgeois family of two centuries later. St. Leon, it is often argued, fails to respect his contract with this family as a space where there is complete openness and "communion of spirit." On the contrary, he speaks of feeling limited by "scene[s] of pastoral simplicity" (209, 177). Yet as Habermas has shown, "the conjugal family's self-image of its intimate sphere collided . . . with the real functions of the bourgeois family" in "the reproduction of capital." As "an agency of society," the family in practice disciplined the individual according to "societally necessary requirements," while maintaining the "illusion of freedom." The family, and indeed the very notion of an "intimate" sphere, were "profoundly caught up in the requirements of the market."[84] Hegel too had tried to theorize marriage as "the 'substantial' union of hearts" and the family as a "community of personal and private interests," but had had to concede their role in maintaining "property . . . industry, [and] labour."[85] The economic role of the family in maintaining a middle class that would not threaten global finance is clear in Hegel's account of the Dutch (or *deutsch*) home as "simple, attractive, and neat . . . unassuming and content in its wealth" (*A*, 2.886). The Novel is of course intimately tied to the discourse of the family, as novels often start with an account of the protagonist's family origins. In Habermas's analysis, the public sphere and its institutions, including the Novel, are formed by "private people com[ing] together as a public." The corollary is that the category of the private, including the "feelings," exists only in public: to "the degree that state and society permeated each other" the private is itself discursively formed for the convenience of the public.[86] In the later nineteenth century it was the Novel that emerged as the very epitome of this public subjectivity and, therefore, as an institution intimately tied to the nation as well as the family.

Perhaps, then, we should not simply retreat in shock when St. Leon anticipates, as a result of his immortality, that by "the death of her I most loved, my affections should be weaned from my country . . . [and] I would then set out upon my travels" (167). Godwin sees the extent to which family responsibilities, by limiting the spirit of adventure, dampen speculation and keep things as they are. Critiquing Habermas (1962) *avant la lettre*, Hannah Arendt in, 1958, had already seen the death of the political in any meaningful sense in "the social," as the expansion of domestic values into the public sphere under cover of a politically expedient sentimentalism. For Arendt the "emergence of society—the rise of housekeeping, its activities, problems, and organizational devices—from the shadowy interior of the household into the light of the public sphere" has changed "almost beyond recognition" the meaning of the word "political." This ubiquity of the social, correlated as it is with "the emergence of mass society" and the end of history, has also meant the end of "individuality" as other than an exchangeable commodity.[87] Arguably the Novel is an important moment in the globalization of domestic values, which has now culminated in a middle-class narcissism focused on "culture" and practices of everyday life.

Against the grain of this emergent genre, Godwin's second novel is an experiment with a character who is progressively unbound from nation and family. In the spirit of experiment the character he invents is a paper character: St. Leon does not really seem affected by the ruin of his family or his repeated imprisonments, even though he spends twelve years in jail at the hands of the Inquisition. He never really suffers, nor can we believe at the end that he really is, like Mandeville or Fleetwood, a shattered man. For the novel is not "really" a confession either. Rather, it plays with the responses the reader might have given its generic categorizaton as confession or, alternatively, adventure-novel. The realist novel, as both Mary Shelley and Habermas recognize, depends on an equivalence of intra- and extradiegetic worlds that is essentially conservative. Because we "use the relationships" between characters in the text "as substitute relationships for reality,"[88] we cannot allow a character to do anything that we would not want to see done in real life. But although Godwin's novel is often teasingly realistic in its detail, St. Leon is hardly like "[our]selves and [our] friends."[89] Nor does the reader, despite Godwin's anticipation of Shelley's novel, really suffer from the loss of St. Leon's family, as we do in *The Last Man*. For if we treat St. Leon's alchemical claims with incredulity, then we also cannot believe at a profound affective level, as so many critics do, that he has ruined his family, since both are part of the same story.

Moreover, there is the curious way the story is reopened by the domestic interlude with which it closes. St. Leon, in his last act, uses his wealth to secretly arrange Charles's future with Pandora, thus providing his "somewhat melancholy story" with a "pleasing . . . termination" (478). In settling this last family obligation, he also shifts the problematic of debt and obligation onto Charles, since it is now Charles who labors under the illusion that a man can "be author of his own existence" (193). It is Charles who, despite epitomizing his mother's middle-class self-reliance, has not moved with the times and remains fixated in the ethos of the Crusades in his attitude to the Turks. As St. Leon is now free of his son, so too is Godwin free of the Novel: he has discharged his debt to the institution of the Novel by ending with the required marriage, which, as Pandora's name indicates, may well be a can of worms. As important, Godwin has discharged the reader from the obligation to condemn St. Leon's treatment of his son, thus freeing us to read St. Leon's past more adventurously in the future.

But this is not to say that we "approve" of St. Leon, which would be another form of "realism." After all, since St. Leon's wealth is fictitious, the happy ending is a hypothesis. The text, in true Kantian spirit, is an experiment with reading adventurously: a critique of our reasons for reading as we do. From the hero's chance meeting with the stranger to his escapes from prison, *St. Leon* refers to the picaresque genre of "adventures" (160) so as to call into question our reading of it within the genre of the Novel. To read the text realistically is to see St. Leon's life as following a logic of repetition that forecloses progress to a future.[90] But the story can just as much be seen as organized by a logic of escape. St. Leon's first brush with the law occurs when he is unjustly imprisoned in Switzerland at the instigation of Grimseld (122). Later, in Constance, he has a narrow escape when the police come to his house in search of the stranger; then he is jailed on suspicion of murdering the stranger, imprisoned by the Inquisition, and confined a fourth time in the castle of Bethlem Gabor, for no reason other than that he embodies the principle of hope (416). Each time he escapes, he is given a second chance at eluding the ideological discipline of the realist novel. Incredible as these escapes increasingly are, if we believe he has escaped, we must once again believe that Godwin's idea might succeed. But since we cannot but believe that St. Leon has escaped if we continue reading, the very fact of our reading is the paralogical proof that the idea might be true. This is not to say that we know, or even need to know, the precise form to be taken by these "ambitious and comprehensive" plans for improving "nations and mankind" (434). The philosopher's stone, as a short-cut around the problems men like Law actually encountered in increasing the supply of money, is a fantasy that functions like Kant's transcendental schematism in that it "constitutes" or provides the "co-ordinates" for desire. For as Slavoj Žižek argues, in seeing fantasy as a Kantian, self-critical faculty, fantasy does not imagine the attainment of its object; rather, by mediating between "the formal symbolic structure and the positivity of the objects we encounter in reality" it "teaches us how to desire."[91] In providing through the philosopher's stone a "schema" for an (im)possible Pure Reason, Godwin too constitutes a specifically Romantic form of the novel wherein narrative, instead of being the reproduction of capital, is the production of desire.

CHAPTER SIX

Whose Text?

Godwin's Editing of Mary Wollstonecraft's The Wrongs of Woman

IN 1798 GODWIN PUBLISHED *The Wrongs of Woman; or, Maria. A Fragment* as part of his attempt to collect the loose ends of his wife's remarkable career. In contrast to the novel's title, this larger gathering is entitled *Posthumous Works of the Author of "A Vindication of the Rights of Woman,"* and is accompanied in the same year by Godwin's *Memoirs of the Author of "A Vindication of the Rights of Woman."* The novel had been left unfinished at Wollstonecraft's death, and in "revising [it] for the press" Godwin combined two states of the manuscript to create what we would now call an eclectic text (*W*, 72).[1] What he gives us is not a clean text, as with Mary Shelley's *Valperga,* which he also prepared for publication. On the contrary, the text is punctuated with notes, parenthetical clarifications, and asterisks, all of which are clearly marked as separate. In addition to the fragmentary "Preface, by the Author," it includes Godwin's Preface and a "Conclusion, by the Editor." Yet the consequences of Godwin's editing have not been systematically explored. For a text that displays the signs of its editing is not one but two texts (or more). As we read, we are reading what Wollstonecraft wrote and also what Godwin did with the text in marking it at crucial points as unfinished, inchoate, unprocessed. On the one hand, Godwin's philological scrupulousness evinces an honesty about the state of this text, the roughness of which makes visible something more fundamental about textuality and narrativity. On the other hand, one cannot quite say that the editor has given us "the words, as well as ideas, of the real author," or that his editing "has intruded nothing of himself into the work" (72). If there is no grand narrative organizing Godwin's editorial work, there are mininarratives that develop from his different intrusions, which at crucial points mediate our sense of what Wollstonecraft is doing.

It would be too easy to critique Godwin for substituting *his* deconstruction of Wollstonecraft's text for *her* voice.[2] Godwin's editing cannot be totalized in that way. And indeed, this is characteristic of philology, which Nietzsche described as *"ephexis* [undecisiveness] in interpretation."[3] Still less, given his insistence that a text's meaning consists in its "effect(s)," can the *effects* of Godwin's editing be totalized. To a degree, his interpolations interrupt the institution of *Wrongs* within what we would now call liberal or democratic feminism.[4] This difference between Wollstonecraft and Godwin is intimated in his *Memoirs* of Wollstonecraft, where he prefers to think of her as an "author," while she prefers to be seen as a Female Philosopher,[5] in the double sense of an enlightened intellectual and a radical philosophe.[6] Thus Godwin has reservations about Wollstonecraft's political writings, which he sees as products of their moment, and he is at pains to distinguish her novel, which she revised again and again, from the more hastily polemical *Vindications*. The *Vindication of the Rights of Woman*, he insists, is an "unequal performance," though it "forms an epocha" in the history of feminism (*MV*, 83–84). Godwin the biographer saw Wollstonecraft as a subject-in-process who should not be reduced to a character "pro tempore," which was not her "fixed and permanent character" (82). Rather, he wants to see her as one of the "names of history" in Deleuze and Guattari's sense: a "zone of intensity" rather than the origin of a fixed corpus of beliefs.[7] Yet arguably, through his famous comments on her *Letters from Norway*, Godwin did at times impose on Wollstonecraft his own fixed characterization of her as an icon of sensibility (129). One of the effects of this sentimentalization has been to feed into devaluations of Maria/Wollstonecraft for falling victim to sensibility, based on the uncertain role of Darnford/Imlay, to which Godwin draws attention in his editing. This devaluation, an invisible and certainly unintended effect of Godwin's mediation, is an aspect of the very rights-based liberal feminism that he sought to trouble in not making the *Vindication* Wollstonecraft's central achievement. Without Godwin's portrayal of Wollstonecraft, later generations might not have seen the sensibility he foregrounds, to temper the positivism and activism of the *Vindication* (129), as being such a problem for her.[8] This portrayal includes not only an intimate detailing of her relationships with Fuseli and Imlay in the *Memoirs* but also the publication of her letters to Imlay in the *Posthumous Works:* letters that collapse the distance between Wollstonecraft and Hays and the distance Godwin himself sought to impose on Hays. Thus, curiously, in emphasizing Wollstonecraft's sensibility, Godwin and the liberal feminists who have critiqued Wollstonecraft in our own time (and whose discourse of rights Godwin questions *avant la lettre*) collude in occluding a feminism to which I try to give voice in reading the courtroom scene in chapter 17 outside of Godwin's editing.[9]

But all these readings—Godwin's and others'—are simply scenarios for narrating "Wollstonecraft." For the edited nature of the text means that we can never read *Wrongs* as we read *Memoirs of Emma Courtney,* by identifying too completely with its passions and polemics. It also means that if we are to respect Godwin's "most earnest desire, to intrude nothing of himself into the work," we must be vigilant about the narratives that emerge from *his* editing, since by indicating where he has taken "libert[ies]" with the text, he also withdraws from the assumptions he makes in inserting "the additional phrases" that inevitably do mediate the text (*W,* 72). Wollstonecraft's text, Godwin's editing, and others' readings of the text over time, all form part of an archive that includes both her writing and the thinking that has been and still can be done around her work. Nor is "archive" merely a metaphor, since Godwin's work on Wollstonecraft is literally archival. His editing of the *Posthumous Works* in the same year that he wrote the *Memoirs* involved a careful archiving of (almost) everything Wollstonecraft left behind and a similar archiving of the details of her life, however uncomfortable.

At the same time this archive, as Godwin conceives it, is not limited to the already said. We can take our cue here from a later venture into philology by Godwin, his *Lives of Edward and John Philips, Nephews and Pupils of Milton* (1815). Godwin had written a life of Chaucer in 1804. The *Lives,* however, is not a life of Milton but an afterlife of his influence on his two nephews: the elder one, Edward, who institutionalized Milton's legacy in a classical direction, and the younger nephew, John, whose work ranged more rhizomatically through a number of cross-cultural and interdisciplinary contact zones. This curious text constructs an archive of the nephews' work *and* lives that is partly historical and occasionally fictitious, reflecting Godwin's sense of the archive as a space for what could have been done as well as a tallying of what has (not) been accomplished. For at least in one case, Godwin's census of the nephews' work includes an item that does not exist: John Philips's *The English Fortune-Tellers*. Through this fictitious insertion Godwin calls in question the very notion of a census as tallying, counting up, accounting for a life. Correspondingly, Godwin's text approaches "Milton" as one of the names of history not by gathering together his work but by allowing its effects to be scattered, disseminated through the very different ways it is picked up by the life and work of the more traditional elder nephew and the more anarchic younger nephew. In this sense Godwin's archiving of the nephews' work as "prose," which Jean-François Lyotard describes as "ungraded supply of phrases from all regimens" (*D,* 158), releases a narrativity embedded in the philological process.

❧

Godwin makes thirty-two interventions, of which twenty-one might be considered significant. These range from his Preface, Conclusion, and an "Appendix" inserted after chapter 14, which he curiously entitles "Advertisement" (*W,* 186); to asterisks and dashes in the text, or footnotes indicating where he has "connect[ed] the more finished parts with the pages of an older copy" (72); to seventeen parenthetical insertions, often seemingly minor. Thus, in chapter 3, Godwin introduces a sentence into the narrator's account of the growing intimacy between Maria and Darnford: "[By degrees, Darnford entered into the particulars of his story.]" The addition interrupts our progress to the next sentence: "In a few words, he informed her that he had been a thoughtless, extravagant young man; yet, as he described his faults, they appeared to be the generous luxuriancy of a noble mind" (94). The added sentence is unnecessary and at odds with Wollstonecraft's own phrase "in a few words," but it serves to slow down the impetuousness of Darnford's and Maria's relationship.

Again, in the courtroom scene, Godwin makes two insertions into Maria's plea:

> To this person, thus encountered, I voluntarily gave myself, never considering myself . . . to transgress those laws to which [the policy of artificial society has] annexed [positive] punishments. (197)

The insertions are in the spirit of Maria's plea, but once again the second one is not needed and seems intended to put the scene in dialogue with

Political Justice. More specifically, it evokes Godwin's opposition to all forms of "positive institution," which, "by its very nature . . . has a tendency to suspend the elasticity and progress of mind" (*PJ,* 1.146). To be sure, Wollstonecraft's view of punishment here is Godwin's, and she does echo him on the right of "private judgment" later in the chapter (*W,* 198). Yet, as we shall see, it is not clear that she shared Godwin's total opposition to positive institution, an example being their different views on a system of national education.[10] It is more likely that she might have seen institutions, or a certain instituting of practice, as also necessary. Such a view of institution is taken by Deleuze, for whom institution must be distinguished from law: "law is a limitation of actions, institution a positive model for action": "Contrary to theories of law which place the positive outside the social (natural rights), and the social in the negative (contractual limitation), the theory of the institution . . . presents society as essentially positive and inventive. . . . Such a theory will afford us the following political criteria: tyranny is a regime in which there are many laws and few institutions; democracy is a regime in which there are many institutions, and few laws." No doubt Wollstonecraft would not have been as sanguine about the realities of the social as Deleuze is in the abstract. But in the case of education, for instance, she did see specific advantages in the instituting of a national system of (co)education, including the training of women in male subjects such as anatomy, medicine, and political science.[11]

Each time Godwin marks a phrase by a parenthesis or a footnote, he isolates a small part of the text and forces us to consider it with unusual care. These micro "units of reading" are called *lexias* by Roland Barthes, who famously divides Balzac's *Sarrasine* into a number of *lexias,* ranging from a word to several sentences. The effect is to "star the text, separating . . . the blocks of signification of which reading grasps only the smooth surface, imperceptibly soldered by the movement of sentences, the flowing discourse of narration, the 'naturalness' of ordinary language." By cutting up the text in this way, Barthes ensures that its parts cannot be "delegated to a great final ensemble" and that we "gain access to [it] by several entrances, none of which can be authoritatively declared to be the main one."[12] Because these units are without complete semantic value, they must be linked back into the text from which they have been disjoined. Godwin's cutting out of a more limited number of *lexias* therefore raises in an exemplary way the larger issue of phrasing: of what is at stake in any choice of links, be it his or Wollstonecraft's or ours.

In what follows I suggest that Godwin's editing is not a binding of the text but a form of "(de)composition" that reduces it to the phrases from which it is assembled. Godwin's archiving of the text, in other words, deconstructs it as a novel and returns it to being "prose," which, according to Lyotard, is "not a genre" but an "ungraded supply of phrases from all regimens and of linkages from all genres" (D, 158). Lyotard's notion of phrases and phrase regimes, unlike Foucault's "discourse," introduces a certain mobility into the constructivism of language. Despite Foucault's attempts in *The Archeology of Knowledge* to represent discourse differently from the unifying paradigms he is critiquing, in his genealogical studies discourses acquire a historical inevitability and functional hegemony as forms of linguistic and material institution. By contrast Lyotard, in distinguishing between *genres* of discourse, shifts the ground to aesthetics, making discourse a matter of judgment and judgment a matter of choice in reading. For Lyotard a genre of discourse provides a "phrase regimen," or set of rules for ordering heterogeneous phrases. A "phrase 'happens'" and we "link onto" it through a phrase regimen such as knowing, recounting, or questioning, so as to assimilate it into a "genre of discourse." Each such genre, the "cognitive" and "speculative" being examples, has its particular "stakes" and is a system for linking phrases aimed at "attaining certain goals" (D, xii). That Godwin means to raise the question of linkage can be inferred from the fact that he does not always add the "additional phrases . . . requisite" to complete the meaning (W, 72). At four points, for example, he actually foregrounds the gaps in the text by inserting or leaving in asterisks and dashes. No doubt, in the three instances that involve Darnford (175, 189), Godwin's aim is to convey Wollstonecraft's uncertainty, at the very level of phrasing, about the character of Maria's lover. But in many of these cases it is also a question of his own phrasing. Thus, in the insertion "*By degrees,* Darnford entered into the particulars of his story," we see Godwin himself linking onto the text in a particular way: through the phrase regimen of "recounting," which shifts the episode into the cognitive rather than the enthusiastic genre.

The marking of the text as a draft thus has the effect of halting any premature phrasing of its episodes within a genre such as sentimental romance or feminist communal narrative. One such instance of unphrasing occurs in chapter 9, which ends abruptly:

> If the state of this child affected me, what were my feelings at a discovery I made respecting Peggy   ?*

Godwin adds a footnote saying that the manuscript is "imperfect here" and that an episode "seems to have been intended, which was never committed to paper" (150). What is interesting is that this is not the first time he intervenes in connection with Peggy. Peggy's "tale" had been told in chapter 7 (132). It is a generic tale of unrelieved distress such as we find in Wordsworth's *Ruined Cottage,* beginning with the loss of Peggy's husband, who is pressed into military service and dies, and then the loss of all her possessions. Maria settles some money on Peggy, in one of those philanthropic gestures that we also find in *Mary,* where "schemes of usefulness, and projects of public interest" may themselves be part of the narcissism of sensibility (186, 133). Godwin prefaces the story in chapter 7 with the following: "[The incident is perhaps worth relating on other accounts, and therefore I shall describe it distinctly]" (130). The addition is completely superfluous but shows an anxiety to make us notice the episode lest we screen out Peggy's "tale" as a distraction from the more substantial "narrative[s]" of Darnford and Maria (95, 98). Godwin certainly does not "intrude" into the text in any decisive way, but by separating Peggy from the smooth flow of narration, he brings out an irresolution in the novel's title, between its communal voice, concerned with the wrongs of woman, and its personal voice, concerned only with Maria.[13] For the awkward supplementarity of "Peggy" cannot but make us aware of the seams in Wollstonecraft's project of quilting together class and gender within a discourse of rights, even as it reminds us of this discourse as one of the genres available to Wollstonecraft.

Darnford—whose name ominously recalls Mary Queen of Scots' husband Darnley—is notoriously another loose end in the story. No fewer than fifteen insertions involve him, including six of the ten occurrences of dashes and footnotes. Several of these have to do with when exactly Darnford, the libertine turned half-hearted American revolutionary, enters Maria's life. For instance, at the end of chapter 2, when Maria first catches sight of Darnford in the madhouse, Godwin adds the phrase: "[for she recollected, by degrees, all the circumstances of their former meeting]" (90). The addition is consistent with Wollstonecraft's comment about "the coincidence of events which brought them once more together," which is at the point in chapter 3 where the more finished copy breaks off (93). But Godwin's insertion draws attention to Darnford as a lacuna in the text, especially when we read it together with a further note at the end of the chapter, describing his "introduction . . . as the deliverer of Maria in a former instance" as an "after-thought." Godwin adds that this "has occasioned the omission of any allusion to that circumstance in the preceding narration" (97), indicating that he does not see "the coincidence" that *is* alluded to in the more finished copy as truly significant. To be sure, Godwin's intrusions are not always on the side of intimating that Darnford may not fulfill the role imagined for him. For instance, most "criminal conversation" suits (suits brought by the husband against his wife's lover) were undefended by the 1790s, as accused "seducers" fled to Calais or Boulogne to avoid paying punitive damages to the husband.[14] We could easily take Darnford's absence in France during the trial scene to be for this reason, but Godwin adds wording about his inheritance that supports Maria's view of his absence as a necessary joint decision in the interests of securing a financial basis for their future (191).

Or perhaps Godwin's added wording simply clarifies Maria's view, since, taken all together, his interventions do have a definite tendency. Three more occur in chapter 13, at the point when a stranger stops Venables and his attorney from harassing Maria in the lodging-house where she has taken refuge. Godwin prints the scene with a number of asterisks, causing us to notice the incident, while leaving its place in the Darnford-Maria romance unsettled. He further adds a footnote:

> The introduction of Darnford as the deliverer of Maria, in an early stage of the history, is already stated (Chap. III.) to have been an after-thought of the author. This has probably caused the imperfectness of the manuscript in the above passage; though, at the same time, it must be acknowledged to be somewhat uncertain, whether Darnford is the stranger intended in this place. It appears from Chap. XVII, that an interference of a more decisive nature was designed to be attributed to him. (175)

The "more decisive" event to which Godwin refers is mentioned by Venables' attorney, who claims that while he cannot say that Maria knew

Darnford while still living with Venables, "once," when her husband "was endeavouring to bring her back to her home, this man put the peace-officers to flight, and took her he knew not whither" (194). Since Maria does not go off with Darnford after his intervention in chapter 13, it could be that Wollstonecraft did have in mind a further episode that would make Darnford's role in a revolutionary solidarity of gender more convincing. But it could also be that the second incident is Venables' fabrication, since Maria herself says that she met Darnford only in the mad-house (197–98).

The question, then, would be why Godwin takes Venables' attorney to be speaking Wollstonecraft's intentions. In general Godwin does seem to want to suggest that as Wollstonecraft developed the story, she moved closer to imagining a decisive and convincing role for Darnford. The sentimental romance that then seems to swallow up the text's political agenda is all the more doomed, given the strong resemblance of Darnford to Gilbert Imlay: also an adventurer who had gone to America and also someone who betrayed Wollstonecraft while leaving her to conduct his business affairs in Norway, as Maria conducts Darnford's defense in the trial. These resemblances make it all too easy to see Maria's project as doomed by Wollstonecraft's compulsive repetition of her life in her text—and Wollstonecraft does model the character of Darnford on Imlay, as if trying out a figure from the Romantic archive once again. This figure—more brutally presented by Shelley as Nempere—is the freethinking radical whose ideas are compromised by the disregard for morality that in a sense makes those ideas possible. Worse than Imlay, John Wilkes, whose politicizing of the courts lies in the background of *Wrongs,* is another instance of a radical whose behavior was at odds with his principles.[15] But the question is whether we would focus our reading of the text on Darnford in the same way if Godwin's editing did not first emphasize that Wollstonecraft meant to build up his centrality and then draw attention to the nebulousness of his role. Could it not be that Wollstonecraft's inability to insert Darnford properly into the text reflects her sense that he is no more than a placeholder for a scenario to which she is not wholly committed? And that in allowing Maria to articulate her desires through Darnford as part-object, Wollstonecraft herself autonarratively constructs herself through Maria as part-subject? For Wollstonecraft, as for Hays in the relationship of Emma to Augustus, Darnford figures the way love and politics must be (con)fused because women's access to the public sphere is through men. Thus, even in the revised copy, Wollstonecraft has not wholly committed herself to a sustained rather than an accidental role for Darnford, describing him somewhat formally as a "stranger" by whose "timely interference" Maria had been "obliged" (90). As I suggest in analyzing the trial scene, it may be that in the final episode Darnford is beginning to slip out of the text, as Wollstonecraft remembers and works through a fantasy from her life that failed to work out. What the editing of the text does, in returning us to the semiosis that precedes and underlies composition, is to make us aware of the characters as under (de)construction. And indeed Wollstonecraft herself puts any definitive phrasing of the text under erasure, as she ends chapter 14 with the sentence: "Some lines were here crossed out, and the memoirs broke off abruptly with the names of Jemima and Darnford" (185).

୬

The most significant challenge to unworking the effects of Godwin's editing is posed by the trial scene, which follows Maria's escape from the madhouse and a brief period of living with Darnford, with whom "she did not taste uninterrupted felicity" (192). For the remainder of this chapter, I explore how this scene might read if it were not influenced by Godwin's arrangement of the text, bearing in mind that this arrangement cannot be subtracted from the text so much as mapped within the speculative space created by the transmission of *Wrongs* as a palimpsest in more than one handwriting. It is less Godwin's insertions that are the issue here, than his positioning of the trial scene: that he does not end with the last chapter Wollstonecraft completed but concludes with a number of fragments, most of which revert to Darnford. The effect, whether or not intended, is to cover over the daring of this scene, to align it with the angry defeatism of the trial scene that concludes the original version of *Caleb Williams,* and to subtly shift it from the speculative to the cognitive genre.

The trial scene is true to legal practice in that divorce proceedings had to begin with an action for "criminal conversation," that is, a charge of seduction and consequent suit for damages by the husband against the wife's lover. At several points, however, Wollstonecraft strategically conflates different stages in the cumbersome legal-ecclesiastical process of divorce, different stages in the history of the law, and even different kinds of law. To begin with, Maria takes the task of "conducting Darnford's defence upon herself" (194), even though there are counsel for the prosecution and the defense in the room. As John Langbein has shown, the "lawyerization" of criminal trials (though the trial in *Wrongs* is not a criminal trial) had begun in the 1730s: before then the accused conducted his own defense, and lawyers for the prosecution were therefore relatively rare. In the 1730s defense counsel still played only a supporting role, and the accused himself often did cross-examine witnesses and address the jury at the end. However, even though the role of lawyers had greatly increased by the 1760s,[16] the confrontation between Maria and the judge looms so large in the chapter that one must read carefully to discover that there are lawyers for either side in the room. The counsel for the plaintiff provides a brief summary of his case at the beginning of the scene, but there are no witnesses and no cross-examination of witnesses. As for the defense counsel, Maria instructs him "to plead guilty to the charge of adultery; but to deny that of seduction" (194), after which he is completely forgotten, as Maria herself seems to take over the defense. Wollstonecraft, in short, combines the criminal trial system before the 1730s, in which the defendant played an important role as a testimonial resource, with a later system, in which trials were conducted through lawyers. Indeed, criminal conversation suits in common law courts were always conducted by lawyers,[17] so Wollstonecraft also conflates two kinds of trial: criminal trials and trials for adultery, which were not criminal unless they involved bigamy or incest.

Moreover, and even more significantly, Maria conducts Darnford's defense, but by the end of the scene his defense has insensibly become hers. Her defense, moreover, modulates into her vindication; thus she also simultaneously becomes the plaintiff as she argues for a divorce. However, in the complex legal system that prevailed until the Divorce Reform Bill of 1857, a divorce not only was difficult to obtain but also could not result from the action for criminal conversation that is the subject of chapter 17. The trial scene, in short, involves several changes of phrase, produced through a sleight of hand that is itself suspended between what Lyotard calls the speculative phrase and the cognitive phrase, as this dialogue is played out between Wollstonecraft's text and Godwin's editing of it.

In order to grasp how Wollstonecraft plays fast and loose with legal procedures, it is useful to know something about the three-part process necessary to obtain a divorce in England in the late eighteenth century.

Parliamentary divorce had been introduced in 1700 as a way around the refusal of the Anglican church to allow divorce. This meant that, until 1857, divorces could only be granted by an act of Parliament and, with four exceptions (all in the nineteenth century), were never granted to women. England's restriction of divorces (Scotland being a separate case) was unusually stringent for a Protestant country, many of which had already redefined marriage as a civil contract. During the revolutionary period in France, due in part to pent-up demand, there were twenty thousand divorces just in the nine largest cities, many of them granted to women, who, Montesquieu had suggested, should be the only ones allowed the right of divorce so as to rectify the gender imbalance in marriage. The revolutionary period was, to be sure, an interregnum. Until 1792 divorce had been impossible in Catholic France, and the opening of the floodgates in the 1790s led to the enactment of a law in 1803 partially curtailing women's right to divorce, until in 1816 divorce was once again banned entirely. But as short-lived as this liberalization of divorce was—including extraordinarily modern provisions for alimony—nothing similar happened in England. Although the number of divorces granted in the 1790s was more than thrice the number in the previous decade, and although this caused great alarm, this only meant that there were forty-two divorces, or four per year, in the last decade of the century, as opposed to twelve in the period 1780–89 and thirty-four in the 1770s.[18] The process of obtaining a divorce was extraordinarily cumbersome, since canon law, equity law, and common law all had something to say on the subject.[19] For this reason divorce was available only to the relatively affluent, although there were often deeds of private separation or informal separations, as in Wollstonecraft's first novel, *Mary*.

By the late eighteenth century the different procedures for dealing with marital breakdown were being syncretized so as to produce a formidable legal trihedron for those seeking a divorce, whether on their own or through collusion with the spouse. The first stage involved a charge of "criminal conversation" (illicit sexual intercourse), in which the husband sued his wife's lover for adultery and seduction: a procedure introduced in the late seventeenth century but not widely used until the 1760s. Because the husband was seeking damages for an infringement on his property rights, the "crim. con." suit was a civil suit in a common law court, sometimes involving a standing jury of twenty-four "gentlemen of fortune," who dealt rapidly with a number of such cases, and sometimes involving only the chief justice.[20] In 1770 a successful criminal conversation suit was made mandatory for a parliamentary divorce. A further stage was a suit for separation from bed and board in an ecclesiastical court, without permission to remarry. This was possible on grounds of cruelty as well as adultery. The separation trial did not involve a jury but took place before a magistrate. Although a judicial separation covered by canon law did not entail a prior suit for criminal conversation in a common law court, and although success in the latter did not ensure a finding of adultery by the wife in the former, by standing orders adopted in 1798 and 1809 the House of Lords required proof of a successful suit for separation in an ecclesiastical court or an explanation of why none was possible in order to grant a divorce.[21] In effect, then, the suit for separation also became a necessary part of the divorce process. The final stage saw the husband seeking a divorce by private act of Parliament, with adultery by the wife still being the only ground, even a century after Milton's divorce tracts and despite the liberal views of natural law theorists on the subject of divorce. Although wives were not expressly prohibited from seeking divorces, none did so between 1700 and 1800, and over the next four decades only one woman was successful in obtaining a divorce.[22] A divorced wife, moreover, regardless of her husband's culpability, lost all access to her children. The final stage of parliamentary divorce involved an investigation by a committee of the House of Lords, a second reading of the bill, which involved a full trial, a third reading, and then examination by a nine-member committee of the Commons on Divorce Bills. After acceptance by the Commons, the bill was returned to the House of Lords and eventually became law. After parliamentary divorce was introduced, the husband always kept the wife's marriage portion but was required to pay her an annuity, which could be quite small. The equity law of Chancery (alluded to in one of the fragmentary continuations of *Wrongs*) might also be involved at some stage of the process, since Chancery dealt with trusts made by married women to keep their property and with decisions about and enforcement of alimony.[23]

Given these legal complexities and what seems a crushing summation by the judge at the end of chapter 17, one could easily read this chapter as a repetition of the shutting down of dissent in the unpublished ending of *Caleb Williams*. In the original ending Caleb, unable to prevail against the legal system, goes mad in prison. The speculative leap of faith in the revised ending then occurs only on condition of our thinking the resolution completely beyond, before, or outside the antinomies of things as they are, which is to say, outside the juridical or the political. But in *Wrongs* something of the revolutionary background also evoked by Blake in the "Song of Liberty," which concludes his *Marriage of Heaven and Hell,* is present in the judge's allusion to "French principles" (199). This reference, dismissive though it is, draws into the text a contemporaneous horizon of potentiality that is not beyond or outside the present, as in Godwin's novels, but *within* a history that is very much under negotiation and to which the text materially contributes precisely as fiction.

The text's rhetorical shift to the speculative phrase necessary to grasp this potentiality is effected by a number of strategic conflations and paralogisms. First, as we have suggested, the trial scene does not follow the rules of a criminal conversation suit. The plea of guilty to the charge of adultery but not seduction is logical enough, since it is seduction that allowed the jury to assess often punitive damages against the defendant. The testimony about Venables' abusive relationship with Maria is also to be expected, since the "smallest appearance of negligence" on the husband's part absolved the seducer of blame, "if he only took what was no value to him."[24] However, the action in a criminal conversation trial was carried on purely between the two men. The wife, who had no "legal personality" except through her husband, could not testify in her own defense, while even the men could only speak through counsel.[25] This silencing is reflected in Maria's presentation of her defense in the form of a "paper, which she expressly desired might be read in court" (*W,* 195). But in a criminal conversation trial Maria could not actually *be* a witness, whether in person or in writing. The entire scene, then, is based on a paralogism, on the positing of a presupposition that is groundless.

Maria's insistence on making a personal statement short-circuits not only the gendered procedures of the law but also the legal structure of a trial conducted by lawyers, which it both appropriates and sidesteps. On the one hand, as John Bender argues in his study of the relation between law and narrative, the "lawyerization" of the criminal trial participated in a struggle for narrative control by articulating "cases *pro* and *contra.*" The wide-ranging powers of inquiry accorded to the judge in an earlier legal system had been correlated with a narrative structure that conferred

on the narrator, what Adam Smith calls an impartial spectator, "exceptional powers of inquiry, adjudication, and sympathy." The lawyerization
of trials, by contrast, allowed each side to make its case, creating a space
for reflection through the responsibility of judgment to the individual
case.[26] We can see the effects of this lawyerization in *Caleb Williams,* even
though the trials themselves follow the earlier pattern of examination by
a local magistrate in the form of "an unstructured altercation" conducted
in "a relatively conversational way," but giving the judge almost absolute
power.[27] The stories of Caleb and Falkland are constructed forensically as
competing legal cases, which are not presented in court but to the reader,
who then recognizes the differends that foreclose any final and judicious
summation. However, in Godwin's novel, this space for difference in
judgment actually occurs only through a transposition of the adversarial
structure of the later criminal trial into the testimonial form of subjective
narrative, which avoids the negative consequences of lawyerization for
the individual and thus for "private judgment." For the lawyerized trial,
strictly speaking, "silenced" the accused by delegating her case to lawyers
instead of allowing her to speak for herself.[28] In the end, then, it too was
not conducive to recognizing the singularity of the particular case.

For the lawyerized trial participated in a general shift from what Matthew Wickman has described as witness testimony to a more objective
"evidence," weighed by juries. These juries, moreover, gradually changed
from being made up of people who had witnessed the event to men considered impartial judges of the evidence. Evidence, in turn, absorbed the
individual case into a circuitry of rules governed by probability, prece-
dent, and normativity,[29] severely constraining the Godwinian right of
"private judgment," to which Maria appeals in her summation of her
case (*W,* 198).[30] Evidence, in short, was part of the discourse network that
supported what Godwin calls "positive law" and "positive institutions"
(*PJ,* 1.175, 178). And positive law, as Arthur Jacobson argues, is a "non-
dynamic jurisprudence" because it suppresses "the *character* of those en-
gaging in the struggle over rules." Positive law "is written two times: it
is written and then the writing is implemented," such that rules are ad-
ministered "as idols, and obey[ed] . . . out of fear of sanctions." While
the first "writing," in the deconstructive sense that Jacobson uses the
term, puts forward rules as "propositions," the second is writing as
discursive inscription. It is this second writing that gives the law the bio-

political power that Godwin calls "institution," as certain norms are "marked" or "franked" so as to render "the application of norms to cases . . . unproblematic."[31]

In short, Wollstonecraft begins the trial scene by borrowing the adversarial structure of the lawyerized trial as a tool for what Stephen Landsman calls "dynamic individualism." In so doing she alludes to a growing tendency of citizens to use the courts in "efforts to vindicate" or "adjudicate difficult questions of political rights," culminating in the various political cases mounted by John Wilkes and his followers.[32] But Wollstonecraft then has Maria testify on her own behalf in a manner that would not have been possible in a criminal conversation trial conducted through lawyers. This testimony, moreover, is also Wollstonecraft's political testament; for the autonarrative passion in the final scene is a further way of restoring character to the struggle over rules. As I go on to suggest, Maria's "paper," which allows her to be the star witness in her own case, can actually be explained as part of the procedure used in ecclesiastical courts, and it reflects Wollstonecraft's conflation of the criminal conversation suit with a suit for separation from bed and board. But the latter also did not make the wife a"witness" in Wickman's sense of a testimonial rather than a legal witness, since ecclesiastical trials were also highly mediated, not to mention long drawn out. In such trials the written deposition of the wife was only one of many submissions, including written interrogatories of witnesses for the prosecution and defense, who were examined in camera and not in public; and this process, even in an undefended suit, took four to nine months.[33] In *Wrongs*, by contrast, we proceed rapidly from the prosecution's charge to the judge's summation. Moreover, there are no witnesses who are orally cross-examined (as would be the case in a criminal conversation suit), nor is there any reference to their being examined in camera (as would be the case in an ecclesiastical court). The compression of the action and the disappearance of characters who have figured in the preceding narrative (Darnford, Venables, even Jemima) create a focus on Maria that counteracts the wife's absence from normal legal proceedings as a flesh-and-blood character. These intensifications of Maria's presence allow her to conduct her own defense, as in the earlier criminal trials, even though it cannot actually be "her" defense since she has no "legal personality" for purposes of a criminal conversation suit. Moreover, they performatively produce written as oral discourse, as we forget that she is not speaking, which in turn performatively produces the text as action and not just "writing." The point, then, is that the trial scene, to adapt Lyotard's terms, "links" together phrase regimes from canon law, common law, and criminal as well as civil trials to create a passionate enunciatory position for Maria within things as they are. The scene does not follow any of these regimes but uses the space between them to invent the (im)possible as able to happen.

What occurs in the trial scene, then, is an almost invisible series of substitutions: the substitution of Maria for the defense counsel, of the female for the male voice, of the oral for the written phrase, and most importantly, of a plea for divorce for a defense against the charge of seduction. By the end of the chapter we have forgotten that it is Darnford who is being prosecuted, as the judge claims that "the *charges* brought against the *husband*" are "vague" and "supported by no witnesses" (199; emphasis mine). Of course, Maria cannot bring charges against Venables in a suit launched by him against Darnford, but by responding to her charges, the judge allows her to switch positions from defendant to plaintiff and in effect gives her the "legal personality" that, as a wife, she cannot legally have. At issue here is not just Maria's plea for a divorce, but her charge against Venables for imprisoning her in a madhouse (199), given that forcible abduction of the wife and confinement in the home was legal until the late nineteenth century, but imprisonment was not.[34] Conceding that Venables' conduct might "perhaps entitle the lady to a sentence of separation from bed and board" (199), the judge entirely forgets whose case, and what case, he is hearing, allowing us to imagine that he might reluctantly grant her a separation though not a divorce. When he then passes judgment on *Maria* rather than Venables, having allowed her right to charge Venables, it is as if he is evading the charges. But since Maria could not actually have made these charges, Wollstonecraft cleverly substitutes the ethical for the legal issue of the trial. Again, Maria could claim neither a separation nor a divorce in a trial of Darnford for criminal conversation, as Godwin reminds us when he inserts the clarification "[in another court]" in the judge's concession that she might be entitled to a "sentence of separation" (199). But Wollstonecraft's rhetorical acceleration of the long-drawn-out divorce process, and her transference of the right to divorce from the husband to the wife, may well be convincing to twentieth-century readers unfamiliar with eighteenth-century law. In a curiously prophetic way, this proves the claim made by this scene: the claim of literature to invent rather than merely reflect the law.

In Kantian terms, the scene performs a usurpation of the *law*, which operates through rules and established concepts, by an "idea" of *justice*. This idea is dialectically produced by "pure reason" insofar as "in experience nothing . . . corresponding to" it can "be found" (*CPR*, 219). Or rather, nothing quite corresponding to it can as yet be found. Kant, as we have seen in the previous chapter, was cautious about Pure Reason and the paralogisms that make it possible. The post-Kantian enthusiasm that he critiqued as "dialectical and fallacious" occurred when transcendental ideas that could only be regulative were literalized as constitutive (374), through a substitution of the speculative for the cognitive. Yet Kant also insisted that it was "in the highest degree reprehensible" to "deduce the laws which dictate what [one] *ought to do*" from the "rules" governing what "*is done*" (221). And there is a way one can argue, with Lyotard, that in his elaboration of practical reason in the second *Critique,* Kant is attempting to bring about "a language game that would be completely independent of that of knowledge" because there is "no knowledge in matters of ethics . . . [or] politics." This would make Kant a kind of Sophist, but in the service of a certain idealism.[35] Changing phrases from the cognitive to the enthusiastic, however, is not necessarily the radical leap we have seen in Godwin's novels. As already suggested, though Maria could not have made her statement in a trial for criminal conversation, in ecclesiastical courts it was possible for the wife as well as the husband to sue for separation (even if success was less frequent). In the ecclesiastical court the trial proceeded by way of written documents: that is, a written "Libel" by the plaintiff, written documents such as love letters, and private interrogation of witnesses by professional examiners based on written interrogatories prepared by each side. Although canon law excluded the direct testimony of the main participants, the wife could produce a written Libel if she were the plaintiff or an "allegation in rejoinder" if she were the defendant,[36] which in effect is what Maria does. The procedure in ecclesiastical courts was therefore moderately more sympathetic to the wife: a possibility alluded to by the judge when he reluctantly concedes that Venables' imprisonment of Maria cannot "be justified" and "might perhaps entitle the lady [in another court] to a sentence of separation from bed and board" (*W,* 199).

In short, Wollstonecraft cleverly works in two registers, by conflating the procedures in the ecclesiastical and common law stages of the action, which are not really "stages" but a patchwork of different legal codes representing the possibility of shifting moralities even within the status quo. On the one hand, she allows her protagonist to be defeated by the injustice of the male-biased criminal conversation trial, so that she can induce the court of public opinion to revolt against things as they are. On the other hand, unlike Godwin, whose *Caleb Williams* she was rereading as she wrote *Wrongs,* she finds a difference and a loophole within this very status quo. In so doing, rather than opposing justice to a law identified with positive law, as Godwin does,[37] Wollstonecraft tries to access a potential within the common law tradition, which, as Jacobson suggests, was meant to be dynamic, even though in practice it was subject to "positivist distortion." Wollstonecraft, moreover, tries to access this dynamism of the law by using the phrase regimes at hand within the law of her time. But she also does so by using the resources of narrative originally allowed for in the common law tradition. For as Jacobson argues, when common law judges began *writing* opinions, a practice institutionalized in the early nineteenth century, "the content and flavour of their judgments altered," as the judge's opinion acquired the force of "justification," or in Kantian terms, determination. By contrast, transcripts of early common law decisions do not "contain 'opinions' but debates amongst judges," which are more conducive to reflective judgment. Moreover, these decisions also contain "hypotheticals" or "invented facts," which bring up fictive cases that call into question the universalism of the rules.[38] Maria's story is such a case, forwarded by "invented" procedures.[39]

This right to "invent" is the crucial point made by the scene. For in contrast to the angry fatalism of mimesis that governs Maria's telling of her story in her memoir, its restaging in the politically charged environment of the trial scene is accompanied by other *(im)possibilities* that challenge the Novel as a form of governmentality. First, Maria has incredibly easy access to the funds needed to take control of her life, even though her uncle's fortune has been left to her child. Married women's property became that of their husbands, and in leaving his fortune in trust to the child, Maria's uncle had taken "every step" to "enable [Maria] to be mistress of his fortune, without putting any part of it in Mr. Venables' power" (180). But we have no reason to think that the child is still alive

(190) and must therefore wonder whether her uncle's friend could indeed have advanced Maria sufficient funds to live comfortably, pay for Darnford's trip to France, and support Venables' illegitimate child by a maidservant (192, 195). Nor would it have been within her uncle's power to make Maria the child's "guardian" (180). These are, however, mechanical objections, for throughout the later part of the story, Maria's access to money is governed by natural justice rather than legalism.[40]

Second, criminal conversation suits could only be heard in London at the Courts of King's Bench or Common Pleas and were relatively expensive.[41] It is not entirely clear that the bankrupt Venables would have had the funds to undertake such a suit, even though he might stand to be awarded exorbitant damages and might want to get his hands on the fortune Darnford is about to inherit. Still less is it likely that he would have had any interest in, let alone funds for, a parliamentary divorce, as intimated in one of the continuations of the story, where Maria is "divorced by her husband" (202); indeed, parliamentary divorces were largely the prerogative of the aristocracy. Yet Venables somehow does what is fictionally necessary to open the road to divorce, which in turn is a figure for other kinds of emancipation, including the extension of rights to the middle classes. Nor is it relevant how he might "really" have acted, since at this point he exists only as a narrative convenience, for the purpose of getting rid of what he represents. Indeed Venables, whose power, like that of Jove in *Prometheus Unbound,* has been hastily dismantled at the end of chapter 16, is not even present at the trial—at least not diegetically. All in all, despite its resemblance to the pessimistic first ending of *Caleb Williams,* this last finished part of Wollstonecraft's text is deeply revolutionary in its affect, offering a sketch and first outline for emancipation. A sketch: meaning that, like closet drama, it cannot yet be performed and has not been thought through, giving the text's incompleteness a strategically enthusiastic quality. But a sketch that nevertheless, if (im)possible at the level of the text's own plot, is not impossible in the larger context of changes that were happening or could be anticipated in 1797.[42]

🝊

Chapter 17 is, of course, not where the published text ends, with a case so much more straightforward than Caleb's that it can easily claim for literature a positive power as unacknowledged legislation. Godwin appends to the manuscript several "hints" for the continuation of the story, which is thus recast within his philological story about what the unconcludedness of the manuscript means. These hints consist of "two detached sentences," four "scattered heads for the continuation of the story," and a longer passage, which "appears in some respects to deviate from the preceding hints" (201–2). Darnford, who was absent from chapter 17, figures prominently in all these fragments. In one of them "he obtains a part of his property" and "Maria goes into the country": an inconclusive conjunction of events, which at least does not preclude a conventionally romantic ending. In five of the six brief fragments, however, Darnford's loyalty is in doubt. In three Maria becomes "once more pregnant," but in two she has a miscarriage, also associated with the "miscarriage of some letters" between her and Darnford (201). In the last of the six brief fragments miscarriage is followed by suicide, while in the longer continuation Maria awakes from having taken a dose of laudanum, thinking or perhaps deliriously imagining her child to be alive. Uncertain about the existence or prospects of either the past or future child, we are left uncertain about whether there is anyone to inherit Maria's political legacy. Also in question are the further legal details of her story. In three of the fragments there is a trial for adultery, in two a separation results, but in one we are not told the outcome of the trial. In one fragment Maria's fortune is "thrown into chancery" (201); in another there is both a criminal conversation suit and a separation from bed and board, which are not clearly distinguished; and in a fourth fragment mention is made of divorce.

Collectively these fragments sketch a personal future and legal situation more tangled than Maria assumes in the trial scene. The most hopeful of the continuations is the first of the "scattered heads," in which she "defends herself" in her trial for adultery, is granted a separation, and goes to the country, perhaps to be reunited with Darnford, who has regained some of his property. That Maria's "fortune is thrown into chancery" (201), perhaps because of a challenge from her brother (180) or because alimony after separation was adjudicated by the court of Chancery, may mean that she will recover some of her inheritance. But it also suggests interminable delays and raises the question, skirted in the main text, of the husband's legal right over the wife's money, which Maria assumes he does not have (180). Other continuations are bleaker, displacing the text's action from a public sphere, where it claims the rights of woman, to a domestic space repetitively brought back to the wrongs of woman.

In short, by deciding not to end the *Wrongs* with its last relatively complete chapter, not to publish a "clean" text of the novel, Godwin radically changes the effect of the narrative. For in chapter 17 Maria, whose story has been interlaced with those of Jemima and Darnford, takes center stage. Not only is Venables absent from the diegesis, but Darnford, who at times has seemed more a symbolic position in the text's archive of characters than a flesh-and-blood character, also drops away into irrelevance and becomes no more than an alibi for Maria's plea. He is described somewhat casually as "this person, thus encountered" (197), even though in the previous chapter she had "called him by the sacred name of 'husband'" (190). Maria's plea, moreover, is for divorce, not romantic love. But in the various continuations, Darnford, by his very absence, is given the power to foreclose on Maria's future. These fragments represent her life either as defined by him or, in the longer sequel, in which Maria decides to form a community with Jemima and "live for my child" (203), they represent her future as defined by a reactive female community constituted as a supplement around the only role given women in the Symbolic order: namely, motherhood. Either way women remain, in Simone de Beauvoir's famous phrase, the second sex.

What is equally significant about these sequels is the way they revert fatalistically to Wollstonecraft's own life. In the trial scene Darnford was absent not out of disloyalty but because he had gone to France to deal with the "ruffians" who had imprisoned him while trying to gain possession of a property, inherited from a relative who had died intestate (191–92). Whereas his absence in chapter 17 conveniently puts Maria in a position of agency, the continuations remind us that Wollstonecraft herself had gone to Scandinavia to handle Imlay's business and that this separation had been the prelude to his desertion. Also in the background of these fragments is Wollstonecraft's own suicide attempt after Imlay had abandoned her with their child, and her survival, only to die later in childbirth. Indeed, this fatality is marked by the somber context of the text's publication, as part of Godwin's production of the mortuary remains of her life in the *Posthumous Works* and in his bleak "natural history" of his wife in the controversial *Memoirs of the Author of "A Vindi-*

cation of the Rights of Woman."[43] As Samantha Matthews argues, the genre of "literary remains" was to become ubiquitous in the nineteenth century. The trope was often used to sublimate the link between "immortal genius or spirit" and "decaying corporeal substance," as "disparate 'writings'" were gathered "into 'an organic whole . . . informed with new life,'" wherein a body of work was "both consummated and transcended" as material body.[44] But there is none of this for Godwin, as the fragments in the Conclusion rather suggest a scattering of energy. Transmitted in this way, any attempt to continue the text and write beyond its ending now seems marked by its author's death, like Shelley's last poem, *The Triumph of Life,* which, as de Man sees it, inscribes the very contingency of its author's death in the materiality of the manuscript as a fragment left permanently unfinishable by its author's drowning.

Altogether, the effect of these continuations is to darken the reformist enthusiasm of the trial scene. Godwin had already moved in this direction in the previous chapter by adding the phrase "in another court," to suggest the complexity of the legal process on which Maria had embarked. Indeed, if the trial scene proceeds by linking phrases to create new discursive possibilities, the continuations unwork what Wollstonecraft has effected. They do so in an almost tangibly material way, by *delinking* the phrases that have yet to be put together and by doing this on the page itself. The "Conclusion, by the Editor" thus functions somewhat like Godwin's account of the composition of *Caleb Williams* in exposing the tenuousness of any story constructed out of the text's events, except that this Conclusion is included *in the text* and given the last word. By extension this segment, which is a conclusion by the editor about the nature of the text as a whole, returns Wollstonecraft's emancipatory project to where it had been before she began the process of "adjust[ing] my events into a story" (71), as if it might be necessary to begin the process of linkage all over again.

For Godwin is also at pains to remind us that the novel was to have three volumes and was not to have been the short, passionate statement we might take it to be. In the Appendix that follows chapter 14, he informs us that the "performance, with a fragment of which the reader has now been presented, was designed to consist of three parts" (186), even though the title page describes the text as being "In Two Volumes" (69, 141). He further describes the first fourteen chapters as "constituting one of those parts" (186), even though volume 2 begins in chapter 9. With eight chapters in one volume and nine in the second, the story may have been close to its end, in the form it had assumed as a narrative manifesto strategically suspended between the judge's summation and the verdict of the jury.[45] A manifesto: because the absence of the jury from the diegesis interpellates us as jury, "in another court," which is that of public opinion. Nevertheless, Godwin wants to represents Maria's history as very far from its conclusion. Again, at the very end of the text he reminds us that Wollstonecraft's intention was "to have filled . . . a number of pages, more considerable than those which have been already presented" and raises the question of "how it could have been practicable" to fill up these pages (203–4). In effect Godwin takes a revolutionary fragment, an "outline" (71), like one of the "unnam'd forms " in Blake's *Marriage of Heaven and Hell,* that is "cast into the expanse" to catalyze thought. And he insists that it was to be a novel in the three-volume format that allowed novels to be "arranged in libraries" (E, 40; 15). This cautionary realism is all the more surprising, even poignant, given the way Godwin himself had found it possible to combine speculation and mimesis in *St. Leon* just a year earlier. For the genre of the novel disallows to the text the dramatic force of a "performance" that Godwin at times gives it (*W,* 186): a force evoked in his own description of Caleb's life as "a theatre of calamity" (*CW,* 59) and implicit in his insistence that the meaning of a work consists in its "effect," which "cannot be completely ascertained" except performatively "by the experiment."[46] A force, moreover, that Wollstonecraft herself gives the text in her Preface when she speaks of "great misfortunes" as having a "*stage-effect*" (*W,* 74) and thus a publicly transformative potential.

There are many reasons why Godwin might have chosen to convey the text as he does. He is clearly anxious not to elide the underlying contradictions that unsettle overly facile "conclusions" of the text: be they imaginary resolutions, which allow Darnford and Maria to live happily ever after or symbolic resolutions, which see reform of the divorce laws as an answer to the wrongs of woman. In the *Memoirs* Godwin emphasizes that Wollstonecraft's "other works were produced with a rapidity, that did not give her powers time fully to expand," but that *Wrongs* was begun several times and "written slowly and with mature consideration" (*MV,* 171–72). Wollstonecraft had written *A Vindication of the Rights of*

Men in less than a month but had already spent a year on the unfinished *Wrongs*. Whether the pace of composition and the kind of reading a text elicits are directly related is unclear: *Caleb Williams* is endlessly reflexive but does not seem to have been written slowly. However, what is clear is that Godwin does not want us to read the *Wrongs* enthusiastically, as a premature or adolescent text. He wants to see it as the result of a process of slow thought and ongoing revision, which calls for an equal reflective-ness on the part of the reader.

This reflection, I suggest, may have something to do with Godwin's own cautious view of the discourse of rights. Godwin raises the question of rights by giving the edition that contains *The Wrongs of Woman* the title *Posthumous Works of the Author of "A Vindication of the Rights of Woman"* and by publishing in the same year his *Memoirs of the Author of "A Vindication of the Rights of Woman."* He also emphasizes that, despite Wollstonecraft's plans for a sequel to *A Vindication*, "she has scarcely left behind her a single paper, that can, with any certainty, be assigned to have had this destination." The *Vindication*, despite "form[ing] an epoch in the subject to which it belongs" and despite being likely to "be read as long as the English language endures," is "undoubtedly a very unequal performance," which leaves in its wake much unfinished busi-ness (*MV*, 99, 83–84).[47] In effect, then, it is *Wrongs* that becomes the sequel: *Wrongs* that Godwin wants to see as bearing a corrective relation-ship to *The Rights of Woman*, despite Wollstonecraft's early "aversion" to being seen "in the character of an author" (64) and her preference for being considered a 'female philosopher.' Indeed Godwin, who persistently valorizes Wollstonecraft's literary over her political texts, is also at some pains to demythologize other cornerstones of a fame based on arguing for "rights" (83). *The Vindication of the Rights of Men*, he tells us, also "ob-tained extraordinary notice." But it was composed with Wollstonecraft's customary "rapidity" and "impetuousness," in "the first burst of indig-nation" against Burke. It was "even sent to the press, as is the general practice when the early publication of a piece is deemed a matter of im-portance, before the composition was finished," and is "certainly charge-able with a too contemptuous and intemperate treatment of the great man against whom its attack is directed" (75–77).

This is not to say that Godwin does not support Wollstonecraft's dem-ocratic ideals and "sentiments of liberty" (75), but what is in question is the sufficiency of the discourse of rights for imagining freedom and, more particularly, the law as a forum for achieving this freedom. At issue here is the relation between positive law, natural law, natural rights, and justice. Positive law, which is the subject of critique within an Idealist tradition that includes Godwin's *Political Justice* and Hegel's *Natural Law*,[48] proceeds through the enforcement of what is written down. As Jacobson argues, it insists that "law achieves order" by a "force" that Godwin calls institution. Positive law is thus a "non-dynamic jurisprudence," and insofar as its notion of law is "restrictive," it cannot be the basis of rights, which are "permissive." Natural law is not inherently nondynamic, as Jacobson claims.[49] Based on the principle of natural rights, which need no religious sanction, and thus homologous with deism, it asserts that law achieves order naturally, according to the norms of a rational nature. But although natural law theorists such as Hugo Grotius and Samuel Pufendorf were liberal for their time on the matter of divorce, to us they still seem constrained by custom.[50] Wollstonecraft recognizes the danger in natural law of naturalizing what are actually social norms when she supplements the title of Thomas Paine's *Rights of Man* with her own *A Vindication of the Rights of Woman*. *A Vindication*, however, remains an appeal to a more original, fundamental form of natural *rights*, the "inherent rights of mankind."[51] As has often been noted, it contains its own middle-class blindnesses, which are acknowledged in *Wrongs* by the inclusion of Jemima, a true "*outlaw*" (*W,* 156) or outsider to the law. But having included Jemima, Wollstonecraft then awkwardly sublimates issues of class in a myth of feminist solidarity. Still, this does not necessarily constitute a wrong that decisively stops the discourse of rights, as is the case between Caleb and Falkland. For Wollstonecraft still thinks of the narratives of Maria and Jemima as parallel, even if the parallel lines cannot yet meet.

For Wollstonecraft, natural law is still the site of a potentially dynamic jurisprudence based on a natural justice that forces us to perpetually rethink rather than entrench concepts of natural rights. Maria would not disagree with Paine's famous dictum that "every civil right grows out of a natural right" or, more utopically, that natural rights can be posited as civil rights and that civil rights can be expanded. By contrast, for Godwin rights result in demands, which, from an ethical perspective "obscure duties." As F. E .L. Priestley argues, Godwin therefore uses the language of rights with that of "duties," or perhaps we should say "responsibility."[52] Or as Nancy, who uses the same vocabulary of "rights" and "duties," insists: "The rights of freedom today do not cease to complicate indefinitely their relations with the duties of the same freedom." This is not to depreciate the importance of rights, "the suppression or even suspension of which we know opens directly onto the intolerable itself."[53] But it is to mark the way that Maria's narrative in chapter 17 obscures that of Jemima. For Jemima would hardly be helped by divorce reform, since women of her class often did not have the privilege of marriage, and when they did, such marriages were ended by desertion rather than divorce. Among the various fragmentary sequels, the last one draws us back to Jemima. It reminds us that Jemima, who has been useful to collectivize the problem of wrongs, has not really found a place in the text subtitled "Maria": neither in the climax, nor in the continuations, only one of which even remembers her.

Unlike Wollstonecraft, then, Godwin could not be sanguine about the emancipatory finality of positive or "active" rights. Instead he preferred to argue for "negative" or "passive" rights, such as the right of private judgment or the right "to a certain sphere of discretion," which should "not be infringed by [one's] neighbours" (PJ, 1.158–82). This could include the right not to be bound to a marriage, but not as a right in the Wilkite sense claimed by Maria. As important, as we have seen in *Caleb Williams*, is Godwin's understanding of wrongs, which are in no sense symmetrical with rights. For wrongs, as Lyotard defines them, cannot be put into a discourse shared by both parties and thus redressed by the granting of rights. A wrong is not the subject of a litigation in which the "victim" becomes a "plaintiff" and which results in "damages." The wrong comes from "the damages not being expressed in the language common to the tribunal and the other party" and in there thus being some remainder, some differend, wherein the "referent of the victim's phrase" is not even "the object of a cognition properly termed" (D, 28).

The "emancipation" of Jemima provides an example of this differend, whose referent eludes phrasing. After their flight from the madhouse, Jemima tells Maria, hesitantly yet defiantly, that she has "perhaps no right now to expect the performance of your promise," on which it "depends to reconcile me with the human race" (W, 189). Maria's promise, made after hearing her story, had been to "procure" for her "a better

fate" and to teach her child to consider Jemima "as a second mother"—
two different promises in fact, one limited and the other unlimited (121).
As the performance of this promise Jemima "insists" on being "considered
as [Maria's] housekeeper" and receiving "the customary stipend": "On
no other terms would she remain with her friend" (191). One imagines
from the upright tone of the last sentence that Wollstonecraft actually
saw making Jemima Maria's housekeeper as the rectifying of a potential
wrong: perhaps that of using Jemima as unpaid labor. But this granting
to Jemima of a right (to what, it is not clear) only conceals further wrongs.
For not only is it wrong for one's "friend" to be one's housekeeper; that
the relationship of the women must be put on a right footing through a
monetary arrangement also nervously concedes that Jemima is not really
a "friend." On the other hand, it is equally hard to say what Maria *should*
do to perform her "promise": hardly a simple promise, to reconcile
Jemima with the human race. In short, it is difficult to see how the wrongs
of Jemima's position, which are of a biopolitical and not just a juridical
order, can be righted within the phrase regimes the women struggle to
share. The genres of discourse in question are incommensurable: For one
is economic and the other ethical; one is limited and allows amends to be
made to Jemima through fair employment, while the other, which is that
of friendship, is unlimited.

The editorial scrupulousness with which Godwin marks the text's gaps
draws us back to the many loose ends left in the story. It does not necessarily invalidate the affective climax of the trial scene but does result in
"*ephexis* [undecisiveness] in interpretation," to return to Nietzsche's description of philology. By emphasizing how Wollstonecraft herself began
the text, "in several forms, which she successively rejected, after they
were considerably advanced," Godwin means us, too, to read "many
parts of the work again and again" (*MV*, 172), so as to experience this
ephexis. But there is also something more going on in "The Conclusion,
by the Editor," something more conclusive. This Conclusion has all the
more insensibly inflected readings of the text in proportion as it has not
itself been much noticed. For in the fragments, as we have seen, Maria is
once again defined through Darnford; she reverts to being the sentimental
heroine of whom Wollstonecraft has been uneasily critical. Correspondingly, in contemporary readings of the novel, even when they recognize

that the actual manuscript ends with the judge's summation, Wollstone-craft is criticized for "transcrib[ing]" "the suffragette . . . as the seduc-tive." This, even though Maria's reference to Darnford as her "husband" is in the previous chapter (*W,* 190), while in the trial scene the male characters are used only transpositionally to facilitate her birth as a po-litical subject.[54]

Thus, according to Virginia Sapiro, Wollstonecraft could not imagine how to translate " 'private pains' within a particular oppressed social group . . . into political action." And according to Mary Poovey, despite her valiant attempts to "abort the sentimental structure of *Maria* in order to reassert" a "political purpose" that Poovey identifies purely with Jemima, even Maria's plea is only further evidence of women's ineffectu-ality. For this plea, as Poovey sees it, foregrounds "the feeling heart" (and not reform of the law, as we have been arguing). Hence it simply "in-stitutionalize[s] female feeling as a new rationale for the old covenant of marriage."[55] In short, the Conclusion's effect has been to confirm the phrasing of the text as sentimental romance, and then, through the auto-biographical identification between Maria and Wollstonecraft, to con-struct Wollstonecraft herself as a sentimental rather than a political sub-ject. A curious variant of the autobiographical transference is at work here, though one that is not uncommon in the reading of women and, more broadly, "Romantic" authors. In general, it is the proper name of the author that is used to confirm the authenticity of the character, but here it is the character who is used autobiographically to settle the iden-tity of the author, even though the author is using the character autonar-ratively as a self-projection: a way of phrasing her own character as still fundamentally unsettled.

If twentieth-century readers are critical of Wollstonecraft for not mak-ing the move from the sentimental to the political, Godwin's arrangement of the text rather narrates the inevitable relapse of politics into sensibility through the foreclosure of Wollstonecraft's life by her death. Godwin's editing of his wife's literary remains is powerfully mediated by his memoir of her, published in the same year as the *Posthumous Works* and reflect-ing a view of his mournful task very different from that of the monumen-tal history proposed in Wordsworth's *Essays on Epitaphs.* For Words-worth writes that the character of the deceased should be seen through a "tender haze or a luminous mist, that spiritualizes and beautifies it."[56] By contrast Godwin seems to have seen the task of writing a memoir as a kind of demythologization. We do not know what Wollstonecraft would have done had she lived longer, but we do know that at the point when her life ended she could not imagine a future for Maria outside of her relationship with Darnford. And we do know that when Wollstonecraft wrote the *Vindications* she had just entered what Keats calls the "Chamber of Maiden Thought." In our first entry into this pre-maturity, Keats says, "we become intoxicated with the light and the atmosphere." But as in the career of another revolutionary, Rousseau, narrated by Wollstonecraft's future son-in-law in the *Triumph of Life,* among the effects of this intoxication is "that tremendous one of sharpening one's vision into the heart and nature of Man—of convincing one's nerves that the World is full of Misery and Heartbreak, Pain, Sickness and oppression." The result is what Lyotard calls a "darkening of . . . the Enlightenment," in which, to quote Keats again, "many doors are set open" but are "all dark—all leading to dark passages."[57]

For Godwin this "darkening of the universalism of the Enlightenment" is associated with a turn from politics to literature: a turn he himself made after the failure of *Political Justice,* and which he saw Wollstonecraft as about to make in her writing of *Wrongs.* But even this potential is denied to her, as the fragments at the end turn into the record of a death that cannot be aestheticized. For if death eluded Wollstonecraft when she sought it in what she described as "one of the calmest acts of reason,"[58] it returns as the accident that cuts off her life just as she, like Maria in the trial scene, is about to begin a new chapter. This death, to adapt de Man on Percy Shelley, is not anything that is "represented or articulated," but it is "present in the margin of the last manuscript page," and it becomes "an inseparable part" of the text through Godwin's editing.[59] For although we do not know when the fragments were composed, their placement at the end of the text affectively telescopes the time of writing with the time of the diegesis, like the omission of the final full-stop in the manuscript of the first ending of *Caleb Williams.* The effect is to make the fragments uncannily contemporaneous with Wollstonecraft's own death, as if she herself was hesitating between suicide and survival when the question was decided for her. Rather than a memoir, a conversation between the characters, or a story told in the third person, the text thus becomes a kind of autobiography, but one that bears the mark of a definitive interruption.

It would not be too much to say that the Conclusion does to *Wrongs* what de Man's "Shelley Disfigured" does to *The Triumph of Life*. In de Man's powerfully physical-cum-rhetorical term, it "dis-figures" any attempt to dispose meaningfully of its author's remains: any attempt to monumentalize the text as a positive achievement. In another essay de Man takes up the trope that arguably subtends autobiography: that of a speaking voice that authorizes the referentiality of the text by linking it to a real rather than a fictitious person. For de Man autobiography is not just a discrete genre. As "a figure of reading or of understanding that occurs, to some degree, in all texts," it is the "tropological structure that underlies all cognitions" and that occurs "whenever a text is stated to be *by* someone and assumed to be understandable to the extent that this is the case." De Man deconstructs this trope through an uncanny doubling of autobiography with epitaph: a mode that withdraws the living voice and exposes it as produced by a prosopopeia. But Godwin in the Conclusion already writes Wollstonecraft's autobiography as her epitaph by conveying it to us as part of her "literary remains," reminding us that any claim to know what the text means is based on "the fiction of an apostrophe to an absent, deceased, or voiceless entity."[60]

But is there any reason to privilege this Conclusion, given that its exact manuscript provenance is unknown? In 1798, in the aftermath of his grief, the compulsive repetition of Wollstonecraft's life in the margins of her text becomes Godwin's compulsive repetition of her death in her life through his editing. Godwin thus accords the fragments a certain finality in their traumatic incompleteness when he writes that "to understand these minutes, it is necessary the reader should consider each of them as setting out" from the same point at the end of chapter 17 (201n), where the manuscript breaks off after the judge's summation and before the jury's decision. However, we do not actually know whether these continuations are part of the second or first manuscript stage, or whether they belong to an even earlier stage of conception: whether they are to be thought of as an aftermath or an *avant-texte*. It may be that after the trial the revolutionary narrative relapses into the conventional Symbolic plot of nineteenth-century novels described by Rachel Blau DuPlessis, which gives women only two choices: death or marriage.[61] Or it may be that Wollstonecraft, seeing the hold of such plots on the sentimental imagination, set these continuations aside as possibilities and revised the text so as to move it towards the trial scene. What we do know is that Godwin found the manuscript as a collection of loose sheaves but did not, and of course could not, publish it as such. From the way he describes the different manuscript stages, we gather that he had an intimate knowledge of the text as it was being written, and he knew that certain parts were more "finished" than others. Prior to Wollstonecraft's death, he had "read or edited" the manuscript on three occasions.[62] But his note on the continuations implies that he may have been unfamiliar with them: "Very few hints exist respecting the plan of the remainder of the work. I *find* only two detached sentences and some scattered heads for the continuation of the story" (201; emphasis mine).

In fact, despite Godwin's note, the fragments do not all set out from the end of chapter 17, as some repeat what has already happened in the preceding story. For instance, in the third fragment Maria provides for her father, though she had already settled his debts in chapter 13 (182). In this continuation she is also "sued by her husband," who is awarded "damages," although damages could only be awarded in the criminal conversation suit, which had already been the subject of chapter 17, and not in the suit for separation, which is its logical sequel. And in this fragment she is "shunned" for being open about her relationship with Darnford (202), something that had already happened in chapter 16 (192). In short, the continuations overlap with the later chapters and may be alternatives, not sequels, to chapter 17. For the earliest likely reference to *Wrongs* in Wollstonecraft's correspondence is in a letter to Godwin from July 21, 1796, in which she sends him "as requested, the altered M.S." This letter is written not long after one on May 13, 1796, which is strikingly echoed in the last of the fragments, where Maria, having swallowed laudanum, declares: "The conflict is over!—I will live for my child" (203). In this letter to Gustav, Graf von Schlabrendorf, Wollstonecraft speaks of her betrayal by Imlay and her desire to "leave England forever," but she also says, "yet I will live for my child."[63] This is not to say that she wrote the fragments when she first began work on the text in 1796, rather than in 1797, just before her death, but that possibility must at least be entertained.[64]

To unbind the Conclusion from its place in the text is to release a narrativity: a potential for different linkages from those Godwin creates, both within the story and between the text and its author's life. This performativity is also part of Godwin's own aesthetics. In "Of Choice in Reading" Godwin argues that the text's meaning consists in its "tendency" rather than in any "moral" or intention stated by the author (or editor). The "formal" moral or "lesson" required by a certain socially produced utilitarianism, as in the morals "annexed" to Aesop's *Fables,* is generally "one of the last inferences that would have occurred to" anyone.[65] As against this prospective or retrospective attempt to simplify the text, the tendency is "the actual effect" produced upon the reader, which can only be known "by the experiment" and will "be various according to the various tempers and habits of the persons by whom the work is considered." The effect, in other words, cannot be totalized because it consists of the different ways readers link on to the text and because we cannot foresee where the text's "principal power of attraction [will] be found."[66] As the metaphor of magnetism underlying the term "attraction" implies, there is also in this "effect" an unpredictable chemistry between different minds and the philological particles, or phrases, they encounter. As Godwin writes elsewhere about the elective affinities governing the process of linkage, "We go forth into the world," and on our return we "produce the materials we have collected abroad, and, by a sort of magnetism, cause those particulars to start out to view in ourselves, which might otherwise have lain for ever undetected" (HR, 455; also cf. 458).[67]

From this perspective it is interesting to consider the ways we link onto Wollstonecraft's letter to George Dyson through the various recontextualizations, which cause its different particulars to start out to view. The letter to Dyson—the only person to whom Wollstonecraft showed her work other than Godwin—is initially part of what Gerard Genette calls the epitext: that part of the paratext that is "at least originally" located at some distance from the book," in interviews, conversations, and private communications.[68] The letter exists in four forms: Wollstonecraft wrote to Dyson on May 15, 1797; she copied the letter onto the back of a letter to Godwin on the same day, as if wanting to preserve it; it is then partially cited in the fragmentary "Author's Preface," and finally, different parts of it are cited in Godwin's Preface. The original letter is a nervously passionate response to Dyson's criticisms of the manuscript, which, interestingly, only went up to the end of chapter 14 at that point (71n), breaking off at the end of Maria's memoirs and before Darnford's response to reading them at the beginning of chapter 15. Dyson's criticisms focus on the lack of interest held by Maria's situation and the fact that Jemima speaks in a more educated way than is realistic—a criticism similar to the one Coleridge will make of Wordsworth's *Lyrical Ballads*. Wollstonecraft insists that Dyson's insensitivity to the importance of Maria's story is because he "[is] a man." She is "not convinced that [his] remarks concerning the style of Jemima's story is just [*sic*]," but she promises to "reconsider it."[69] This empty symbolic gesture betrays her unspoken sense that the focus on diction is an alibi and reveals her resentment at the woman writer being put in the position of a novice. The copying of the letter to Godwin assumes a more sympathetic audience, but it also functions as a form of semipublication, wherein we see Wollstonecraft's defensive position becoming the occasion for a certain assertiveness. This shift is not unlike the changing of phrases that occurs in the trial scene, as Maria moves from defendant to plaintiff. Significantly, the trial scene was written after the partial manuscript of fourteen chapters that Wollstonecraft showed Dyson. The change in the way both Wollstonecraft and the reader link onto the letter is effected even more strongly in the Author's Preface. Wollstonecraft drew most of her Preface from the letter. But given her polemical purpose she does not repeat the criticisms of Jemima, reproducing only the defense of Maria, which now becomes a manifesto against "matrimonial despotism" and "the peculiar Wrongs of Woman" (73).

Finally, Godwin also quotes part of the letter in his Preface, but he reproduces neither the criticisms of Jemima nor the defense of Maria. Instead he cites Wollstonecraft's comments about how she is aware "that some of the incidents" "ought to be transposed" and how she "wished in some degree to avail [her]self of criticism" before she "began to adjust my events into a story, the outline of which I had sketched in my mind" (71). The phrases Godwin chooses from the letter, in other words, have to do with the form rather than the politics of the text. As a formal commentary, they could be read simply as conceding the unfinished nature of the text, and in the original letter they had indeed been preemptively apologetic. But when re-cited in proximity to the "Author's Preface" they convey a certain enthusiasm in Wollstonecraft's writing, wherein inspiration runs ahead of composition, producing speculative forms that await a more detailed development. These forms would be like Kant's "ideas," which can be either "rational" or "aesthetic": either concepts that cannot yet be represented or representations and affects that have not found expression in concepts (*CJ,* 157). Moreover, this enthusiasm of the idea is something Godwin produces through the very prosopopeia he eschews in the Conclusion: that is, by *quoting* Wollstonecraft and thus giving renewed voice to an absent or deceased entity.

The re-citing and "transposition" of parts of the letter to Dyson provides a model for the process of linking made possible throughout by Godwin's de-composition of the text. For Godwin himself, we can argue, links onto the unfinishedness of the text in different ways at different points: Godwin as implied reader, as one of only two people to whom Wollstonecraft showed the text, cannot be consolidated into a unified interpretive position. To be sure, the Conclusion dissolves and dissipates the activism of the trial scene. But in the Preface, even though Godwin represents Wollstonecraft as an "inexperienced author" (71), his publication of "these unfinished productions of genius" is mobilized by her sense that they are "capable of producing an important effect" (71). In this Preface Godwin constitutes the text within its own Romantic genre, that of the "sketch" or "outline," the "conception," which is to be "filled up" later (71). The outline, according to Deleuze, is the "preparatory work" that precedes yet "belongs to" aesthetic production, and as such it "marks out possibilities of fact" that "do not yet constitute a fact."[70] Or as Lyotard says of Kant's aesthetic ideas, outlines are "scenarios or simulations." The outline permits "possible, probable, or improbable stories" to be told, "regardless of their verisimilitude, in anticipation of what could be the case" (*D,* 148). To provide a different kind of example, (de)constructive rather than enthusiastic: Wollstonecraft's foreshortening of the three-part divorce process in the trial scene is based on a fallacious though just presupposition, namely, that Maria can be her own witness. Godwin draws attention to this paralogism by inserting the phrase "in another court," thus putting the brakes of realism on Wollstonecraft's enthusiasm. At the same time it is his editorial decomposition of this pa-

ralogism that also decomposes the hegemony of the law into its overdetermined, moveable components, by suggesting a scenario in which there
is another court—a possibility of fact that does not exist in the original
ending of *Caleb Williams.*

In short, Godwin's editing returns the text to the preparatory work
that precedes its unification into a *genre* that "imprints a unique finality
onto a multiplicity of heterogeneous phrases by linkings that aim to procure the success proper to that genre" (129). The "story" promised in the
letter to Dyson would be one such genre, a story being, in Godwin's
words, a narration put together "with great artifice and appearance of
consistency" (*CW,* 437). But *Wrongs* has not necessarily established itself
within a genre. Rather than being a novel, the text, including its Prefaces
and Conclusion, is what Lyotard calls "prose": an "ungraded supply of
phrases" from all genres (*D,* 158). A phrase, as Lyotard argues, "comes
along," and the question is, within what genre or "genre of discourse will
it take its place?" The phrase that "comes along is put into play within a
conflict between genres of discourse" and becomes the subject of a "differend" or difference in judgment (129, 136). Thus the phrase "in another
court" could intimate that Wollstonecraft has confused different stages of
the divorce process and could imply a judgment on her naiveté. Or it
could point to a verdict different from the moral judgment passed by the
judge. The first way of linking onto Godwin's insertion phrases it in the
"cognitive genre" of things as they are, which falls under the regulation
of the Kantian faculty of "understanding"; the second transfers it into
"the dialectical genre" of "speculative reason," or things as they could be
(137). By putting the phrase in parentheses, Godwin impedes its seamless
absorption into any one discourse and allows us to see, not only that "the
linking of one phrase onto another is problematic," but also that this
problem is one of "politics," our politics (xiii). The same problem of linkage arises with regard to the text's literary genre, which could be that of
the story, whose forensic criteria of unity and plausibility Wollstonecraft
fails to meet. Or it could be that of the sentimental romance or emancipatory program, which, in their different ways, evade these criteria. Or indeed it could be the genre of literary remains. All these genres, including
the ways Wollstonecraft's critics have linked onto them, "inscribe [the
phrase] into the pursuit of certain stakes," which result in other linkages
being "neglected, forgotten, or repressed possibilities" (136).

By phrasing the text in the editorial genre Godwin makes the linkages that produce genre themselves an object of reflection. For philology, as Hegel says, focuses on "small details which can be recombined in various ways," thus making us aware that interpretation is a moving army of metaphors and metonymies. Philology is the poetry of scholarship: a form of *enjambement* or hanging back. This hanging back, or *différance,* as Derrida would call it, releases a certain narrativity within the edited text that configures it as a potential—rather than a mimetic—space. Hegel goes on to describe how the skepticism of philology as a site of differends in judgment is neutralized, as its "combinations gain a footing first as historical hypotheses, but soon after as established facts."[71] Through the process that Godwin calls institution, philology becomes a form of positivism. But it is the potential for recombination that Godwin's editing retrieves, since he not only foregrounds the process of linkage by describing how he has joined chapters from different manuscript stages to produce a reading text but also emphasizes that there are links at the level of characters and events that have not been made. Philology for Godwin is an-archic, in the root sense of the word as meaning "before *arche*," before foundation or institution. In short, the editorial genre, by presenting the text and its reading as not yet established, lets us treat the text as an archive of possibilities, thus returning literature as the work of culture to its creative functioning. But in this respect philology, with its molecular care for the particular, simply foregrounds what is true of all texts, namely, that when we consider them in detail we discern phrases that could be said differently, and thus "possible phrases [that] remain unactualized" (*D,* xii).

Philology, then, shifts the text from the narrative to the speculative or deliberative genre, or rather rephrases narrative *as* deliberative. Narrative, as Lyotard admits, contains a "heterogeneity of discourses." Nevertheless, for Lyotard, unlike Bakhtin, it is the genre within which this heterogeneity has "the easiest time passing unnoticed." This is because narrative, which Lyotard equates with story, is governed by "the diachronic operator or operator of successivity," whose "finality is to come to an end." Wherever in "diegetic time" the story "stops, its term makes sense and retroactively organizes the recounted events," "'swallow[ing] up' the event and the differends carried along by the event." As a result the "unleashing of the now," of the "occurrence, with its potentiality of differends," is "domesticated by the recurrence of the before/after" (151–52). This linearity makes narrative, according to Lyotard, "a genre, whereas deliberation is a concatenation of genres" and phrase regimes (149). But as narrative *Wrongs* is already quite different from its precursor, *Mary.* Wollstonecraft's first novel is "an artless tale, without episodes,"[72] which unfolds chronologically under the rule of the diachronic operator. It is told strictly in the past, such that the narrating is subsequent to the action. *Wrongs,* by contrast, switches between several modes of conveying events, none of which do in fact reach a term. There is the episode that is brought to a conclusion but is still part of a longer story, for example, Maria's account of her marriage to Venables. There is the conversation in which stories are interchanged and sometimes interrupted, as in the case of Jemima's history. These stories re-cite the past within the urgency of the present and are not told as past. Finally, there is Maria's memoir, which is sufficiently finished to be passed on to readers but is still in process when she is abducted, thus becoming more like a diary in which the action and the narrating of it are simultaneous. At first the memoir, because of its length, stands apart from the other stories, as the *possibility* of a completed story, in which the action would be prior to its narration. But in fact the memoir is "interpolated" in another action.[73] When the memoir breaks off, the narration of Maria's story passes to a heterodiegetic narrator. Although this narration is left unfinished because of Wollstonecraft's death, the text itself has already phrased stories as *inherently* incomplete and ongoing: lacking in the completion that Godwin attributes to the "story" (*CW,* 59, 432, 437). In addition, the text contains not just Maria's story but also her vindication of the rights of woman in the court scene, as well as several shorter political statements, mostly clustered in the later chapters. We could therefore phrase *Wrongs* as a political manifesto supported and impassioned by being in narrative form. Or we could phrase it as an abstract political program submitted to the deliberative test of concrete events.

Nor is there a single narrative voice in the text. There are three autodiegetic narrators who tell their own stories: Maria, Darnford, and Jemima. But in addition there is also the heterodiegetic narrator, who opens the text, puts its characters in conversation, and takes up the narration again when Maria's memoir, which begins in chapter 7, breaks off at the end of chapter 14. The switch between Maria and this narrator suggests different ways of linking onto Maria's story: from inside or through the sympathetic yet judgmental gaze of a second voice, which condemns her for succumbing to the ethos of sentimental romance. This division does not simply contain Maria's sensibility within the more sensible voice of the narrator. It allows us to link onto the heterodiegetic narrator in different ways—to link onto "Wollstonecraft" in different ways. For the narrator, like the author of *A Vindication,* is an advocate of women's rights who tries to work beyond Maria's stock responses to a truly "rational" feminism. She condemns Maria for reading her own situation through Rousseau (81, 89), for her excessive passions (91), and for "mistakes of conduct" that are perhaps excused by her youth (99). She refers critically to the delusions of "imagination" (101). By the same token, the narrator is influenced by a certain propriety, which does not correspond to the revolutionary way Wollstonecraft, like Hays, lived her own life.

It is this side of the Jacobin woman writer—reckless, passionate and experimental—that Godwin emphasized in his first version of the *Memoirs,* with their candid unveiling of Wollstonecraft's relationships with Fuseli and Imlay. In the *Memoirs* Godwin comments on a certain conventionalism in Wollstonecraft's work, a recourse to "homily-language," which she imbibed from writing for periodicals (69). He takes aim, *avant la lettre,* at the Habermasian construction of an *Öffentlichkeit* in which even the "private" exists for the convenience of the public. On the contrary, Godwin tries to counteract this "respect for establishments" (74) by making Wollstonecraft's life as much a part of her cultural work as her writings. Reading *Wrongs* through the *Memoirs,* which were published in the same year, we link on to the heterodiegetic narrator's nervously proper voice as itself discursively constructed. For Maria herself links on to her story in different ways: sentimentally and narcissistically, when she begins writing her memoir, and then polemically, when she retells it in court. These different re-citations of her story show Maria developing in ways that make the narrator's reduction of her to a sentimental heroine a moral at odds with the text's tendencies. Even the narrator herself seems undecided about the degree of authorial distance she should maintain from her character. Just before the escape from the madhouse, she criticizes Maria for her "imagination" and for "see[ing] what we wish." But then she unexpectedly writes: "Maria now, imagining that she had found a being of celestial mould—was happy,—*nor was she deceived*" (*W,* 189; emphasis mine). The chapter then ends in dashes, as Wollstonecraft sets aside the decision about sensibility: whether it is a trap or whether it can be part of a radical politics. In short, in constructing Maria as a part-object with whose behavior she does and does not identify, the narrator (and Wollstonecraft herself) finds herself reciprocally reconfigured as a part-subject.

Perhaps the reason Maria is not "deceived" is not because her investment in Darnford is going to be repaid. Perhaps it is because the accident of his entry into her life allows the text to spin out a thread in the plot that may lead nowhere but that functions as fantasy or part-narrative. In elaborating on the curious retraction, "nor was she deceived," the narrator continues: "He was then plastic in her impassioned hand—and reflected all the sentiments which animated and warmed her" (189). The plasticity, or Coleridge might say "esemplasticity," of narrative, the narrator seems to allow, lets us accept scenarios that are not deceptive precisely because they do not imagine the attainment of their object; they simply teach us the coordinates of desire, as Žižek argues of fantasy. Even at the cost of calling into question his own hypotheses about how the text might play out, Godwin's editorial destructuring of *Wrongs,* by shifting it from the level of mimesis to that of semiosis, recognizes the poetry in narrative.

NOTES

Introduction

1. Ian Duncan, *Modern Romance and Transformations of the Novel.*

2. See Clifford Siskin, *The Work of Writing*, 196. But as Siskin recognizes, the gendering of genre is highly unstable and, as Mary Favret points out, was already in flux ("Mary Shelley's Sympathy and Irony," 24–25).

3. Mary Favret, "Telling Tales about Genre," 154, 158.

4. Mary Wollstonecraft, *The Wrongs of Woman; or, Maria: A Fragment* (1798), in *"Mary" and "The Wrongs of Woman,"* 82. Hereafter cited as W.

5. Lennard Davis argues that the novel emerges as part of a discourse network that values the new and the news (*Factual Fictions*). This view can be taken back to Mikhail Bakhtin's argument that the novel introduces a new sense of time distinct from that of the past-oriented epic ("Epic and Novel," 3–40). Davis deals only with the genre of the novel. However, Bakhtin's notion of "novelization" extends the *episteme* of the novel to other genres, thus offering a poetics of the novel, rather than the more limited sociology of the genre that has come to dominate Anglo-American studies in the past three decades. Finally, the linkage of the novel with the new(s) can also be traced back to Friedrich Schlegel's use of the term *"Roman"* synonymously with a "progressive universal poetry" that is associated with the "new" and is "still in the state of becoming." For Schlegel the progressive is that which "often negates itself but also immediately creates itself again." Importantly for my use of narrative here, Schlegel also equates the novel with *"romantische Poesie"* ("Atheneum Fragments," 11, 31–32; *Literary Notebooks, 1797–1801,* ed. Hans Eichner [Toronto: University of Toronto Press, 1957], 32. Translations mine).

6. Siskin, *Work of Writing*, 176–85; Jürgen Habermas, *The Structural Transformation of the Public Sphere*, 43, 50.

7. Peter Brooks, *Reading for the Plot.*

8. Tilottama Rajan, "Romanticism and the Death of Lyric Consciousness," 194–207; idem, "The Web of Human Things," 85–107.

9. See Irving Ehrenpreis, *The "Types Approach" to Literature*, 16.

10. Harold Bloom, "The Internalization of Quest Romance," 13–36; Karl Kroeber, *Romantic Narrative Art.*

11. Cleanth Brooks' *The Well Wrought Urn: Studies in the Structure of Poetry* (New York: Reynal and Hitchcock, 1947), which represents Romanticism by Wordsworth's "Intimations of Immortality," is the classic example of the New Criticism's close reading of single short poems or short extracts from longer poems. Its most obvious Romantic follower is Earl Wasserman's *The Finer Tone.* For the historicist identification of Romanticism with Wordsworth, see James Chandler, *Wordsworth's Second Nature,* and Alan Liu, *Wordsworth: The Sense of History,* as well as Marjorie Levinson, *Wordsworth's Great Period-Poems,* which, curiously, follows the New Critical model of autonomous chapters devoted to the close reading of single poems. Siskin also sees lyric as playing a key role in the professionalization and "specialization" of literature (*Work of Writing,* 131–33). See also Liu for the association of Wordsworth with a lyric moment of "local transcendence" ("Local Transcendence," 87).

12. Paul Ricoeur, "Narrative Time," 165–86; Hayden White, "The Value of Narrativity in the Representation of Reality," 1–24; Teresa de Lauretis, "Desire in Narrative," 103–12.

13. D. A. Miller, *Narrative and Its Discontents;* J. Hillis Miller, *Ariadne's Thread.*

14. Gary Kelly had already set this division in place two decades ago, in making Scott and Austen the only novelists deserving of full chapters in his *English Fiction of the Romantic Period 1789–1830.*

15. Habermas, *The Structural Transformation of the Public Sphere,* 27, 51.

16. Immanuel Kant, *Anthropology from a Pragmatic Point of View,* 3–4; Gianni Vattimo, *The Transparent Society,* 14.

17. For further discussion of these issues, see Tilottama Rajan, "In the Wake of Cultural Studies," 67–88; idem; "The Prose of the World," 479–504.

18. Andrew Elfenbein, *Byron and the Victorians,* 89.

19. Marc Redfield, *The Politics of Aesthetics,* 9–18. See also Redfield's *Phantom Formations.*

20. De Lauretis, "Desire in Narrative," 105.

21. David Carroll, *Paraesthetics,* 39.

22. Samuel Taylor Coleridge, *Biographia Literaria,* 1.304.

23. Joel Faflak, "Speaking of Godwin's *Caleb Williams,*" 121; Ross Woodman, *Sanity, Madness, Transformation.* I discuss Woodman's concepts further in chapters 2 and 3.

24. Percy Bysshe Shelley, *A Defence of Poetry,* in *Shelley's Poetry and Prose,* 512. Unless otherwise noted, all references to Shelley's poetry and prose are to this edition and will be cited parenthetically; *DP* refers to *A Defence of Poetry,* and *PU* refers to *Prometheus Unbound.*

25. Rudolf Haym, quoted in Walter Benjamin, *The Concept of Criticism in German Romanticism,* 173; Friedrich Schlegel, "Gespräch Über die Poesie," 209.

26. Benjamin, *The Concept of Criticism,* 173–75.

27. Giorgio Agamben, *The Idea of Prose,* 40–41. Kristeva describes the semiotic in terms of "discrete quantities of energy" that move through the body of a "subject who is not yet constituted as such" and that are " 'energy' charges as well as 'psychical' marks" (*Revolution in Poetic Language,* 25). This text is hereafter cited as *R*.

28. Allen Tate, "Tension in Poetry," 62–64.

29. Michel Foucault, *The Order of Things,* 300.

30. W. B. Yeats, "The Circus Animals' Desertion," in *Collected Poems,* 392.

31. Gerald Prince, "The Disnarrated," 1–8.

32. Michel Foucault, *"The Archaeology of Knowledge" and "The Discourse on Language,"* 128–30.

33. Jacques Derrida, *Archive Fever,* 10.

34. William Godwin, *Caleb Williams,* 434. Hereafter cited as *CW*.

35. Godwin, "Of History and Romance," in *CW,* 467. This essay is hereafter cited as HR.

36. Jean-François Lyotard, *The Differend: Phrases in Dispute,* 3–11. Hereafter cited as *D*.

37. Tilottama Rajan, "Framing the Corpus," 423; G. W. F. Hegel, *The Philosophy of Nature,* 437.

38. Ian Duncan, "Adam Smith, Samuel Johnson, and the Institutions of English," 39. On the entry of novels into the curriculum see Paul G. Bator, "The Entrance of the Novel into the Scottish Universities," 89–102.

39. Robert Crawford, *Devolving English Literature,* 20.

40. Theodor W. Adorno and Max Horkheimer, *Dialectic of Enlightenment,* 3–42; David Simpson, *The Academic Postmodern and the Rule of Literature,* 24, 120–24.

41. Duncan, "Adam Smith, Samuel Johnson, and the Institutions of English," 40.

42. Adam Smith, *Lectures on Rhetoric,* 110; Thomas Love Peacock, *The Four Ages of Poetry,* 17–21.

43. David Simpson, *Romanticism, Nationalism, and the Revolt against Theory,* 8–11.

44. Jacques Derrida, "Sendoffs (for the Collège Internationale de Philosophie)," *Eyes of the University,* 243.

Chapter One: The Trauma of Lyric

1. Unless otherwise noted, all references to Shelley are to *Shelley's Poetry and Prose,* edited by Donald H. Reiman and Neil Fraistat. *Prometheus Unbound* is hereafter cited as *PU*; *A Defence of Poetry* is cited as *DP*.

2. Shelley, *Note Books of Percy Bysshe Shelley,* ed. H. B. Forman, 2:102.

3. Allen Tate, "Tension in Poetry," 62–64.

4. William Keach, *Shelley's Style,* 81–82.

5. William Godwin, *Caleb Williams,* 434.

6. The word is not Shelley's, but is widely used, beginning with Earl Wasserman, *Shelley: A Critical Reading,* 11–21. Before Wasserman's influential reading, which describes *Alastor* as "an elegiac biography narrated by a dramatic speaker who has his own fictional identity" (11) and then goes on to describe this speaker as the Narrator, the Narrator and Poet were generally confused. See, for instance, Harold Bloom, *The Visionary Company,* 280; Ross Woodman, *The Apocalyptic Vision in the Poetry of Shelley,* 13. This confusion is a symptom of the poem's intension and inwardness. Though they do not take up narrative as a problem within the text, readings after Wasserman always refer to a Narrator: see, for example, my own reading, which sees the Poet and Narrator as positions on a spectrum rather than sharply differentiated characters (*Dark Interpreter,* 75–83); Lloyd Abbey, *Destroyer and Preserver,* 21–30; Jerrold Hogle, *Shelley's Process,* 57.

7. Mary Favret, "Mary Shelley's Sympathy and Irony," 17–19, 29. For a less binary and polemical reading of Mary Shelley's editorial relationship to Percy's work, see Susan Wolfson's essay in the same volume, "Editorial Privilege: Mary Shelley and Percy Shelley's Audiences" (39–72).

8. Søren Kierkegaard, *"The Present Age" and Two Minor Ethico-Religious Treatises,* 8–17, 34–41; Matthew Arnold, "The Function of Criticism at the Present Time," 9–34.

9. In *Romantic Moods: Paranoia, Trauma, and Melancholy,* Thomas Pfau compellingly argues for the relationship between lyric and "a traumatic . . . disturbance of the subject" in the period 1800–15 (21; see also 192–94). In *Alastor,* I am suggesting, lyric is a trope for trauma.

10. Paul Ricoeur, "Narrative and Hermeneutics," 153.

11. Paul de Man, "Shelley Disfigured," 100, 110–20.

12. Giorgio Agamben, *The Idea of Prose,* 41; Alexander García Düttmann, "Integral Actuality," in ibid., *The Idea of Prose,* 3.

13. Friedrich Schlegel, "Gespräch Über die Poesie," 209.

14. Walter Benjamin, *The Concept of Criticism,* 173–75; see also Düttman, "Integral Actuality," 17–18; Andrew Phelan, *"Fortgang and Zusammenhang:* Walter Benjamin and the Romantic Novel," 69.

15. Agamben, *The Idea of Prose,* 40–41; Benjamin, *The Concept of Criticism,* 154, 158, 178–79.

16. Rodolphe Gasché, "The Sober Absolute," 55.

17. Jerome McGann, *The Romantic Ideology,* 1.

18. Wasserman, *Shelley,* 15–21.

19. Gasché, "The Sober Absolute," 51–52, 67–68.

20. Robert Browning, "An Essay on Percy Bysshe Shelley" (1852), in *Peacock's "Four Ages of Poetry," Shelley's "Defence of Poetry," Browning's "Essay on Shelley,"* ed. H. F. B. Brett-Smith (Oxford: Blackwell, 1921–53), 63–67, 82.

21. According to Richard Woodhouse in an 1819 letter to John Taylor, Keats thought *Isabella* "mawkish" (Hyder Rollins, ed., *The Keats Circle,* 1.:90).

22. Agamben, *The Idea of Prose,* 40–41. On the connection between lyric and turning back as part of verse or *versus,* see also Heather Dubrow, *The Challenges of Orpheus,* 27–31.

23. Browning, "Essay," 63, 66.

24. Gasché, "The Sober Absolute," 65.

25. Walter Benjamin, "The Storyteller," 91. The Narrator's "tale" of course cannot have the other characteristic Benjamin associates with the form, that of reinforcing community around an orally shared experience, since the Narrator is already part of the world of writing and solitude that Benjamin associates with the novel (87, 99).

26. Quotations are from Wordsworth and Coleridge, *Lyrical Ballads.*

27. In the first "Essay upon Epitaphs" (1810), Wordsworth writes that the character of the deceased should be seen through a "tender haze or a luminous mist, that spiritualizes and beautifies it; that takes away indeed, but only to the end that the parts that are not abstracted may appear more dignified and lovely" (*Literary Criticism of William Wordsworth,* 101).

28. Northrop Frye, *Anatomy of Criticism,* 249.

29. Arthur Schopenhauer, *The World as Will and Representation,* 1.248–51; Friedrich Nietzsche, *The Birth of Tragedy,* 36–46; For a discussion of Nietzsche's concept of mood see Stanley Corngold, "Nietzsche's Moods," in *Nietzsche and Romanticism,* ed. Tilottama Rajan, *Studies in Romanticism* 29.1 (1990), 67–90.

30. Sharon Cameron, *Lyric Time,* 204, 250.

31. Ibid., 23; Theodor W. Adorno, "Lyric Poetry and Society," 62.

32. For Lacan the "Symbolic" in contrast to the "Imaginary" is the order of language and the law in which the subject finds himself inscribed and displaced. Kristeva adds a third category to this dyad in the "semiotic," which is associated with physiological drives and pulsions whose residual presence disrupts language and which is felt in terms of absence, contradiction, silence. Where the Symbolic is patriarchal, the semiotic is associated with the mother's body, so the feminine resistance to male *logos* is not pleasure (as in Hélène Cixous's valorization of the Imaginary) but rather a de-idealized difference (*R,* 25–30).

33. Jacques Derrida, *Positions,* 26.

34. Benjamin, "The Storyteller," 86, 97; Paul Ricoeur, "Narrative Time," 170–73.

35. William Wordsworth, *The Excursion;* further references are given in the text. Wordsworth, "Preface to 'Lyrical Ballads,' with Other Poems (1800)," 21.

36. The various stages and states of the text (literally a text and not a work in Roland Barthes's sense) and their complicated history can be found in William Wordsworth, "The Ruined Cottage" and "The Pedlar," edited by James Butler, whose "Introduction" to the various texts (3–36) is an indispensable resource. References to "The Baker's Cart" and "Incipient Madness" are also from this edition.

37. Samuel Taylor Coleridge, *Biographia Literaria,* 2.156.

38. The phrase is used by de Selincourt and Darbishire in the Notes to their edition of *The Excursion* (365).

39. In its earliest form MS B, according to Butler, was a 528-line poem, ending with "she died,/Last human tenant of these ruined walls," followed by the words "The End." Wordsworth then started drafting and adding lines about the Pedlar's early education and his developing philosophy of the "One Life"; as these additions made the bleakness of the original ending inappropriate, he made several attempts at a reconciling conclusion ("Introduction," 17–20). Alternatively, the attempts at a conclusion may have come first, and the supplementary material on the Pedlar may have been added later to make the conclusion more credible (21). Interestingly, in her copying Dorothy did not copy all the Pedlar material (19), thus evincing a certain uneasiness about its superfluity. In MS D, Wordsworth does indeed remove much, but not all of the Pedlar material to the verso of the text.

40. Butler, "Introduction," 9; Browning, "Essay on Shelley," 65.

41. Rodolphe Gasché, *The Tain of the Mirror,* 6.

42. "The Baker's Cart" and "Incipient Madness" are sometimes assumed to precede MS A, but Butler dates the former before and the latter after the first stammering draft of Margaret's story. Butler's dating, however, refers to the completed and titled fragment "Incipient Madness." Even according to his argument, Wordsworth was drafting the fragment and MS A simultaneously, and he "eventually decided" to transfer the latter to "the opposite verso" (9). The point is that the two are connected: the very transference of "Incipient Madness" to the verso is the condition of possibility for writing the further poem which is in some sense answerable to, reflected back into, the space of this de-jection. Similarly but somewhat differently, Joel Faflak suggests that the fragments constitute the "primal scene" of *The Ruined Cottage,* or rather *The Recluse* (*Romantic Psychoanalysis,* 80). But the point is that this primal scene is not just the trauma (real or fantasized) that underlies composition but also its inspiration, its creative condition.

43. To write, according to Blanchot, is "to surrender to the fascination of time's absence . . . . The time of time's absence is not dialectical. In this time what

appears is the fact that nothing appears. What appears is the being deep within being's absence." This absence is the absence of the work, which makes the writer "a survivor, without work," *désouevré* ("The Essential Solitude," in *The Space of Literature*, 24, 30).

44. Samuel Taylor Coleridge, "Frost at Midnight," *The Complete Poetical Works of Samuel Taylor Coleridge*, 1.9, 15–19.

45. Parenthetical references are to *The Complete Poetry and Prose of William Blake*, ed. David V. Erdman; hereafter cited as E, and referred to by page and plate number.

46. Parenthetical references to *The Fall of Hyperion* are to *The Poems of John Keats*, ed. Jack Stillinger.

47. Wordsworth, miscellaneous Dove Cottage mss, quoted in Butler, "Introduction," 17.

48. Butler, "Introduction," 11. Butler speculates that Lamb may have seen an early and/or later text of MS B.

49. "The Ruined Cottage" was in fact offered to Joseph Cottle in 1798 and was slated for publication, but instead Cottle printed the *Lyrical Ballads* (Butler, "Introduction," 21–22). One can only speculate on how differently Wordsworth might have been perceived if he had been known by this poem rather than *The Excursion*.

50. For the relation between music and the body in Nietzsche and Kristeva, see Tilottama Rajan, "Language, Music, and the Body," 147–69.

51. John Crowe Ransom, "Criticism, Inc.," 349; idem, "Humanism at Chicago," 100–101; idem, *The New Criticism*, 25, 267–75.

52. Keach, *Shelley's Style*, xii-xiii. Keach is actually quoting from Frederick Pottle, "The Case of Shelley," *PMLA* 67 (1952): 601; and David Perkins, *The Quest for Permanence* (Cambridge, MA: Harvard University Press, 1965), 168.

53. Keach, *Shelley's Style*, 80, and more generally, 79–183.

54. Benjamin, *The Concept of Criticism*, 129; Gasché, "The Sober Absolute," 57.

55. Gasché, *The Tain of the Mirror*, 13–22. Gasché's critique of Romantic reflection both here and in "The Sober Absolute" places him in a long line of thinkers who have reservations about "romantic irony" from Hegel to Karl Schmitt. In a disciplinary sense, his outlining of absolute or speculative reflection in Hegel configures speculative philosophy in such a way as to make it more analytically acceptable, whether or not Hegel himself fully achieves this goal (35ff.).

56. I am not using the term *extensiveness* here in the same sense as Tate's *extension*, which involves, as Murray Krieger argues, "the precision of [a poem's] denotations as well as the inevitable pattern of its logical relations," both of which are sacrificed by intension (*The New Apologists for Poetry* [Bloomington: Indiana University Press, 1963], 147).

57. Agamben, *The Idea of Prose*, 40–41.

58. Gasché, *The Tain of the Mirror*, 16.

59. Agamben, *The Idea of Prose*, 40. Strictly speaking enjambment is the completion, in the next line, of a clause or grammatical unit begun in the previous line. But for Agamben the pause, or "caesura," also creates a certain holding back or recursiveness.

60. Maurice Blanchot, "Sleep, Night" and "Orpheus' Gaze," in *The Space of Literature*, 265, 171.

61. Tilottama Rajan, "Romanticism and the Death of Lyric Consciousness," 198–200.

62. Thus the Narrator writes of the Poet: "Many a wide waste and tangled wilderness/Has lured his fearless steps" (78–79; see also 107). The echo of Wordsworth is symptomatic, but the effect is actually the opposite, since Shelley uses the "has" to break the continuity of the simple past tense and introduce a sense of a past that repeats itself as we read the poem.

63. Ricoeur, "Narrative and Hermeneutics," 152.

64. The doubling of the Poet's story has not generally been noticed. However, Thomas Weiskel suggests that the Poet's journey falls into "two phases, an upward, regressive journey to origins (ll.222–468), and a downward course, following a river that is meant to image the progress of his life" (*The Romantic Sublime*, 146).

65. J. Hillis Miller, *Fiction and Repetition*, 6.

66. Harold Bloom, "The Internalization of Quest Romance," 13–36.

67. Blanchot, "Death as Possibility," in *The Space of Literature*, 104.

68. On lyric and childhood, see Dubrow, *The Challenges of Orpheus*, 35.

69. André Green, *The Work of the Negative*, 45, 71, 261.

70. Jean-Luc Nancy, *The Ground of the Image*, 1–3. By "distinct" Nancy does not mean the clear as opposed to the indistinct. The distinct, as he explains, "is distinct according to these two modes: it does not touch, and it is dissimilar" (2).

71. Agamben, *Infancy and History*, 82.

72. Nancy, *The Ground of the Image*, 2–3.

73. For a more detailed discussion of how Keats works through the contradictions between Classical and Romantic or, one could say, objective and subjective images of the writer, see my discussion of the poem in *Dark Interpreter*, 169–71, 186–203, and also in "Keats, Poetry, and 'The Absence of the Work,'" 346–51.

74. Nancy, *The Ground of the Image*, 2.

75. Ibid., 2–3.

76. Blanchot, "Orpheus' Gaze," in *The Space of Literature*, 171.

77. Ibid., 172. Blanchot comments that to "kill oneself is to mistake one death

for the other": to mistake the death "that is not linked to *me* by any relation of any sort" and "toward which I do not direct myself" for the "power that has its source in the end" and is correlated with "freedom" and "possibility" ("Death as Possibility," 95, 100, 104).

78. Mary Shelley included *Alastor* in her *Posthumous Poems of Percy Bysshe Shelley* because it had gone out of print. But although she included other poems for the same reason, in her 1839 "Note on Alastor" she does also confer on it a certain posthumousness by associating it with "the death which he had often contemplated during the last months as certain and near" (in Percy Bysshe Shelley, *Poetical Works*, ed. Thomas Hutchinson, 31). Further citations from Mary Shelley's Prefaces and notes are from this edition.

79. Neil Fraistat, "Shelley Left and Right," 106, 108. In a different turn on this reduction of Shelley to lyric, Julie Carlson argues that Shelley, in an attempt to transcend life, life-writing, and his "embeddedness" within his literary family, constructs himself as the "Poet" and specifically the lyric Poet, thus "intentional[ly] and inadvertent[ly]" eclipsing the reputations of Godwin, Wollstonecraft, and Mary Shelley, "an eclipse that holds to this day" (*England's First Family of Writers,* 257–60). I am completely in agreement with the broader goals of Carlson's important study, which tries to retrieve the writers in her title as "England's first family" by disturbing the "idealization of lyric" as a definition of classic romanticism" and by valorizing various forms of life-writing and subjectivity that have not been recognized by the New Criticism, deconstruction, or cultural studies. But it will be obvious that I take a different view of Percy Shelley's place in this family.

80. Mary Shelley, "Note on *Prometheus Unbound*," 272; "Preface to First Collected Edition, 1839," x; "Note on The Cenci," 337.

81. Fraistat, "Shelley Left and Right," 108.

82. Wolfson, "Editorial Privilege," 49–54; Mary Shelley, "Preface to First Edition," ix.

83. On the Victorian pathologization of Romantic poetry, see Dino Felluga, *The Perversity of Poetry,* particularly 1–8.

84. Mary Shelley, "Preface to the Volume of Posthumous Poems Published in 1824," xiii.

85. The phrase *"retrait du politique"* is used by Philippe Lacoue-Labarthe and Jean-Luc Nancy to describe a form of the political intimately connected to philosophy but one that retreats from the total "domination" of the contemporary scene by the political and its reification as "politics" (*Retreating the Political,* ed. Simon Sparks, 95–99). As Simon Sparks explains in his "Introduction: Politica ficta," this *retrait* is not a "simple withdrawal" but is "a matter of the effacement of any assignable and specific meaning" to the political, which, "accompanying

and operating on the basis of the first sense of the retreat as the withdrawal of meaning, 'would thus retrace the contours of this specificity, whose actual conditions would need to be reinvented' " (xxv-vii).

86. Mary Shelley, "Preface to Posthumous Poems," xii; "Preface to First Edition," xi. Note also her description of the world's reaction to Shelley's death in the 1839 Preface: "He died, and the world showed no outward sign" (xi); and in the 1824 Preface: "The ungrateful world did not feel his loss, and the gap it made seemed to close as quickly over his memory as the murderous sea above his living frame" (xiii).

87. Ranita Chatterjee uses the term "psychonarration" in taking up my discussion of "autonarration" in my article (an early and different version of chapter 3 of this book) "Autonarration and Genotext in Mary Hays' *Memoirs of Emma Courtney*," 149–76. Psychonarration, as she defines it, is a process midway between the libidinal and the discursive, wherein material is circulated between "partial subjects who are intimately invested in each other," such that their texts refer to "other published texts written by family members"—or, one could add, by members of a literary community. The consequence of both auto- and psychonarration is that texts "are not stable objects to be understood; they are sites for author-readers to produce themselves as narrative" ("Filial Ties," 30–32).

88. Mary Jacobus, *Psychoanalysis and the Scene of Reading*, 168, 197, 199; Tilottama Rajan, "Mary Shelley's *Mathilda*," 43–68. Jacobus's reading takes up my analysis of the text's negativity but suggests that for me "Matilda's resistance and negativity ultimately remain just that: unproductive and unusable" because I see the text as unreadable, an aesthetic failure (167–68). On the contrary, I see the text's failure as its power, and although my essay does not give poetry the attention that Jacobus does, our readings are fundamentally in accord. To read a text as unreadable is still to read it, but the point about "unusable negativity" in Bataille's and Blanchot's sense is precisely that one must be careful not to economize it within a genre or protocol of reading, a care that Jacobus indeed takes in arguing that the "enigmatic poetics of pathological mourning brings psychoanalysis and poetry into the same room with the phantom of analytic failure" (165). Where the style of our readings differs is that mine is more focused on what Jacobus calls the "buried parental secret" and its incommunicability, and hers is more focused on poetry or lyric as the "bearer" of that secret (165).

89. Jacobus, *Psychoanalysis and the Scene of Reading*, 165, 197. In citing Jacobus, who tacitly identifies lyric and poetry, I do not mean to conflate the two in the case of Mary any more than in the case of Percy Shelley. For Mary Shelley, too, lyricism is simply the shell or signifier of a "poetry" that has yet to be grasped, even as it is also a specific capacity to "listen" or "hear" that poetry. Implicit in Jacobus's association of lyric with listening is a claim about its importance to

psychoanalysis. But if poetry is an anagram for psychoanalysis, narrativity is as important to this poetry as lyric.

90. Dubrow, *The Challenges of Orpheus,* 12. Dubrow discusses the various mythological figures who have been used to thematize lyric, including Orpheus, Arion, Amphion, and Pan (18–26). She specifically discusses Amphion and Orpheus in the context of the ability to move "rocks and stones" (19).

Chapter 2: Shelley's Promethean Narratives

1. All parenthetical references are to Percy Bysshe Shelley, *"Zastrozzi" and "St. Irvyne,"* ed. Stephen C. Behrendt.

2. My decision to discuss the earlier novels after the later *Alastor,* while logical in a book largely oriented to prose, is obviously at odds with the chrono-logic of Shelley's corpus. It can easily have the counterintuitive effect of making the novels seem more "mature" than the poem. It is important to remember that if the novels are the first site of Shelley's uneasiness about a pure poetry, which is often attributed to him, they are written in a form that also deconstructs "prose" as an alternative to poetry. Beneath this construction of prose as a self-consuming artifact, in other words, lies what will subsequently emerge as a pressure to reimagine poetry in a way that will not reduce it to the clichés to which it is nervously reduced in Shelley's anticipatory echoes of his later work.

3. According to Stephen Behrendt (in an e mail correspondence), the copies brought out in 1822 were probably ones that remained from the original print run.

4. As Žižek explains, "deep ecology" can take two forms, both of which remain powerfully anthropocentric despite their claims to the contrary. On the one hand is a seemingly "anti-anthropocentric Spinozian Deep Ecology, for which all forms of life are strictly equivalent, so that the rights of all elements of a biosphere, rivers and rocks included, have ultimately the same weight as the rights of man." On the other hand is a "New Age animist spiritualism, which conceives of the entire universe as a living organism whose development has culminated in man, its Omega-point, its steward- guardian," and which thus claims to stand "on the brink of a new cosmo-spiritual alteration which will deliver man from his narrow egoism and bring about a new solidarity of Life." But in both cases the very demand that deep ecology "addresses to man to sacrifice himself for the entire biosphere confers on him the exceptional status of universal being." Žižek's critique seems particularly pertinent to the last act of *Prometheus Unbound* ("Of Cells and Selves," in *The Žižek Reader,* ed. Elizabeth Wright and Edmond Wright, 304–5).

5. Jürgen Habermas, *Philosophical-Political Profiles,* 71.

6. Julia Kristeva, "The Adolescent Novel," 8–11, 22.

7. Ibid., 21.

8. G. W. F. Hegel, *Aesthetics: Lectures on Fine Art*, 1: 76–77. Hereafter cited as *A*. The *Aesthetics* was edited in 1835 and 1842 by H. G. Hotho, based on lectures given by Hegel in 1823, 1826, and 1828–29.

9. Associating adolescence with the advent of the symbol (in the sense of a certain distancing and self-consciousness), Kristeva disagrees with what she says is Hanna Segal's view (linked to Melanie Klein but also to Freud's theory of mourning), that the symbol comes out of the "depressive" position. She suggests that symbolic activity also "sustains itself" "from a *manic* position" (11). Both Segal and Kristeva allude here to Klein's three-part schema, in which the paranoid-schizoid position gives way to the depressive position, as a turning inward that also involves a taking stock and greater realism: a withdrawal of hysterical projections, which then leads to reparation. However, Segal's account of symbolic activity in terms of object-relations theory is far more complex than Kristeva allows. Segal begins by noting that "Klein links symbolism with projection and identification" and "agrees with Sandor Ferenczi that symbolism starts with projection of parts of the infant's own body into the object." However, she goes on to distinguish two kinds of "symbolic function." One is *"symbolic equation,"* which "underlies schizophrenic concrete thinking" and in which "the symbol is so equated with the object that the two are felt to be identical." In this form of symbolic activity "boundaries are lost" and "part of the ego is confused with the object." In *"symbolic representation,"* however, "the symbol represents the object but is not entirely equated with it." It is "with the advent of the depressive position, the experience of separateness, separation and loss, that symbolic representation comes into play," as "projective identifications" are withdrawn, and there is a "greater awareness of one's own psychic reality and the difference between internal and external" ("Symbolism," 35, 38, 40). I want to suggest that the fetishism of symbolic equation characterizes what Hegel calls the Symbolic; the Romantic, by contrast, deploys symbolic representation.

10. Kristeva, "The Adolescent Novel," 22.

11. Georg Lukács, *The Meaning of Contemporary Realism*, 27, 39.

12. Tilottama Rajan, "Toward a Cultural Idealism," 51–72.

13. Jacques Derrida, *Negotiations: Interventions and Interviews, 1971–2002*, 242.

14. Slavoj Žižek, *The Plague of Fantasies*, 14, 32.

15. According to Bataille base materialism, in contrast to dialectical materialism, which has its starting-point in German Idealism, takes over the Gnostic conception of matter "as an *active* principle having its own eternal autonomous existence as darkness . . . and as evil" ("Base Materialism and Gnosticism," 45, 47).

16. Michel Foucault, "Fantasia of the Library," 87–88, 91; Clifford Siskin, *The Work of Writing,*.

17. Foucault, "Fantasia," 88. Hegel sees his own period as characterized by "the prose of actuality" or, in effect, by modernity (*A*, 525).

18. Peter Brooks, *Reading for the Plot*, 101.

19. Samuel Taylor Coleridge, *Biographia Literaria*, 1.304.

20. The question of whether the novels were initially "intended" as seriously as we might take them in the light of Shelley's later work is, to my mind, a red herring for the purposes of this argument. If one must determine intention, what Shelley is doing in these texts operates in a grey area somewhere between blindness and insight. But more important is the fact that the novels have self-reflexive effects, especially when read in relation to Shelley's larger corpus. Moreover, a deconstruction of cultural norms is embedded in the Gothic genre as Shelley receives it, again at a level that is between blindness and insight, and that has to do with the symptomatic role of the genre as a whole in culture rather than with the intention of any single author.

21. Slavoj Žižek, *The Plague of Fantasies*, 35. As Žižek comments, perversion has an "intermediate status . . . between psychosis and neurosis, between the psychotic's foreclosure of the Law and the neurotic's integration into the Law" (34).

22. Peter Brooks, *The Melodramatic Imagination*, 105.

23. Julia Kristeva, *Le texte du roman*, 19.

24. The concept of non-synchronicity or uneven development was introduced, though in a less theoretical and structural way, by Ernst Bloch in "Nonsynchronism and the Obligation to Its Dialectics," 22–38.

25. Fredric Jameson, *The Political Unconscious*, 29, 32, 37, 39. Jameson's point contra Althusser is that structural causality is still a practice of mediation, because the concept of semiautonomy still "*relate[s]*" as much as it "*separates*" the parts or levels (41).

26. Ibid., 77. Jameson uses "imaginary" and "symbolic" resolution somewhat interchangeably (e.g., 77, 80, 252). The terms do, nevertheless, refer to different aspects of the Lacanian triad of the Imaginary, the Symbolic, and the Real, which I will capitalize when referring to Lacan. We could therefore think of a symbolic resolution as a false resolution of contradictions imposed by the "Symbolic" order of family and kinship, Emma Courtney's marriage to Montague in Mary Hays's *Memoirs of Emma Courtney* being an example. An imaginary resolution, by contrast, would be a fantasized resolution, such as the union of Prometheus and Asia in *Prometheus Unbound*.

27. For further elaboration, see my article "(Dis)figuring the System," 120–27.

On the preludia, see Julia Wright, *Blake, Nationalism, and the Politics of Alienation*, 89–110.

28. Jameson, *The Political Unconscious*, 50–52.

29. Žižek, *The Plague of Fantasies*, 20.

30. Žižek, *The Sublime Object of Ideology*, 78–79.

31. Žižek, *The Plague of Fantasies*, 7.

32. In the final chapter Zastrozzi mockingly asks Matilda: "Did you think it was from friendship I instructed you to gain Verezzi?" He goes on to disclose that it was he who led Julia to Matilda's house, "foreseeing the effect it would have upon the strong passions of your husband" (155–56).

33. Kristeva, "The Adolescent Novel," 22.

34. Ibid., 11, 18, 22. Joel Faflak, "Speaking of Godwin's Caleb Williams," 121.

35. Ross Woodman, *Sanity, Madness, Transformation*, 6–7; Slavoj Žižek, *The Indivisible Remainder*, 52. Insofar as he implicitly sees critique as a kind of *poiesis* and not just a discipline, Žižek is one of the few "cultural" critics to think culture Romantically.

36. Immanuel Kant, *Critique of the Power of Judgment*, 192. Hereafter cited as *CJ*.

37. Segal, "Symbolism," 42.

38. It is Nempere who first asks why we are "taught to believe that the union of two who love each other is wicked, unless authorized by certain rites and ceremonials" (230).

39. Wolfstein is "the heir of a wealthy potentate in Germany" (113) but also the brother of Eloise, whose home, St. Irvyne, is in France (185). Moreover, when he meets Ginotti again and hears his story, he seems to be in Bohemia, where he has gone to claim the estate of his uncle (165), but at the end of the story Ginotti expects Wolfstein to meet him at midnight in France (185).

40. Žižek, *The Sublime Object of Ideology*, 87.

41. As Steven Bruhm suggests in discussing the tortured body in Shelley and Godwin, Zastrozzi's body finally remains "unreadable," even though the violent explicitness of the ending apparently reverses the earlier treatment of him, in which he is always masked and obscure. For where the Gothic departs from a sentimental aesthetic in which the "body broadcasts an internal state" and where torture therefore violently tries to "get inside" the unreadable Gothic body, Zastrozzi's body remains a "shield, an impediment to the truth." Bruhm also points out that the inquiry-by-torture comes *after* Zastrozzi's confession (*Gothic Bodies*, 101–3). As in *Caleb Williams*, in which Falkland is put on trial after the reader has found him guilty, the effect is to render the logic of judgment that subtends the genre of the Novel incoherent.

42. Mary Shelley, *Valperga*, 430.

43. Nicholas Abraham and Maria Torok, "Qui est Mélanie Klein?" 189–90. Translation mine.

44. Søren Kierkegaard, *The Concept of Irony*, 278.

45. Donald Ault, "Re-Visioning The Four Zoas," 105–40.

46. The term is used by Gerald Prince to signify what has not happened but could have happened ("The Disnarrated," 1–8).

47. The suggestion is made by L. J. Zillman in *Shelley's Prometheus Unbound*, 12.

48. More specifically, the manuscript comprises three notebooks. MS E1 begins with act 4 on the right-hand side of the page and continues to line 427. At this point Shelley begins act 1 on the left-hand pages and continues to insert the rest of act 4 on the right-hand side. This notebook ends in the middle of the scene involving the Furies. MS E2 begins with the remainder of act 1 on the left-hand side. Several pages on the right side are left blank, and it is not until he reaches the middle of act 2 scene 2 that Shelley returns to his eccentric practice of dividing the text between left and right sides of the notebook. Having placed all of the dialogue between Asia and Panthea (2.1) and part of the next scene involving the Semichorus of Spirits (2.2.1–63) on the left side, Shelley suddenly switches the remainder of 2.2 to the right side. Thus the first part of 2.3 (Asia's dialogue with Panthea as they approach the volcano) is placed on the left side beside the remainder of 2.2 (the dialogue between the Fauns: ll.64ff.). The second half of 2.2 does not occupy as much space as the first half of 2.3, so Shelley leaves one of the right-hand pages blank as he continues scene 3 up to the end of the sisters' conversation prior to their entry into the Cave of Demogorgon (2.3.53). The remainder of 2.3 is now shifted from the left to the right side. Thus the crucial interview between Asia and Demogorgon (2.4) now occupies the left side, while the remainder of scene 3 (the Song of the Spirits: ll.54ff.) is placed opposite it. Finally, MS E3, which is far simpler, begins at 2.4.124 and continues straightforwardly to the end of act 3, sometimes, but not always, leaving the left-hand pages blank for corrections.

49. C. D. Locock, *Shelley Manuscripts in the Bodleian Library*, 28–29.

50. F. W. J. Schelling, *Ideas for a Philosophy of Nature*, 272.

51. Paul Ricoeur, "Narrative and Hermeneutics," 149, 153.

52. I discuss the reflexiveness of the play at length in *The Supplement of Reading*, 305–22.

53. Ibid., 310–14.

54. Carlos Baker, *Shelley's Major Poetry*, 107; cf. also Kenneth Neill Cameron, "The Political Symbolism of *Prometheus Unbound*," 119–20.

55. Steven Cohan and Linda Shires point to the role of metaphor in the con-

figuration of plot: "A story paradigmatically replaces one event with another to organize signifying relations of selection and substitution, thereby operating like metaphor in a linguistic structure" (*Telling Stories*, 54).

56. Jerrold Hogle, "'Frankenstein' as Neo-Gothic," 178.

57. The use of inset poems is of course characteristic of Radcliffe. In parodying her, Shelley draws attention to Gothic as the repository of a poetry—sentimentally protected from the genre's psychic violence—that it does not quite know how to bring back into the work of culture.

Chapter 3: Unbinding the Personal

1. Mary Hays, *Appeal to the Men of Great Britain*, 70, 67.

2. Though he was not romantically interested in Hays, Frend had taken the initiative in approaching her, praising her maiden publication *Cursory Remarks* (1791), published under the pseudonym "Eusebia," after it was attacked in a highly gendered way by Gilbert Wakefield. For this part of Hays's story, including her misunderstanding of Frend's interest in her, see Gina Luria Walker, *Mary Hays*, 44–53.

3. Friedrich Schiller, *Naive and Sentimental Poetry*, 106–7.

4. Julia Kristeva, *Revolution in Poetic Language*, 59–60. Hereafter cited as *R*.

5. Joel Faflak, "Speaking of Godwin's *Caleb Williams*," 121; Ross Woodman, *Sanity, Madness, Transformation*, 3–7. For a discussion of poetry in Shelley as a faculty of perpetual deconstruction, see my chapter "World within World: The Theoretical Voices of Shelley's *Defence of Poetry*," in *The Supplement of Reading* (277–97).

6. Jean-Paul Sartre, *Critique of Dialectical Reason*, 67, 318.

7. Letter to Godwin, February 6, 1796, included in Mary Hays's *Memoirs of Emma Courtney*, 239. Further references to the novel and the letters are from this edition and will be given parenthetically in the text, with references to the novel being indicated by *M*, and references to the letters being indicated by "L."

8. The epitext according to Gerard Genette is that part of the paratext that is "at least originally" located at some distance from the book," in interviews, conversations, and private communications (*Paratexts*, 5).

9. See, for instance, Claire Tomalin, *The Life and Death of Mary Wollstonecraft*, 241, 245; James Foster, *History of the Pre-Romantic Novel in England*, 259–60. Another example of the automatic dismissal of Hays is provided by Allene Gregory, who deals with Hays by absorbing her into Godwin, despite her concession that the novel by Godwin to which *Memoirs* bears a "striking resemblance" was published much later (*The French Revolution and the English Novel*, 223).

10. William Godwin, "Of Choice in Reading," 132–33, 136–38. I discuss this essay in the next chapter. Godwin's essay was published in the same year as Hays's novel. It is hard to know whether she had read the essay, and the word "tendency," though most rigorously theorized by Godwin, was widely used.

11. I use the word "error" as Stanley Corngold does, when he writes that "Error is not *mistake*"; instead error is a constitutive, creative misprision, a trope, so that "the skew of error implies a truth" ("Error in Paul de Man," 92).

12. *Collected Letters of Mary Wollstonecraft*, ed. Ralph M. Wardle, 376.

13. Rachel Blau DuPlessis argues that nineteenth-century novels about/by women uniformly end in the heroine's recontainment through marriage or death (*Writing beyond the Ending*, 1–4).

14. I use this term in the sense used by Lacan and Kristeva, to indicate the order in which we are constructed as speaking subjects: the order of syntax, which is also the order of law and family. This order is "Symbolic" in the sense that the individual's identity within it is always other: a representation of her as something else, for and by someone else.

15. Sometime late in 1795 Godwin suggested that Hays set down the thoughts she had communicated to him in her letters in a work of fiction, and she agreed on condition that he read her work. In January 1796 Hays then asked Frend to return her letters because she wanted to incorporate them in a work of fiction. He did not reply. Hays tells Godwin, in a letter of February 6, 1796, that she has "only some imperfect copies of the papers in question" (L, 245). In other words, it seems that she kept drafts of at least some of the letters for re-citation. She did, of course, have access to the letters she had written to Godwin.

16. Augustus's phrasing is ambiguous enough that it might refer to a social "engagement" (157) that has prevented him from answering Emma's importunate letters more promptly. But the word "attachment" used of a social engagement is surely odd enough to suggest that he is, in a veiled way, trying to alert Emma to his situation.

17. Nicola Watson, *Revolution and the Form of the British Novel*, 20, 25–26, 44–49.

18. Ibid., 42.

19. Felicity Nussbaum, *The Autobiographical Subject*, 179–80.

20. Hays refused to divulge Frend's identity to Godwin, but she is referring here to her decision to move into her own apartment when her family decided to move farther away from London, which would have meant being at a greater distance from Frend.

21. Hays, *Appeal to the Men of Great Britain*, 70, 67.

22. Judith Butler, *Subjects of Desire*, 186.

23. Slavoj Žižek "The Eclipse of Meaning," 208–9.

24. Butler, *Subjects of Desire*, 186–87, 192–98.

25. Jean Hyppolite, *Genesis and Structure of Hegel's Phenomenology of Spirit*, 162–68.

26. Butler, *Subjects of Desire*, 9.

27. The phrase is Kristeva's (*R*, 210). The translation reflects the double meaning of the French "*en procès.*"

28. Godwin retained the advantage in their correspondence by asking that Hays write to him but by answering her only in person. But in the novel Francis is not given this immunity from public scrutiny.

29. Sigmund Freud, "Psychopathic Characters on Stage," 7:308–10.

30. I refer here to Coleridge's poem "Constancy to an Ideal Object" (1825?), in *The Complete Poetical Works of Samuel Taylor Coleridge*, 455–56. Hays herself also uses the phrase "a purely ideal object" (*L*, 251).

31. Slavoj Žižek, *The Sublime Object of Ideology*, 74–76. "Enjoyment," it is necessary to point out, is not the best translation of "*jouissance*," which is as much painful as pleasurable: what Nietzsche in *The Birth of Tragedy* calls the original "oneness," its "pain" and "contradiction" (25, 33).

32. Note the frequent use of certain proto-Romantic words and concepts: "image" and "imagination" (*M*, 55, 86), "ideal" or "romantic" (81, 92, 110, 114, 132), and "visionary" (81, 114).

33. See David Farrell Krell, *Contagion*, 47.

34. Linda Kauffman, *Discourses of Desire*, 92–97, 160–78.

35. Ruth Perry, *Women, Letters, and the Novel*, 72–84, 111.

36. Godwin, "Of Choice in Reading," 136–38.

37. Žižek, *The Sublime Object of Ideology*, 76.

38. William Godwin, *Faulkener*.

39. See Tilottama Rajan, "Mary Shelley's Mathilda," 48–61; idem, "'Something Not Yet Made Good.'"

40. Michel Foucault, *The Archaeology of Knowledge*, 128–30. My interest here is in the word "corpus" and the distinction Foucault makes, but I will continue to use the word "archive" as he uses it in "Fantasia of the Library" (1967). Indeed, Foucault's later use of "archive" is a disciplining and repression of his earlier and more radical use of it to include what Derrida calls the archiviolithic (*Archive Fever*, 10). Derrida's reference in *Archive Fever* to "burn[ing] the archive" harks back to Foucault's earlier "conflagration of the archive," in 1967. However, in the silent debate between Derrida and the later Foucault, *Archive Fever* (1995) is a critique of Foucault's use of the term in *The Archeology of Knowledge* (1969), as well as a critique of his genealogical work, especially his various lectures at the Collège de France, which in effect submit to *habitus* and the process of institution by being purely descriptive. Derrida is tacitly recall-

ing this later Foucault's use of "archive" to mean a set of practices when he refers to the archive superintended by the *archons* as consisting of the "documents" that "in effect speak the law . . . recall the law and call on or impose the law." The archive in this sense "forgets" the "memory which it shelters" (2) and must become the object of an "archiviology" (34) rather than a genealogy.

41. Walker, *Mary Hays*, 134.

42. Seymour Chatman, *Story and Discourse*, 9.

43. Fredric Jameson, *The Political Unconscious*, 35, 81–82.

44. Augustus refers to Emma as his sister (*M*, 100, 105), the role which Mrs. Harley also assigns her (101, 183), even though she also imagines them as husband and wife (103), thus marking the incestuous and forbidden nature of this union within the terms of the Symbolic order. Similarly, Emma Jr. and Augustus Jr. are brought up as brother and sister (220), this brother-sister "incest" signifying a typically Romantic and impossible union of the self with what is most like itself.

45. Walker, *Mary Hays*, 112.

46. The scandalous memoirs are discussed by Felicity Nussbaum, who describes them as the first significant form of women's self-writing other than spiritual autobiography (180). Nussbaum sees the scandalous memoirists as confirming and resisting the dominant ideology, further noting the conflicted position of these writers, given the relegation of "unlicensed sexuality to the lower classes" (179). I would further argue that the memoirists' identification of desire with sexuality aborts the emergent radicalism of their texts and that Hays's representation of a love that is and is not sexual is a way of retaining her right to address a middle-class liberal audience.

47. Jacques Derrida, *Archive Fever*, 11.

48. In "The Adolescent Novel" Kristeva might seem to take a different view of narrative as revolt and polymorphous perversity. However, this essay can still be summed up by her statement in *Revolution* that the "subjectal structure" of narrative, while producing an "infinite" series of " 'masks' and protagonists corresponding to the signifying process' abutments against parental and social structures," is still "locked in place to the extent that the parental and social network is applied to it" (91).

49. The Imaginary and the Symbolic can be seen as different ways of relating to an identity that is always already specular. In the Imaginary the subject identifies with the image (or imago) in the mirror. In the Symbolic she is uneasily aware of it as a representation.

50. Žižek, *The Sublime Object of Ideology*, 132.

51. Watson, *Revolution and the Form of the British Novel*, 48.

52. Jameson, *The Political Unconscious*, 242.

53. Another example of this motif is Matthew Arnold's poem "Tristan and Iseult," in which the dark, passionate Iseult is repeated as Tristan's paler, fairer, and more domestic second love. Arnold's poem parallels Victorian novels such as *David Copperfield* in its linking of repetition to the domestication of the Romantic, the conversion of revolutionary energy into evolutionary caution.

54. Katharine Goodman, *Dis/Closures*, 77.

55. Habermas argues that the public sphere is formed by "private people com[ing] together as a public," which is to say that for him there is no such thing as the private: the private is simply the sphere of the feelings as they exist for and are managed for public convenience (*Structural Transformation*, 27, 51–56, 150–51).

56. Watson, *Revolution and the Form of the British Novel*, 42; Perry, *Women, Letters, and the Novel*, 93–118; Roy Roussel, "Reflections on the Letter," 375–99.

57. Goodman, *Dis/Closures*, 79.

58. Wollstonecraft writes to Godwin: "I think you wrong. . . . You judge not in your own case as in that of another. You give a softer name to folly and immorality when it flatters—yes, I must say it—your vanity, than to mistaken passion when it was extended to another—you termed Miss Hays' conduct insanity when only her own happiness was involved" (*Collected Letters*, 404).

59. Mary Jacobus, *Psychoanalysis and the Scene of Reading*, 209–10, 212.

60. D. W. Winnicott, *Playing and Reality*, 5, 9, 41.

61. Michel Foucault, "Nietzsche, Genealogy, History," 148.

62. Winnicott, *Playing and Reality*, 3, 97. In a letter of February 6, 1796, Hays writes to Godwin: "Mine, I believe, is an almost solitary madness in the 18th century" (L, 240).

63. On this subject see Tilottama Rajan, *Dark Interpreter*, 186–203; idem, "Keats, Poetry, and 'The Absence of the Work,'" 346–51.

64. Francis and Emma meet before she meets Augustus, but he is called to London and suggests a correspondence. After the unraveling of her friendship with Augustus, Francis is attentive to her during her "sickness of the soul" (M, 166, 179), but when Mrs. Harley dies and Emma finds herself in need of help, it turns out Francis has abruptly left on a continental tour (191). He never reappears.

65. D. W. Winnicott, "The Fate of the Transitional Object" and "Notes on Play," in *Psychoanalytical Explorations*, 57, 60–61.

66. Winnicott, *Playing and Reality*, 94; Roy Schafer, *Bad Feelings*; Joan Riviere, "Hate, Greed, and Aggression," 3–56. Post-Kleinian analysis, however, does want to put bad feelings back into a recuperative dialectic in which aggression and depression are followed by "reparation." Thus Winnicott writes: "The

object is always being destroyed. This destruction becomes the unconscious back-cloth for love of a real object" (94). The point is valid but elides the legitimacy of the self-love involved in bad feelings.

67. Walker, *Mary Hays*, 64–65, 133.

68. This mourning frames the text, since Maria's separation from her daughter is the occasion for her imprisonment and subsequent woeful tale. But one could also argue that Maria can only move on to become a political subject once the daughter and associated motherhood plot are out of the way.

69. I understand the term "wounded masculine" to mean at once that part of the female psyche that is both disallowed from accessing its "masculine" potential and forced to grasp that potential in warped ways; *and* that part of the male psyche that is warped into certain forms of masculinity as well as resistance to such forms, such that it, too, is disallowed from accessing its " feminine" potential. The wounded masculine, in other words, is an androgynous concept but in the mode of negativity.

70. Mary Hays, *Letters and Essays, Moral and Miscellaneous*, 92.

71. In addition to the letters already cited, which focus on Caleb and Falkland as parallels for Emma's strong passions, Gina Luria Walker also argues that Hays's second novel, *The Victim of Prejudice*, devises "an alternative story for Godwin's character, Emily Melville." It revisits a subplot of *Caleb Williams* so as to retrieve from Emily's death a strength that Godwin allows her, without quite recognizing it (Walker, *Mary Hays*, 191–93).

72. The phrase is used by Godwin himself in arguing that Wollstonecraft, as a subject still in process, should not be judged according to her character "*pro tempore*" (*Memoirs of the Author of "A Vindication of the Rights of Woman*," 82).

73. Derrida, *Archive Fever*, 5, 12, 26–31.

74. Ibid., 34.

75. Michel Foucault, "Technologies of the Self," 27.

76. Derrida, *Archive Fever*, 29–30.

77. Janet Gezari, *Charlotte Brontë and Defensive Conduct*, 33–34.

78. Peter Melville Logan, *Nerves and Narrative*, 72. Although Logan does here present the text as unresolved, in general his reading closes down its narrativity by sharply distinguishing the older from the younger Emma and by focusing on the narrative frame, which he sees both as "making it clear from the start that the narrative is a cautionary tale" and as "discarding an agency based on sexuality" associated with the earlier Emma and "substituting one based on reproduction" (65, 70). This reading, in turn, is based on a depreciation of the younger Emma's desire, which assumes that her desire is identical with her sexuality rather than that this sexuality is itself a trope. While the older Emma's turning upon her younger self is thus painful, according to Logan, at least this new "voice,"

however "tentative and unstable, is nonetheless more substantial than the fiction of agency in the younger Emma's illusions" (72).

79. Virginia Woolf, *A Room of One's Own*, 70–74.

Chapter Four: The Scene of Judgment

1. William Godwin, *Enquiry Concerning Political Justice*, 1.2. Hereafter cited as *PJ*.

2. Foucault uses the term "governmentality" to describe the techniques by which individuals are rendered as governable subjects. Insofar as governmentality extends even to such apparently private and subjective matters as acts of kindness, his use is clearly anticipated by Godwin's use of the term "government" (Michel Foucault, "What Is Critique?" 156).

3. According to Robinson Godwin can serve as "an excellent bridge between the two hostile systems of empiricism and German idealism." Kant is an avowed "Republican," and his system has had "a vast effect in freeing the Mind from all shackles of prejudice—-Revelation, forms of Government, all are criticised" (*Crabb Robinson in Germany*, 105, 113). Despite their profound affinity, which will be pursued further in the next chapter, it is impossible to know whether Godwin read Kant, which he probably could not have done by the time of the first edition of *Political Justice*, since Kant was first translated only in 1798. On the knowledge of Kant in England, see René Wellek, *Immanuel Kant in England, 1793–1838*. Wellek mentions Baader's interest in Godwin during the period of his interest in Kant (28).

4. Immanuel Kant, *Critique of the Power of Judgment* (1790), 66–67. David Collings also discusses Godwin alongside Kant in one of the best articles on Godwin, "The Romance of the Impossible," 850–54. Collings, however, focuses on the uncompromising stance of the Kantian categorical imperative as read through Lacan on Kant and Sade, rather than on the micrological nuances of judgment. While distinguishing Godwin's ethics from Kant's, he also sees in Godwin's "determination to liberate his society from unreason, whether people want him to or not," a similar "violence" and "aggression" on the part of pure reason (853–54). Nevertheless, while constructing Godwin as a fanatic rather than a sceptic in *Political Justice*, Collings does also see Godwin's "experience of writing" as contradicting "his claims about immutable reason," particularly as he unravels the first into the second ending of *Caleb Williams*, thus performing a kind of autocritique of himself as Caleb in the process of writing (859). As will be apparent, my reading of the novel, while also assigning the revised ending the role of an autocritique, differs in the level of intentionality it attributes to Godwin and in reading the second ending as more than a negative, (self)critical moment.

5. By contrast Kant, in "What Is Enlightenment?" (1786), does seem to separate conscience from conduct when he gives the example of the soldier who, as a "private" individual, must obey orders, although in his "public" role as a scholar he cannot be prevented from criticizing the government (*"To Perpetual Peace" and Other Essays*, 42–43). Kant's use of the terms "private" and "public" is the opposite of Godwin's more normal usage and thus may contain a veiled irony. While Kant's position is different from that of Godwin, one should not too easily jump to the conclusion that Kant's distinction between public and private is a form of temporizing. For as Derrida emphasizes, Kant saw censorship as a "critique that has power" (*Eyes of the University*, 46); in other words, the censorship imposed on the private individual is a necessary part of the debate that must occur in the public sphere over what would otherwise be enthusiasm.

6. Jean-Luc Nancy, "The Inoperative Community," 9–12.

7. Immanuel Kant, *Critique of Pure Reason*, 219; hereafter cited as CPR.

8. Immanuel Kant, *Essays and Treatises on Moral, Political, and Various Philosophical Subjects.*

9. Jacques Derrida, *Negotiations*, 242.

10. I would limit Derrida's criticism to *The Critique of Pure Reason*. As I have argued elsewhere, in the first *Critique* Kant deals only with transcendental ideas and thus focuses on the *distance* of the idea(l) from actuality. He concentrates on two things: on the idea as operating on the side of freedom because it transcends experience, and on the dangers of hypostatizing this idea through an identification of representation with reality (*CPR*, 219–21, 373–75). In the Third *Critique*, however, Kant deals with "aesthetic" and "rational" ideas, and thus with the difference within these ideas *now* rather than their distance from the real (*CJ*, 192–95). For a fuller discussion, see Tilottama Rajan, "Toward a Cultural Idealism," 51–72.

11. On the one hand, anarchy "awakens thought," but on the other, Godwin sees it as a threat to personal security that may result in the counterreaction of despotism (*PJ*, 2.368–70). Though Godwin's discussion of anarchy is largely critical, as he points out, all peoples were "in a state of anarchy, that is, without government, previously to their being in a state of policy" (1.371): thus there may be nothing intrinsically wrong with anarchy, and its effects and desirability may vary depending on the state a particular society was in before it fell into anarchy (2.370–71). Of course, Godwin's concern about anarchy is not necessarily a dismissal of *anarchism*. The contemporary tradition of thinking about justice to which I link him here is often described as "pre-original" or "anarchic" in the root sense of going back before any *arche*, foundation, or institution of thought. Nevertheless, if Godwin believes philosophically in anarchism (and has therefore been seen as a founding thinker of anarchism), it is still the case that he is practi-

cally ambivalent about it. Hence I suggest that Godwin's anarchism is better thought of as the absence of institution than as an actual practice or "ism."

12. Jacques Derrida, *Negotiations,* 242.

13. William Godwin, "Of History and Romance," in *Caleb Williams,* 466–67. The essay, meant for a second edition of *The Enquirer,* was never published, though parts of it appear in revised form in the Preface to *Cloudesley.*

14. Godwin, Preface to *Fleetwood,* in *Caleb Williams,* 444.

15. Slavoj Žižek, *The Plague of Fantasies,* 7.

16. B. J. Tysdahl, *William Godwin as Novelist,* 132.

17. *Caleb Williams,* 169.

18. Interestingly, towards the end of the first volume Caleb starts putting Collins' narration in quotation marks: "I shall endeavour to state the remainder of this narrative in the words of Mr. Collins" (166). It would seem that Caleb at first makes himself the narrator of Falkland's story in order to claim an inside view of his patron, but he then returns the narration to Collins in order to mark his (Caleb's) difference from Falkland. After the conclusion of that part of Falkland's history that falls outside the diegesis, Falkland becomes a character in Caleb's story. The point is that Falkland's story is always mediated through Caleb.

19. Angela Esterhammer, "Godwin's Suspicion of Speech Acts," 554–56.

20. Jean-François Lyotard, *The Differend,* 151, 1.

21. Godwin, Preface to *Fleetwood,* 448; idem, Preface to *Cloudesley,* 7.

22. Lyotard's word for "event" is "*événement,*" which in contemporary French philosophy signifies a "now" with an explosive surplus of affect/effect, which cannot be placed within a syntagm (such as plot, which is a form of causality and thus rationality). An event is something like a "happening." In the passage cited, Lyotard's word for what is rendered in the English translation as "narrative" is actually "*récit*" (story). While his initial account of *récit* as containing a number of differends is closer to my definition of "narrative," his account of the genre as closing down this difference is consistent with his use of the term *récit* and my use of the word *story* (Lyotard, *Le Différend,* 218–19).

23. Shlomith Rimmon-Keenan, *Narrative Fiction,* 15–16.

24. See, for instance, *CW,* 59, 145, 179, 184, 210, 216, 235, 246, 254, 403, 431, 432. Godwin, it should be noted, does not himself distinguish "narrative" in the way I am doing from tale and story (e.g., 210). However, as is indicated by descriptions such as "unanswerable" (*St. Leon,*188), "plain and unadulterated," and "artless and manly" (*CW,* 431, 432), Godwin does associate "tale" and "story" with a certain feigned unity and integrity.

25. Gavin Edwards takes up Godwin's use of the terms "character" and "story," noting his uneasiness with the "narrative idea" but insisting that Godwin is in the end "committed to this idiom himself" ("William Godwin's Foreign

Language," 542). Edwards argues that character for Godwin is not interiority but a representation of oneself or perception of oneself within the public sphere (540–41), in other words, a form of institution. Nevertheless, he sees Godwin as wanting to distinguish a true from a false story, a true from a false character (544), and suggests that in the published ending of the novel Caleb "succeeds" in vindicating his character (546). Of particular interest is a passage from *Political Justice* that Edwards cites, which succinctly articulates character as a principle of totalization and predictability that facilitates the seamless operation of judgment: "The character of any man, is the result of a long series of impressions, communicated to his mind and modifying it in a certain manner, so as to enable us . . . to predict his conduct" *(PJ* 1.370). Yet Godwin is quite clear at the beginning of the text that such character is the effect of "political institution" on a "ductile," impressionable "substance" (1.26, 47), and indeed his Humean epistemology is what allows for his relentless probing, in his fiction, of character as an index of the fantasies a culture has about itself.

26. Esterhammer, "Godwin's Suspicion of Speech Acts," 554–56.

27. William Godwin, "Of Choice in Reading," 132–33, 136–38.

28. Godwin, Preface to *Cloudesley,* 7.

29. Godwin, Preface to *Fleetwood,* 445–48.

30. Jean Bellemin-Noel, *Le texte et l'avant texte,* 15.

31. Godwin, Preface to *Fleetwood,* 446.

32. Ibid., 446.

33. Giorgio Agamben, *The Coming Community,* 10.

34. William Godwin, *Memoirs of the Author of "A Vindication of the Rights of Woman,"* 83–84. Hereafter cited as MV.

35. The trial in both versions is not a jury trial or a public trial with attorneys as in *The Wrongs of Woman,* but a hearing at the house of the magistrate, designed "to find a medium between the suspicious air of a private examination and the indelicacy, as it was styled, of an examination exposed to the remark of every casual spectator" (426). In the original ending the magistrate does intervene (436, 438). In the revised ending, he does not speak at all.

36. Pamela Clemit, *The Godwinian Novel,* 64.

37. Jean-François Lyotard, "The Sign of History," 396.

38. On the complexities of Godwin's novel as a contribution to "the pamphlet debate on the French Revolution," see Clemit, *Godwinian Novel,* 36, and more generally, 35–69.

39. Lyotard in "The Sign of History" (408) describes the French Revolution as a hypotyposis, which Kant defines as a figure for a "concept which only reason can think, and to which no sensible intuition can be adequate" *(CJ,* 225). A paralogism occurs when an argument unfolds logically but is based on a groundless

presupposition. For a discussion of paralogism in Kant and Lyotard, see the next chapter. As Antonio Negri says, "the only justification for the hypothetical, hypostatic falsity of the paralogism is that it follows on from a real and irrepressible need" (*The Constitution of Time*, 37).

40. Godwin, Preface to *Fleetwood*, 448.

41. Jacques Derrida, *Points . . . Interviews*, 212.

42. Foucault, "What Is Critique?" 29.

43. Jean-Paul Sartre, *Being and Nothingness*, 105–8.

44. Joel Faflak, "Romanticism and the Pornography of Talking," 104–9; Michel Foucault, "Technologies of the Self," 244–45; idem, *The History of Sexuality*, 58–65. Faflak's reading of *Caleb Williams* is very different from my own, in that Faflak sees Godwin as nervously complicit with the "enlightenment" of psychoanalysis as a form of moral management, and he argues that "whatever knowledge" Godwin's novel produces simply "preys on itself" in the form of an interminable analysis for its own sake, which becomes predictable and ultimately evasive of the novel's traumatic core (118–19).

45. For a more detailed reading of *Mandeville*, see my essay "The Disfiguration of Enlightenment."

46. Johann Wolfgang von Goethe, *Elective Affinities*, 52–53. The term "affinity" had traditionally meant the attraction of like for like. It was only later that it came to mean the attraction between opposites, or in the nineteenth century, between electronegative and electropositive substances, leading to decomposition (Trevor Levere, *Transforming Matter*, 35, 89).

47. William Godwin, *Fleetwood*, 268. MacNeil's behavior is consistently puzzling. Even though he seems to have the perfect family, he unaccountably decides to set sail for Italy with his wife and two of his daughters. When the boat capsizes, the captain is able to save two passengers, but MacNeil decides that the entire family should perish together, even though he has left one daughter, Mary, behind (267–68). Not only does the drowning fulfil a death wish, but it seems as if Macneil wants to render Mary an orphan.

48. See Tilottama Rajan, "Mary Shelley's *Mathilda*," 52–54.

49. Søren Kierkegaard, *The Concept of Irony*, 276.

50. Jean Baudrillard, *Symbolic Exchange and Death*, 149.

51. Or, as Kierkegaard puts it in describing the utopianism of irony, irony as infinite absolute negativity is "negativity because it only negates; it is infinite because it negates not this or that phenomenon; and it is absolute because it negates by virtue of a higher which is not" (278).

52. It is significant here that Godwin makes Henrietta the ineffectual mouthpiece for the utopian side of necessitarianism when he has her say: "Consider that man . . . is just what his nature and his circumstances have made him. . . . He is

to be pitied therefore, not regarded with hatred; to be considered with indulgence, not made an object of revenge; to be reclaimed with mildness, to be gradually inspired with confidence" (153).

53. William Godwin, *St. Leon*, 475.

54. John Gibson Lockhart, "Review of *Mandeville*," 271.

55. Jon Klancher, "Godwin and the Genre Reformers," 32.

56. On the (Hegelian) dialectical logic of Scott's historical novels, see Georg Lukács, *The Historical Novel*, 26–29, 57–58.

57. Slavoj Žižek, *The Sublime Object of Ideology* (London: Verso, 1989), 87–89.

58. Slavoj Žižek, *The Plague of Fantasies*, 216.

59. Ibid., 18, 27.

60. Gary Handwerk, "History, Trauma, and the Limits of the Liberal Imagination," 72–82.

Chapter 5: Gambling, Alchemy, Speculation

1. Parenthetical references to Godwin's novel are to *St. Leon*, ed. Pamela Clemit; hereafter cited as *St.L.* For a comparison of *St. Leon* and Mary Shelley's *The Last Man*, see Jan Plug, *Borders of a Lip*, 148–52.

2. On Kant's ambivalent attitude to secrecy, especially as regards political activity (in which St. Leon is engaged in Hungary), see Hannah Arendt, *Lectures on Kant's Political Philosophy*, 48–49.

3. One of the earlier titles of Godwin's novel was *Opus Magnum* (see Clemit, *The Godwinian Novel*, 88 n. 54).

4. As foreigners, the St. Leon family are excluded from the compensation afforded by the government when they lose their few possessions in a storm and are "reduced . . . to the necessity of a second emigration" (96–97). Switzerland is thus for Godwin, unlike Williams, an example of the continued "coercive regulations" of government (97).

5. Thomas Kavanagh, *Enlightenment and the Shadows of Chance*, 44, 47. Kavanagh convincingly analyses ancien régime gambling in terms of Marcel Mauss's theory of the gift, as a way of not imposing on it "a set of concepts and values that were themselves generated by the emerging bourgeoisie as weapons in their campaign . . . to discredit the ethos of the traditional nobility." He writes that the "all but universal condemnation of gambling now subscribed to with surprisingly equal enthusiasm by the voices of the social sciences and of common sense forecloses any real understanding of what that practice represented in the context of the eighteenth century" (62). But we might add that what that practice represented in novels such as *The Mysteries of Udolpho*, which contain scenes of gambling, is the double bankruptcy both of ancien régime and bourgeois values.

6. Thomas M. Lennon, *Reading Bayle*, 153–62.

7. Kavanagh, *Enlightenment*, 67. Kavanagh argues that Law's scheme cleverly got round the French nobles' resistance to printing money and worked on their attachment to land. However, land had been at the core of his economic theory from 1705 onwards. Law was well aware of the dangers of inflation or devaluation in changing the equivalence between money and GDP; he was not an advocate of credit in the sense of pure promise: "Credit that promises a Payment of money, cannot well be extended beyond a certain proportion it ought to have with the Money" (*Money and Trade*, 60). His scheme of backing money with land actually aimed to increase the supply of money so as to draw out potential in the economy, which was currently untapped through unemployment, but without the dangers of inflation, since land, as he saw it, was there, would not decrease in quantity, and unlike metal, could be used as money while still being used for agriculture (45–51, 60, 90–93). The irony is that, although the land was there in Scotland, the land Law used as backing in America was not there (or was not owned by France), and thus his scheme was in the end a form of trading in futures, not to mention imperialism (which St. Leon avoids by using the philosopher's stone rather than land as his backing).

8. Quoted in Kavanagh, *Enlightenment*, 91.

9. Ibid., 87; John Law, *Money and Trade*, 60–61, 113.

10. Quoted by Kavanagh, *Enlightenment*, 88.

11. Edmund Burke, *Reflections on the Revolution in France*, 149, 143–44, 209. That Burke has Law in mind is evident from his reference to "the Mississippi and South Sea" (209). Law's company was often called the Mississippi Company, although its correct name was the Compagnie des Indes (Kavanagh, *Enlightenment*, 258 n. 2).

12. Kavanagh, *Enlightenment*, 72.

13. Burke, *Reflections on the Revolution in France*, 185–86.

14. According to *The Oxford English Dictionary* (16.172), speculation is "buying and selling goods, and stocks, and shares, etc., in order to profit by the rise or fall in the market value, as distinct from regular trading or investment; engagement in any business enterprise or transaction of a venturesome or risky nature, but offering the chance of great or unusual gain." The *OED* cites Horace Walpole (1774) and Adam Smith (1776): "Sudden fortunes, indeed, are sometimes made . . . by what is called the trade of speculation." The word "speculation" was used as the name of a card game by 1804, if not earlier: "Cards. A round game of cards, the chief feature of which is the buying and selling of trump cards, the player who possesses the highest trump in a round winning the pool."

15. Samuel Johnson, *A Dictionary of the English Language*. Further references are to this edition, which is, of course, alphabetic.

16. David Simpson, *Romanticism, Nationalism, and the Revolt against Theory*, 5, 52–53.

17. It should be said that manufacturing gold coins is not the same thing either as printing money or as borrowing money to cover a deficit, since the gold itself has some value. Though Burke treats French gold as a valueless paper currency, it seems that France had more wealth than Burke gives it credit for.

18. Kavanagh, *Enlightenment*, 88, 86.

19. Terry Mulcaire, "Public Credit," 1033.

20. Karl Jaspers, *Kant,* ed. Hannah Arendt, trans. Ralph Mannheim (New York: Harcourt, Brace, and World, 1952), 46.

21. Friedrich Schlegel, "Atheneum Fragments," 25–26.

22. Peter Fenves, *A Peculiar Fate*, 4. According to Manfred Kuehn, who traces the links between Kant and Scottish Common Sense philosophy, there is a greater affinity between the two than is normally thought: "In Kant's critical philosophy the struggle (or dialectic) between common sense and philosophy emerged as an important formative influence. And Kant's thought . . . may be considered as a sustained attempt to balance the aspirations of both common sense and critical reason" (*Scottish Common Sense in Germany,* 246). Of course, Kant's Scottish roots may also include enthusiasm, for example, via Thomas Wright, whose astronomical theories he takes up in *Universal Natural History and Theory of the Heavens.*

23. F. A. Nitsch, *A General and Introductory View of Professor Kant's Principles Concerning Man,* 56.

24. Immanuel Kant, "On a Newly Arisen Superior Tone in Philosophy," 51, 62, 71 n. 6.

25. Fenves discusses Kant's reservations about this "enthusiasm" in his notes to "On a Newly Arisen Superior Tone in Philosophy," which was written as a polemic against the annotated translation of Plato published in 1795 by Johann Georg Schlosser (72–75).

26. Immanuel Kant, *The Conflict of the Faculties,* 153.

27. Gregory Johnson, "Introduction" to Immanuel Kant, *Dreams of a Spirit-Seer and Other Writings,* xiii-xxi.

28. Immanuel Kant, "Announcement of the Near Conclusion of a Treaty for Eternal Peace in Philosophy," 88.

29. Immanuel Kant, *Essays and Treatises on Moral, Political, and Various Philosophical Subjects.*

30. Nitsch, *A General and Introductory View,* 131 (emphasis mine); A. F. M. Willich, *Elements of the Critical Philosophy,* 15, 77.

31. Neither Nitsch nor Willich takes up the *Critique of Judgment;* both are concerned exclusively with *The Critique of Pure Reason,* though Willich is obvi-

ously aware of the *Critique of Practical Reason* and other writings by Kant on ethics. On the way in which Kant's attitude to the "ideas" of Reason shifts from the first to the third *Critique*, and on Kant's reaction to Hegel more generally, see my essay "Toward a Cultural Idealism," 51–72.

32. Nitsch, *A General and Introductory View*, 59; Samuel Taylor Coleridge, *Biographia Literaria*, 1.155, 30, 147, 154. Coleridge's distinction between fanaticism and enthusiasm is in keeping with Kant's distinction between *Schwärmerei* and *Enthusiasmus*. See Fenves, *A Peculiar Fate*, 241–43.

33. Simpson, *Romanticism, Nationalism, and the Revolt against Theory*, 94–97.

34. Quoted in ibid., 95.

35. Ibid., 30–31, 95.

36. Peter Fenves, "The Topicality of Tone," in *Raising the Tone of Philosophy*, 31.

37. Immanuel Kant, "To Perpetual Peace: A Philosophical Sketch," in *Raising the Tone of Philosophy*, 109. Interestingly Kant, unlike Burke, sees credit as an English invention (109).

38. Kant, "On a Newly Arisen Superior Tone," in ibid., 51, 56.

39. Kant, "Other Exaltations," in ibid., 105.

40. Immanuel Kant, *Anthropology*, 84.

41. Ibid., 4–6, 20, 27, 82.

42. Willich, *Elements of the Critical Philosophy*, 77.

43. William Wordsworth, "Preface to *Lyrical Ballads*," 21; Samuel Taylor Coleridge, *The Friend*, 1.20, 132, 179.

44. Kant, *Anthropology*, 105.

45. On the growing legal emphasis on objective "evidence" rather than personal "testimony," see Matthew Wickman, *The Ruins of Experience*, 69–89.

46. Jean-François Lyotard, *The Postmodern Condition*, 61–62.

47. Kant, "To Perpetual Peace," 111, 117; idem, "Idea for a Universal History with a Cosmopolitan Intent," in *"To Perpetual Peace" and Other Essays*, 20, 34, 38.

48. Slavoj Žižek, *Tarrying with the Negative*, 126–130.

49. Immanuel Kant, "Speculative Beginning of Human History" (1786), in *"To Perpetual Peace" and Other Essays*, 49.

50. Kant, "Idea for a Universal History," 30, 38–39; idem, "Speculative Beginning," 49, in ibid.

51. Arendt discusses Kant's spectatorial attitude in relation to the French Revolution and the 1798 Irish Uprising in *Lectures on Kant's Political Philosophy*, 44–68. This spectatorship means that, on the question of rebellion against

an unjust government, Kant can condemn "the very action whose results" he can also affirm from the sidelines "with a satisfaction bordering on enthusiasm." Arendt argues that the reason why "you should not engage in what, if successful, you would applaud, is 'the transcendental position of publicness' which rules all political action" (48): in other words, the need to keep politics in the realm of debate and ideas.

52. Theodor W. Adorno, Kant's "Critique of Pure Reason," 38.

53. See also Arendt, Kant's Political Philosophy, 24.

54. Susan Meld Shell, The Embodiment of Reason, 176.

55. In "An Old Question" Kant proposes three models of history: (1) "continual retrogression towards wickedness"; (2) "perpetual progression toward improvement," which he calls eudaemonism or chiliasm; and (3) "stagnation" or "eternal rotation" around the same point, which he calls abderitism (The Conflict of Faculties, 145). In effect he sees chiliasm and abderitism as not inconsistent with each other, and he defers the dialectical resolution of the antinomy between them to a future point (147–57).

56. Kant, "To Perpetual Peace," (109). In view of Burke's association of credit/debt with the French, it is interesting that Kant associates the "credit system" with the British, quite correctly, given that it was a Scotsman who brought it to France. In fairness to Kant it should also be said that he disliked credit because of the way it is used to finance wars. On the other hand, Burke, in insisting that the British economy was backed by a growing GDP whereas the French economy was not, entirely ignored the fact the British GDP was growing because of colonial wars, which were in turn sustained by credit. The relationship between credit and war is the other, darker side of the much more general correlation I am arguing for between credit and Romanticism.

57. Friedrich Schlegel, "Atheneum Fragments," 31–32; idem, "Gespräch Über die Poesie," 209.

58. St. Leon enters Hungary in 1560 (373). At the time, as Chatillon he is twenty-two, but as St. Leon he is fifty-five (386). We do not know exactly how long the Hungarian episode, culminating in St. Leon's imprisonment by Bethlem Gabor, his escape, and his facilitating of the marriage of Charles and Pandora, lasts. However, when he writes his memoir, "Hungary has resounded for thirty years with the atrocities of the Sieur de Chatillon" (476). It therefore seems reasonable to assume that St. Leon is about eighty-five at the time he writes his memoirs.

59. Mark Philp, Godwin's Political Justice, 7–11, 99.

60. Paul Hamilton, Metaromanticism, 80.

61. Arendt, Kant's Political Philosophy, 40, 49.

62. Ibid., 19.

63. Bernadette Bensaude-Vincent and Isabelle Stengers, *A History of Chemistry*, 22–23, 41.

64. Hamilton, *Metaromanticism*, 81. My analysis is indebted to Hamilton, who links Godwin to Habermas, though not Kant, on the subject of the public sphere (85). Hamilton, however, treats the novel's endless "bluffs" as irony or double negation, whereas I approach the text's mode of communication as a paradox that provokes (dis)belief.

65. Bensaude-Vincent and Stengers, *A History of Chemistry*, 51.

66. Kant, *Dreams of a Spirit-Seer*, 4.

67. Jean-François Lyotard and Jean-Loup Thébaud, *Just Gaming*, 76.

68. Bensaude-Vincent and Stengers, *A History of Chemistry*, 21.

69. Immanuel Kant, *The Metaphysics of Morals*, 70. Kant cites Adam Smith, but Smith was familiar with Law. Kant's argument in this passage, that money facilitates trade and that goods other than money are used as means of exchange "only in a nation where there is little trade" (71), was made by Law well before Smith.

70. Having defined alchemy as the more subtle and occult part of chemistry, Johnson goes on to add a derogatory comment by Hooker.

71. *Encyclopédie, ou Dictionnaire raisonné des sciences, des arts et des métiers.*

72. Jürgen Habermas, *The Structural Transformation of the Public Sphere*, 57.

73. Clara Reeve, *The Progress of Romance*, 1.111.

74. Kavanagh, *Enlightenment*, 107–20.

75. Ibid., 118–20.

76. On the mediocre hero in Scott see Georg Lukács, *The Historical Novel*, 34–37. Based on his use of the mediocre hero, Lukács notes that "it is completely wrong to see Scott as a Romantic writer" unless one uses the term in a purely chronological sense (34). As already noted, Gary Kelly marks the later curricular prominence of Scott and Austen in making them the only two novelists to whom he accords full chapters in *English Fiction of the Romantic Period,* and Ian Duncan associates Scott with a definitive taming of romance by the Novel. Ina Ferris links Scott to an emergent professionalization of the novel and to a masculinization of what had earlier been a form that catered to female readers (*The Achievement of Literary Authority: Gender, History, and the Waverley Novels* [Ithaca: Cornell University Press, 1991], 79, 104).

77. Ruth Bernard Yeazell has recently written on the sustained analogies drawn between Dutch genre painting and the realist novel in the nineteenth century, noting Scott's application of the parallel to Austen and its application to his own work (*Art of the Everyday*, 1–17).

78. It is worth noting that Reeve's *The Progress of Romance* takes up the terms as different, but just a few years earlier Johnson's *Dictionary* had defined "Novel" as "a small tale, generally of love," and "Romance" as "a military fable of the middle ages; a tale of wild adventure in war and love." The key difference here seems to be scope and size, not realism.

79. Mary Shelley, "Modern Italian Romances," 245, 250, 258. Later than Shelley, Hyppolite Taine (1863–64) is also critical of Austen and "the novel of manners" for her "minute copying" in the mode of Dutch painting, which is "incapable of the great divinations and wide sympathies that open up history" (quoted by Yeazell, *Art of the Everyday,* 5).

80. Reeve, *The Progress of Romance,* 2.104, 41.

81. Habermas points out that "opinion" was originally associated with a judgment that lacked certainty and thus seemed antithetical to rationality (*Structural Transformation of the Public Sphere,* 89–90). In England, where the division between "opinion" and "critique" was less sharp than in France, Locke's identification of opinion with conscience helped to uncouple it from prejudice; in France it was when the physiocrats ascribed *opinion publique* to the *publique éclairé* that the concept "receive[d] the strict meaning of an opinion purified through critical discussion" (89–92).

82. Reeve, *The Progress of Romance,* 2.86.

83. For example, Pamela Clemit, *The Godwinian Novel,* 91.

84. Habermas, *Structural Transformation of the Public Sphere,* 47, 55.

85. G. W. F. Hegel, *Philosophy of Mind,* 255–56.

86. Habermas, *Structural Transformation of the Public Sphere,* 27, 51, 150–1.

87. Hannah Arendt, *The Human Condition,* 36–49.

88. Ibid., 50.

89. Mary Shelley, "Modern Italian Romances," 258.

90. Handwerk, "History, Trauma, and the Limits of the Liberal Imagination," 72–75.

91. Slavoj Žižek, *The Plague of Fantasies,* 7.

Chapter 6: Whose Text?

1. In fact the "more finished" copy (*W,* 72) provides relatively little of the text: it runs only from the beginning to the middle of chapter 3 (75–93), and from the beginning to the middle of chapter 5 (102–15). Most of Godwin's parenthetical additions are in the less-finished version, but one is in the more-finished part (90), indicating that the role of Darnford was still unresolved in the copy that he described as having received Wollstonecraft's "last corrections" (115n).

2. I take this line in ventriloquizing Mary Shelley's implicit reading of her fa-

ther's editing of her mother's work two decades earlier, when she sends her own novella *Mathilda* to Godwin for publication ("Mary Shelley's *Mathilda*," 58–59). I have taken up Godwin's editing of Wollstonecraft's novel on other previous occasions: see also "Is There a Romantic Ideology?," 70. *The Supplement of Reading*, 179–83, and "Framing the Corpus," 516–18. Each time I have returned to the problem, I have read the relationship between Wollstonecraft's text and Godwin's editing of it differently. The result is the present chapter, which neither privileges not criticizes Godwin's editing but rather explores the complexities of the relationship between and within the text's two voices.

3. Friedrich Nietzsche, *The Antichrist*, 169.

4. For examples of this reading of Wollstonecraft, see Maria J. Falco, ed., *Feminist Interpretations of Mary Wollstonecraft*. See in particular the essays by Penny A. Weiss, 15–32; Virginia Muller, 47–60; and Dorothy McBride Stevenson, 165–77.

5. William Godwin, *Memoirs of the Author of "A Vindication of the Rights of Woman,"* Hereafter cited as *MV*.

6. Barbara Taylor elaborates on the term "philosopher," the double meaning of which itself supports Godwin's view of Wollstonecraft as a subject-in-process. Wollstonecraft, she suggests, "saw herself as a philosopher in the sense that liberal Britons gave to the term for most of the eighteenth century: that is, as an abstract reasoner of enlightened disposition, concerned to comprehend and elucidate general truths." But she also saw herself as a "proponent of revolutionary demoracy" in the line of the radical philosophes (*Mary Wollstonecraft and the Feminist Imagination*, 26–30, 50–54, 149). Wollstonecraft's "aversion" to being considered an author (*MV*, 64) probably had to do with being dismissed as an "authoress," which is not what Godwin means by the term.

7. Gilles Deleuze and Félix Guattari, *Anti-Oedipus*, 21.

8. In general liberal feminists blame Godwin's frank representation of Wollstonecraft's life and loves in his *Memoirs* for the subsequent decline in her reputation. Yet in doing so they are curiously complicit with the conservative reaction against her work by Richard Polwhele and others, which was catalyzed by Godwin's portrayal. That is, they either see Godwin's portrayal of Wollstonecraft as incorrect and as an attempt to put her down (rather than to bring out her complexity), or they accept it and see Wollstonecraft as falling short of true feminism. See, for example, the essays by Falco, Weiss, and Wendy Gunther-Canada in Falco, *Feminist Interpretations*, 5, 24, 214.

9. This feminism is appropriately described by Gary Kelly's phrase "revolutionary feminism." Kelly is one of the few who does not critique Wollstonecraft for compromising a rights- based feminism by falling into the trap of sensibility. However, he reads *Wrongs* straightforwardly as an expression of revolutionary

feminism, without taking account of the greater complexity disclosed and produced by Godwin's editing (*Revolutionary Feminism,* 1–2, 206–23).

10. Godwin is absolutely against a system of national education (*PJ,* 2:290–301). Seeing the drawbacks of both public and "private" (home) schooling, Wollstonecraft favors a combination of both, and indeed favors coeducation (*A Vindication of the Rights of Woman,* 5:229–50). Interestingly, Wollstonecraft is also not as dismissive as Godwin of another institution, that of marriage, if set on a correct basis (ibid., 237; *PJ,* 2:506–10).

11. Gilles Deleuze, "Instincts and Institutions," 19–20; Wollstonecraft, *Vindication,* 263–64.

12. Roland Barthes, *S/Z,* 11, 13, 12, 5. Barthes contrasts the "semiology" of *lexias* with a "philology" that "declar[es] every text to be univocal" (7), but my point is that philology is precisely a semiology.

13. According to Susan Lanser, who valorizes "communal" over "personal" voice, *Wrongs* fails because "it remains in paralyzed suspension between individual and communal narrative" (*Fictions of Authority,* 225, 231). More sympathetically, Taylor also sees the communal concern with the wrongs of different classes of women as marking the "beginnings of modern feminism" (*Mary Wollstonecraft,* 236–45).

14. Lawrence Stone, *Road to Divorce,* 235–36.

15. On Wilkes, see Susan Staves, *Married Women's Separate Property in England,* 170–75. Wilkes, then twenty-two, married Mary Mead, a woman ten years his senior, in 1747. He turned out to be something of a libertine, and in 1756 they privately negotiated a separate maintenance agreement, in which Mary gave up much of the property she had brought into the marriage, and was given an allowance of £200 per annum. Heavily in debt, Wilkes in 1758, after having used the agreement to get Mary's property, tried to get the allowance disallowed, and when he failed, he tried to argue that the maintenance agreement was unenforceable, hoping that he could get Mary to live with him again so that he could eventually claim the £100,000 she would inherit from her mother (the case failed). While Wilkes's action against his wife preceded his radical career, in a somewhat ingenuous expression of freethinking, he questioned being bound to a marriage contracted in his "non-age."

16. John Langbein, "The Criminal Trial before the Lawyers," 311–15; idem, "Shaping the Eighteenth-Century Criminal Trial," 124–32. For a chronology of the evolution of adversarial procedure see also Stephen Landsman, "The Rise of the Contentious Spirit," 497–609.

17. Stone, *Road to Divorce,* 234. Trials for criminal conversation became common only in the 1760s.

18. Roderick Phillips, *Untying the Knot,* 58, 65, 74–80.

19. Stone, *Road to Divorce,* 24.

20. Ibid., 246–47, 233–34.

21. Ibid., 297, 323–24.

22. A Mrs. Addison was successful in obtaining a divorce on grounds of her husband's incestuous adultery with her married sister in 1801. But between 1800 and 1840, there were only six more divorce suits by women, all unsuccessful, as male adultery was not considered a ground for divorce (ibid., 360–61).

23. Ibid., 340–41, 323–24, 25. Married women could only retain access to their property through the agency of a trustee, since a married woman's "legal personality" was absorbed into that of her husband (150).

24. L. Simond, *A Journal of a Tour and Residence in Great Britain during the Years 1810 and 1811, by a French Traveller* (quoted in Stone, *Road to Divorce,* 231).

25. Stone, *Road to Divorce,* 234.

26. John Bender, *Imagining the Penitentiary,* 155–57, 175–76. The trial in *Wrongs* is not a criminal trial. Criminal conversation suits were always conducted by lawyers, though they did not become popular until the 1760s and 1770s, which coincidentally is also the period when lawyers, introduced into the criminal trial in the 1730s, came to strongly dominate this procedure.

27. Langbein, "The Eighteenth-Century Criminal Trial," 123–24. See also Landsman, "The Rise of the Contentious Spirit," 504–9.

28. Langbein, "Shaping the Eighteenth-Century Criminal Trial," 130. Landsman also notes that by the 1780s more and more defendants left the defense to their counsel, and they were even chided for contributing to it ("The Rise of the Contentious Spirit," 547, 557).

29. Matthew Wickman, *The Ruins of Experience,* 25–34.

30. Bender makes this point about the negative side of lawyerization in classically Foucaultian terms: "The genius of modern forms of bureaucratic control is that they appropriate the heteroglossic diversity of the metropolis by keeping track of it and absorbing it into a container of authority projected as systematic rules, a controlled framework within which polyglossic discourse can be allowed liberal freedoms" (*Imagining the Penitentiary,* 177).

31. Arthur J. Jacobson, "The Idolatry of Rules," 110–11, 130–31.

32. Landsman, "Rise of the Contentious Spirit," 582, 580–91. Landsman sees adversarial procedure as crucial to the development of "dynamic individualism" and political liberty (503, 580–91), whereas Bender takes a more Foucaultian view of the adversary system's potential to reentrench a power that is ubiquitous and cleverly dispersed. Despite Wollstonecraft's sidestepping of counsel and rules of evidence, Landsman's point about the usefulness of an adversarial court system to radical reformers concerned with freedom of speech, the abolition of slavery,

and adequacy of political representation is obviously relevant to the trial scene in *Wrongs.*

33. Stone, *Road to Divorce,* 196–97. A sense of these libels, depositions, exhibits and interrogatories can be gathered from *Trials for Adultery* (1779–80); see n. 21.

34. A frequent way around the illegality of imprisonment was the use of private madhouses. Confinement of the wife in a private madhouse that was, in effect, a prison was often used between 1660 and 1774, when parliament tried to put a stop to the practice by licensing madhouses (Stone, *Road to Divorce,* 164–68). If the madhouse in *Wrongs* is unlicensed, this would explain the sudden collapse of its panoptical power and Maria's and Darnford's unexpected escape, as well as the fact that Venables then tries to sue Darnford for damages rather than confining Maria again.

35. Jean-François Lyotard and Jean-Loup Thébaud, *Just Gaming,* 73.

36. Stone, *Road,* 195–97; idem, *Broken Lives,* 224.

37. Mary Wollstonecraft, *Collected Letters,* 381. It is worth noting that, unlike *Caleb Williams, Wrongs* is clearly set in the years after the French Revolution and thus in a period of social upheaval and possible change. The trial scene therefore does not simply confirm the force of law, as in the original ending of Godwin's novel; it does not, as Nancy E. Johnson argues, "reaffirm a dichotomy between morality and the legal system" (*The English Jacobin Novel,* 149). Rather, it participates in the Wilkite project of usurping the public space of the courts to forward political reform. Such reforms were occurring, at least de facto. Often wives in successful divorce cases married their lovers, and by the 1790s many criminal conversation suits involved collusion between the husband and the lover to release all parties from an arrangement that was not working. According to Stone, by the 1790s most criminal conversation suits were undefended: the lover did not come to the trial, and the husband, intending to release the wife, accepted damages but returned the money. Thus, even though one cannot imagine Venables except as a Blakean Nobodaddy, the text certainly evokes the historical reality of what Stone describes as an increasing skepticism about "the religious foundations of the indissolubility of marriage" (*Road to Divorce,* 26, 235, 297). See also n. 25.

38. Jacobson, "Idolatry of Rules," 134–35.

39. Gary Kelly suggests in a note to his edition of *Wrongs* (230n) that Wollstonecraft got her information on "trials for adultery and damages" from *Trials for Adultery.* The full title of this collection is worth citing:

TRIALS FOR ADULTERY: OR, being THE HISTORY of DIVORCES. being SELECT TRIALS at DOCTOR'S COMMONS, for ADULTERY, FORNICATION, CRUELTY, IMPOTENCE, &c. From the Year 1760 to the present Time. Including the whole of the Evidence on each Cause. TOGETHER WITH, The LETTERS &c., that have been intercepted between the amorous parties. The whole form-ing a complete History of the PRIVATE LIFE, INTRIGUES, and AMOURS of many Characters in the most elevated sphere: every scene and transaction, however whimsical, ridiculous, or extraordinary, being fairly represented, as becomes a faithful Historian, who is fully determined not to sacrifice *Truth* at the Shrine of *Guilt* and *Folly*.

Bladon's seven-volume collection is interesting in several respects. It does indeed combine accounts of separation suits with the occasional criminal conversation suit (e.g., *Abergavenny vs. Lyddel*, or *Cibber vs. Sloper*, in volume 7—the volumes are not continuously paginated). It thus puts suits in which a woman could be the plaintiff on the same basis as ones in which only men could be involved, much as Wollstonecraft does. Second, despite the moralistic tone assumed in the Preface, which justifies the sensationalistic publication of details on so many trials for separation by arguing that the volumes are meant to discourage divorce, the vol-umes clearly function as a form of incitement, by showing the just causes that exist for separation in a variety of cases. Indeed, there are no cases in the volumes that do not result in a separation (though in some cases no "sentence" is pro-vided), and in a roughly equal number of cases the separation is granted to the woman. In the transcripts of crim. con. suits, damages also vary widely, between £10 (Cibber) and £10,000 (Abergavenny). This is to say that the *Trials* are an instance of narrative actually putting pressure on the law through the adducing of overwhelming numbers of cases in which a separation is justified or in which damages should only be pro forma. Finally the words "separation" and "divorce" are used synonymously throughout: an indication that although divorces were legally very difficult to obtain, the *idea* of divorce was already commonplace. Indeed, the appetite for accounts of separation suits demonstrated by the publica-tion of these volumes suggests that public opinion on the subject of marriage was more flexible than the law suggests.

40. One could argue that Wollstonecraft's knowledge of the law was impre-cise. However, she appears to know the "partial laws enacted by men" well enough in chapter 10 (150–51). In the case of the legacy from Maria's uncle, I am less inclined to see Wollstonecraft as ignorant of the law than to see her as invent-ing it, by polemically eliding the distinction between the role of trustee and that of "guardian." Maria's uncle could not have appointed a guardian for Venables' child; he could appoint a trustee for the estate he bequeaths to the child, but he could not have appointed Maria, a woman, as trustee. Nevertheless, Maria has the active role here, while the uncle's male friend (presumably the legal trustee, though he is never given authority by being named as such) is merely an interme-

diary. In other words, Wollstonecraft cleverly reverses a regime of trusteeship in which, as Susan Staves, says, "men alone appeared publicly as the owners of property" while women were simply "transmitters of inheritance" (*Married Women's Separate Property in England*, 194).

41. Stone, *Road to Divorce*, 247.

42. If one takes the issue of married women's separate property discussed by Staves, earlier in the century women had actually begun to acquire a quasi-legal personality through "separate maintenance contracts," which replaced status law with a more egalitarian contract law and which allowed husband and wife to live separately without going through the courts. These contracts were made between the man and the woman, and it was only in the postrevolutionary reaction of the 1790s that the courts made such contracts invalid, insisting on contracts between the husband and trustees for the wife, and thus making the disposition of the woman's property once again something that happened between men (*Married Women's Separate Property in England*, 166–67, 186–95). The more liberal regime is evident in the prerevolutionary *Mary* (1788), where it seems that Mary and her husband must have concluded a separate maintenance agreement that allows them to live separately and her to have an income. In the postrevolutionary *Wrongs* the law is decisively male, but the greater autonomy accorded women in the earlier novella is in the background as a future potential.

43. I discuss natural history as a mode of writing transposed from science and place Godwin's *Memoirs* within the genre in "Dis-Figuring Reproduction," 232–38.

44. Samantha Matthews, *Poetical Remains*, 1, 3. "Literary remains," as the genre emerged in the nineteenth century, consisted of a selection of fragments, extracts from published works, a biographical introduction, passages from letters, and sometimes the author's last wishes (4). Godwin's editing of Wollstonecraft could be considered one of the earliest examples of this genre, and while it does contain letters, it does not contain any previously published work, and is completely unframed, lacking the extravagance or sentimentality of the later instances of the genre.

45. Since the manuscript up to chapter 14 was what Wollstonecraft showed George Dyson in May of 1997 (*W*, 71n), it is also possible that at one point she intended the first part to end here but then changed her mind.

46. William Godwin, "Of Choice in Reading," 136.

47. Describing *A Vindication* as concerned with a "few simple principles," Wollstonecraft promises a second volume that will go into greater detail and will take up, among other things, marital law (*Vindication*, 70, 215). As Barbara Taylor suggests, that second volume may well be *Wrongs* (*Mary Wollstonecraft*, 231).

48. Hegel's critique of positive law is slightly different, and has to do with his

notion of positive sciences as "finite" where philosophical thinking is "infinite." The "positivity of legal science" consists in one "sphere isolat[ing] itself," so that "civil law, for example, which is concerned with possession and property, becomes wholly absorbed in itself." As a result of this "formalism" in which particular spheres of the law fetishize themselves instead of recognizing themselves as part of a larger organic whole, the law "become[s] perverted and corrupted" (*Natural Law*, 123–25).

49. Jacobson, "Idolatry of Rules," 110, 130–31. On restrictive vs. permissive notions of law see F. E. L. Priestley, Introduction to Godwin, *Political Justice*, 3.34n.

50. Phillips points out that Pufendorf and Grotius still regarded procreation as the principal reason for marriage and did not go as far as Milton in stressing the companionate aspects of marriage as central and in thus making incompatibility a ground for divorce (*Untying the Knot*, 52–53).

51. Wollstoncraft, *Vindication*, 67, 247.

52. Thomas Paine, *The Rights of Man*, in Burke and Paine, *"Reflections on the Revolution in France" and "The Rights of Man,"* 306; Priestley, Introduction to Godwin, *Political Justice*, 3:34. Godwin defines duty as "the treatment I am bound to bestow on others" and right as "the treatment I am entitled to expect from them" *(PJ*, 1.148).

53. Jean-Luc Nancy, *The Experience of Freedom*, 1–3.

54. Virginia Sapiro, *A Vindication of Political Virtue*, 151; Nicola Watson, *Revolution and the Form of the British Novel*, 53. More recently Nancy E. Johnson has been critical of the tendency to treat *Wrongs* as a sentimental rather than political novel. However, she approaches it as an unproblematic claim for rights focused on the issue of women and property (*The English Jacobin Novel*, 140–52).

55. Sapiro, *Vindication of Political Virtue* 268; Mary Poovey, *The Proper Lady and the Woman Writer*, 102–8.

56. William Wordsworth, "Essay upon Epitaphs (1810)," 101.

57. Jean-François Lyotard, *Heidegger and "the Jews,"* 5; Keats, *The Letters of John Keats*, 143.

58. Wollstonecraft, *Collected Letters*, 317.

59. Ibid.; Paul de Man, *The Rhetoric of Romanticism*, 120. De Man refers to figures of sailboats that Shelley doodled in the margins of the poem's last pages and that uncannily foretell his death by drowning, just as Maria's suicide in one of the fragments seems to foretell her author's death.

60. De Man, *Rhetoric of Romanticism*, 93–95, 120–23; 68, 70, 75–76.

61. Rachel Blau DuPlessis, *Writing beyond the Ending*, 1–4.

62. Wollstonecraft, "Mary" and "The Wrongs of Woman," 215n. The dates

Gary Kelly gives, based on Godwin's journal, are July–September of 1796, and January 26 and April 27–30, 1797.

63. Wollstonecraft, *Collected Letters,* 331, 330.

64. Continuing with this hypothesis, according to Godwin Wollstonecraft showed Dyson some version of the first fourteen chapters of *Wrongs* in May, 1797 (*W,* 71n). In July of 1796, then, she would have drafted less of the manuscript, and the fragments could therefore belong to a very early stage.

65. Godwin, "Of Choice in Reading," 132–33. Pointing to the utilitarian criteria underlying "morals," Godwin says: "It is in a very different temper that the bookmaker squeezes out what he calls his Use, from that in which the reader becomes acquainted with the circumstances of the fable" (133).

66. Ibid., 136–37, 3–34.

67. The term "elective affinities" is famously explained by Goethe in his novella of that name. These affinities do not involve communion or identification, but friction: they "become interesting only when they bring about divorces" (*Elective Affinities,* 53).

68. Gerard Genette, *Paratexts,* 5.

69. Wollstonecraft, *Collected Letters,* 391–92.

70. Gilles Deleuze, *Francis Bacon,* 99, 101.

71. G. W. F. Hegel, *The Philosophy of History,* 280.

72. Mary Wollstonecraft, *Mary: A Fiction,* xli.

73. On the possible relations between the "narrating instance" and the story, see Gerard Genette, *Narrative Discourse,* 216–17.

WORKS CITED

Abbey, Lloyd. *Destroyer and Preserver: Shelley's Poetic Skepticism*. Lincoln: University of Nebraska Press, 1979.

Abraham, Nicholas, and Maria Torok. *L'Écorce et le Noyau*. Paris: Flammarion, 1987. See esp. "Qui est Mélanie Klein?," 184–99.

Adorno, Theodor W. *Kant's Critique of Pure Reason* (1959). Edited by Rolf Tiedemann. Translated by Rodney Livingstone. Stanford: Stanford University Press, 2001.

———. "Lyric Poetry and Society." Translated by Bruce Mayo. *Telos* 20 (1974): 56–71.

Adorno, Theodor W., and Max Horkheimer. *Dialectic of Enlightenment* (1944). Translated by John Cumming. New York: Continuum, 1987.

Agamben, Girogio. *The Coming Community*. Translated by Michael Hardt. Minneapolis: University of Minnesota Press, 1993.

———. *Infancy and History: Essays on the Destruction of Experience* (1978). Translated by Liz Heron. London: Verso, 1993.

———. *The Idea of Prose* (1985). Translated by Michael Sullivan and Sam Whitsitt. Albany: State University of New York Press, 1995. Includes Preface by Alexander García Düttmann, "Integral Actuality."

Arendt, Hannah. *Lectures on Kant's Political Philosophy*. Edited by Ronald Beiner. Brighton: Harvester Press, 1982.

———. *The Human Condition* (1958). 2nd ed. Chicago: University of Chicago Press, 1998.

Arnold, Matthew. "The Function of Criticism at the Present Time." In *Matthew's Arnold's Essays in Criticism: First and Second Series*, 9–34. London: J. M. Dent, 1964.

Ault, Donald. "Re-Visioning *The Four Zoas*." In *Unnam'd Forms: Blake and Textuality*, edited by Nelson Hilton and Thomas Vogler, 105–40. Berkeley: University of California Press, 1986.

Baker, Carlos. *Shelley's Major Poetry: The Fabric of a Vision*. Princeton: Princeton University Press, 1948.

Bakhtin, Mikhail. "Epic and Novel." In *The Dialogic Imagination: Four Essays*.

Translated by Caryl Emerson and Michael Holquist, 3–40. Austin: University of Texas Press, 1981.

Barthes, Roland. *S/Z: An Essay.* Translated by Richard Miller. New York: Farrar, Straus, and Giroux, 1974.

Bataille, Georges. "Base Materialism and Gnosticism," in *Visions of Excess: Selected Writings, 1927–1939.* Edited by Allan Stoekl. Translated by Allan Stoekl, with Carl Lovitt and Donald M. Leslie, 45–52. Minneapolis: University of Minnesota Press, 1985.

Bator, Paul G. "The Entrance of the Novel into the Scottish Universities." In *The Scottish Invention of Literature,* edited by Robert Crawford, 89–102. Cambridge: Cambridge University Press, 1998.

Baudrillard, Jean. *Symbolic Exchange and Death.* Translated by Iain Hamilton Grant. London: Sage, 1993.

Bellemin-Noel, Jean. *Le texte et l'avant texte: Les brouillons d'un poème de Milosz.* Paris: Librairie Larousse, 1972.

Bender, John. *Imagining the Penitentiary: Fiction and the Architecture of Mind in Eighteenth- Century England.* Chicago: University of Chicago Press, 1987.

Benjamin, Walter. *The Concept of Criticism in German Romanticism* (1920). In *Selected Writings.* Vol. 1, *1913–1926.* Edited by Marcus Bullock and Michael W. Jennings. Translated by David Lachterman, Howard Eiland, and Ian Balfour, 116–200. Cambridge, MA: Harvard University Press, 1996.

———. "The Storyteller: Reflections on the Work of Nikolai Leskov" (1936). In *Illuminations.* Edited by Hannah Arendt. Translated by Harry Zohn, 83–110. New York: Shocken Books, 1969.

Bensaude-Vincent, Bernadette, and Isabelle Stengers. *A History of Chemistry.* Cambridge, MA: Harvard University Press, 1996.

Blake, William. *The Complete Poetry and Prose of William Blake.* Edited by David V. Erdman. Rev. ed. Berkeley: University of California Press, 1982.

Blanchot, Maurice. *The Space of Literature* (1955). Translated by Ann Smock. Lincoln: University of Nebraska Press, 1982.

Bloch, Ernst. "Nonsynchronism and the Obligation to Its Dialectics" (1935). *New German Critique* 11 (Spring 1977): 22–38.

Bloom, Harold. *The Visionary Company: A Reading of English Romantic Poetry.* New York: Doubleday, 1961.

———. "The Internalization of Quest Romance." In *The Ringers in the Tower: Studies in Romantic Tradition,* 13–36. Chicago: University of Chicago Press, 1971.

Brooks, Peter. *The Melodramatic Imagination: Balzac, Henry James, Melodrama, and the Mode of Excess.* New Haven: Yale University Press, 1976.

———. *Reading for the Plot: Desire and Intention in Narrative.* New York: Vintage, 1985.

Bruhm, Steven. *Gothic Bodies: The Politics of Pain in Romantic Fiction.* Philadelphia: University of Pennsylvania Press, 1994.

Burke, Edmund. *Reflections on the Revolution in France* (1790), in Edmund Burke and Thomas Paine, *"Reflections on the Revolution in France" and "The Rights of Man,"* 15–266. New York: Doubleday Anchor, 1973.

Butler, Judith. *Subjects of Desire: Hegelian Reflections in Twentieth-Century France.* New York: Columbia University Press, 1987.

Byron, George Gordon, Lord. *Cain.* In *Lord Byron's "Cain": Twelve Essays and a Text, with Variants and Annotations,* edited by Truman Guy Steffan, 151–258. Austin: University of Texas Press, 1968.

Cameron, Kenneth Neill. "The Political Symbolism of *Prometheus Unbound.*" In *Shelley: Modern Judgments,* edited by R. B. Woodings, 102–29. London: Macmillan, 1968.

Cameron, Sharon. *Lyric Time: Dickinson and the Limits of Genre.* Baltimore: Johns Hopkins University Press, 1979.

Carlson, Julie. *England's First Family of Writers: Mary Wollstonecraft, William Godwin, Mary Shelley.* Baltimore: Johns Hopkins University Press, 2005.

Carroll, David. *Paraesthetics: Foucault, Lyotard, Derrida.* London: Methuen, 1987.

Chandler, James. *Wordsworth's Second Nature: A Study of the Poetry and Politics.* Chicago: University of Chicago Press, 1984.

Chatman, Seymour. *Story and Discourse: Narrative Structure in Fiction and Film.* Ithaca: Cornell University Press, 1978.

Chatterjee, Ranita. "Filial Ties: Godwin's *Deloraine* and Mary Shelley's Writings." *European Romantic Review* 18.1 (2007): 29–42.

Clemit, Pamela. *The Godwinian Novel: The Rational Fictions of Godwin, Brockden Brown, Mary Shelley.* Oxford: Clarendon Press, 1993.

Cohan, Steven, and Linda Shires. *Telling Stories: A Theoretical Analysis of Narrative Fiction.* New York: Routledge, 1988.

Coleridge, Samuel Taylor. *The Friend* (1818). Edited by Barbara E. Rooke. 2 vols. Princeton: Princeton University Press, 1969.

———. *The Complete Poetical Works of Samuel Taylor Coleridge.* Edited by E. H. Coleridge. 2 vols. Oxford: Clarendon Press, 1912. Reprint, 1975.

———. *Biographia Literaria; or, Biographical Sketches of My Literary Life and Opinions* (1817). Edited by James Engell and Walter Jackson Bate. 2 vols. in 1. Princeton: Princeton University Press, 1983.

Collings, David. "The Romance of the Impossible: William Godwin in the Empty Place of Reason." *ELH* 70 (2003): 847–74.

Corngold, Stanley. "Error in Paul de Man." In *The Yale Critics: Deconstruction in America,* edited by Jonathan Arac, Wlad Godzich, and Wallace Martin, 90–108. Minneapolis: University of Minnesota Press, 1983.

———. "Nietzsche's Moods." *Nietzsche and Romanticism,* edited by Tilottama Rajan. *Studies in Romanticism* 29.1 (1990): 67–90.

Crawford, Robert. *Devolving English Literature.* Oxford: Clarendon Press, 1992.

———, ed. *The Scottish Invention of Literature.* Cambridge: Cambridge University Press, 1998.

Davis, Lennard. *Factual Fictions: The Origins of the English Novel.* New York: Columbia University Press, 1983.

De Lauretis, Teresa. "Desire in Narrative." In *Alice Doesn't: Feminism, Semiotics, Cinema,* 103–57. Bloomington: Indiana University Press, 1984.

Deleuze, Gilles. *Francis Bacon: The Logic of Sensation* (1981). Translated by Daniel W. Smith. New York: Continuum, 2003.

———. "Instincts and Institutions." In *Desert Islands and Other Texts: 1953–1974.* Edited by David Lapoujade. Translated by Michael Taormina, 19–21. New York: Semiotext(e), 2004.

Deleuze, Gilles, and Félix Guattari. *Anti-Oedipus: Capitalism and Schizophrenia.* Translated by Robert Hurley, Mark Seem, and Helen R. Lane. Minneapolis: University of Minnesota Press, 1983.

de Man, Paul. *The Rhetoric of Romanticism.* New York: Columbia University Press, 1984. See esp. "Autobiography as Defacement" (1979), 67–82; "Shelley Disfigured" (1979), 93–124.

Derrida, Jacques. *Positions* (1967–71). Translated by Alan Bass. Chicago: University of Chicago Press, 1981.

———. *Points . . . Interviews, 1974–1994.* Edited by Elisabeth Weber. Translated by Peggy Kamuf et al. Stanford: Stanford University Press, 1995.

———. *Archive Fever: A Freudian Impression* (1995). Translated by Eric Prenowitz. Chicago: University of Chicago Press, 1996.

———. *Negotiations: Interventions and Interviews, 1971–2002.* Edited and translated by Elizabeth Rottenberg. Stanford: Stanford University Press, 2002.

———. *Eyes of the University: Right to Philosophy 2.* Translated by Jan Plug et al. Stanford: Stanford University Press, 2004. See esp. "Sendoffs (for the Collège Internationale de Philosophie")" (1982), 43–63; "Vacant Chair: Censorship, Mastery, Magisteriality" (1984), 216–49.

Dubrow, Heather. *The Challenges of Orpheus: Lyric Poetry and Early Modern England.* Baltimore: Johns Hopkins University Press, 2007.

Duncan, Ian. "Adam Smith, Samuel Johnson and the Institutions of English." In Crawford, *The Scottish Invention of Literature,* 37–54.

————. *Modern Romance and Transformations of the Novel: The Gothic, Scott, Dickens*. Cambridge: Cambridge University Press, 1992.

DuPlessis, Rachel Blau. *Writing beyond the Ending: Narrative Strategies of Twentieth-Century Women Writers*. Bloomington: Indiana University Press, 1985.

Edwards, Gavin. "William Godwin's Foreign Language: Stories and Families in *Caleb Williams* and *Political Justice*." *Studies in Romanticism* 39.4 (2000): 533–42.

Ehrenpreis, Irving. *The "Types Approach" to Literature*. New York: King's Crown Press, 1945.

Elfenbein, Andrew. *Byron and the Victorians*. Cambridge: Cambridge University Press, 1995.

Encyclopédie; ou, Dictionnaire raisonné des sciences, des arts, et des métiers (1754–80). Vol. 1. Reprint. Stuttgart-Bad: Frommann, 1966.

Esterhammer, Angela. "Godwin's Suspicion of Speech Acts." *Studies in Romanticism* 39.4 (2000): 553–78.

Faflak, Joel. "Romanticism and the Pornography of Talking." *Nineteenth-Century Contexts* 27.1 (2005): 77–97.

————. "Speaking of Godwin's *Caleb Williams:* The Talking Cure and the Psychopathology of Enlightenment." *English Studies in Canada* 21.2–3 (2005): 9–122.

————. *Romantic Psychoanalysis: The Burden of the Mystery*. Albany: State University of New York Press, 2007.

Falco, Maria J., ed. *Feminist Interpretations of Mary Wollstonecraft*. University Park: Pennsylvania State University Press, 1996.

Favret, Mary. "Mary Shelley's Sympathy and Irony: The Editor and Her Corpus." In *The Other Mary Shelley: Beyond Frankenstein*, edited by Audrey A. Fisch, Anne K. Mellor, and Esther Schor, 17–38. New York: Oxford University Press, 1993.

————. "Telling Tales about Genre: Poetry in the Romantic Novel." *Studies in the Novel* 26.2 (1994): 153–62.

Felluga, Dino. *The Perversity of Poetry: Romantic Ideology and the Popular Male Poet of Genius*. Albany: State University of New York Press, 2005.

Fenves, Peter. *A Peculiar Fate: Metaphysics and World-History in Kant*. Ithaca: Cornell University Press, 1991.

————. "Introduction: The Topicality of Tone." In *Raising the Tone of Philosophy: Late Essays by Immanuel Kant, Transformative Critique by Jacques Derrida*, edited by Peter Fenves, 1–48. Baltimore: Johns Hopkins University Press, 1993.

Foster, James. *History of the Pre-Romantic Novel in England*. New York: Modern Language Association, 1949.

Foucault, Michel. *"The Archaeology of Language" and "The Discourse on Language" (1969)*. Translated by A. M. Sheridan Smith. New York: Pantheon, 1972.

———. *The Order of Things: An Archeology of the Human Sciences* (1966). No translator. New York: Vintage Books, 1973.

———. *Language, Counter-Memory, Practice.* Edited by Donald F. Bouchard. Translated by Sherry Simon and Donald F. Bouchard. Ithaca: Cornell University Press, 1977. See esp. "Fantasia of the Library" (1967), 87–112; "Nietzsche, Genealogy, History" (1971), 139–64.

———. *The History of Sexuality.* Vol. 1, *An Introduction* (1976).Translated by Robert Hurley. New York: Vintage, 1980.

———. "Technologies of the Self" (1982), in *Ethics: Subjectivity and Truth.* Edited by Paul Rabinow. Translated by Robert Hurley et al., 223–52. New York: New Press, 1997.

———. "What Is Critique?" in *The Politics of Truth.* Edited by Sylvère Lotringer and Lisa Hochroth, 23–82. New York: Semiotext(e), 1997.

Fraistat, Neil. "Shelley Left and Right: The Rhetorics of the Early Textual Editions." In *Shelley: Poet and Legislator of the World,* edited by Betty T. Bennett and Stuart Curran, 105–13, 289–91. Baltimore: Johns Hopkins University Press, 1996.

Freud, Sigmund. "Psychopathic Characters on the Stage." In *The Standard Edition of the Complete Psychological Works of Sigmund Freud.* Vol. 7, *"A Case of Hysteria," "Three Essays on Sensuality," and Other Works,* 303–10. Translated under the general editorship of James Strachey, 1901–5. London: Hogarth Press, 1901–5.

Frye, Northrop. *Anatomy of Criticism: Four Essays.* Princeton: Princeton University Press, 1953.

Gasché, Rodolphe. *The Tain of the Mirror: Derrida and the Philosophy of Reflection.* Cambridge, MA: Harvard University Press, 1986.

———. "The Sober Absolute: On Benjamin and the Early Romantics." In *Walter Benjamin and Romanticism,* edited by Beatrice Hanssen and Andrew Benjamin, 51–68. New York: Continuum, 2002.

Genette, Gerard. *Narrative Discourse: An Essay in Method.* Translated by Jane E. Lewin. Ithaca: Cornell University Press, 1980.

———. *Paratexts: Thresholds of Interpretation.* Translated by Jane E. Lewin. Cambridge: Cambridge University Press, 1997.

Gezari, Janet. *Charlotte Brontë and Defensive Conduct: The Author and the Body at Risk.* Philadelphia: University of Pennsylvania Press, 1992.

Godwin, William. *Enquiry Concerning Political Justice and Its Influence on Morals and Happiness* (rev. ed. 1798). Edited by F. E. L. Priestley. 3 Vols. Toronto: University of Toronto Press, 1946. See esp. Introduction, by F. E. L. Priestley.

———. *Caleb Williams* (1794). Edited by Gary Handwerk and A. A. Markley. Peterborough, ON: Broadview Press, 2000.

———. *St. Leon* (1798). Edited by Pamela Clemit. Oxford: Oxford University Press, 1994.

———. "Of History and Romance" (1798). In Handwerk and Markley, *Caleb Williams*, 453–467.

———. "Of Choice in Reading," in *The Enquirer: Reflections on Education, Manners, and Literature in a Series of Essays* (1798), 129–46. Reprint. New York: A. M. Kelley, 1965.

———. *Memoirs of the Author of "A Vindication of the Rights of Woman"* (1798). Reprint. Oxford: Woodstock Books, 1993.

———. *Lives of Edward and John Philips, Nephews and Pupils of Milton* (1804). London: Longman, Hurst, Rees, Orme, and Brown, 1815.

———. *Fleetwood* (1805). Edited by Gary Handwerk and A. A. Markley. Peterborough, ON: Broadview Press, 2001.

———. *Faulkener: A Tragedy as It Is Performed at the Theatre Royal, Drury Lane, London.* London: Richard Phillips, 1807.

———. *Mandeville: A Tale of the Seventeenth Century in England* (1817). Vol. 6 of *The Collected Novels and Memoirs of William Godwin*. Edited by Pamela Clemit. London: Pickering and Chatto, 1992.

———. Preface to *Cloudesley: A Novel* (1830). Vol. 5 of *The Collected Novels and Memoirs of William Godwin*. Edited by Pamela Clemit, 6–8. London: Pickering and Chatto, 1992.

———. "Preface" to the "Standard Novels" edition of Fleetwood" (1832). In Handwerk and Markley, *Caleb Williams,* 443–50.

Goethe, Johann Wolfgang von. *Elective Affinities* (1809). Translated by R. J. Hollingdale. Harmondsworth, UK: Penguin, 1971.

Goodman, Katharine. *Dis/Closures: Women's Autobiography in Germany between 1790 and 1914.* New York: Peter Lang, 1986.

Green, André. *The Work of the Negative.* Translated by Andrew Weller. London: Free Association Books, 1999.

Gregory, Allene. *The French Revolution and the English Novel.* London: G. P. Putnam, 1915.

Habermas, Jürgen. *The Structural Transformation of the Public Sphere: An Inquiry into a Category of Bourgeois Society* (1962). Translated by Thomas Burger and Frederick G. Lawrence. Cambridge, MA: MIT Press, 1996.

———. *Philosophical-Political Profiles* (1971). Translated by Frederick G. Lawrence Cambridge, MA: MIT Press, 1985.

Hamilton, Paul. *Metaromanticism: Aesthetics, Literature, Theory.* Chicago: University of Chicago Press, 2003.

Handwerk, Gary. "History, Trauma, and the Limits of the Liberal Imagination: William Godwin's Historical Fiction." In Rajan and Wright, *Romanticism, History, and the Possibilities of Genre,* 64–85.

Hays, Mary. *Letters and Essays, Moral and Miscellaneous* (1793). Edited by Gina Luria. New York: Garland Press, 1974.

———. *Memoirs of Emma Courtney* (1796). Edited by Marilyn L. Brooks. Peterborough, ON: Broadview Press, 2000.

———. *Appeal to the Men of Great Britain in Behalf of Women.* London: Joseph Johnson, 1798.

Hegel, G. W. F. *Natural Law: The Scientific Ways of Treating Natural Law, Its Place in Moral Philosophy, and Its Relation to the Positive Sciences of Law* (1802). Translated by T. M. Knox. Philadelphia: University of Pennsylvania Press, 1975.

———. *The Philosophy of Nature* (1816). Translated by A.V. Miller. Oxford: Clarendon Press, 1970.

———. *Aesthetics: Lectures on Fine Art* (1823–29). Translated by T. M. Knox. 2 vols. Oxford: Clarendon Press, 1975.

———. *Philosophy of Mind* (1830). Translated by William Wallace. Oxford: Clarendon Press, 1971.

———. *The Philosophy of History* (1830–31). Translated by J. Sibree. New York: Dover, 1956.

Hogle, Jerrold. *Shelley's Process: Radical Transference and the Development of His Major Works.* New York: Oxford University Press, 1988.

———. " 'Frankenstein' as Neo-Gothic: From the Ghost of the Counterfeit to the Monster of Abjection." In Rajan and Wright, *Romanticism, History, and the Possibilities of Genre,* 176–210.

Hyppolite, Jean. *Genesis and Structure of Hegel's Phenomenology of Spirit.* Translated by Samuel Cherniak and John Heckman. Evanston, IL: Northwestern University Press, 1974.

Jacobson, Arthur J. "The Idolatry of Rules: Writing Law According to Moses, with Reference to Other Jurisprudences." In *Deconstruction and the Possibility of Justice,* edited by Drucilla Cornell, Michael Rosenfeld, and David Gray Carlson, 95–151. New York: Routledge, 1992.

Jacobus, Mary. *Psychoanalysis and the Scene of Reading.* Oxford: Oxford University Press, 1999.

Jameson, Fredric. *The Political Unconscious: Narrative as a Socially Symbolic Act.* Ithaca: Cornell University Press, 1981.

Johnson, Nancy E. *The English Jacobin Novel on Rights, Property, and the Law: Critiquing the Contract.* New York: Palgrave Macmillan, 2004.

Johnson, Samuel. *A Dictionary of the English Language* (1755). London: Times Books, 1983.

Kant, Immanuel. *Dreams of a Spirit-Seer* (1766). *"Dreams of a Spirit-Seer" and Other Writings*. Translated by Gregory R. Johnson and Glenn Alexander Magee, 3–66. West Chester, PA: Swedenborg Foundation Publishers, 2002. See esp. "Introduction," by Gregory Johnson, xi-xxxvi.

———. *Critique of Pure Reason.* 2nd ed. (1787). Translated by J. M. D. Meiklejohn. London: J. M. Dent, 1934. Reprint 1991.

———. *Critique of the Power of Judgment* (1790). Edited by Paul Guyer. Translated by Paul Guyer and Eric Matthews. Cambridge: Cambridge University Press, 2000.

———. *Raising the Tone of Philosophy: Late Essays by Immanuel Kant, Transformative Critique by Jacques Derrida.* Edited by Peter Fenves. Baltimore: Johns Hopkins University Press, 1993. See esp. "Announcement of the Near Conclusion of a Treaty for Eternal Peace in Philosophy"(1796), 83–100; "On a Newly Arisen Superior Tone in Philosophy" (1796), 51–82; "Other Exaltations" (1780–1796), 51–82.

———. *The Conflict of the Faculties* (1798). Translated by Mary J. Gregor. Lincoln: University of Nebraska Press, 1992.

———. *Anthropology From a Pragmatic Point of View* (1798). Translated by Victor Lyle Dowdell. Carbondale: Southern Illinois University Press, 1996.

———. *The Metaphysics of Morals* (1798). Translated by Mary Gregor. Cambridge: Cambridge University Press, 1996.

———. *Essays and Treatises on Moral, Political, and Various Philosophical Subjects by E. Kant.* Translated by John Richardson. 2 vols. London, 1798–99.

———. *"Perpetual Peace" and Other Essays.* Translated by Ted Humphrey. Indianapolis: Hackett Publishing, 1983.

Kauffman, Linda. *Discourses of Desire: Gender, Genre, and Epistolary Fiction.* Ithaca: Cornell University Press, 1986.

Kavanagh, Thomas M. *Enlightenment and the Shadows of Chance: The Novel and the Culture of Gambling in Eighteenth-Century France.* Baltimore: Johns Hopkins University Press, 1993.

Keach, William. *Shelley's Style.* London: Methuen, 1984.

Keats, John. *The Poems of John Keats.* Edited by Jack Stillinger. Cambridge, MA: Harvard University Press, 1979.

———. *The Letters of John Keats.* Edited by Maurice Buxton Forman. 2nd ed. London: Oxford University Press, 1935.

Kelly, Gary. *English Fiction of the Romantic Period, 1789–1830.* London: Longman, 1989.

———. *Revolutionary Feminism: The Mind and Career of Mary Wollstonecraft*. New York: St. Martin's Press, 1992.

Kierkegaard, Søren. *The Concept of Irony*. Translated by Lee M. Capel. Bloomington: Indiana University Press, 1965.

———. *The Present Age*. In *"The Present Age" and Two Minor Ethico-Religious Treatises*. Translated by Alexander Dru and Walter Lowrie. London: Oxford University Press, 1949.

Klancher, Jon. "Godwin and the Genre Reformers: On Necessity and Contingency in Romantic Narrative Theory." In Rajan and Wright, *Romanticism, History, and the Possibilities of Genre*, 21–38.

Krell, David Farrell. *Contagion: Sexuality, Disease, and Death in German Idealism and Romanticism*. Bloomington: Indiana University Press, 1998.

Krieger, Murray. *The New Apologists for Poetry*. Bloomington: Indiana University Press, 1963.

Kristeva, Julia. *Le texte du roman*. The Hague: Mouton, 1970.

———. *Revolution in Poetic Language* (1974). Translated by Margaret Waller. New York: Columbia University Press, 1984.

———. "The Adolescent Novel." In *Abjection, Melancholia, and Love: The Work of Julia Kristeva*, edited by John Fletcher and Andrew Benjamin, 8–23. London: Routledge, 1990.

Kroeber, Karl. *Romantic Narrative Art*. Madison: University of Wisconsin Press, 1960.

Kuehn, Manfred. *Scottish Common Sense in Germany, 1768–1800*. Montreal: McGill-Queen's University Press, 1987.

Lacoue-Labarthe, Philippe, and Jean-Luc Nancy. *Retreating the Political*. Edited by Simon Sparks. London: Routledge, 1997.

Landsman, Stephen. "The Rise of the Contentious Spirit: Adversary Procedure in Eighteenth-Century England." *Cornell Law Review* 75.3 (1990): 497–609.

Langbein, John. "The Criminal Trial before the Lawyers" *University of Chicago Law Review* 45.2 (1978): 263–316.

———. "Shaping the Eighteenth-Century Criminal Trial: A View from the Ryder Sources" *University of Chicago Law Review* 50.1 (1983): 1–136.

Lanser, Susan. *Fictions of Authority: Women Writers and Narrative Voice*. Ithaca: Cornell University Press, 1992.

Law, John. *Money and Trade Considered with a Proposal to Supply the Nation with Money* (1705). Reprint. New York: Augustus M Kelley, 1966.

Lennon, Thomas M. *Reading Bayle*. Toronto: University of Toronto Press, 1999.

Levere, Trevor. *Transforming Matter: A History of Chemistry from Alchemy to the Buckyball*. Baltimore: Johns Hopkins University Press, 2001.

Levinson, Marjorie. *Wordsworth's Great Period-Poems*. Cambridge: Cambridge University Press, 1986.

Liu, Alan. *Wordsworth: The Sense of History*. Stanford: Stanford University Press, 1989.

———. "Local Transcendence: Cultural Criticism, Postmodernism, and the Romanticism of Detail." *Representations* 32 (1990): 75–113.

Lockhart, John Gibson. Review of *Mandeville*. *Blackwood's Edinburgh Magazine* 2 (Dec. 1817): 268–79.

Locock, C. D. *An Examination of the Shelley Manuscripts in the Bodleian Library*. Oxford: Clarendon Press, 1903.

Logan, Peter Melville. *Nerves and Narrative: A Cultural History of Hysteria in Nineteenth-Century Prose*. Berkeley: University of California Press, 1997.

Lukács, Georg. *The Historical Novel*. Translated by Hannah and Stanley Mitchell. Harmondsworth, UK: Penguin, 1976.

———. *The Meaning of Contemporary Realism* (1957). Translated by John and Necke Mander. London: Merlin Press, 1963.

Lyotard, Jean-François. *The Postmodern Condition: A Report on Knowledge* (1979). Translated by Geoff Bennington and Brian Massumi. Minneapolis: University of Minnesota Press, 1984.

———. "The Sign of History" (1982). In *The Lyotard Reader*, edited by Andrew Benjamin, 393–411. Oxford: Basil Blackwell, 1989.

———. *Le Différend*. Paris: Les Éditions de Minuit, 1983.

———. *The Differend: Phrases in Dispute* (1983). Translated by Georges Van Den Abbeele. Minneapolis: University of Minnesota Press, 1988.

———. *Heidegger and "the Jews"* (1988). Translated by Andreas Michel and Mark Roberts. Minneapolis: University of Minnesota Press, 1990.

Lyotard, Jean-François, and Jean-Loup Thébaud. *Just Gaming*. Translated by Wlad Godzich. Minneapolis: University of Minnesota Press, 1985.

Matthews, Samantha. *Poetical Remains: Poets' Graves, Bodies, and Books in the Nineteenth Century*. Oxford: Oxford University Press, 2004.

McGann, Jerome. *The Romantic Ideology: A Critical Investigation*. Chicago: University of Chicago Press, 1983.

Miller, D. A. *Narrative and Its Discontents: Problems of Closure in the Traditional Novel*. Princeton: Princeton University Press, 1981.

Miller, J. Hillis. *Fiction and Repetition: Seven English Novels*. Cambridge, MA: Harvard University Press, 1982.

———. *Ariadne's Thread: Story Lines*. New Haven: Yale University Press, 1992.

Mitchell, W. J. T., ed. *On Narrative*. Chicago: University of Chicago Press, 1981.

Mulcaire, Terry. "Public Credit; or, The Feminization of Virtue in the Marketplace." *PMLA* 114.5 (1999): 1029–42.

Nancy, Jean-Luc. *The Inoperative Community*. Edited by Peter Connor. Translated by Peter Connor et al. Minneapolis: University of Minnesota Press, 1991. See esp. "The Inoperative Community" (1986), 1–42.

———. *The Experience of Freedom* (1988). Translated by Bridget McDonald. Stanford: Stanford University Press, 1993.

———. *The Ground of the Image*. Translated by Jeff Fort. New York: Fordham University Press, 2005.

Negri, Antonio. "The Constitution of Time." *Time for Revolution*. Translated by Matteo Mandarini, 21–128. New York: Continuum, 2003.

Nietzsche, Friedrich. *The Birth of Tragedy* (1870–71). In *"The Birth of Tragedy" and "The Genealogy of Morals."* Translated by Francis Golffing, 1–146. New York: Doubleday, 1956.

———. *The Antichrist* (1888), in *"Twilight of the Idols," "The Antichrist."* Translated by R. J. Hollingdale, 113–87. Harmondsworth, UK: Penguin, 1968.

Nitsch, F. A. *A General and Introductory View of Professor Kant's Principles Concerning Man, the World, and the Deity*. London: J. Downes, 1796.

Nussbaum, Felicity. *The Autobiographical Subject: Gender and Ideology in Eighteenth-Century England*. Baltimore: Johns Hopkins University Press, 1989.

Paine, Thomas. *The Rights of Man* (1790). In Edmund Burke and Thomas Paine. *"Reflections on the Revolution in France" and "The Rights of Man,"* 267–515. New York: Doubleday Anchor, 1973.

Peacock, Thomas Love. *The Four Ages of Poetry* (1820), in Percy Shelley and Thomas Love Peacock. *"A Defence of Poetry," "The Four Ages of Poetry,"* edited by John E. Jordan, 3–21. Indianapolis: Bobbs-Merrill Co., 1965.

Perry, Ruth. *Women, Letters, and the Novel*. New York: AMS Press, 1980.

Pfau, Thomas. *Romantic Moods: Paranoia, Trauma, and Melancholy, 1790–1840*. Baltimore: Johns Hopkins University Press, 2005.

Phelan, Andrew. "*Fortgang and Zusammenhang*: Walter Benjamin and the Romantic Novel." In *Walter Benjamin and Romanticism*, edited by Beatrice Hanssen and Andrew Benjamin, 69–82. New York: Continuum, 2002.

Phillips, Roderick. *Untying the Knot: A Short History of Divorce*. Cambridge: Cambridge University Press, 1991.

Philp, Mark. *Godwin's Political Justice*. Ithaca: Cornell University Press, 1986.

Plug, Jan. *Borders of a Lip: Romanticism, Language, History, Politics*. Albany: State University of New York Press, 2004.

Poovey, Mary. *The Proper Lady and the Woman Writer: Ideology as Style in the Works of Mary Wollstonecraft, Mary Shelley, and Jane Austen*. Chicago: University of Chicago Press, 1984.

Prince, Gerald. "The Disnarrated." *Style* 22 (1988): 1–8.

Rajan, Tilottama. *Dark Interpreter: The Discourse of Romanticism.* Ithaca: Cornell University Press, 1980.

———. "Romanticism and the Death of Lyric Consciousness." In *Lyric Poetry: Beyond New Criticism,* edited by Patricia Parker and Chaviva Hosek, 194–207. Ithaca: Cornell University Press, 1985.

———. "Is There a Romantic Ideology? Some Thoughts on Schleiermacher's Textual and Hermeneutic Criticism." *Text: Transactions of the Society for Textual Scholarship* 4 (1988): 59–77.

———. *The Supplement of Reading: Figures of Understanding in Romantic Theory and Practice.* Ithaca: Cornell University Press, 1990.

———. "The Web of Human Things: Narrative and Identity in *Alastor.*" In *The New Shelley: Later Twentieth Century Views,* edited by G. Kim Blank, 85–107, 251–252. New York: Macmillan, 1991.

———. "Mary Shelley's *Mathilda*: Melancholy and the Political Economy of Romanticism." *Studies in the Novel* 26 (1994): 43–68.

———. "Language, Music, and the Body: Nietzsche and Deconstruction." In *Intersections: Nineteenth-Century Philosophy and Contemporary Theory,* edited by Tilottama Rajan and David L. Clark, 147–69. New York: State University of Albany Press, 1995.

———. "(Dis)figuring the System: Vision, History, and Trauma in Blake's Lambeth Books." In *William Blake: Images and Texts,* edited by Robert N. Essick, 107–36. San Marino, CA: Huntington Library, 1997.

———. "Keats, Poetry, and 'The Absence of the Work.'" *Modern Philology* 95.3 (1998): 334–51.

———. "Framing the Corpus: Godwin's 'Editing' of Wollstonecraft in 1798." *Studies in Romanticism* 39.4 (2000): 511–32.

———. "In The Wake of Cultural Studies: Globalization, Theory, and the University." *Diacritics* 31.3 (2001): 67–88.

———. "Dis-Figuring Reproduction: Natural History, Community, and the 1790s Novel." *CR: The New Centennial Review* 2.3 (2002): 211–51.

———."Toward a Cultural Idealism: Negativity and Freedom in Hegel and Kant." In *Idealism without Absolutes: Philosophy and Romantic Culture,* edited by Tilottama Rajan and Arkady Plotnitsky, 51–72. Albany: State University of New York Press, 2004.

———. "The Prose of the World: Romanticism, The Nineteenth Century, and the Reorganization of Knowledge." *Modern Language Quarterly* 67.4 (2006). 479–504.

———. "The Disfiguration of Enlightenment: War, Trauma, and the Historical Novel in Godwin's *Mandeville.*" In *Godwinian Moments,* edited by Victoria

Myers and Robert Maniquis. Toronto: University of Toronto Press, forthcoming.

———. "'Something Not Yet Made Good': *Cain,* Godwin, Mary Shelley." In *Byron, Freedom, and Terror,* edited by Piya Pal-Lapinski and Matthew Green. London: Palgrave, forthcoming.

Rajan, Tilottama, and Julia Wright, eds. *Romanticism, History, and the Possibilities of Genre: Re-forming Literature, 1789–1837.* Cambridge: Cambridge University Press, 1999.

Ransom, John Crowe. "Criticism, Inc." *The World's Body.* Port Washington, NY: Kennikat Press, 1938.

———. "Humanism at Chicago." *Poems and Essays,* 81–101. New York: Vintage, 1955.

———. *The New Criticism.* Norfolk, CT: New Directions, 1941.

Redfield, Marc. *Phantom Formations: Aesthetic Ideology and the Bildungsroman.* Ithaca: Cornell University Press, 1996.

———. *The Politics of Aesthetics: Nationalism, Gender, Romanticism.* Stanford: Stanford University Press, 2003.

Reeve, Clara. *The Progress of Romance, through Times, Countries, and Manners* (1785). *"The Progress of Romance" and "The History of Charoba, Queen of Aegypt,"* i–xvi, 1–104. Reprint. New York: Facsimile Text Society, 1930.

Ricoeur, Paul. "Narrative Time." In Mitchell, *On Narrative,* 165–86.

———. "Narrative and Hermeneutics." In *Essays on Aesthetics: Perspectives on the Work of Monroe C. Beardsley,* edited by John Fisher, 149–59. Philadelphia: Temple University Press, 1983.

Rimmon-Keenan, Shlomith. *Narrative Fiction: Contemporary Poetics.* London: Methuen, 1983.

Riviere, Joan. "Hate, Greed, and Agression" (1937). In Melanie Klein and Joan Riviere. *Love, Hate, and Reparation,* 3–56. New York: Norton, 1964.

Robinson, Henry Crabb. *Crabb Robinson in Germany, 1800–1805: Extracts from His Correspondence.* Edited by Edith J. Morley. Oxford: Clarendon Press, 1929.

Rollins, Hyder, ed. *The Keats Circle: Letters and Papers and More Letters and Poems of the Keats Circle.* Vol. 1. Cambridge, MA: Harvard University Press, 1965.

Roussel, Roy. "Reflections on the Letter: The Reconception of Presence and Distance in Pamela." *ELH* 41 (1974): 375–99.

Sapiro, Virginia. *A Vindication of Political Virtue: Mary Wollstonecraft's Political Theory.* Chicago: University of Chicago Press, 1992.

Sartre, Jean-Paul. *Being and Nothingness: An Essay in Phenomenological Ontology* (1943). Translated by Hazel E. Barnes. New York: Washington Square Press, 1956.

————. *Critique of Dialectical Reason* (1960). Translated by Alan Sheridan-Smith. London, Verso, 1976.

Schafer, Roy. *Bad Feelings: Selected Psychoanalytic Essays.* New York: Other Press, 2003.

Schelling, F. W. J. *Ideas for a Philosophy of Nature* (2nd ed., 1803). Translated by Errol E. Harris and Peter Heath. Cambridge: Cambridge University Press, 1988.

Schiller, Friedrich. *Naive and Sentimental Poetry.* In *"Naive and Sentimental Poetry" and "On the Sublime."* Translated by Julis A. Elias, 83–190. New York: Frederick Ungar, 1966.

Schlegel, Friedrich. "Atheneum Fragments" (1798). *Philosophical Fragments.* Translated by Peter Firchow, 18–93. Minneapolis: University of Minnesota Press, 1991.

————. "Gespräch Über die Poesie" (1800). *Kritische und theoretische Schriften.* Edited by Andreas Huyssen, 165–224. Stuttgart: Reclam, 1984.

Schopenhauer, Arthur. *The World as Will and Representation.* Translated by E. F. J. Payne. 2 vols. New York, Dover 1966.

Segal, Hanna. "Symbolism," in *Dream, Phantasy, and Art,* 31–48. London: Tavistock; New York: Routledge, 1991.

Shell, Susan Meld. *The Embodiment of Reason: Kant on Spirit, Generation, and Community.* Chicago: University of Chicago Press, 1996.

Shelley, Mary. "Modern Italian Romances." *Mary Shelley's "Literary Lives" and Other Writings.* Vol. 4. Edited by Pamela Clemit, 227–60. London: Pickering and Chatto, 2002.

————. *Valperga; or, The Life and Adventures of Castruccio, Prince of Lucca.* Edited by Tilottama Rajan. Peterborough, ON: Broadview Press, 1998.

Shelley, Percy Bysshe. *Poetical Works.* Edited by Thomas Hutchinson. Oxford: Oxford University Press, 1904.

————. *Shelley's Poetry and Prose.* Edited by Donald Reiman and Neil Fraistat. 2nd ed. New York: Norton, 2002.

————. *Note Books of Percy Bysshe Shelley.* Edited by H. B. Forman. 3 vols. Boston: Bibliophile Society, 1911.

————. *"Zastrozzi" and "St. Irvyne."* Edited by Stephen C. Behrendt. Peterborough, ON: Broadview Press, 2002.

Simpson, David. *Romanticism, Nationalism, and the Revolt against Theory.* Chicago: University of Chicago Press, 1993.

————. *The Academic Postmodern and the Rule of Literature: A Report on Half Knowledge.* Chicago: University of Chicago Press, 1995.

Siskin, Clifford. *The Work of Writing: Literature and Social Change in Britain, 1700–1830.* Baltimore: Johns Hopkins University Press, 1998.

Smith, Adam. *Lectures on Rhetoric and Belles Lettres*. Edited by J. C. Bryce. Oxford: Oxford University Press, 1983.

"Speculation." Defs. 8 & 10. *The Oxford English Dictionary Online*. Oxford: Oxford University Press, 2001.

Staves, Susan. *Married Women's Separate Property in England, 1660–1833*. Cambridge, MA: Harvard University Press, 1990.

Stone, Lawrence. *Road to Divorce: England, 1530–1987*. Oxford: Oxford University Press, 1990.

———. *Broken Lives: Separation and Divorce in England, 1660–1857*. New York: Oxford University Press, 1993.

Tate, Allen. "Tension in Poetry" (1938). *Essays of Four Decades*, 56–71. Chicago: Swallow Press, 1968.

Taylor, Barbara. *Mary Wollstonecraft and the Feminist Imagination*. Cambridge: Cambridge University Press, 2003.

Tomalin, Claire. *The Life and Death of Mary Wollstonecraft*. London: Weidenfeld and Nicholson, 1964.

Trials for Adultery. London: S. Bladon, 1779–80. Reprint. New York: Garland, 1985.

Tysdahl, B. J. *William Godwin as Novelist*. London: Athlone Press, 1981.

Vattimo, Gianni. *The Transparent Society*. Translated by David Webb. Baltimore: Johns Hopkins University Press, 1992.

Walker, Gina Luria. *Mary Hays (1759–1843): The Growth of a Woman's Mind*. Aldershot: Ashgate, 2006.

Wasserman, Earl. *The Finer Tone: Keats' Major Poems*. Baltimore: Johns Hopkins University Press, 1953.

———. *Shelley: A Critical Reading*. Baltimore: Johns Hopkins University Press, 1977.

Watson, Nicola. *Revolution and the Form of the British Novel, 1790–1825*. Oxford: Oxford University Press, 1994

Weiskel, Thomas. *The Romantic Sublime: Studies in the Structure and Psychology of Transcendence*. Baltimore: Johns Hopkins University Press, 1976.

Wellek, René. *Immanuel Kant in England, 1793–1838*. New Haven: Yale University Press, 1931.

White, Hayden. "The Value of Narrativity in the Representation of Reality." In Mitchell, *On Narrative*, 1–24.

Wickman, Matthew. *The Ruins of Experience: Scotland's 'Romantick' Highlands and the Birth of the Modern Witness*. Philadelphia: University of Pennsylvania Press, 2007.

Willich, A. F. M. *Elements of the Critical Philosophy* (1798). Reprint. New York: Garland, 1977.

Winnicott, D. W. *Playing and Reality*. London: Routledge, 1971.

———. *Psychoanalytical Explorations*. Edited by Clare Winnicott, Ray Shepherd, and Madeline Davis. Cambridge, MA: Harvard University Press, 1989.

Wolfson, Susan. "Editorial Privilege: Mary Shelley and Percy Shelley's Audiences." In *The Other Mary Shelley: Beyond Frankenstein,* edited by Audrey A. Fisch, Anne K. Mellor, and Esther Schor, 39–72. New York: Oxford University Press, 1993.

Wollstonecraft, Mary. *Collected Letters of Mary Wollstonecraft*. Edited by Ralph M. Wardle. Ithaca: Cornell University Press, 1979.

———. *A Vindication of the Rights of Woman* (1792). Vol. 5 of *The Works of Mary Wollstonecraft*. Edited by Janet Todd and Marilyn Butler, 79–266. 7 Vols. London: Pickering and Chatto, 1989.

———. *Mary* (1788). *"Mary" and "The Wrongs of Woman."* Edited by Gary Kelly, 1–68. Oxford: Oxford University Press, 1980.

———.*The Wrongs of Woman; or, Maria: A Fragment* (1798). Kelly, *"Mary" and "The Wrongs of Woman,"* 71–204.

Woodman, Ross. *The Apocalyptic Vision in the Poetry of Shelley*. Toronto: University of Toronto Press, 1964.

———. *Sanity, Madness, Transformation: The Psyche in Romanticism*. Edited by Joel Faflak. Toronto: University of Toronto Press, 2005.

Woolf, Virginia. *A Room of One's Own*. New York: Harcourt, Brace and World, 1957.

Wordsworth, William. *"The Ruined Cottage" and "The Pedlar."* Edited by James Butler. Ithaca: Cornell University Press, 1979.

———. *Literary Criticism of William Wordsworth*. Edited by Paul M. Zall. Lincoln: University of Nebraska Press, 1966. See esp. "Preface to *Lyrical Ballads,* with Other Poems" (1800), 15–32; "Essay upon Epitaphs—I" (1810), 90–106.

———. *The Excursion* (1814). *The Poetical Works of William Wordworth*. Edited by Ernest de Selincourt and Helen Darbishire. 5 vols. Vol. 5. Oxford: Clarendon Press, 1949.

Wordsworth, William, and Samuel Taylor Coleridge. *Lyrical Ballads*. Edited by R. L. Brett and A. R. Jones. London: Methuen, 1971.

Wright, Julia. *Blake, Nationalism, and the Politics of Alienation*. Athens: Ohio University Press, 2004.

Yeats, William Butler. *Collected Poems*. 2nd ed. London: Macmillan, 1950.

Yeazell, Ruth Bernard. *Art of the Everyday: Dutch Painting and the Realist Novel*. Princeton: Princeton University Press, 2008.

Zillman, L. J., ed. *Shelley's Prometheus Unbound: A Variorum Edition*. Seattle: University of Washington Press, 1959.

Žižek, Slavoj. *The Sublime Object of Ideology*. London: Verso, 1989.

———. *Tarrying with the Negative: Kant, Hegel, and the Critique of Ideology.* Durham, NC: Duke University Press, 1993.

———. *The Indivisible Remainder: An Essay on Schelling and Related Matters.* London: Verso, 1996.

———. *The Plague of Fantasies.* London: Verso, 1997.

———. "Of Cells and Selves." In *The Žižek Reader,* edited by Elizabeth Wright and Edmond Wright, 302–20. Oxford: Blackwell, 1999.

———. "The Eclipse of Meaning: On Lacan and Deconstruction." In *Slavoj Žižek: Interrogating the Real,* edited by Rex Butler and Scott Stephens, 206–30. New York: Continuum, 2005.

Page numbers in **bold** refer to definitions.

Charke, Charlotte, 100
Chatterjee, Ranita, psychonarration, 224n87
closet literature: closet drama, xiii, 75, 193; closet novels, xiii, xix, 56–57, 62–66, 75
Coleridge, Samuel Taylor, xvi, 17, 19, 52, 55, 93–94, 207, 213; *Christabel*, 46; on Kant, 151–54. *See also* autonarration; novel(s)
Collings, David, 236n4
Common Sense philosophy, 149–52, 155, 243n22; *sensus communis* (Kant), xv. *See also* theory
Crabb Robinson, Henry, 118, 236n3
Crawford, Robert, xxiii
criminal conversation. *See* divorce
criticism, 8–9; Benjamin on, xvii, 7, 26; Victorians on, xv, 4, 8
critique, 118, 122, 129–30, 132, 135, 237n5; Derrida on, 135; Foucault on, 135; in Kant, 153–54
cultural studies, xiv–xv, xxiii, 4, 63. *See also* literature; theory

Dacre, Charlotte, 52
Damon, Foster, 73
Dante, 44
de Lauretis, Teresa, xiii
Deleuze, Gilles, 178, 208. *See also* Deleuze and Guattari
Deleuze, Gilles and Félix Guattari, 175
de Man, Paul, 5, 26, 87, 196, 203–4
De Quincey, Thomas, *The Dark Interpreter*, 68
Derrida, Jacques, xxiv, 14, 53–54, 76, 210; on Kant, 120–21, 237n10. *See also* archive; critique
dis-figuration, 5, 9, 23, 37, 52–54, 116, 204
disnarrated, xxi, 74, **229n46**
divorce, 183, 190, 199–200, 251–52n39; criminal conversation, 181, 184–87, 189, 191–99, 205, 251n37; parliamentary, 185–86, 193; separation from bed and board, 186, 189–91, 205; and women, 185–86, 250n22
Dubrow, Heather, 45
Duncan, Ian, xi

Du Plessis, Rachel Blau, 205
Dyson, George. *See* Wollstonecraft, Mary

Edwards, Gavin, 238–39n25
Elfenbein, Andrew, xv
Eliot, T. S., 95
empiricism, xxii, 151, 236n3
epistolary form/epistolarity, 86, 88–89, 92, 107–8. *See also* Hays, Mary
Esterhammer, Angela, 123
event, 123–24, 132–33, 210, 238n22
evidence, 158, 167, 188

Faflak, Joel, xvi, 83–84, 100, 135, 240n44
fantasy, xvi, 39, 63–64, 83, 121, 213; the fantastic, 52; in Godwin, 139–40; in Hays, 84, 109; in Shelley (Percy), 48–49, 61–62; traversal of the fantasm, 61–62, 132; Žižek on, 61–62
Favret, Mary, xi, 3–4, 42
Ferris, Ina, 246n76
Fichte, J. G., 7
Fontenelle, Bernard de, *Plurality of Worlds*, 168
Foucault, Michel, xviii, xxi, 41, 55, 109, 118, 236n2; care of the self, 114; confession, 135–36; discourse, 179; governmentality, **236n2**. *See also* archive; critique; literature
Fraistat, Neil, 42
Frend, William. *See* Hays, Mary
Freud, Sigmund, 55, 89, 113–14
Frye, Northrop, 11, 73
Fuseli, Henry. *See* Wollstonecraft, Mary

Gasché, Rodolphe, 7, 18, 26–27, 221n55
Genette, Gérard, 207
genotext, 101–2, 103–6, 108. *See also* phenotext
Gezari, Janet, 115
Gide, André, 69
Godwin, William, xiii, xvi–xvii, xx–xxiv, 2, 4, 35, 42, 45, 101, 117–173, 191 —*Caleb Williams*, 93, 112, 122–37, 140, 142–43, 146, 163, 188, 192, 196–99; "Choice in Reading," 84, 93, 124, 126, 193, 206; *Deloraine*, 94; ending of, 122, 129–34, 183,

186–87, 193, 203; *Enquiry Concerning Political Justice*, 93, 117–19, 121–22, 126, 142, 178, 199, 203; *Faulkener*, 94; *Fleetwood*, xxii, 94, 122, 134–35, 137–38, 142, 240n47; "History and Romance," 121, 128, 159, 168; *Lives of Edward and John Philips*, 176–77; *Lives of the Necromancers*, 153; *Mandeville*, xxii, 122, 134, 136, 138–43, 146; *Memoirs of Wollstonecraft*, 174–76, 195, 197–98, 202–3, 212; *St. Leon*, xxiii–xxiv, 50, 71, 80, 135, 140, 144–50, 155–57, 161–73, 197
—anarchism, 120, 237n11; character, xxi, 114, 124, 125, 127–28, 140, 142, 156, 238–39n25; confession, xxiv, 121, 134–37, 141; editing of Wollstonecraft, xxv, 174–84, 190, 194–98, 201–9, 213, 247n1, 247–48n2, 253n44; and Hume, 128, 239n25; institution, **xxi**, 83, 92, **117–18**, **129**, 139, 142, 178, 189, 199, 210; and Kant, 118–20, 145, 150–51, 155–56, 159–60, 162–64, 172, 236n3–4, 237n5; misanthropy in, 94, 136–40; necessity/necessitarianism, 59, 143, 240–41n52; rights, 198–200; right of private judgment, 118–19, 124, 178, 188, 200; on trials and juries, 119; trials in, 122, 129–30, 134, 239n35; and Wollstonecraft, 96–97, 112, 116, 130, 212, 249n10. *See also* autonarration; fantasy; Hays, Mary; law; part-objects/part-subjects; repetition; romance; Shelley, Mary; Shelley, Percy; story; tale
Goethe, Johann Wolfgang von, 52, 137; elective affinities, 240n46, 255n67
Gothic, xvi, 48, 50, 52, 55, 62, 66–68, 81, 227n20; Gothic romance, 46
Green, André, 381
Greimas, A. J., xv
Grotius, Hugo, 199

Habermas, Jürgen, xii, xiv, 52, 107, 167, 169–71, 212, 247n81
Haller, Albrecht von, 43

Hamilton, Paul, 163–64, 246n64
Handwerk, Gary, 143
Hardenberg, Friedrich von. *See* Novalis
Haym, Rudolf, xvi
Hays, Mary, xvii, 124, 182
—*Appeal to the Men of Great Britain*, 82, 87, 98; *Memoirs of Emma Courtney*, xiii, xx–xxi, 82–116, 138, 176
—desire in, xx, 87–93, 95, 98, 103, 107, 113, 116, 233n46; epistolary form in, 86–89, 107–13, 115; and Frend, William, xx, 82, 85, 87, 89, 98–99, 105–6, 110, 231n15; and Godwin, 84–85, 87–89, 91, 94–95, 98, 108, 110, 112, 116, 231n15, 232n28; letters, 84–85, 89–93, 108–10, 231n15; passion in, 84, 86, 91–92, 105, 107, 112; sexuality in, 90–91, 95–96; violence in, 105–6, 111, 116; and Wollstonecraft, 84, 91, 108, 111–12, 176, 212. *See also* autonarration; fantasy; madness; part-objects/part-subjects; repetition
Hegel, Georg Wilhelm Friedrich, xxiii, 7, 38, 43, 52, 59, 106, 117, 121, 153, 170, 199, 210; Dutch painting, 167–68; positive law, 253–54n48; prose of actuality, 55, 167–68; Romanticism, 161, 168; Symbolic and Romantic art, xix, **52–54**, 58, 88, 161, 168, 226n9. *See also* Kant, Immanuel; Novel, the; novel(s); prose; romance
Hogle, Jerrold, 81
Hölderlin, Friedrich, xviii
Hume, David. *See* Godwin, William
Hyppolite, Jean, 88

Idealism. *See* post-Kantian Idealism
Imaginary and the Symbolic, the, **233n49**
Imlay, Gilbert. *See* Wollstonecraft, Mary
intension, 6, 9, 25, 27; vs. ex-tension, xviii, xxii, 2, 128, 221n56

Jacobson, Arthur, 188–89, 192, 199
Jacobus, Mary, 44, 108–9, 224n88, 224–25n89
Jameson, Fredric, 57–59, 87, 97, 106; and symbolic and imaginary resolution, **227n26**

Jaspers, Karl, 151
Johnson, Gregory, 152
Johnson, Joseph, 98
Johnson, Samuel, 150, 166. *See also*
theory
Jonson, Ben, 166
Jung, Carl, 146

Kant, Immanuel, xv, xxii, xxiv, 27,
65, 76, 88, 133–35, 151–58, 172,
245nn55–56
—*Critique of Judgment*, 118–19, 160,
237n10; *Critique of Pure Reason*,
151–55, 160, 191, 237n10; *Dreams
of a Spirit-Seer*, 152–53; essays (political and historical), 120, 153, 158–61
—aesthetic and rational ideas, 65, 208,
237n10; enthusiasm, 133–34, 152,
154; and French Revolution, 133,
152, 160, 239n39, 244–45n51; and
Hegel, 153–54, 159–60, 165; on
history, 245n55; hypotyposis, 134,
156, 158, 239n39; idea(s), 120–21,
158–59, 191, 237n10; judgment, xv,
xxii, 118–20, 192; pragmatic anthropology, xiv, 156; reason vs. understanding, 119–20, 151, 153–54,
159, 209; *subreptio*, 155. *See also*
Coleridge, Samuel Taylor; Common
Sense philosophy; critique; Derrida,
Jacques; Godwin, William; paralogism; romance
Kauffman, Linda, 91, 107
Kavanagh, Thomas, 147–48, 150,
167–68, 241n5, 242n7
Keach, William, 25
Keats, John, xii, 3, 8; *Fall of Hyperion*,
xviii–xix, 9, 19, 29, 39–41, 44, 73,
94, 110, 203. *See also* autonarration
Kelly, Gary, 246n76, 248–49n9
Keynes, John Maynard, 164
Kierkegaard, Søren, 4, 72; on irony, 138,
240n51
Kittler, Friedrich, xiv
Klancher, Jon, 141
Klein, Melanie, 38, 53, 66, 111, 226n9;
post-Kleinian analysis, 234–35n66
Kristeva, Julia, 23, 57, 66, 81, 83, 98,
115; adolescent novel, xix, 52–53,

168, 233n48; genotext (vs. phenotext), 101; narrative, novel, 52, 63;
semiotic, xvii, 14, 63, 217n27,
219n22. *See also* poetry
Kuehn Manfred, 243n22

Lacan, Jacques, 57, 69, 87–89, 136; on
the Imaginary and the Symbolic, 14, 91,
104, 231n14; on the Real, 64, 83. *See
also* Imaginary and the Symbolic, the
Lacoue-Labarthe, Philippe, and Jean-
Luc Nancy, 43; *retrait du politique*,
223–24n85
Lamb, Charles, 19, 94
Landsman, Stephen, 189, 250–51n32
Langbein, John, 184
Lanser, Susan, 249n13
Law, John, 147–48, 150, 161, 165, 168,
172, 242n7, 246n69
law, 209; common, 192; ecclesiastical,
191–92; Godwin on, 117, 119, 122–23,
129, 131, 134; and institutions, 178;
and justice, 132, 191–92; lawyerization of trials, 184, 187–88, 250nn26,
30; Lyotard on, 123, 130; natural,
199; positive, 188–89, 192, 199,
253–54n48; and women's property,
186, 192, 250n23, 253n42. *See also*
divorce; evidence; testimony
Letters of a Portuguese Nun, 92
literature, 2, 4, 8, 10, 18–19, 38–39, 44,
122; in cultural studies, xii, xiv; and
death, xviii; Foucault on, xviii; Scottish Enlightenment concept of, xxiii
Locke, John, xxii
Lockhart, John Gibson, 140
Logan, Peter Melville, 116, 235–36n78
Lukács, Georg, 53; mediocre hero, 246n76
Lyotard, Jean-François, xxv, 8, 96, 120,
132–34, 158, 177, 191, 203, 208,
238n22; damages vs. wrongs, 130,
200; differend, xxii, 123, 130, 200,
209; on narrative, 123–25, 210–11,
238n22; on phrase regimes, xix, 55,
125, 133–34, 179, 184, 190; on phrasing, 209; and Jean-Loup Thébaud,
165. *See also* law
lyric, lyricism, xviii, 2–4, 10–13, 17,
20–24, 39–40, 42, 44–45, 224–25n89;

and autonomy, 30; as avoidance of history, 5; and childhood, 38; compression, brevity, 12, 14, 27, 31; as figure for poetry, 3, 42, 224–25n89; as ideality, identity, xiii, xix, 11–13; identified with Romanticism, xii; and interiority, 12–13, 25; as involution, xix; as transcendence, 9, 12; and trauma, xviii, 5, 31, 45
lyricization, xii, 12–13

madness: Blanchot on, 41; in Godwin, 122, 136–37; in Hays, 84, 109–10; of plot, 104; in Shelley (Percy), 33, 41, 63–64; Winnicott on, 110; Woodman on, 63, 83; in Wordsworth, 18
Matthews, Samantha, 196
McGann, Jerome, xiii, 7, 48
Mill, John Stuart, xv
Miller, D. A., xiii
Miller, J. Hillis, xiii, 33
Milton, John, 176–77, 186
Montesquieu, Charles Louis, Baron de, 185
Mulcaire, Terry, 150

Nancy, Jean-Luc, xviii, 39–40, 200; community vs. society, 119; and Philippe Lacoue-Labarthe, 43, 223–24n85
narrativity, xii, xv, xix–xxii, xxv, 2, 4, 10, 42, 48, 71, 86, 129, 131, 177; and philology, 210
narratology, xiii, xv, xx, 3, 5–6, 57, 61, 73–74, 82, 96, 111, 138, 140
negative, work of the, xvi–xvii, xx, 54, 82, 88, 108, 111; and idealization, 38–39
negativity, xviii, 87–88, 99, 146; infinite absolute, 72, 138, 247n51; unusable, 19, 224n88; and wounded masculine, 235n69
Nerval, Gérard de, xviii
Newton, Isaac: alchemy, 164
Nietzsche, Friedrich, 12, 23, 71, 175, 201
Nitsch, F. A.: on Kant, 151–54
Novalis (Friedrich von Hardenberg): romanticization, 91
Novel, the, xii, xx, 2, 55, 63–64, 87, 157–58, 166–67; and aesthetic ideol-

ogy, xv, xxiii; and anthropology, xxiii, 157; and credit, 151; as disciplinary apparatus, governmentality, xxiii, 121, 169, 192; and education, xxiii; as epistemic practice, xxiii; and the family, xxiv, 169–70; gendering of, xi, 169; Godwin and, 171–72; Hegel on, 161, 167–68; and judgment, xxii, 121; of manners, xiv–xv, 157–58, 167; as normalization, xxii, 81; and periodization, xiv; vs. prose fiction, xiii–xiv, 169; and publicness/public sphere, xiii, xxii; realist, 144; Regency, 86; vs. romance, 167; Victorian, xii, xv, 83. *See also* novel(s)
novel(s), xi, 215n5; Coleridge on, 158; Hegel on, 168; Kant on, 157–58; vs. the Novel, 169; Shelley (Mary) on, 168; and speculation, 63, 158; Wordsworth on, 157–58. *See also* closet literature; Kristeva, Julia; prose
novelization, xi, xix, 48, 215n5
Nussbaum, Felicity, 87

overdetermined form, 49, 56–60, 65, 70, 75

Paine, Thomas: *Rights of Man*, 199
paralogism, 134, 158–59, 161, 172, 208; Kant on, 156, 187, 239–40n39
part-narrative, xiii, xxv, 17, 95, 213
part-objects/part-subjects, 7, 111, 224n87; in Godwin, xxii, 136–37, 139; in Hays, 110; in Shelley (Mary), 4, 94; in Shelley (Percy), 3, 21, 36, 81; in Wollstonecraft, 182, 213; in Wordsworth, 19–20
Peacock, Thomas Love, xix, 3–4, 49; *Four Ages of Poetry*, xv, xvii, xxiii
Perry, Ruth, 93
perverse identification, xxii, xxiv, 89, 94, 136–38
perversion, perversity, 52, 56, 61–64; Žižek on, 54, 64, 227n21
Pfau, Thomas, 131–32, 218n9
phenotext, 101–2, 108, 111. *See also* genotext; Kristeva, Julia
philology, xviii, xxv, 175, 177, 201, 210, 249n12. *See also* narrativity

Philp, Mark, 162
phrases/phrasing, xix, xxi, xxv, 50,
    55–56, 74, 77, 113, 130, 132–34,
    143–44, 149–50, 177–84, 191–92,
    196, 201–2, 207, 209–11; cognitive,
    133, 143, 179, 184, 191, 209; moral,
    149; speculative/dialectical, 133, 144,
    149, 184, 187, 209–10; unphrasing,
    180. *See also* Lyotard, Jean-François.
Pilkington, Laetitia, 100
Plato, 120, 151–52
plot, xiii, xxii, 5, 14, 17, 26, 38, 66, 74,
    77, 104–6, 121, 127, 129; emplot-
    ment, 77; reading for plot, xii, 65,
    100, 123
poetry, xix, 5–9, 23, 26, 37–41, 44, 48,
    63–64, 83–84, 101, 225n2; and com-
    mercial society, xvii; as epistemic
    practice, xii, xvi, 6; feminization of,
    xi; as the idea of prose, xvi–xvii, 6–7,
    20, 121; and institution, 114; Kristeva
    on, 63; and narrative, 48; philology
    as, 210; Romanticism identified with,
    xiv–xv, xix; Shelley (Percy) on, xvi,
    2–4, 6, 15–17, 72, 81, 83, 94–95; and
    untimeliness, 39, 45; Wordsworth on,
    17; and worklessness, 18–19. *See also*
    Browning, Robert; lyric; prose; Schle-
    gel, Friedrich; Shelley, Mary
poiesis, xvi, xxi, 48, 63, 109–10, 120;
    and pathology, 138, 141
Poovey, Mary, 202
post-Kantian Idealism, xxii, xxiv, 77,
    151, 153, 161, 191, 199, 236n3
Priestley, F. E. L., 199–200
Prince, Gerald, xxi
Propp, Vladimir, xv
prose, xiii, 6–8, 25–26, 37, 42, 81, 96,
    177, 179, 225n2; as epistemic prac-
    tice, xii–xiv, xvi–xvii, 6; as the idea of
    poetry, xvii, 6–7; and modernity, xvii.
    See also Hegel, Friedrich; Shelley,
    Mary
prose fiction, xiii, 5
Pufendorf, Samuel, 199

Radcliffe, Anne, xi, 46, 147, 230n57;
    Mysteries of Udolpho, 47, 60, 146,
    166

Rajan, Tilottama, xii, 44, 218n6, 222n73,
    224n88, 237n10, 243–44n31, 247–48n2
Ransom, John Crowe, xviii, 25
Redfield, Marc, xv, xxiii
Reeve, Clara: *The Progress of Romance*,
    167–69
reflection, 7, 9, 18–19, 26–27, 31, 41,
    221n55
repetition, 27, 33; in Godwin, 204; in
    Hays, 106–7; in Shelley (Percy),
    27–28, 32–36, 49, 57; in Wollstone-
    craft, 182
Ricoeur, Paul, xiii, 5, 16–17, 32, 77–78
Rilke, Rainer Maria, xviii
Rimmon-Keenan, Shlomith, 124
romance, xxiii, 134, 140, 161, 167, 169,
    247n78; Godwin on, 121, 159; Hegel
    on, 168; Kant on, 158, 160; sentimen-
    tal, xxv; and women, xi, 84, 182. *See
    also* Novel, the
Rousseau, Jean-Jacques, 84, 137, 212

Sapiro, 202
Sartre, Jean-Paul, 84, 88, 135
Saussure, Ferdinand de, 5
Schelling, Friedrich, 43, 63, 77, 91
Schiller, Friedrich, 7; sentimental poetry,
    82–83
Schlegel, A. W., 52, 161
Schlegel, Friedrich, 6, 152, 161, 169,
    215n5; "romantic" poetry, xvi–xvii
Schopenhauer, Arthur, 12, 91
Scott, Sir Walter, xi, xiv, 139–41, 167,
    246n76
Segal, Hanna, 66, 226n9
Shelley, Mary Wollstonecraft, xx,
    94–95, 168, 171; editing of Percy
    Shelley, 3–4, 41–43, 223n78, 224n86;
    Falkner, 94; *Frankenstein*, 50, 71, 79,
    107; and Godwin, 94–95, 174; *Last
    Man*, 4, 43, 94, 171; *Mathilda*, 3–4,
    44–45, 94; and poetry, 43–45; and
    prose, xvii, 42; *Valperga*, 72, 94.
    See also autonarration; part-objects/
    part-subjects; novel(s)
Shelley, Percy Bysshe, xiii, xv–xvii, xxi,
    1–81, 83, 94–95, 114, 120, 143, 223n79
    —*Adonais*, 3, 7, 10, 29, 49, 81; *Alas-
    tor*, xii, xvii–xix, 2–45, 49, 52, 60,

Woodman, Ross, xvi, 63–64, 83, 122, 137. *See also under* madness
Woolf, Virginia, 116
Wordsworth, William, xii, xviii, 3, 7–8, 40–41, 50, 93–94, 166, 207, 219n27; "Baker's Cart," 17, 220n42; *Essays on Epitaphs*, 202–3; "Incipient Madness," 17–18, 220n42; Lucy poems, 10–11, 38; *Ruined Cottage*, xviii, 17–20, 39, 44, 180, 220nn39, 42; "There was a boy," 11, 13, 29–31, 37–38. *See also* autonarration; madness; novel(s); part-objects/part-subjects; poetry; story; tale
wounded masculine, 94, 111–12, 235n69. *See also* negativity

Yeats, W. B., xix, 5, 67
Young, Arthur, 150

Žižek, Slavoj, 54, 61–62, 64, 69–70, 104, 121, 132, 141–42, 158, 172–73, 213; deep ecology, 225n4; *sinthome*, 89–90. *See also* fantasy; perversion